# SALVATION LIES WITHIN

## 别 慌

叶志刚 著　高赫飞 译

U0368489

清华大学 出版社
**Tsinghua University Press**
北京 Beijing

**图书在版编目（CIP）数据**

别慌 = Salvation Lies Within：英文 / 叶志刚著; 高赫飞译. — 北京：清华大学出版社，2024.2

ISBN 978-7-302-65682-1

Ⅰ.①别… Ⅱ.①叶… ②高… Ⅲ.①青少年—心理健康—健康教育—研究—英文 Ⅳ.①G444

中国国家版本馆CIP数据核字(2024)第040610号

责任编辑：杨爱臣
封面设计：赵雷勇
责任校对：王荣静
责任印制：沈　露

出版发行：清华大学出版社
　　　网　　　址：https://www.tup.com.cn，https://www.wqxuetang.com
　　　地　　　址：北京清华大学学研大厦A座　　邮　　编：100084
　　　社 总 机：010-83470000　　　　　　　邮　　购：010-62786544
　　　投稿与读者服务：010-62776969，c-service@tup.tsinghua.edu.cn
　　　质量反馈：010-62772015，zhiliang@tup.tsinghua.edu.cn
印 装 者：北京雅昌艺术印刷有限公司
经　　销：全国新华书店
开　　本：130mm×197mm　　印　　张：16.125　字　数：613千字
版　　次：2024 年 3 月第 1 版　印　　次：2024 年 3 月第 1 次印刷
定　　价：128.00元

产品编号：103926-01

# *Preface*

I started my career in education in 2003. As of before the publication of this book, my team and I had trained outstanding successors for over 300 families. More than 60 thousand employees in their family businesses were even more convinced of the bright future of the companies, and their vast family assets had successors. Based on the excitement of the parents, I even started to wonder whether our education indirectly drove the sustained growth in the stocks of 17 companies. These are largely due to our education following the guiding principles outlined in this book.

Since then, the society has undergone rapid changes, and various educational technologies and concepts are also changing. However, the principles that I proposed in this book are still practical and effective today. Parents still buy this book for the positive changes that teachers bring to their children: the eagerness to obtain knowledge, greater happiness, increased sense of responsibility, closer relationship with the parents, etc. These shall remain unchanged for all the parents in the world.

In this era where there are almost no handwritten letters, I unexpectedly received many handwritten letters from their parents. They attributed their children's current achievements to meeting me back then.

Mr. Zhou Erliu, former Vice President of Peking University, said to me, "Zhigang, I think the most unique aspect of your education is its effectiveness."

I view our uniqueness in this way:

We prioritize creative action as our primary responsibility. We only hire the most capable guys. A first-class business requires the use of first-class talents.

I try my best to let the talents bring out their full potential in the work. We are people who love honesty from the bottom of our hearts. We detest people who play tricks, flatter, domineer, and show off in their work. We praise people who work diligently, objectively, and seriously. We always remember not to complain about whom the parents entrust their children to. We pay attention to keeping family secrets confidential. Parents do not appreciate teachers who leak their privacy, nor do they like a teacher to claim credit for it. Taking credits from the parents is an abominable behavior. We are unprecedentedly concerned about the effectiveness of education, and making changes is our mission.

Our communication with the parents is positive and easy to understand. We refuse to use academic words, such as Imageless Thought, Two-factor Theory, Wilcoxon Sign Rank Test, etc. Even more, we refuse to use expressions that make us sound less manly, such as "healing, inner, psychological umbilical cord, care for life, introspection, present, and the joy of abundance", and so on and so forth. I often tell team members that if we cannot explain our education plan clearly to an illiterate person, our education is not about educating people.

Before meeting us, students and parents switch between well-known educators and psychological counseling institutions, and here we will be their last stop. When we see the students rejuvenate in our hands, that kind of pride cannot be taken away by anyone.

Every teacher should work in my field for two years before starting their education career. At that time, in any education book, with just a glance, he can determine whether the author has actual educational experience.

Normally, most of my education programs are based on surveys—they are as effective today as they were back in 2003.

Thanks to meticulous market research, I successfully started my own business in college. In the words of Director Cai of the cafeteria, I was the wealthiest student. Afterwards, I became a teacher, and as far as I know, I am the only remaining teacher who relies on investigation as the foundation of education. This fact always makes me examine educational work from the perspective of an investigator. What follows are the most valuable experiences I have learned.

1. Successful education is a craft that relies partly on love and inspiration, but essentially on knowledge and diligence. If you have the talent and are willing to work hard to make your wallet full, that's how you have longevity in this field.

2. The difference between one type of education and another is measured by "human lives", which is called "people die when compared to people, goods are thrown away when compared to goods."

3. It's worth spending more time researching students before you start your education.

4. The key to earning the favor of the parents lies in the benefits you bring to them—for example, the children are enrolled to Tsinghua University or Peking University through their own hard work, the children expressed genuine care for the parents, or the children became self-sufficient and happy without the parents' worrying about them, etc.

5. The effect of great education usually lasts for many years without losing its influence. Back in 2003, I helped Xiaomin to establish his life goal of "entering politics through the college entrance examination and becoming a village official to benefit the people", which led him to strive for 10 years. After graduating from university, he took charge of the industry in the town. In 2006, I helped Haonan establish his life goal of "studying abroad and pursuing business, inheriting the family business to repay society", which has been his pursuit ever since. In 2013, the family group went public, and father and son worked together to ring the bell.

Although the educational principles and techniques in the book are still effective on children today, I kindly ask parents and educators not to blindly apply the examples I have provided in the book. Principles and technologies can be applied universally, while their interpretation and implementation vary from person to person.

Since I stepped onto the stage of education, Zhigang Education has always regarded "setting students' life goals and shaping their life spirit" as its own responsibility and dedicating itself to the everlasting foundation of the family business.

Let's work together towards a common goal: for the sake of the happiness of the families, as well as the continuation of the families' glory, we provide safe and effective education.

Yes Gunn

# Contents

## Part I  My Education Practice

# Part II  My Education Thoughts

# Part I
# My Education Practice

# Chapter 1

# How to Educate Children
# with Internet Addiction

### Xiaomin's bazar biography

At the end of 1998, Xiaomin became addicted to the Internet. He often skipped school to go to the Internet cafe and later he would spend 16 hours online every day. He became silent, feeling extremely insecure. He even beat, scolded his parents, and bullied his classmates. He broke his tutor's eyeglasses several times, watching blood flow from the corner of his tutor's eye. He's extremely picky about his food. He would slam the bowl into the caretaker's face if he didn't like the food. And when he shows up in the living room wearing a long face, relatives leaning on the sofa watching TV will reflexively jump up.

- In April 2003, Xiaomin was persuaded to leave the Municipal Experimental High School due to prolonged skipping classes.
- On June 22, 2003, I first met Xiaomin.
- On July 10, 2003, all the tutors were driven away by Xiaomin, except me.
- On September 14, 2003, Xiaomin sold his video game account.
- On March 4, 2004, Xiaomin went to the First Complete Middle School, ranking 1024.
- On March 26, 2004, Xiaomin was expelled from the First Complete High School.
- On April 10, 2004, he returned to the First Complete Middle School.

- On May 14, 2008, Xiaomin voluntarily donated all his savings to the Wenchuan earthquake-stricken area in Sichuan Province.
- In July 2008, he was admitted to a key university of finance and economics.
- In 2023, Xiaomin served as a leader of a unit in Panjin City.

From a severe Internet-addicted teenager who beat, scolded his parents, closed down and felt inferior, to a diligent, filial, and positive top-tier high school student, and then to a gentle and versatile key university student, Xiaomin has completed dramatic life changes one after another within merely five years.

How did Xiaomin quit his Internet addiction in less than half a year, and complete a full seven-year course from third grade of elementary school to fourth grade of junior high school within 14 months, and was admitted to a key high school? How did he do it? Let's turn our attention back to June of 2003.

## This kid is doomed—A close contact with Internet-addicted teenagers.

In June 2003, I heard that there was a child who was unanimously recognized by the teachers of the Municipal Experimental High School as the most difficult child to educate since its founding. It is said that his name was Xiaomin. His father was the chairman of a company, and his mother was the general manager of a large catering chain. He was their only child.

It is said that he dropped out of school and stayed at home for a year, 24 hours a day, with 16 hours spending on the Internet. He worried all day, without saying a word. It is said that due to long-term and severe Internet addiction, Xiaomin's body was close to collapse. The hospital diagnosis was:

*1. Iron deficiency anemia (severe);*
*2. Malnutrition, pectus carinatum.*

It is said that anyone who disagreed with him, whether classmates, teachers, relatives, friends, or parents, was either verbally insulted or physically assaulted. His mother and grandmother were beaten the most, and their relatives were afraid of him. The nanny was also particularly afraid of him. If the taste of the food cooked by the nanny did not meet his expectations, he would smash the food onto the nanny's face.

It is said that he would run around the room deliberately during tutoring sessions. It took 40 minutes of the 45-minute class to get him to sit down. He would smash the tutor's glasses if he was pissed off, smile and then look at the bleeding corners of the tutor's eyes and said, "Go, ask my mom to get you a pair of crystal glasses!"

When his mother awkwardly rolled up her sleeves in the luxurious hotel office and showed me the purple scars on her arms from her child's beating, I finally believed that all the rumors above were true!

Another problem with Xiaomin was that he never communicated with others. Apart from what to eat and buy, he did not speak a word, no one really knew what he was thinking about.

How are you supposed to help him if you don't even understand him? I thought I needed to make every second count, so I started my first move: infiltration.

At that time his mother hired four tutors for math, physics, chemistry, and English. The English tutor was so angry with the child that he quitted, so I came into contact with the child in the name of his English tutor.

When I first met Xiaomin, he was in a physics class. He was lying in bed with his eyes closed. Next to him was a male tutor who was in his 60s, kneeling at his bedside, with a textbook in hand. He would smile from time to time and say: "Come on, let's open eyes and take a look at this formula." Xiaomin opened one eye and said: "Bring the book closer!" 18 days later, Xiaomin suddenly said that he did not want to learn anything. He kicked all the tutors out of the door, except me.

(A letter from Xiaomin's grandmother)

### Is it Internet addiction to be online for 16 hours a day?

Children with Internet addiction have a symptom of being online excessively, but the causes of such addiction are dramatically different. Thus, the plans for helping them quit the addiction and return to a regular life path are dramatically different as well. If we want to quit Internet addiction, we need to first figure out whether the child is really addicted to the Internet.

First of all, we need to understand what addiction is.

"Addiction" is a special state of life composed of two factors: Firstly, the habits harm one's interests. Secondly, one wants to change but finds oneself powerless to do so. These two factors are indispensable.

If someone likes doing something, for example, playing mahjong, one doesn't take it seriously even though one's health suffers from indulging in it. One finds joy in it and doesn't want to make a change. Instead of addiction, it is considered a bad habit. On the other hand, it would be an addiction when one has trouble pulling away from it.

These are two completely different concepts. Thus, we need to treat them differently. If it wasn't confirmed as an addiction but we acted on the family's disapproval, it would be no different from making Churchill quit smoking or making Li Bai quit drinking, which would have serious consequences.

Back then, Xiaomin remained silent all day without talking to anybody, and he played video games until 10:00 pm, and he woke up at around 6:00 the next morning to keep playing. He had never talked to anyone about his ideals or his worries, and nobody knew what he was thinking about. Therefore, the first thing to understand was whether Xiaomin had the willingness to change.

**With a sigh—Without investigation, there is no right to speak.**

Without investigation, there is no right to speak. Revolution is like this, and so is education. But how can we find the answer? To find the answer, one must delve deep into children's lives.

Shortly enough, I moved in with him, and another "Internet-addicted youth" appeared in the luxury home.

One day a month later, I woke up at five o'clock in the morning and read in the study. At six o'clock, I heard a noise coming from Xiaomin's bedroom. He had woken up but stayed in bed. Everything was so quiet as the morning sun shone through the window screen into the room. At this moment, I heard a sigh coming out of his bedroom. "Alas!" I felt a shock in my heart when I heard it! My mind is thinking rapidly: Why did Xiaomin sigh? What kind of person sighs? Or under what situation would a person sigh?

I thought it is only when a person's inner thoughts are inconsistent with the reality he was in, and he feels powerless to change, that he sighs! So, I came to a very definite conclusion: Xiaomin wanted to change from the bottom of his heart. He was not satisfied with his current situation that he was an Internet addict!

**There is no Internet addiction, but only the main contradiction.**

Xiaomin's parents believed that the reason their children developed Internet addiction was that he was not interested in learning. They believed that in order to quit Internet addiction, it is necessary to cultivate their child's interest in learning and ask the best teachers to give them extra classes.

After analyzing the phenomenon of Xiaomin wanting to change but beating and scolding his parents, even private tutors, and driving out many teachers but only leaving me behind, I made the following three judgments: Firstly, Xiaomin's main contradiction was not between learning and Internet addiction. Otherwise, he would not have accepted his parents arranging teachers to make up for him before. Secondly, he needed someone to help him resolve his inner conflicts. Otherwise, he wouldn't ask me to stay. Thirdly, academic failure, symptoms of severe Internet addiction, and physical abuse of those around him masked the true contradictions. These statements directly clarified the direction of my next stage of work: eliminating interference and continuing to understand the truth. T. S. Eliot said, "We must never stop exploring, and the end of all exploration is to return to the starting point and have a first-time understanding of it."

**The answer has surfaced, uncovering the bitterness
behind Internet addiction.**

One day, we were playing video games together. Xiaomin suddenly spoke up and said to me, "You're pretty good at playing games!"

I said, "This is nothing. I'm not only good at playing games but also predicting the future!" Xiaomin stopped and grabbed my hand, saying "I'm only convinced if you can guess one thing right!" He took out a framed photo from the bottom of his wardrobe, on which was a graduation group photo. "This is the graduation photo of my elementary school, and there is a girl I like in it. If you can guess which one it is, I'll tell you all my secrets! If not, don't brag to me in the future!"

I said it was easy. I took the framed photo, and there were four rows of people on it. I pointed at the top row and said, "It's definitely not in this row."

"Obviously! It's all guys!" Xiaomin said.

I pointed at the bottom row, "and definitely not in this row."

"Obviously! It's all teachers! Can you guess or not!" Xiaomin was running out of patience. I pointed to one girl from the middle two rows and said, "It's her!" Time seemed to freeze, and a surprised expression appeared on Xiaomin's face for the first time. He grabbed the framed photo, hugged it tightly to his chest, and started running around in the ginormous living room, with tears dripping down his cheeks onto the marble floor. When he appeared in front of me again exhausted, his eyes were full of trust in me. He asked me, "Brother Ye, I'm convinced. No one knew about this. How did you guess it?"

I looked at him and said, "Tell me your story."

It turned out that when Xiaomin was in the third grade, his desk mate was a girl named Xiaojing, and their families lived very close.

Xiaojing often helped Xiaomin with his study, and explained the questions he didn't understand, even reminding him to finish the homework. Xiaomin was grateful to her, and he brought her snacks and helped carry things for her on their way to school.

Gradually, Xiaomin realized that he couldn't help looking at Xiaojing during classes. Every morning, he woke up hoping to see her earlier. Xiaomin knew he had fallen in love with Xiaojing, but he didn't dare to tell her. He was afraid that if Xiaojing didn't agree, they wouldn't even be able to be friends. There is no airtight wall. Xiaojing still knew it. She refused Xiaomin, saying that they were too young and should focus on studying.

Xiaomin said, "Well, let's still be friends and I'll marry you when I grow up!" She got shy and looked away. But not long after, he heard from his classmates that Xiaojing was dating with Xiaobin. Xiaobin was a well-known problem student in his school. Xiaomin found it hard to believe that the Snow White in his heart would be together with someone like Xiaobin. She broke her original "promise"!

When Xiaomin saw Xiaobin and Xiaojing appearing in front of him, Xiaomin collapsed. At first, he tried to talk to Xiaojing, who always avoided him. Later, Xiaojing turned around and ran away as soon as she saw Xiaomin from a distance.

Not long after, one afternoon after school, Xiaomin was attacked by several delinquent youths who ambushed him at the school gate.

From then on, Xiaomin refused to go to school. He didn't want to see Xiaojing again and recall everything from the past.

He tried his best to surf on the Internet, not giving himself any free time. In the painful reality and the murky online world, five years passed in the blink of an eye!

"Brother Ye, it's been so long. It's the first time I feel like I'm a man!"

Five years have exhausted Xiaomin's confidence and dignity. To drag Xiaomin out of the quagmire, not only should he have confidence in me, but also in himself!

How to make a teenager have confidence in himself? I conclude in two phrases: Say what you want to say and do what you need to do. I planned an action:

At 7:30 pm, I said to Xiaomin, "Do you miss Xiaojing?"

"Yeah, pretty bad!"

"Do you have something to say to her?"

"Yeah! A lot! I want to say that... (a few hundred words are omitted here), but I dare not to face her!"

"You need to organize your speech. How many key points do you have?" (Summarizing skills are important. It needs to be developed through life.)

"Umm...there are three. Firstly, I like you. Secondly, break up with Xiaobin. And thirdly, I'm willing to do anything to be with you!"

"Take action!"

"What are you talking about, Brother Ye?"

"Do you know where the pain of the vast majority of men originated?"

"No."

"Thinking too much and doing too little!" (Teach philosophy of life in difficult situations.)

I took him downstairs immediately and arrived at Xiaojing's house shortly after. I encouraged him to go upstairs and knock on the door himself, and there he went without any hesitation. He came down from upstairs with an excited expression 15 minutes later.

"Have you covered all the three key points?" (If not, I'll let him go up-stairs and say it again.)

"Yeah, Brother Ye. It was really cool!"

"What did Xiaojing say?" I laughed.

"Her whole family were shocked and dumbfounded. They just listened to me, but later her father got pissed off and told me to get away!"

"How are you feeling now?"

"It's been so long that this is the first time I feel like a man, Brother Ye!" Xiaomin hugged me tightly and cried loudly.

After a while when he calmed down, I asked him, "Why do you want Xiaojing to leave Xiaobin and be with you?"

"Because he's a trouble kid and I'm way better than him!"

"Better in what ways?"

"I'm kinder!"

"Well, did you know that Xiaojing and Xiaobin have already broken up and she's with Xiaozhou now? Do you know Xiaozhou?"

"Xiao Zhou? He used to be in the top ten in my class, and he's quite nice."

"How are you better than him?" (Point out the conflict, trigger thinking and promote changes)

"..."

"A man who wants to achieve happiness first asks himself, 'How am I better than the others', then he asks himself, 'What kind of men do women like?' " (Train his thinking)

"Alright."

"I went to your school yesterday (large amounts of preparation and co-ordination with the class teacher), and here is the evaluation of you from your former classmates. Take a look." I handed him a slip.

It reads:

> *Advantages:*
> *1. He is sometimes very enthusiastic about helping classmates.*
> *(Xiaomin's heart was actually very soft and compassionate.)*
> *2. He is generous.*
>
> *Disadvantages:*
> *1. He is too fond of surfing on the Internet.*
> *2. He insults and assaults others.*
> *3. He is always with a worried expression.*
> *4. He never studies.*
> *5. He walks weirdly. (When Xiaomin was young he suffered from malnutrition and the lack of attention from his parents, which caused him to limp)*

"Keep the strengths on the note and correct the weaknesses, and you will be perfect."

"Then I can win Xiaojing over?"

"A boy studies well, has good health, good temperament, comes from a good family, is polite, generous and righteous. Who doesn't like him? You might even win over the boys too!"

"Quit joking around, Brother Ye!"

"I'm not kidding! Think about it. If you change for the better now, and in the future, while attending a decent university, you will hold 99 roses in your hand, wear a suit, in your family's Mercedes, and have a gentle smile on your face to pick up Xiaojing. What kind of scene should it be! (Describe a delicate, almost real visible scene to inspire children.)

In the darkness, Xiaomin's eyes sparkled with urgency. "Alas! I probably can't do it alone. Can you help me, Brother Ye?" (The symbol of successful education—children actively seek help!)

"Well, that depends on if you're worth helping!" (An American politician Paine once said, "Those that come too easily will not be cherished. Only by paying the price can everything gain value.)

"I'll prepare your foot bath!" (No one will cherish things gained without a price. Educators need to keep a dynamic balance with the subject's pay and return.)

"Alright."

Xiaomin slept quite well on that evening, while I was in the neighboring study, brainstorming one plan after another to help him break his five bad habits.

The next day, Xiaomin said that in his dream last night, he saw himself holding a rose from a prestigious school and walking towards Xiaojing from the Mercedes. Xiaojing also smiled and ran towards him...

As American writer Marilyn Ferguson once said, "No one can persuade others to change. Each of us guards a door of change that can only be opened from inside. We cannot open the door for others, either by argument or emotional appeal."

## To get rid of the Internet addiction
## is like peeling the silk from a cocoon.

Although Xiaomin actively asked me to help him overcome his five shortcomings, and although I believed that he was sincere, he was still a child, a child with a silver spoon. Children like him are usually extremely self-willed, and tend to start strong but finish weak, unpredictable indeed. How was I supposed to help a kid like that to quit Internet addiction?

The three phases of quitting Internet addiction:

**Phase one: Making Xiaomin focus on one game only.**

After I started living with him, I encouraged him to keep his attention on one type of online game only. I asked him to give up everything from "Legend" and "Red Moon" and focus on "Stone Age". (Later, Xiaomin's essay recorded the situation at that time.)

I encouraged him, helped him, and even played this online game with him, which ultimately helped him gain more and more satisfaction from the game and he became more and more obsessed with this game. The account of this game was equivalent to his life.

We finally reached level 140, which was the highest level of this game! Our reputation in the game ranked first in the three northeastern provinces at that time.

At this moment, there were voices from Xiaomin's family who couldn't understand my approach and believed that not only did their child not improve academically, but also I plunged him into deeper Internet addiction. This kind of criticism kept coming, and at that time I was under a lot of pressure.

Take fishing as an example. Before fishing, people will first find some things that the fish love to eat, make these things suitable for the fish to bite, and then choose the appropriate time of the day to throw them into the fishpond with the fishing hook. But in the eyes of birds, these steps are extremely inconsistent with the purpose.

Even in situations where no one could understand my approach, Xiaomin's parents still maintained absolute trust in me. They encouraged me to follow my own ideas and believed that I had my reasons, and in the end, I would succeed. Looking back now, this kind of trust from beginning to end was actually a prerequisite for the complete transformation of Xiaomin.

Why do I encourage him to only play one type of online game at first? Because this will allow the child to devote all their time and energy to one thing, which is equivalent to having the child put all their eggs in one basket. This way, when I quit online games in the future, it will be easier for me to concentrate on this goal and avoid awkward situations where I need to use force from left to right and disperse my efforts to deal with multiple goals.

Secondly, the development of anything goes through a process from weakness to strength and from prosperity to decline. The same goes for playing online games. Our initial goal when playing online games is to become the top expert. However, when you become the top expert and seek defeat alone, it is precisely when the game brings you the least joy and is also the easiest time to leave. So I believe that completely quitting Internet addiction must start from being deeply addicted to it.

We should not isolate children or send them to a training camp to suffer when it comes to Internet addiction. Our goal is to encourage children to use the Internet reasonably rather than keep them away from it.

Educators should accompany children and guide them to step out of the

Internet. It is absolutely worthwhile to spend time on this process. After quitting Internet addiction, teenagers with Internet addiction will have a better understanding of many things than their peers and avoid taking detours. So, they seem to have wasted time on the Internet, but their past tortuous growth experiences will also save them time on the path of life in the future. Therefore, I often say to children that there are no detours for men.

After I successfully made Xiaomin addicted to only one game, it was time for the next phase.

**Phase two: From online games to single-player games.**

Single-player games refer to electronic games that can run independently using only one computer. Single-player gamers can play games on their own computers without being connected to the Internet and can also compete with other computers in the same room, which is different from playing online games.

Because it is not played on the Internet, its interactivity is slightly worse, but stand-alone games are often more delicate than online games, and the plot is more rich and vivid. The series of game experiences unfolding in the background of the game theme often gives people a feeling of being there.

The benefits of single-player games are also that they are less addictive, and they do not involve too much time and energy and focus more on leisure and entertainment. The appeal of online games lies in:

Firstly, it allows a brand-new start at a low cost.

In a survey on 100 'Stone Age' players done in 2003, I found that 96% of them had in-game characters that were more morally excellent than the players themselves in real life.

Game players will reflect the parts of their personality that need to be changed in real life on the game characters they operate on, and fully promote their personality that has not been fully utilized in real life in the online world.

For example, if a person with Internet addiction is very isolated in life and doesn't have many friends, he will definitely make more friends online. A person who is cowardly and is often bullied in real life will make their online characters heroic, generous, and even lend a helping hand when faced with injustice.

Such dramatic change only costs about two yuan per hour. What a deal! On the Internet, life can be turned back. If you fail, you can start over at any time. Online games have made up for these shortcomings that are difficult for us to make up for in real life.

Secondly, sincere and close connections with others. The large number of online players and vast gaming territories in online games enable players to always find their favorite friends, who spend time together and fight side by side. "Vibe" is their only criterion for making friends. It's such a pure friendship.

Thirdly, a fair gaming environment is the foundation of everything in the online gaming world, and everything is based on numbers, which is very transparent. The pros and cons are all visible. If you want to succeed, you need to buy more cards and spend more time. Transparency is only one path to success, and anyone can take it. All of this creates an orderly and fair social environment that people aspire to.

Fourthly, a timely digital incentive system is in place in the game. Every time you kill enemies or monsters and every second you spend in the game is accurately recorded. You can see your progress every moment through the increasing numbers. If you take a break from work and return online, your wealth and experience will not shrink. Everyone warmly welcomes you when you come back! All of these bring you confidence and warmth every moment.

Therefore, online gaming is a dramatic reoccurrence of the society. The incentive system of online games is the fundamental reason why quitting Internet addiction cannot start by cultivating learning interest. Internet-addicted teenagers are all ambitious children who hope to make changes and are not afraid of hardship.

Children are not playing computer games, but playing with people, so quitting Internet addiction is equivalent to quitting the connection with the people they trust. It's so difficult to quit these things! Unfortunately, the Internet is ultimately empty, and the gap between reality and virtuality cannot be bridged. So Xiaomin's Internet addiction must be quitted. After sorting out the above, I made some preparations and planned the following actions.

I carefully selected a few people to eat and live with me and Xiaomin. We went to the same Internet cafe every day to play games. In the beginning, we played our own games, but for half an hour before leaving, we played the same game: "*Battlefield 1942*".

We ate together, lived together, and charged forward together every day. We played in the dark every day, and that kind of happiness quickly merged us into a family. Gradually, we spent less time playing online games and more time playing single-player games. Why was this? Because playing games online together made up for the shortcomings of single-player games compared to online games, replacing the advantage of close connections between people in online games, and was more realistic than in online games, representing people in real life.

These Internet-addicted teenagers who are excluded by the mainstream school group naturally go online to find friends to play with. Although making friends online is sincere, their interactions are still quite limited.

Nowadays, Xiaomin not only played games, but also had access to the live operators behind each soldier on the computer screen and lived with them. We paid close attention to Xiaomin, provided suggestions for his shortcomings, and gave timely and collective encouragement to every progress of Xiaomin.

So, did he like online games or single-player games more? Or did he like living in the virtual world or did he like the reality that I had created for him? Gradually, he felt that online games were not as attractive and enjoyed being with us every day.

This basically completed the transition between online games and single-player games. But this transition was not thorough. He was still a child, and children would not make up their minds to completely quit online games. So, how can he completely quit online games? I thought, what could cause changes to a boy who's in love? There was only one answer to it, a girl.

"Men change the world, and women change the men's view of the world."

Start taking action!

At 3:00 pm.

"Come here, Xiaomin. I got something to say to you."

"Yeah. What's up?"

"I feel like it's a little boring for you to live with a bunch of men all day, Xiaomin! You should pursue your own happiness!"

"Are you talking about me and Xiaojing? I miss her a lot, but I don't even get to see her, and there's nothing I can do." Xiaomin shook his head with disappointment.

"Do you want to see her every day? Every time you see her, do you want her to smile at you?"

"Of course! I owe you, Brother Ye! I've always dreamed of it! Do you really have a way?" Xiaomin rushed over and hugged my leg.

"I'll ask Xiaojing's mother to take her to a film studio to take a set of photos, and I will enlarge the photos and make it crystal painting and print them life-size. What do you think of it?"

"Great!" Xiaomin ran around the room out of excitement. "But how is it possible? Her mom wouldn't agree to that, would she?" Xiaomin suddenly stopped.

"I'll deal with it, but there surely is a problem."

"What problem is it?"

"Money!"

"How much, Brother Ye?"

"5000 Yuan."

"Piece of cake! Money isn't a problem!" Xiaomin looked at me proudly. (Don't get proud too early, I thought.)

"But my parents took my New Year's money a little while ago." (I arranged.)

"Oh yeah?"

"I could definitely get it though, if I go to my grandparent's house."

"Alright, go ahead!"

At 7:00 pm.

"Oh, you're back, Xiaomin."

"Damn, it's a bit unlucky." Xiaomin looked dejected.

"What's up?"

"They both got sick, and I managed to get a total of 200 Yuan!" (Again, I arranged, and the whole family cooperated.)

"That's really hopeless. We need to take two sets. Keep one for ourselves and give Xiaojing's mother one set. Our set of photos also needs to be made into crystal paintings, and 5000 yuan is already the lowest price."

"Brother Ye, I'll think of another way." Xiaomin was very frustrated.

The next morning at 2:00 am, I was awakened by someone poking me in the darkness.

"Brother Ye, wake up. I've thought it over and decided to sell my Internet account."

"How much is your Internet account worth?"

"My account has the highest level and reputation, and there is some top-notch equipment in the game. If this account is sold at market price now, it can probably be sold for over 8000 yuan."

(I thought, damn, he'd still have 3000 left afterward. Maybe he would buy something else to play with later.)

"Is anyone buying it?"

"I don't know. It hasn't been sold before. Why don't you help me sell it?"

"Sure. I'll do it, but I can only go to the Internet cafes to ask, not sure how much I can get for it. Don't blame me for not getting what you wanted."

"Oh no, I won't. I know I can't get much if I'm rushing to sell it." (I wasn't expecting him to understand this.)

"Okay, as long as you have a plan in mind."

I was afraid that Xiaomin would turn back, so I immediately got up and went out with the account and password.

I asked around in the Internet cafe and made sure the account was worth the amount.

Then I took out my phone and made a phone call.

"Hello, Xiaomin's dad, are you in town?"

"Hello, Mr. Ye. I just got home. It's so late. What's up?"

"I'll sell you Xiaomin's online game account for 5000 yuan. I'll take the money now."

"… All right! Where are you? I'll deliver it to you right away!"

Ten minutes later, Xiaomin's father drove to the agreed location. He hopped out of the car before I had the chance to move towards him, grabbed my hands and said, "Is my son quitting the Internet?"

I nodded.

"Mr. Ye, you've worked hard!" Through the street lamp, I saw an excited face and a pair of tearful eyes, filled with gratitude.

A few days later, on a Sunday morning at 6:30, I woke up Xiaomin and said to take him to a place. We arrived at the pedestrian street. When he couldn't believe it, he saw Xiaojing's mother taking her into the studio to take photos. Xiaomin stared at me blankly and said, "Brother Ye, you are my own brother!"

Human beings have a commonality: once they put in all their efforts on something, they will regard it as a treasure and take care of it in every way possible. If the thing unfortunately dies prematurely, it is difficult to have the courage to start over, and they are even unwilling to see anything related to it again.

So is Xiaomin. Since then, he has never touched online games again. He had no inner trauma because he was voluntary and believed that all of this was worth it. Through this incident, not only did Xiaomin quit online games (Note that quitting online games does not mean learning to use the Internet reasonably), but also our relationship deepened. For children with Internet addiction, it is best not to force or isolate them. Solving their main inner conflicts is the best strategy to help them break free from Internet addiction. Xiaomin has completed 100% of the tasks from online games to single-player games. Now we can start the third goal.

**Phase three: From single-player games to rational games.**

For educators, a problem always lies before us, which is the issue of "revolutionary leadership"! Because in human society, the issue of revolutionary leadership has always been an important issue from small businesses to large countries. How can we establish the position of an educator in the hearts of these problematic children? Firstly, it is the children's trust in your abilities, and secondly, they have love for your personality. The greater your abilities, the more attractive your personality. The greater your personal charm, and the greater your leadership. Some children have been influenced by their parents since childhood, and their horizons even surpass those of ordinary adults. Moreover, time waits for no one, and relying on "seeing people's hearts over time" to establish an image is inefficient. So the establishment of leadership is very skillful.

I have summarized eight words: To earn the respect in a short period.

How difficult it is to achieve these seven words! Because this involves the learning and accumulation of various professional fields such as education, behavioral psychology, personality psychology, sociology, philosophy, economics, Chinese language and literature, history, geography, colorism, rhetoric, military science, physical training, fashion, etc. Each aspect affects the personal quality of teachers and the speed of student growth, with basic disciplines such as literature, history, and geography having the greatest impact on people.

Leadership is definitely not something that can be achieved through hard work. The establishment of leadership must come from their genuine admiration for you. And in the process of children's change, leadership must be absolute. Undoubtedly, leadership was now in my hands. I would immediately make a three-rule agreement:

Firstly, although we no longer played online games, we fully invested in single-player games. Secondly, it was better to go to the Internet cafe and play happily, day and night. (Xiaomin was startled upon hearing this.) Thirdly, I would decide when to go to the Internet cafe. To ensure smooth management, it is necessary to make the public feel that they have received practical benefits.

I have set three-time slots for us to go every day: from 11:30 pm to 2:30 am the next day. The second is from 11:30 pm to 2:30 pm, and the third is from 5:00 pm to 7:00 pm. Eight hours per day.

What a strange rule! Xiaomin thought to himself. But he calculated that if we went to play, we usually waked up at 8:00 am in the morning, tidied up at 8:30 am, had breakfast at 9:00 am, played from 9:00 am to 11:30 am for two and a half hours, and then went home for dinner at 11:30 am and took a nap at noon. We played from 1:30 pm in the afternoon to 5:00 pm for three and a half hours, at home for dinner, and played for six hours a day.

According to Ye's schedule, it will be from 11:30 am to 2:30 pm, for three hours. Then from 11:30 pm to 2:30 am, it takes another three hours! From 5:00 pm to 7:00 pm in the evening, we played eight hours a day. What a great deal! Although the time may seem strange, a deal is a deal.

"Alright, let's do it."

So how did I come up with these three segments to go to the Internet cafe to play? I'll explain the last two first, from 11:30 pm to 2:30 am, and from 5:00 pm to 7:00 pm. The Internet cafe we were going to was right next to the high school where he used to study. School ended at 11:30 am and 5:30 pm. At noon, students came home for dinner. Every time after school, many students who would lie about getting out of school late today rushed into the Internet cafe, threw their backpacks on chairs, and then eagerly started surfing on the Internet.

Every time these peers rushed in wearing school uniforms, laughing and joking, they would strongly stimulate Xiaomin: they come to surf on the Internet after school, and I drop out to surf on the Internet! (Utilize comparisons)

This kind of emotional vibration was most evident when we played online games. Whenever the students rushed in from outside, Xiaomin would perform poorly, and he immediately lost aims. The mortality rate of the character he played increased.

Because we were in the same game, I was there right behind him in the game. It was especially apparent to me.

It was even more awkward when we met his old classmates. But the rules were the rules, he didn't have a say in where or when we played video games.

Every time the students rushed in after school not long after we sat down, Xiaomin would feel very frustrated, frowning and sighing incessantly.

The significance of the first segment from 11:00 pm to 2:30 am, is that humans have a commonality that it is easy to trigger thinking when it is quiet at night. People reflect on the day, the past times and their own lives. They think about what they have been busy with during the day, and what their peers have done, and people who have a hard time in life also like to numb themselves with alcohol at this time.

Whenever this happens, I found that Xiaomin's condition was very poor, often frowning and playing, sometimes appearing absent-minded.

What would he be thinking about? Every day, besides surfing on the Internet, it was all about eating, sleeping, surfing on the Internet and then eating again...

He was stimulated during the day while reflecting on the situation in the early morning. After being tormented for two months like this, one day, when we were preparing to leave for the Internet cafe again, Xiaomin said, "Brother Ye, I don't want to go anymore."

"What do you want to do then?" I asked.

He said he just wanted to sleep, and he'd like to sleep every day in the future. He didn't want to go anymore. He just wanted to take a walk in the park or downstairs.

Throughout history, we can find that before any revolution in society erupts, there will always be a revolution of thought, just like the Enlightenment Movement prepared for the bourgeois revolution and the May Fourth Movement prepared for the new democratic revolution.

Does the revolution of thought appear out of a sudden? No. It is a result of the ever-cumulating emotions. Before Xiaomin truly took the step to make the change, he must have this long-term emotional accumulation. And he should be the one to take the step on his own. This way of giving children space to make their own decisions can achieve the best results. In this way, Xiaomin spontaneously took a step towards a bright future and completely quitted Internet addiction. During this period, Xiaomin made improvements academically and physically simultaneously. I have tailored an education plan for Xiaomin that suited him. In the beginning, Xiaomin was very lazy and lacked enthusiasm for life. Why was this happening? Because his life had no goals yet.

In the long history of the Chinese education system, the need for motivation has long been overlooked and even denied. People always assume that only pure willpower and unremitting effort are needed. In practice, ignoring motivation means that we seek help from external forces, from the authority of teachers or the prestige of textbooks, from the fear of punishment or failure, from surpassing others, from the fear of not being able to advance, seek care for future success in adult life, seek rewards, and so on. Educators become helpless when they realize that the students are immune to these motivations.

In fact, all we need to do is understanding the meaning of the words "purpose", "method", and "life goal". Purpose refers to the final stage of an activity equal to its final or concluding period. Method refers to the earlier stage of an activity, which is the stage before the end of the activity.

The terms "method" and "purpose" only refer to the two stages of an activity, while the meaning of life goals lies in the ability of an action process, a job, or a profession to completely attract a person. So, establishing life goals is of utmost importance for children!

Since I took over Xiaomin's transformation work, I have gradually taken him to travel to many places. After arriving in various places, we did not just go sightseeing, but gained a deep understanding of many people he had never seen before. Some started by working hard to earn money. Some started by relying on knowledge to develop high-tech industries, and some struggled in the vortex of money.

I took Xiaomin on a study tour to deepen my understanding of society. At the end of 2003, I took Xiaomin on an inspection trip to Jiangsu and saw college students coming to rural areas to serve as grassroots cadres, leading the villagers to become wealthy. Their down-to-earth and hard-working spirit, which overcame all difficulties, left a deep impression on us. After returning to Liaoning, Xiaomin eventually established the life goal of "taking the college entrance examination to enter politics and becoming a village official to benefit the local community". The first way to achieve this goal was to be admitted to a key high school in the city, which was his own choice.

From the perspective of children, the biggest waste in school is that they are completely unable to fully and freely utilize the experiences gained outside school. At the same time, he cannot apply what he has learned in school in his daily life. That is the phenomenon of school isolation between school and life.

During this period, I engaged in extensive philosophical contemplation with Xiaomin on 24 important and ordinary topics such as life, justice, love, death, and money, forming a common understanding.

Common understanding is the foundation of our communication, and it helps us to respect each other. Educators tend to have the illusion that teenagers are just immature and yet to mature, shallow in knowledge yet to be deepened. His experience is narrow and needs to be expanded, and his duty is to passively accommodate or accept. When he is docile and obedient, our duty is fulfilled.

Teenagers and the truth in books are two sides of a coin. The process of continuing to transform from the existing experiences of teenagers to the truth in textbooks is education. The child's Internet addiction had been quit and good study habits had been established, but the problems of hitting people, cursing, frowning, and walking in strange postures had not changed yet.

I believed that the changes to these shortcomings, like Internet addiction, could not be achieved through verbal preaching. In order for children to truly change, they need to change in their lives and in society.

### Getting beat up in the Internet cafe, the price within the mirror

Xiaomin had a habit of hitting and cursing people since childhood, and he never changed his behavior. He even scolded people regardless of time, place, or character. Even in the Internet cafe, the person who was insulted never said anything back because we usually outnumbered them.

In order to prevent this bad habit from causing a big disaster, in the later stage of Xiaomin's addiction to the Internet, one night I sent away all the people who lived with us and secretly set him up in the Internet cafe.

# CHAPTER 1

"Xiaomin!"

"What's up, Bother Ye?"

"Let's go gaming."

"Are we still going this late?"

"Yeah, let's play a few, just the two of us."

"Alright!"

When we arrived at the Internet cafe upstairs, Xiaomin found only one computer unoccupied. I told him to get on it and then made an excuse and left.

Half an hour later, people on the first floor started running upstairs, saying that a child had been beaten. I took out my phone and called the police.

It turned out that Xiaomin started playing Counter-Strike with the people on the second floor and cursing casually after I left. He forgot that his family were not at the Internet cafe, and when two angry youths were about to teach him a lesson, Xiaomin was still provoking them with indifference.

When blood dripped from the corner of his mouth, Xiaomin panicked. It was too late for him to run away. He got a solid beating and then the two youths were pulled apart by the people that I've put around them. Later, the police arrived, and the relevant personnel were taken to the police station. In the police station, Xiaomin saw the cost of beating someone. In the mirror, Xiaomin saw the cost of cursing someone. Starting from that night, Xiaomin completely changed his bad habit of hitting and cursing people at will.

## The anger of the masses is difficult to calm.

If a child is always worried and unhappy, how will he get along with people in the future? In March 2004, Xiaomin was transferred to a new school and the opportunity came. The classmates were all disgusted by his long face. Finally, someone "brave" decided to solve the issue for the rest of them. He said to Xiaomin after class, "I'm quite annoyed by you. I'm going to get 50 people to finish you tomorrow at noon!"

After Xiaomin returned home, he said to me, "Brother Ye, a classmate wants someone to beat me up tomorrow at noon when I go to school. What should I do?"

"Why did they want to beat you?"

"I don't know."

"You should go ask him the reason this afternoon. Also, you can tell him that we are all men, and it's best for men to solve problems in a man's way. If he wanted to fight, you can 'fight alone' and fight one-on-one."

"Alright, I'll tell him this afternoon."

Xiaomin went to school normally in the afternoon. When he came back from school in the evening, he said to me, "It didn't work, Brother Ye. He said he's annoyed when he looks at me, and the 50 people are all annoyed when they see me!"

"Did you tell him about the one-on-one fight?"

"Yeah, he said that he agreed, but the other 49 people didn't agree. Because they were all annoyed with me, so they decided to beat me together."

"It seems that your face is quite annoying. When are they planning to beat you?"

"He said tomorrow at noon before school." (Students are let out for lunch at noon.)

"Alright, I'll see what I can do."

The next day at noon, I took a taxi to take him to school. It was indeed an unusual day, and the students on duty at the school gate looked flustered.

A group of people at the school gate were rubbing their hands and fists. "Why do they hate me so much?" Xiaomin asked me in frustration when he saw this situation.

"Because your facial expression sucks! I'll take a photo of you and take a look. This is what you look like every day, with an unfriendly long face. Everyone would think that this person doesn't like me! But I know you are a kind-hearted person, and you are willing to help others when they are in trouble. You have to express that. Don't you think so?"

He sighed and said, "I'll change, Brother Ye." He did make a change after the incident. He became someone always with a smile on his face after about a year.

**Blindly copying others and making oneself look foolish.**

People who have watched "Animal World" know that the individual who acts strange in a group setting tends to be alienated and even attacked by their peers. For example, if one of the six ducklings born to a duck mother has wings or feet that are faulty, the other ducklings will continue to bully it until it dies.

Due to malnutrition and the lack of attention from his parents, Xiaoming had developed a limp when he walked. In Zhao Benshan's words, he was "tiptoeing".

Xiaomin was very distressed and said to me, "Brother Ye, I have changed my problem with a worried face, but why can't I change my problem with tiptoeing? Sometimes the more I want to change, the more serious it becomes! My classmates all laugh at me. What should I do?"

I said, "Xiaomin, let's just try our best to improve. Your job as a student is to study. If you don't study well now, tiptoeing is your weakness. When you study well, tiptoeing is your characteristic!" "We can't rush into correcting a bad trait. Sometimes we even need to be grateful for our imperfections. It is those imperfections that help us see the ones who truly love us."

"You're very brave. Being brave doesn't mean you're never afraid, rather being able to persevere when you are afraid."

A year later, in April 2005, after school, Xiaomin rushed to me excitedly and said to me, "Brother Ye! You were so right before! There were two boys in my class who were learning walking on tiptoe with me!"

I thought to myself that let's not mess others' kids up.

It turned out that Xiaomin's grades had risen from 1024 when he was enrolled in 2004 to 388 in 2005. Students were puzzled by Xiaomin's progress, and some male students who had worked hard and had no success did not know the secret to Xiaomin's rapid progress. They believed that it was "tiptoeing" that made Xiaomin's grades improve rapidly, so they all followed suit.

Later on, after long-term dietary adjustments and basketball training, Xiaomin's tiptoeing problem finally disappeared.

As Gandhi once said, they cannot take away our self-respect if we do not give it to them.

## Suicide—the ultimate move of Xiaomin

At the beginning of teaching Xiaomin, I was surprised by Xiaomin's mother's lack of principles in front of Xiaomin. Faced with Xiaomin's unreasonable demands, Xiaomin's mother always kept giving in. In the end, no matter how absurd the demands were, they would be met. Whenever this happened, Xiaomin's mother always had a bitter smile on her face and shook her head helplessly. Finally, one day, I discovered the reason behind it.

I remember it was one morning, Xiaomin, who dropped out of school and was at home, should have taken a physics class. Xiaomin said he didn't want to take it. I asked him the reason, and he said there was no reason, but he didn't want to. I said we had to do whatever we needed. His eyebrows immediately stood up and he said to me, "I'll jump off this building if you keep pushing me!" As soon as I heard this, I immediately began to observe his expression and movements. His eyebrows kept lifting, and he wiped the tip of his nose with his hand. Then he said to me, "Alright then!" He turned around and ran towards the balcony. We lived on the fifth floor, and below was a hard stone road. If you really fall, you will either die or be injured.

In the blink of an eye, Xiaomin's body had already crossed the window of the balcony. He turned around and looked at me with such a firm and cold expression. The crowd downstairs enjoying the cool air screamed. I dashed to him and hugged him tightly. From the side, I saw a twitch in the corner of Xiaomin's mouth. I quickly put my mouth close to Xiaomin's ear and said to him, "Do you know what my mission is? My mission is to help you realize your ideas."

"You wanted to play video games.
I've helped you!

"You wanted to get a girlfriend.
I've helped you!

"You wanted a photo album.
I've helped you!

"You wanted to sell your game account.
I've helped you!

"You wanted to fight someone else.
I've helped you!

"Today you want to die.
I will still help you, and I will still be wholehearted!"

Xiaomin looked at me with an incredulous expression on his face. He remembered my principle of handling things and realized that the person in front of him was someone who played cards without following the rules. The serious expression on my face told him that I meant what I said. A few seconds later, Xiaomin began to plead with me, "Don't do that, Brother Ye, please don't do that! I'm Xiaomin! Please!"

I just replied robotically, "It's okay. I'll help you. I'll help you jump off."

"Brother Ye! I don't want to die! I won't play anymore!" Xiaomin started crying.

"Oh, have you changed your mind?" I pretended to be surprised.

"Hmm, um, I was kidding! Stop playing!"

I pulled him back inside all at once. (I've studied the paper written by Paul Ackerman, a psychology professor at the School of Medicine, the University of California. He devoted his life to studying facial expressions, deception, and emotions. He is the most authoritative expert in this field worldwide.

The raised eyebrows, itchy nose and the twitching lips of Xiaomin indicated one thing, that he was lying. Psychology is the brightest light when handling emergencies. After getting pulled back in, Xiaomin sat in front of the desk, as if nothing had happened before, and asked to keep having lessons. Later down the line, Xiaomin told me that threatening to commit suicide had never failed to work on the adults, and the reason why his mother kept backing off was that she was afraid that Xiaomin's emotions would go out of control. Of the children that I've interacted with, more than half of them had used such a strategy, and this tactic was indeed effective for parents.)

After a while, Xiaomin's mother rushed over, as the neighbor downstairs had called her. As soon as she entered the door, she pounced and lovingly stroked Xiaomin's hair, with tears flickering in her eyes. I asked Xiaomin to look at the woman sitting in the chair trembling slightly and said to him, "This is a woman. She needs to be protected." Xiaomin nodded, and then he never threatened anyone with suicide again.

Xiaomin's mother had calmed down after a bit. After listening to my description of the incident, she gratefully said to me, "I used to think that my kid wasn't properly educated because I didn't have time, and if I had time, I could do your job. Now I know I can't do your job."

Later, there was another time when a student called me late at night and said he wouldn't be back that night. He was about to jump off the bridge and called me to say goodbye. I thought about it and said to him, "After you die, we will have a brief sadness. But your father is still young and handsome, only 40 years old. Your father and your mother are both intelligent people. After you die, they will quickly recover from the sadness, have another child, cultivate him well, and the child would never make the same mistakes as you did. Their family will live a happy life from then on. Oh, by the way, this child will also have the same name, and he'll have your allowance. It's really not too big of a deal if you die. What you need to do now is to get off the bridge, find a tall building with a cement road below, and jump off. Because there is a river under the bridge, you may have attempted suicide and will face double punishments. If you haven't been so foolish yet, go back quickly and don't delay sleeping at night."

20 minutes later, the child returned, washed up and went to bed, as if nothing had happened.

Children often threaten to commit suicide to make the adults compromise. The actions I took when Xiaomin threatened to commit suicide were based on a special response to Xiaomin's personality, which is a special educational action for professionals. Such a professional approach is not recommended to the readers. In fact, none of my approaches are recommended to be imitated, because you have never done such meticulous investigation and preparation in advance like me. For parents, if your children always resort to suicide tactics, you can consider hiring professionals to educate your children, not letting them make such threats all the time.

## Zhongkao (the middle school entrance examination) and Gaokao (the college entrance examination) in China

Xiaomin's parents had concerns about whether their child was suitable for school, as Xiaomin's curriculum fell too far behind. From the third grade of elementary school to the fourth grade of junior high school, there are totally seven years of curriculum. Both Chinese and English are accumulation-oriented subjects, making it difficult to break through. I didn't think it was a problem! I analyzed that firstly, Xiaomin's parents graduated from key universities, and their children's genes are relatively good. Secondly, what kind of children could play an online game to the full level? He must have extraordinary intelligence and endurance. If a child could play games for 16 hours a day, I believed he could study for 16 hours a day!

The standard for evaluating ability and perseverance is precisely how well you play games, not how well you learn. What type of person can play for 16 hours a day? Being capricious also requires courage and strength. I said to Xiaomin, "Not everyone can truly fall in love with learning. For most people, the joy of learning comes from constantly surpassing others. Learning is like a game. No matter how tiring it is, it feels better than losing!" After hearing this, Xiaomin only asked me one question: "Brother Ye, have you forgotten my life goal?" Xiaomin returned to his alma mater. We were ready to get back up from where we fell.

I had a long conversation with Xiaomin's parents and agreed that I would continue to arrange all of Xiaomin's work after going to school. In order to ensure the autonomy of the child's learning, I refused to ask tutors to provide him with tutoring. I demanded that children should learn on their own and ask the teachers at school for help when needed. We started to work tirelessly day and night.

His task was to study hard, while I was responsible for inspiring thinking, identifying problems, developing plans, and providing logistical support.

The content of middle school textbooks may seem difficult, but as long as one is willing to learn, even if he falls behind for a long time, a student can still learn better. And if the child starts learning from the third year of junior high school which is a four-year program, it is not too late. If it is a three-year program, it is not too late to start studying from the second semester of the second year of junior high school.

During the difficult times before the high school entrance exam, I lit three fires for Xiaomin!

**The first one: A single spark can start a prairie fire.**

He had encountered many difficulties since he went back to school.

Firstly, he was embarrassed in front of his old classmates, as they were all in their fourth year of junior high school, but he was still in his third year.

Secondly, he was still working on his facial expressions.

Thirdly, he was often ridiculed for the problem of tiptoeing.

Fourthly, the textbooks were difficult for him to understand, like heavenly books!

And fifthly, he was ranked 811 for the exam on April 6th, 2004, and all the students in the class knew that this newly transferred student was academically poor.

Xiaomin was on the edge of breaking down! At this critical moment, I conducted the first mental encouragement for Xiaomin. The title of my speech was "A single spark can start a prairie fire".

What is fire? It is our determination to strive and our belief in achieving success in learning! We might not necessarily succeed (Lower the self-expectations of ordinary people and relieve stress), but we are still heading forward! Why? Because we are the sons of hardworking individuals. Striving is our innate habit!

Though we are a small lighter now, if we stick together, keep improving every day, and solving new problems in learning every day, one day we will make this flame a blazing fire!

Xiaomin shouted, "I understood. Brother Ye! I'll give it my all!"

(At that time, I bought a Hero 616 fountain pen, the cheapest in the market, 2.5 Yuan. Xiaomin made history with it. The pen was nowhere to be found, but the slip with encouragement on it was still there.)

One month later, Xiaomin moved up 138 in ranking.

Life is like a game, and attitude is the most important.

At this point, the problem I had already anticipated appeared. For such a child who has hardly received any praise since the day of school, after making great progress in exams, the encouragement from teachers, the praise from classmates, family and friends fed his ego and immersed him in complacency every day. What was an educator supposed to do under such circumstances? Was I supposed to remind him constantly? Or, to cool him down with criticisms? No way.

Firstly, as a child, after making significant progress, this impetuousness is normal. Although this mentality clearly leads children to failure and makes parents and teachers anxious, we must believe in one truth: if teachers and parents feel that something is wrong, rest assured that the child would probably have known it long ago. He is just powerless to extricate himself. At this time, there is no need for words, just to educate the child with ironclad facts, as facts are better than eloquence!

Allowing children to experience and practice on their own is called growth. Learning to educate children with facts, is the growth of being parents.

**The second one: A fire in the darkness.**

Just say the keywords once. I said to Xiaomin, "We have now transformed from a small flame into a fire. Under what conditions are we a fire? It is a fire in the darkness!

We can easily see this fire in the darkness, but we need to pay more attention to the endless darkness that surrounds the fire.

We are still in the early stage of the struggle. Even though we moved up to rank 673 from 811, we are still doing poorly and far away from our goal of being admitted to a key high school. That was my reminder to you."

Xiaomin surprised me with his response, "I'll try my best, Brother Ye."

Not surprisingly, Xiaomin ranked 642 in grade in the exam on July 10, 2004, only advancing 31 places.

Xiaomin finally understood that the struggle in learning was actually a struggle against himself! We kept working hard day and night, bravely moving forward! The progress of the child has given hope to the parents of Xiaomin. Their expectations have risen like rockets, from the initial "It's okay as long as he gets into a high school" to "he would be supposed to be in a key high school". How could I not understand the heart of being a parent? But I had to put my feet down and walk one step at a time. On the examination of October 8, 2004, Xiaomin ranked 510 in the whole school, advancing 132 places.

One day, while I was sleeping at night, I heard Xiaomin talking in his sleep. "Father, I will work hard!" Haha, he was pledging to his father! I was so pleased every time I saw him study till late at night. Every time I saw him dedicating himself so wholeheartedly to his struggle, I felt sincerely gratified and felt that through Xiaomin, I had realized my own value. In November 2004, Xiaomin's parents divorced. Xiaomin said nothing and locked himself in a room when he heard the news. Half an hour later, he came out as if nothing had happened and continued his study.

On November 28, 2004, Xiaomin ranked 585 in the unified examination, falling 75 places behind. This was the only time Xiaomin had moved backward, which showed how much influence the family had on their children.

He stared at his report card sadly, "Troubles do come in pairs, huh."

I said, "Is it painful for you to learn about your parents?"

"Yes"

"Are you going to do something about it?"

"Is there anything I can do, Brother Ye?"
(He thought I had a way to get his parents to remarry. Looking at how worried he was, my heart was shattered.)

"The only thing you can do now is to learn from their lessons and prevent the same tragedy from happening to your children!" Xiaomin nodded. Not long after, the sadness was drowned out by the fast-paced life. We were back on our way again!

In the unified school examination on January 15th, 2005, Xiaomin ranked 464, advancing 121 places. During this period, Xiaomin's grandparents, uncles, and aunts came to visit him many times to encourage him. He was enthusiastic but they never stayed for too long so that they wouldn't keep him from studying. Although it was always for a short period, seeing the warm scene of their family together made my heart feel very warm.

### The controversy at the parents' meeting

There was a parents' meeting after every monthly exam. Xiaomin's father was too embarrassed to attend because Xiaomin did poorly. It was always his mother who used to attend the meetings. However, since I stood in this position, this important task quickly fell on my shoulders.

It was the sixth time that I attended the meeting as his cousin. Like the previous five times, the teacher did not mention how much improvement Xiaomin had made. On the contrary, each teacher would focus on reciting the names of a few students who often did not complete their homework at the end of their speeches, including Xiaomin.

Some teachers would even ask the parents of students mentioned to stand up and verify their identities. Finally, it was my turn. The teacher asked angrily, "Who are Xiaomin's parents? Stand up and show me yourself. Why does your child never complete his homework?"

I stood up and walked over to the teacher, standing next to her and facing the other parents. "I am Xiaomin's cousin. May I ask the parents present whose child slept after 2:00 am last night? Please raise your hand." No one did.

"Alright, let me do some calculations. The school closes at 6:30 pm every day, and the students arrive home at 7:00 pm. Even if it takes half an hour to have dinner immediately, 7:30 pm would be the earliest time when they finish dinner. Even if they start doing homework immediately after dinner, it will take at least two hours which is already 9:30 pm because yesterday's Chinese homework had two test papers not including a composition.

"Math homework takes an hour and a half, which would make it 10:30 pm.

"An English paper takes another hour and a half, that would make it 12:00 pm at midnight.

"Physics and chemistry each take an hour, and it's already 2:00 am to finish them all.

"Note that this does not include the class teacher's requirement for students to exercise for half an hour every night in the physical education subject of the middle school entrance examination, daily English, calligraphy, daily Chinese characters in regular script, 15 minutes of English listening every day, plus ten minutes of resting and time for the restroom after completing each subject.

"Therefore, any child who went to bed before 2:00 am today could not complete their homework. Those whose names were not mentioned by the teacher more or less were copying others' homework.

"Your children must have arrived at school early in the morning, right? You must not know what they came to do so early. Let me tell you, they all came to school to make up for their homework because even copying answers took an hour!

"Some of them borrowed answers to copy, while others copied according to their classmates. The most efficient way was for each of the five students to write one subject, and the next morning they switched to copying."

The seated parents looked disturbed.

I continued, "Xiaomin came home on the first day of school and cried to tell me that homework was too much to finish. I said that homework didn't need to be completed because it was for students of different levels. Students need to choose to complete their homework according to their own needs. You just need to complete the questions that I marked in front of you.

"That's why he was able to go to sleep before 11:00 pm and wake up at 5:00 am in the morning, and then he has some time for extracurricular reading, exercising, listening to music, and 20 minutes for breakfast.

"He never copies homework and only arrives at school 10 minutes earlier than the school's required time. We never hire tutors and only ask the teacher for any questions he doesn't understand.

"Xiaomin never falls asleep in class and answers questions very actively. He never slacks off after class and completes homework and household chores I assigned admirably. Every day, he also overcomes his problems of being worried and tiptoeing when walking.

"In the past 10 months, Xiaomin's annual ranking has advanced by a total of 560 places, but he never received any encouragement at the parents' meetings. On the contrary, he was always regarded as a typical poor student. I am sad that if a child like him with courage, integrity, diligence, and honesty cannot be recognized here, then I don't know what type of people this school is cultivating!

"We should bless him, encourage him, embrace him, for he's been nothing but at least an honest child."

"Believe me, one day you will be proud of him. Thank you all."

The room was silent. I walked through the parents and returned to my seat. And on the way, I was greeted by approving gazes.

On March 26, 2005, Xiaomin ranked 436 in the school unified examination, advancing 28 places.

On April 27, 2005, Xiaomin ranked 388 in the school unified examination, advancing 48 places.

It was getting closer and closer to the middle school entrance examination, and the children were getting more and more restless as the tasks piled up.

Every year at this time, the children in the graduation class were extremely excited, and the proportion of early love was increasing. Even in Xiaomin's class, there was an abnormal phenomenon where all the boys in the class made a collective appointment to go out and play basketball at 4:30 am in the morning.

The thoughts of Xiaomin have also undergone tremendous fluctuations. He started to have difficulty in focusing. In this situation, I once again gave him an encouraging speech.

### The third one: Looting a burning house.

"Xiaomin, the high school entrance examination is about to take place in a month, and the temperature is rising. People are feeling anxious, and there is an indescribable sense of restlessness in the class. These emotions are detrimental to learning."

"Whenever we encounter unfavorable situations, we must fully see the positive side. How can we be advantageous? We must be different!"

"If you truly inherited good genes from your parents, and if you have truly grown from the past detours, you can be different!"

"Although you all are classmates now, they will be your competitors in future exams. Therefore, when such unfavorable situations occur, you need to maintain a clear mind instead of drifting off with the flow. You may loot the burning house in the last month! Namely, you should take advantage of the situation and make another big leap in performance while everyone is lost in thought."

"But can we still move forward with great strides like before? It seems not. Why? Even though you don't want to be influenced by the surrounding environment, as a part of the whole, you are still constantly influenced by the environment, and no child can be unaffected by it."

"At this point, students are like on a slope, struggling to advance towards the top of the slope. Many people may lose control of their energy and emotions and perform poorly during this exam. They are like rolling down the slope.

"The closer the middle school entrance exam approaches, the more un-favorable it is for such students because of their bad mentality. Therefore, every day before the exam, such students will regress.

"Of course, there are also some students who are still struggling. These students account for about 1% to 2%."

"So, what is progress? At this stage, progress is about not retreating."

"We need to be the ones who nail to the slope! If you don't move and 100 people fall from the front, you have advanced 100 places. Don't un-derestimate these 100 people. How many places will you advance in your entire school, the Liaohe Oilfield area or the whole city?

"So, it would be great if we could be the defenders in difficult situations."

"I understood, Brother Ye!" Xiaomin said.

One month later, in the final exam before the middle school entrance examination, Xiaomin ranked 140 in grade, improving by 248.

On July 10, 2005, Xiaomin was admitted to a key high school in the city with a score of 756.

Looking back, how long did it take for the beginner to complete all the courses from the third grade of elementary school to the fourth grade of junior high school: 14 months, a little over a year?

Therefore, as long as you truly understand your child, you can act realistically, you help your child establish their own life goals, you can grasp the main contradictions of things, and you win the support of parents, it is completely possible for Internet-addicted teenagers to attend key high schools and universities.

### Be reluctant to part.

People often say that it is difficult to say goodbye when we meet. The relationship between Xiaomin and I was also true. On the third day after Xiaomin received the admission letter, I set off for Beijing, marking the end of our tumultuous years. I thought carefully and left a long letter for Xiaomin.

*Dear Min,*

*As an old saying goes, sending off a thousand miles, but in the end, we must say goodbye! It is time to say goodbye to the two years of our getting along day and night. At the moment of parting, please take my concern for you in writing to keep you moving forward.*

*1. Study, but never forget about her.*

*2. When I was young, my mother always told me to "Work diligently and be an honest person." Don't fantasize about becoming God's favorite. He doesn't have any favorites as far as I observe.*

*3. When facing unfairness, don't complain. Your unfairness may actually be others' fairness. Therefore, it's better to work hard and strive for the most suitable fairness for yourself.*

*4. You do need to learn to be cunning sometimes, but remem-*

ber, and always remember, there is only one trick to be successful in society, and undoubtedly that is strength.

5. If you don't smoke, your energy will be much better than
when you smoke, which is absolutely true.

6. "I love you." No matter how many people you say it to in
the future, make sure it comes from the bottom of your heart, as
it is respecting the ones you love as well as your own emotions.

7. Safety is the top priority for anything. Taking care of yourself and cherishing yourself is very important! Nothing is more
important than health and life. Be sure to pay attention to safety
and cherish yourself.

8. Don't say things like "I'll treat you to dinner." recklessly,
because everyone will take it seriously.

9. "Where am I going?" This is a directional question. The
choice for your future has already begun the moment you step
into the high school. Which career level will you enter, the
blue-collar, white-collar, or gold-collar class, no matter how
you choose, the key to change your destiny is in your own
hands. Opportunities for success always favor those who are
prepared and have a mind.

10. Many things have been notified to you by others, and you
need to say thank you. Don't blame others for not notifying
you, because you should actually figure out those things yourself.

11. Whether male or female overly values appearance as an important thing in high school, they may not suffer losses now, but
sooner or later they will suffer losses, and definitely they will.

12. Cheating depends on others. Occasionally once or twice is not a big deal, but gradually you will understand that sometimes others cannot be trusted, and it will be too late. It's better to rely on yourself as much as possible. Be an honest and trustworthy person!

13. Make sure to take time every day to exercise. Make effective choices based on your own strengths! Persist, and it'll be beneficial in the long run.

14. Don't pick on the teacher. If you think the teacher is not good to you, work hard to learn this course well and let him look at you with new eyes.

15. Many things when you look back are not big deals once they have passed. So, no matter how angry you are at the time, tell yourself that it is not worth it, and you'll realize that it is actually not.

16. Dignity is the most important thing. In middle school, one should understand how to use this space to exercise oneself and have enough tolerance. You should know that society is a place that loves to shatter human dignity the most, and no one will keep it for you except yourself.

17. If your personality makes many people keep a distance from you, then your personality is a failure. The success of personality lies in attraction, not rejection.

18. The easiest way to learn well is to put in a lot of effort, practice well what you should and memorize what you should. When smart people are still looking for a shortcut, the dumb ones are already in the next section. So many smart students exclaims, "He is much dumber than me, but why does he learn

*better than me?"*

19. *Start training your calmness in middle school. This is an ability. It is impressive for someone to come up with a solution calmly when events happen.*

20. *If you consider not to sleep in class as a form of exercise and achieve it, then you are strong. And remember that you should actually be like this. No matter how poor the teacher is, they are stronger than students because they are teachers.*

21. *You need to believe one thing: nothing is impossible! It is true as long as you stick to it. You are a student now, what about ten years or twenty years from now? Think about it.*

22. *Don't complain about all kinds of quizzes and exams, as they are great ways to prove your abilities.*

23. *Everyone has potential energy, but it is easily overshadowed by habits, blurred by time, and consumed by laziness.*

24. *You don't have to like everything. If you cannot change it, you just need to learn to accept it.*

25. *Being impulsive indicates that you still have passion for life while being always impulsive means you don't understand life yet.*

26. *Preparing for the college entrance examination earlier is definitely better than preparing later.*

27. *Don't use foul language, as you know the strength of habits. When you grow up and interact with others, a single or a few random words will greatly diminish your image in their hearts.*

28. You are very courageous now, and I hope you keep the courage in the future. Even if you fail, don't let your life be mediocre.

29. Like yourself, trust your abilities, and do what you think is worth doing.

30. Don't waste money. Your parents earned them with sweat and blood.

31. "I don't think about whether I can succeed or not. Since I have chosen my destination, I'll march forward regardless of hardship. I don't think about whether there will be cold wind and rain behind me. Since the goal is the horizon, what can only be left for the world is the view of my back." This sentence may be useful for you.

32. Regret is an emotion that consumes energy. Regret is a greater loss than loss itself and a greater mistake than mistake itself.

33. Believe in the power of time which can dilute many things.

34. Don't look down on classmates who are not as capable or have good habits as you are. Sometimes a low starting point can bring about a big leap.

35. Smile more. It will make you happy.

36. The friends you make in high school are likely to be a part of your future career. They will help you. But you should also have the ability to help them, so you need to work hard. You and your friends will work together to build a potentially bril

liant career in the future. It sounds great, doesn't it? But you all have to work hard.

37. You should chat with your family, since the life experience of your parents and elders is your wealth, can help you avoid many detours and is a shortcut to your success.

38. Continue to maintain the politeness and etiquette learned earlier, such as dining etiquette. Middle school students are no longer children, and the gentlemanly demeanor is gradually cultivated. Keep working hard.

39. Learn to be a good person. For students, knowledge and methods can be quickly mastered, but good habits, excellent qualities, and noble character are not something that can be achieved overnight. Only by perfectly combining the pursuit of knowledge with being a good person can one truly realize their own value.

40. Be brave enough to learn things you don't know. Some children may not know anything at first, but after a period of time, they may become experts because they seek advice from people they meet. In high school, one must not be ashamed to ask questions and not be afraid of losing face. Otherwise, it is oneself who will suffer.

41. Speak to your classmates about your innovations. Maybe you can join a competition one day.

42. If you plan to live on campus, call your family often. Remember that your mother is always thinking about you.

Above is what I want to tell you. We all have our own life to live. Min, please take care when I'm not around. In this melancholic July, we hastily bid farewell, heading towards our future, without pain or regret, only with eternal longing and blessings towards each other from the bottom of our hearts.

A whistle sounded around into the wilderness. My heart is filled with infinite melancholy and loneliness at the moment of parting with you.

Brother Ye
Night, July 12, 2005

## Xiaomin's smile

Let's take a look at Xiaomin's grades after entering high school.

The second exam in the first semester of the freshmen year: ranking 556. The final exam: ranking 273.

It was July 14th, 2006 when he got the ranking. It had already been a year since Xiaomin was away from me, but I still maintained the state of him still being by my side. Why?

Because even though the environment around Xiaomin had changed, the life goals we explored and set together had not changed and could withstand the test of time. Things that he's learned from me made it easy for him to adapt to life back home.

He's received the "Best Progress Award" as well as a scholarship. His photo was kept in a showcase in the school. He called me with great pride to tell me the good news. I asked him: "Xiaomin, what have you learned from the two years we spent together?"

"Brother Ye, I've learned three things from you. The first one is the way to think. I'm better at it than my peers. The second is never to give up.

The third is that I understand my parents, and this makes me feel happy."
(A postcard written by Xiaomin to his father during middle school,
which was Xiaomin's first time expressing his feelings to his father.)

In July 2008, Xiaomin was admitted to a university of finance and economics.

One day at the end of 2012, I was shopping at the mall, and suddenly I
heard someone calling my name. I turned around, and it was Xiaomin's
grandmother! She came over and hugged me, "Mr. Ye, it was such a
blessing to have had you in my grandson's life! We owe you so much!
You look thin." Her deep emotion touched me, and I felt like the hap-
piest person.

In 2012, after graduating from university, Xiaomin became a village official and realized his childhood ideals. Now he is humble and cautious,
and his life is meticulous and well-organized. He is charismatic and has
a kind attitude. Nothing is going to stop him. He feels unmatched happiness in his work. He is responsible when he is in an inferior position,
and someone would be considered lucky to have him as a superior for his
fairness. He has self-control, and doing the job perfectly is something he
lives by. He lives his life with a burning heart. For someone with such
dedication, there definitely are many successes waiting for him. We can
fully trust him and rely on him. God bless Xiaomin!

# Chapter 2
## How to Educate Rebellious Children

### The frightening sports car

One evening in October 2006, Mr. Chen called to tell me that he had heard about my story with Xiaomin from a friend, and he wanted to meet me out of admiration. We agreed to meet at his home in Beijing next month for a detailed discussion so that I could also visit his child.

After meeting and exchanging greetings, I went straight to the point and asked the parents to introduce their family history.

Their only son Haonan was in the first year of high school. He had a few good friends who often hung out with him. They did not do well in school, although they all came from wealthy families and were considered polite by Haonan's parents.

Haonan's parents had a divorce when he was in the second grade of elementary school, and he seemed to be troubled by it, and sometimes would sneak out in the family car during the night. Moving into adolescence, he started staying out frequently, and argued with his parents whenever things were not going well.

"Haonan is not a bad kid. His greatest strength is kindness. He doesn't have any major problems besides being rebellious and somewhat lazy at school." Mr. Chen took out two coins and told me that it was his son's masterpiece during class.

Mr. Chen told me that he didn't hide anything from Haonan about my visit to Beijing, and the child wanted to meet me alone at a nearby Beijing restaurant to have Tan's cuisine. Haonan drove to pick me up and asked me to wait for him at the west gate for 2 minutes. Standing at the west gate, I suddenly saw a Lamborghini turning from a distant street corner and roaring towards me. At 100 meters, 50 meters, 30 meters, 20 meters, 10 meters, and 1 meter, the car came to a stop 5 centimeters in front of my legs amidst the sharp braking sound.

I stood still, without moving, and the time seemed to be frozen. The driver didn't get out of the car. We stared at each other for two minutes. Then the car door was opened, and a handsome boy emerged from the car. He blushed and bowed to me embarrassed, "I'm Haonan, Mr. Ye."

During dinner, Haonan asked me why I didn't dodge just now. I said, "I trusted you to stop the car." He looked away as tears came to his eyes. (A year later, Haonan finally told me what this sentence meant to him at that time.)

## The prince Haonan

Haonan's secret was hidden within the details of the fright of the sports car and the delicious smell of Tan's dishes. With the consent of the child's father, I conducted an investigation into Haonan. A week later, the information gathered was presented in front of Mr. Chen, and there were too many secrets that were not known to the parents. Haonan had started a crew at the end of 2005. All the members were children with wealthy backgrounds just like him. Haonan was the leader of them. They hung out together all day in entertainment areas, and often fought and caused troubles. When Haonan and his team went to the disco and KTV, they often took ecstasy; before playing Jingwu and Jingle together online, they would consume Kefei and ephedrine. Haonan often raced with his team on the highways in the suburbs of Beijing, testing the maximum speed of all kinds of sports cars.

## "Who leads the revolution?"

Haonan's father looked stressed when presented with the videos and audio recordings. He kept smoking one after another while painfully pulling his hair. Finally, he forcefully extinguished the cigarette in his hand and said, "I didn't expect how efficient your work was. Mr. Ye, thank you! All these indicate that Xiaonan's performance is not very good now, but they don't necessarily mean that my son Xiaonan is the head of a bunch of bad kids. He may also have been dragged in by friends. In addition, he is still a child in middle school, and children inevitably have some minor problems and do things that are beyond the standard. I won't bother you if he is all normal! These don't really mean much. Let's talk about your plan for Xiaonan's academic tutoring." As he spoke, he poured all the files into a trash can.

He agreed with the investigations but still didn't want to believe the results. He thought Haonan's main problem was in academics, and the purpose for inviting me was to improve his academic performance, and everything else was just a child's mischievousness, so there was no need to make a big fuss about it.

I said to Haonan's father, "We should understand what is going on with the kid if we want to help him grow. If education is not based on facts, but on emotions, it is like stepping on clouds, which would cause serious consequences. Please feel free to investigate in person if you still question the truthfulness of the files. If you cannot accept them emotionally, let's wait until the time is right for cooperating." I stood up and left after telling the truth.

The next morning, Haonan's father called to meet me. He apologized to me in person, saying that he saw the materials I provided yesterday and felt mixed emotions in his heart. On the one hand, he was angry at his son. On the other hand, as a father, he deeply felt guilty and felt that he had done something wrong to his child. It was his failed marriage that hurt the child, and his busy career that delayed the child. Therefore, he was unwilling to believe that these were true.

He went through the files again word by word, and believed the fact that his son's situation was serious, and he should face the reality.

I understand the father's lack of understanding towards Haonan. His lack of understanding of the situation of Haonan is certainly related to his limited observation of children. Through my understanding of families like his, I concluded the major difference between children from wealthy families and regular families: they judge the situation and observe one's words and expressions. They are stealthy.

Although the parents of these children rarely have time to spend with their children, they keep the children regulated since childhood, for example, how to speak to certain types of people or how to act in certain types of situations. The children feel an invisible constraint, even in the most laid-back family. The children develop a coping mechanism to predict the parent's thoughts or guess the intentions of other people. Coincidentally they develop the habit of judging the situation and observing one's words and expressions. Regular families tend to have simpler lives, as things are usually in set patterns which give the children less stress. They don't need to predict any behaviors of the adults, as things in life are clear and straightforward.

Humans are social animals. The most advanced skill is to understand the others' intentions, acknowledge their emotions, seize opportunities and predict progressions. The value of this skill lies in the fact that it is not something that can be achieved and cultivated overnight!

Therefore, the parents tend to have a difficult time in believing the fact when someone in such a community makes a huge mistake. Different beliefs make different worlds. Once these children have a positive goal, coupled with the support of their families, their chances of success are extremely high.

Haonan's father spilled his heart to me: He had hinted several times to Haonan that he would study hard and take over the family business in the future. But Haonan seemed not interested in it at all, even a little repulsed. Later Haonan's mother told me that he was going to sell the family business after taking over, open a cafe and then travel around the world with his girlfriend. Even though he was only a child, Haonan's father was deeply worried about the problem of the family business.

Therefore, Mr. Chen decided to let me take over the task of educating and transforming Haonan.

We signed several agreements. It clearly stated that I have the authority to educate Haonan at any time, place, and in any way. Haonan's father hesitated for a moment and said we should change it into our joint research plan. Zhigang should come and implement it. I agreed.

Then a tragedy happened. You all think that Haonan's situation was caused by the lack of attention from his parents, right? Let's take a look at the result of paying attention to him. Haonan's father was opposed to most of my plans and methods. I could not make him understand what type of education was beneficial to Haonan. The most interesting conversation we had was about a schedule on a weekend. He couldn't understand after I repeated myself three times, but he immediately understood Haonan after he said exactly the same words.

Oh my god! Can you believe it?

Haonan's father had gained my full attention since then, and we had many encounters. My plans for Haonan were not able to move forward for three months, which worried me a lot. Words had spread out within the group company that the new teacher of Haonan's was a "Batman", who dared to go head to head with "Mr. Freeze". I felt the support from everyone whenever I showed up at the headquarters.

Finally, one day, exhausted as I was, I decided to end this unfortunate "marriage". However, at this moment, Haonan's father demonstrated his extraordinary decisiveness.

"Zhigang, for the past three months, I have greatly appreciated your abilities, but I don't think you truly understand the heart of a father. I asked myself since you said you were leaving, and I decided to let it go. I hope you can complete what you have started with Haonan. Please stay safe as he is my only son. You know it's a gamble to me."

"You're attached and anxious. I can stay, but only under one condition: Haonan comes to Panjin with me." He asked me how to convince the child to go with me. I told him Haonan would call him in a few days.

Three days later, Haonan called his father and said he wanted to go to Panjin, Liaoning Province with me for a while… Finally, I gained "revolutionary leadership", and the education went back to its normal course. I couldn't fail Haonan's father, so I began to search for the main contradiction right away.

### Spotted the main contradiction through investigation.

What is the main contradiction behind Haonan? Is it an organized group? Is it using drug substances? Is it reckless driving? Is it sexual indulgence? All these are appearances. Only by finding the roots of the problems can we spot the main contradiction and solve the problem. But how? Observing. Patience always pays off. The answer gradually emerged.

## I couldn't feel the love from my family

Haonan was raised by his grandmother as his parents were busy with their own businesses. Later he was sent to a private boarding elementary school. Haonan said that he would miss home every night during that time and cried to call his family every day.

His parents were divorced when he was in the second grade of elementary school, and for young Haonan at that time, his mother was becoming a stranger, and his father was more like an ATM.

Through similar experiences, Haonan found his friends around him were more like a family to him. He never liked when people called his friends "bad friends like foxes and dogs" even though they had done many shady things together. He said that foxes and dogs stay loyal, but humans change.

Gradually Haonan developed a twisted view of the world:

*Ambition—a strong desire to be slandered by enemies when alive, and to be ridiculed by friends after death.*

*Achievement—the end of striving, the beginning of boredom. Life is like a tug of war. Backing up means victory.*

He hated advice from others to the point that he would wear a tag on his chest that read: I am young, and I need your advice, but I don't need you judging me! He would feel an inexplicable sadness in his heart at night, with a strong emotion accumulated inside waiting to burst out.

He loved walking alone through the Victoria Harbor the most. He loved the feasting and the crowd, and he loved watching the spiritual wanderers who were just like him in the busy city. That's the only moment he felt accompanied.

He was afraid of stopping, for stopping only brought him cluelessness in the endless nights.

He would rather be lost than to be clueless! It was the blood-covered shoulders, the craziness caused by the substances, the exhaustion after the indulgence, and the racing cars that would lost control at any moment that made him feel alive!

Everything felt natural when it became a habit. Haonan wanted to escape, but no matter in which direction he ran, it was all darkness ahead. He wrote a slip of paper after waking up once more:

"Listening to the chaotic sounds, it was the laughter from other
people's homes.
Looking carefully into my empty memories, only to find out I
have no home.

A warm home, my own home.
The surroundings are as quiet as a tomb.
I cannot find my way home.
I'm walking on the way home every day,
Only to find there is no home to return to!
The ginkgo trees dance in the evening breeze.
What a lonely sight!

A suffocating darkness surrounds me in the blink of an eye.
I cannot see anything in the pitch-black abyss.
I do not dare to stay.
I inch forward slowly in the endless darkness.
I have never raised flowers,
For it hurts to see it wither quickly.
Fear wriggles in my heart,
Yet I dare not to scream through this eternal darkness."

## CHAPTER 2

## The tragedy of many other Haonans

People say they envy the children from wealthy families. I said, "What we don't have can be obtained through our own efforts, but what these children don't have is something they can't even achieve with their own efforts!" The generation who have experienced hardship tend to underestimate their children's abilities, and generally believe that their success is a coincidence. It was a gift from an era, and it is impossible for their children to recreate their own legends, so they usually have low expectations for their children. Parents whose career success was not related to education have lower expectations for their children.

In addition, during Haonan's growth process, the lack of family care prevented him from developing a good self-identity, making it difficult for him to find his place in society and family. When Haonan needed emotional support and guidance, no one was there to give him a hand.

Even if their parents are not divorced, most second-generation people like Haonan generally lack parental guidance and companionship during their growth. After all, childhood is gone forever!

Haonan's heart was already filled with insecurity, anxiety, confusion, and hatred. He had been socialized, and we could see traces of the adult world in his every move.

What do I do now? I'd ask my Aladdin's lamp without hesitation whenever children like Haonan appeared: to bring the child into an enlightened family to grow up. The results were usually surprising.

For children like Haonan, it is useless to preach or discipline by force, as conventional school education is no longer effective for such children. The way to change such children is to have them accompanied and slowly guided by the people they admire.

What he longs for is love that he trusts and needs to grow up in an enlightened family.

The difference between an enlightened family and an uncultured family mainly lies in the fact that the former considers their impact on children caused by lifestyle and social habits, and they are carefully selective.

When I was in junior high school, I was transferred to Anshan to live with my aunt. The family was harmonious and fun under the leadership of my uncle. My younger cousin was thoughtful. My aunt was kind, and my uncle was wise and provocative. As a filial son, my uncle kept enlightening me traditionally and culturally, and the best part was the storytelling of events in history every night at the dinner table. The historical figures felt alive through his descriptions, and I was mesmerized by them, to the point that my grades plummeted (There was no inevitable connection between the two). During that period, the help and teachings I received from my uncle and cousin have benefited me to this day, and my uncle's understanding of education and life had influenced greatly my view of the world.

I brought Haonan into my family and gave him siblings, uncles, and aunts as well as grandparents. We lived together every day, trying our best to heal his traumatized inner child. In the 24-hour interaction day and night, Haonan was changing slowly and quietly in the love and guidance provided by the family. He wrote in his diary: they were able to change my perspective. I am someone who has confidence and hope. He wrote a letter to his friends in Beijing:

> Standing on the balcony alone at night, looking down at the crowded city, I could not help but feel extremely moved. To survive in the city, one has to have a foundation to strive. But what do I have? My grades are low. I wish I studied harder, but I don't have the courage to face the pain and my academic challenges. Sigh! Life is like a book in which there's a lot of

*confusion, only to be understood after reading. But is there a second chance to read it? No. One will achieve nothing after growing up if one doesn't achieve anything at a young age. We should believe in miracles, but miracles only happen to the ones who are not afraid of pain. I'm overwhelmed with helplessness, emotion and sadness. I will be left alone if I don't keep up with the world. Maybe it is time for us to do something for the future, or the next one to be abandoned might just be you and me.*

### Teaching benefits teachers and students alike.

I weighed around 110 kg before and was on the larger side. Haonan asked me one day: "Mr. Ye, you always say men need perseverance when doing things, and I think there are two types of perseverance. One is perseverance in doing things, and the other is perseverance towards oneself. Your perseverance in doing things goes without saying, but you really don't have much perseverance towards yourself."

"Really? Haonan, how do you say this?"

"Why don't you try to lose weight if you really have perseverance?"

"What's wrong with being a little overweight? It doesn't affect work efficiency."

"To be honest, Mr. Ye, in my eyes, being overweight is a sign of weakness and poverty. There's no one in my family who's overweight. Fat makes one look old too. When you first arrived, my uncle said to me, 'Your father has hired a teacher who is in his 40s, and quite a fat man.' I was desperate when I heard these words. Who would like to live with an overweight middle-aged uncle?"

After listening to Haonan's words, I made a decision to lose weight immediately.

"Alright, Haonan, let me show you how a person with perseverance loses weight."

No one understands you better than yourself. I came up with a plan to lose weight. By running and a balanced diet, I lost nearly a quarter of my weight within four months and weighed 85 kg. Haonan had witnessed the entire process. He said that he was convinced that I should've opened a weight-losing camp because my experience was convincing.

None of my old clothes fit me anymore. My mother said painfully while packing up the clothes, "What a waste! Maybe we can save them for when you get fatter in the future?" Looking into her beautiful eyes, I smiled and asked her, "Do you think I will make myself rebound?" She sighed and told the nanny to take all the clothes away.

Not long after, when I showed up in front of Haonan's father, he couldn't believe his eyes and asked me with concern if I was sick. After understanding the whole story, he expressed his feelings, "Zhigang, each of us has a lot to learn from you. You are the teacher that Haonan admires the most. You have helped my son find his life goal. You are his godfather." It was almost unbelievable to everyone there on that day, and later the vice president of the group company standing beside him quietly told me that Haonan's father had never praised anyone before. The title "godfather" has been stuck with me ever since.

Before Haonan returned to Beijing, he handed me a diary notebook. He once wrote in this diary:

> The end of life is death, but Chairman Mao once said that one's death can either be lighter than a feather or heavier than Mount Tai. I used to think that it'd be the same either way, but now I choose the latter, because we need to live a unique life.

*As for teachers, he is the first one that I've ever seen who puts*
*his heart into it, but I don't want to put my mind into a fight*
*with him now. All I want is to change for the better. I should*
*seize the moment before it is gone for good. I'm going to utilize*
*my youth to start a career, so I don't regret it when I'm old.*

In the peaceful life filled with laughter in Panjin, Haonan gradually
moved away from decadence. He started to cherish time, care for his
family, take things seriously and become responsible. He was so happy
during Christmas in 2007. On New Year's Eve, he wrote down his new
years' resolution:

1. *Spend the year safely. Hope my family does the same.*

2. *Maintain a good position in the family.*

3. *Be filial to my parents.*

4. *Study everything well.*

5. *Take everything seriously.*

6. *Become a responsible man.*

Haonan called his parents separately, which is something he's never done
before, not asking for money, but to tell them that he was doing well
in Panjin, as well as his longing for them. A few days later, his father
couldn't wait to bring his whole family to Panjin to see his son. When he
saw Haonan's New Year's resolution, he burst into tears.

After calming down, Haonan's father said to me, "You saved my only
son, Zhigang. I should've given you all my wealth, but you know it's
impossible, not even half of it. I should let you know what I think, and
I won't repeat myself. Firstly, your love for Haonan, the emotions be-

tween you and Haonan, I might forget but he will not. The entire family is in your debt for what you have done. Secondly, hit me up if you ever find yourself in any trouble. Thirdly, I know that we've had our differences in Haonan's education. If time can turn back, I want you to know that I would've listened to you from the beginning."

It took my breath away after hearing it.

The facts proved that conducting a comprehensive investigation of children is extremely necessary. Many parents believe that the problem is only in academics, but the problem in academics is only solved after solving other relevant problems.

### Haonan's business empire

Setting a life goal is the most important aspect for adolescents, and it was the same for Haonan. I took him to travel around many places. Instead of sightseeing, it was to get to know the various industries like what I did with Xiaomin. There was a particular person that left a huge impact on Haonan: a businessman from Singapore, who was successful in both family life and his career. Haonan was envious of him, and he also wanted to become such a person.

I took Haonan on research trips across the country, and even chatted with people overseas through video calls, and compared the differences between China and foreign countries in various fields, which was shocking to him.

We visited the employees of his father's group company on payday. He saw how happy they were when they received the salary, how proud the wives were of the husbands, and saw the value of a few thousand yuan for an ordinary family, as well as the value of his father's career, and an understanding of his own responsibilities.

Eventually, Haonan decided to study economics and finance abroad in order to take over the family business in the future. In 2009, he scored 6.5 in the IELTS exam and went to the UK. His goal was the University of Manchester. He lived simply and plainly in the UK. He wrote to welcome me to the restaurant where he worked because I would see a handsome young man doing dishes in the back. No one knew that the young man had enough money to buy the entire restaurant. He had his own understanding of life and money, and he worked hard for his goals. In 2013, his family had another listed company, and Haonan, who had returned from University of Manchester, and his father sounded the bell together. My student, Haonan, had an outgoing personality and active thinking. He focused on cultural cultivation and was full of passion for life.

His positive view on life, future and love was influential to others. He always brought out the best of the people around him. He's interested in many fields including literature and traveling, but he doesn't like it when others interfere with his freedom. He's always ready for adventures both spiritually and physically. He likes to be involved in many things at the same time. But reckless behavior often brings him trouble. He is generous and selfless to the ones he admires, and he wishes satisfaction and happiness for everyone around him.

Haonan likes to invite friends to his home and try to help them in any way possible. As a result, he will meet many influential figures in society and receive strong support and protection in his life and career.

Haonan is particularly concerned about current affairs news, enjoys insightful ideas and viewpoints, and is good at expressing his own opinions on them. He is praised by many for his cheerful and outgoing personality. He is good at working with others, and his ability to inspire others makes him easy to get along with. But sometimes his inner contradiction draws attention from others.

Haonan likes to work out ideas and plan trips for his family while considering everyone's independence and freedom of movement. He likes to know about the details instead of being confused, and he doesn't like to be vague or ambiguous. He is undoubtedly honest when he raises his wine glass.

Honor weighs the most in Haonan's heart. He is certainly going to become a great father, a beloved family leader, and a well-respected citizen in the future. Keep up the good work, Haonan. I am proud of you.

# Chapter 3
## How to Educate Children Failing to Study Abroad

*If you love him, bring him to New York, for it is heaven.*
*If you hate him, bring him to New York, for it is hell.*
　　　　—The TV series *A Native of Beijing in New York*

China has become the world's largest exporter of international students. Amongst the countless students studying abroad, many of them are no longer like those who used to be thrifty, with excellent grades, and relying on part-time jobs to earn their tuition fees.

These children from affluent families traveled overseas to study, with the habits formed back at home, and gradually changed the impression that the locals used to have of Chinese international students.

A lot of Americans ask me: Brother Sway, are they real Chinese? Are the Chinese really that rich? Is there really such a domineering person among Chinese people? I always tell them that they are not ordinary Chinese people, and they are Chinese people of the "ancestral" level, nurtured by several generations of wealthy and powerful people.

They are the educated generation, growing up in private schools that were established by foreigners. They can curse in particularly authentic American English. If we don't say anything else, it sounds like a drunken old black man cursing, with a strong African flavor that makes black Americans inevitably homesick.

They are the only generation who dare to treat the United States as a paper tiger. They have completely conquered and scared the strong but weak Americans really with money and various credit cards, allowing them to hear the shocking voice—the Chinese people are standing up!

As soon as they land in America, they buy a villa worth several million dollars at Beverly Hills and it takes more than ten minutes just to get out the off-drive way. They drive Ferrari, Porsche, Maserati, and Lamborghini. They collect the latest purse releases of the Hermes, Prada and Louis Vuitton.

They buy wines in tens of cases and handmade cigars on the entire shelf. After they leave, the shops look like being robbed.

They are bossy for having a dozen white shop assistants following them as they shop, female shop assistants making coffee and echoing everyone's response. The Americans don't see themselves as inferiors, but they reply with a "Yes, sir!" After loading the car, they give each shop assistant a $200 tip, which are usually their two-day salary! The shop assistants gaze with tearful eyes at the wealthy Easterners in front of them, who are as rich as in the fairy tales. The envy, admiration, and gratitude are exactly the same as how the Chinese people looked at Americans back in the 1980s.

> They proved with their action that, in today's global economic crisis, only Chinese people are so wealthy, and only China is the hope of the world people. The American Dream is nothing, while the Chinese Dream is the way.
>
> —Cui Baoyin

My student Ah Long is one of them, but he's not just another wealthy Chinese. He is the offspring of the powerful. In July 2011, I received a call from a director of a business school saying that he wanted me to meet a parent. I told my assistant to send over a Student Growth Survey Form on the child. I took a second look afterward. The child was already 20 years old.

I met with his parents the next day. His name was Zhiguo, and his nickname was Ah Long. It was obvious that his parents had much expectation for him. His father sat across from us smiling arrogantly, as if unwilling to seek help from us. He was experienced and skillful in controlling the flow of the conversation.

We talked for three hours, and I've learned a lot of negotiation skills. Some important details I've gathered about the child can be concluded as "failing to study abroad and severe Internet addiction". I suggested meeting with the child at home in the evening.

I arrived on time, following Ah Long's father's instructions to change shoes, and wash hands and then sit down on a spot he had arranged. The door to the room on the right side of my seat was sealed shut. Dinner was served not long after, but Ah Long wasn't present. His mother called twice, but there was no movement. I was a little confused. Then all of a sudden, with a "clang" sound, the door to my right side was pulled open violently. A young man with a head of long hair and a big beard came out, with a weird smell. He went straight to the refrigerator, took out a 1.25-liter pack of chilled Sprite and chugged it. He took a quick look at me and sat down at the table. His father quickly introduced, "This is Uncle Ye, a good friend of mine." Ah Long wasn't bothered by it. He picked up three pieces of hairtail with chopsticks, took two bites on each piece, throw them aside, and left for his room, with a loud bang, closing the door. The entire process was no longer than three minutes.

Ah Long's father was obviously embarrassed. He sighed and became more easy-going to make up for his son. From 7:30 pm to 10:30 pm, I started asking for more details, but he was still defensive. He didn't want to talk in depth about the family matter and interrupted me for several times. He asked me what to do in a situation like Ah Long based on my previous experience. After I explained the significance of my investigations and understanding, the couple slowly talked to me about their pain and Ah Long's ruthlessness. And that was when Ah Long's most serious problems appeared.

Ah Long has always been a clever, talented child. He attended the top elementary school and won multiple awards in various levels of Olympiad math competitions in Grade Five. All high schools in the city opened their doors to him. But Ah Long was lifted by his excellent performance in math Olympiad and didn't study much since he got into Grade Six. After entering Beijing 101 Middle School, his English teacher even skipped Level A of textbook, and the first class started directly from Level B for the students who were well prepared, but Ah Long could not even write 26 letters. His grades in English always fell behind in the class. He thought that nothing else would matter if his English was bad and he began to give up on himself completely. His father was so disappointed that they would often argue.

He grew tall and strong by the time he entered Grade Nine. In one argument he accidentally knocked his father over when he realized that he didn't have to obey his father any longer.

In high school, Ah Long completely gave up his study and idled around all day. Half of his classmates went abroad when he was in Grade 12. He's heard that the environments are much better overseas, and schools are a lot more manageable, which got him to look forward to joining them and not want to participate in the college entrance examination anymore.

Though most of his friends and colleagues sent their children abroad, Ah Long's father was well aware of his son's character and insisted that Ah Long should stay in China. During another argument, Ah Long smacked his father in the face. His father didn't hit him back and that encouraged him to get even worse as the whole "revolutionary situation" changed completely.

Ah Long left home for three days and his parents were too embarrassed to tell anyone, so they took days off from work to look for him street by street. They couldn't find him after searching in every Internet cafe in the Chaoyang District and the Dongcheng District. Eventually, they found him in an Internet cafe located in the Chongwen District as he was planning to spend the night there. Any person with a right mind would've guessed that he was going to get disciplined, but surprisingly his father only tapped on his shoulder, smiling just like playing a hide and seek, and said, "I've found you!" Ah Long turned around and glanced at his father. The two of them returned home one after another.

Anyway, when it comes to studying abroad, Ah Long's father was determined not to let him go and that was nonnegotiable. But soon Ah Long found a trick: he decided to stand in the courtyard and cursed at his parents loudly by name and surname, until all his neighbors heard him before giving up.

Ah Long's father had no other options but to compromise. Then he prepared to send Ah Long overseas after entrusting one of his friends with his son. But Ah Long was hard to deal with. He got rid of that friend of his father's with minimum effort. Ah Long has a unique personality. He doesn't care about the crowd in New York. Rather, he likes the beautiful nature of New Zealand. He doesn't care about the wealthy kids who look like celebrities living in mansions, buying designer clothes and driving supercars. Rather, he befriends the sincere ones. He doesn't like driving his Porsche and Ferrari down the mountains with his friends, and his Lamborghini was parked in the garage for the entire year. The engine sounded like the cough of a pulmonary fibrosis patient when he moved it to sell. He didn't care about how much it was sold for.

He favors tank tops and basketball shorts, instead of Zegna and Givenchy. He thinks the Vertu phones are weak compared with Nokia. He hates the kind of love that's easy to get and thinks it's all a game. He looks down on the friends who hire gunmen to attend classes or take exams. He thinks that a man should be decisive and aboveboard, and if he doesn't want to study then he doesn't study. He locks himself indoors and takes his phone battery out, only communicating with his friends through an online app and spending his days playing DOTA against the Polish clans. He doesn't like mansions or luxurious apartments. Rather, he loves the way of the Maoris family. Foods are microwaveable, fast and simple.

Ah Long settled with a Maori family on the North Island, and he did not take the initiative to call his parents even once a year. They had to only speculate on his recent situation through the social media posts forwarded by his cousin.

His journey of studying abroad was a failure. He got even more indifferent to his family after returning to China. They were almost like strangers and wouldn't say a word for a week. His mother told him that his grandmother, who had raised him since childhood, was seriously ill. He angrily shouted, "Can you tell me something related to me?"

Ah Long got even more isolated. He hired a teacher from the Central Academy of Fine Arts to paint the walls of the room all black, with two giant spider-man figures painted on them. The room was completely in dark with the curtains up. He drew a group of friends with similar experiences and played DOTA in their own circle day and night and isolated themselves deep in the world of gaming.

As Ah Long's father was speaking, his face darkened, and his words changed. He stared at me in the eyes, "Because Ah Long, I have come into contact with too many people in your field in recent years. Among those who work in education and psychology, nine out of ten are con artists. You can only prove yourself to me by making my son go with you willingly."

What he asked seemed easy but was extremely difficult for students who never ask for help willingly, and you can never wake up someone who doesn't want to be woken up. Prior to this, many masters in the fields of psychology and education were invited from various places, but no one was able to call Ah Long out of his room. I knew that he would not take anyone seriously. But birds of a feather flock together. I was sure Ah Long must admire people who are more skilled at playing games. But I can't play DOTA. What should I do?

Suddenly, I remembered an experience of dressing up that I had for a social experience.

I have always enjoyed dressing up as people of various professions for social experience activities. That was a late winter night many years ago. I disguised myself as a homeless man and came to the underground video studio of the train station. Soon, I met a young boy named Xiaotao inside. Xiaotao was an orphan, and his parents died. When he was young, he was sold to a brick kiln to be a laborer and often suffered from beatings, leaving scared all over his body. His ultimate skill was to buy a train ticket. After getting on the train, he took off his clothes and all the people were startled. A few hundred meters away, he walked from the front to the back of the train, crying and getting a few hundred yuan. In the afternoon, he took a nap in a small hotel, and at night, he went to a restaurant to have a good meal. After dinner, he would spend half of the night watching videos at the store, and the second half gaming in an Internet cafe. And he would repeat the same the next day.

Xiaotao took me to the Internet cafe at night. He greeted almost everyone there as we walked in. He told me that everyone there had their own unique way of surviving. I asked who he thought was the most impressive, he pointed at a young man in yellow without hesitation, "It's him! He's a pickpocket. But he's set the record in this place of staying up for seven days and nights. He finished his game on the 8th day and stood up cheering but blacked out as blood came out from his nose. Anyways the record is his, and he's our superstar here." This indicated that anyone who can stay up for extended periods can earn the respect of an Internet addict.

Looking at Ah Long's father, I said to him, "I'll give it a try." I asked him to tell Ah Long that I was going to stay at their home for a few days.

07 / 23

I went to Ah Long's home, and his mother opened the door for me. She said that Ah Long would've not opened the door if she wasn't in. Ah Long texted his mother to ask how long I was going to stay there. I greeted him briefly and left, saying that I stayed up all night being busy.

07 / 24

I went to Ah Long's home in the afternoon. He opened the door for me unexpectedly, but quickly went back to his room. I knocked at the door and walked in to greet him, and then left quickly again while telling him that I hadn't slept in two days.

07 / 25

Ah Long was going out. I tried to send him on his way, and then saw his mother on our way down. She was touched by my actions. Ah Long saw that I was exhausted and insisted that I take a rest at his home. That was the first time he smiled at me. It was also the first time he left his door open when I was there. Soon I received a call and left, telling him that I stayed up all night again.

07 / 26

I met the middleman who introduced me to Ah Long. He was surprised by the amount of money that I charged them, as well as our slow progression. Ah Long was on his trip.

07 / 27

Ah Long came back home. I spoke with his parents in the morning for two hours about details and contracts. His father refused to sign contracts and insisted that they were useless compared with the results. He said, "Though I don't need him financially, I would still love to have him care for me when I'm old. If he could do that, I would be so glad."

That evening, Ah Long's father expressed his dissatisfaction as planned. Ah Long started crying. I tried to calm him, but he asked me to beat his father, but then he realized something after looking at my face, "Uncle Ye, haven't you slept at all while I was gone?" I told him, "I haven't slept in five days." He was touched, stopped crying and started laughing.

07 / 28

I haven't shut my eyes for five days and five nights. On July 28th, like never before, Ah Long came out of the building, got into my car, and we left for Panjin. He called his father on the way, "I'm going to Panjin with Uncle Ye. I don't know when I'm coming back but I'll call you when I want to."

We arrived in Panjin at 1:30 pm. Ah Long then read books for the next five hours. He ate slowly and was picky about dishes too. He actively helped with carrying stuff. He was positive and respectful, and even stayed to chat after he had done eating. He only bought water and snacks for himself from the service areas on the highway.

07 / 29

Ah Long woke up at 4:00 am and read until 8:00 am, and then was on the Internet for two hours. He took reading and doing housework seriously, but severely needed sleep, as well as a haircut and a shower. He got to bed at 12:00 pm, talked to his friend on the Internet about wanting to leave, was about to take 200 Yuan and leave by train, and he went to sleep around 1:00 am.

07 / 30

Waking up at 11:00 am and going to my parents' house at noon. Mrs. Hao tried to talk to him in the afternoon. In the evening, he stayed off the computer, and I gave him a speech on My Struggle for 20 minutes.

07 / 31

This was an important day. Ah Long woke up at 9:00 am and read for the entire day. At 9:00 pm, he asked me, "Uncle Ye, when do you want me to go back?" I asked him, "When do you want to go back?" He said that he hadn't thought about it yet, and I said I hadn't either but let's chat.

We went back to the bedroom after a little while. He looked at me from the side. I asked him, "What do you want to do in the future?" He said that he hadn't thought about it. I asked him who he thought was not to think about it, since the prerequisite for enjoying rights was to take responsibility. Ah Long said that he understood. He said that he got annoyed even when he saw his parents. His dad was abnormal, for he wrote about the contradiction and his not studying in his grandfather's 9th anniversary memorial, and deliberately showed it to him.

Ah Long said he actually regretted falling behind step by step to where he was today. His grades were good other than English, but he thought it would be useless unless his English was good. Then everything went down and even had to repeat the same level for a year, which was one year behind his peers. Being in New Zealand caused him to be another year behind and coming back to China added even one more to that. He wanted to catch up from being three years behind but never acted on it.

His eyes were filled with tears as he spoke. He said that he never liked his parents since he was young and grew apart from his grandmother as he got older. He said that he's willing to get help and get in touch with people from different fields and establish life goals. I told him that he could be an author if he didn't want to work hard, for he could rant in his writings and still make a living. He laughed. We made a rule that anything should step aside from making contact with people in the future. He agreed with a smile.

08 / 01

Ah Long was happy to see Uncle Fu, and even said he was going to exercise after he got back. At the dining table he acted accordingly, poured water for the guests and even drank alcohol with them. He went to sleep at 10:30 pm.

Below is Ah Long diary for that day.

*08 / 01 / 2011*

*First of all, the Guobaorou at the Meiyuan Xincun Restaurant is definitely more delicious than the takeout.*

*Today, Uncle Ye took me to meet his elementary school class-mate. He is currently working hard at Southeast University to-wards the title of associate professor. Compared with him, I feel like, in conclusion, I was lazy. I heard this dude was good in all subjects like morality, intelligence, physical fitness, aesthetics, and labor skills. He got a grade of 'very good' from grade 1 to 12, and then went to the US to study, and got back two years later. I feel that he has a bright future ahead. But there are quite a few similarities between us. I graduated from elementary school with a very good grade, middle school with the lowest* grade, and high school with the lowest grade. I went to New Zealand to study at my own expense, and now I have been back for a year. My future is pitch dark. Maybe the ones who study hard every day all expect the same result? He said that he only had two choices now: work hard for two years to become an associate professor, and work hard for who knows how long to become a professor, and then he's done. Or going into government to work. What even is that? I really don't know. But he said that he might go for something stable. What is stable? It's like waking up in the morning already knowing what is happening in the day, or a week, a month, even four or five years. He said that it's a horrible way to live. Geez. That's the life that I want... maybe the so-called stable is what I consider happiness to be. Oh, I almost forgot that he ended up with the girl he was with because he had good grades in middle school. I feel bad for not having good grades back then... whatever.

Ps. I haven't even done raids yet since I transferred to this server, and I want to raid.

08 / 02

Today is a big day. He woke up at 6:00 am, had breakfast, read, without desire to play games.

He had lunch, read and then went to sleep again. He woke up in the afternoon and told me that he wanted to leave and asked me to take him to the station. I told him that we were going to have dinner with Uncle Zhou before leaving. He followed disdainfully and told me that he was no good and that I shouldn't waste my time on him. I called Uncle Zhou to cancel the appointment, but Zhou collapsed on the phone. Then I drove Ah Long to a spot behind my high school dormitory, parked the car and started disciplining him.

In today's world, the most privileged class is the student class, who rely on their young ignorance and academic pursuits as their top priority. They prey on their parents and look down upon others.

Will the privileged class voluntarily give up the privilege? Or how do we make them treat their power and obligation correctly? I only know one thing: All power is the result of struggle, and only facts can change attitudes. Teachers should not avoid struggle. We should not only dare to struggle, but also be good at it. In the struggle with educational elements, we will never give up using force on principle issues. Take a look at the effect, as it was the turning point of his fate.

Afterwards, Ah Long cried to me about past experiences and told me about his girlfriend Irene that he had in middle school. Later, he went upstairs to have dinner with the Zhou family and had a great conversation. Uncle Zhou shared his past experiences, and we were deeply moved. Ah Long had four bottles of beer and got tipsy. We held on to each other as we got home. On the way, Ah Long confided in me:

"Uncle Ye, I feel that I've failed my parents. It's like they were in the same boat as Uncle Zhou. I feel sorry for my parents. Their situation over the years is extremely similar to that of Uncle Zhou after he failed the college entrance examination." I told him to call his parents, but he refused. Ah Long also told me that his ex-girlfriend called to borrow some money, and he didn't know what to do when she asked for more in the future. He said that he needed to have a skill. He shouted in the car: "How come everyone said that I was smart growing up, but I turned out to be the one doing the worst? Thank you, Uncle Ye, for the encouragement today. Thank you!"

At 10:30 in the evening, Ah Long got up and wrote the diary as below, then went back to sleep after midnight.

*08 / 02 / 2011*

*Today Uncle Ye took me to one of his friends for dinner. I heard that only true friends would invite you to their homes for dinner. I recalled my entire life, and it was unpleasant.*

*Uncle Zhou was a soldier and now he's higher in the ranks. He made me realize that being in the military is almost identical to jumping into a fire pit, except for his name. Only very few could climb out of it! It seemed that he did it, though. He must be different from those who were doomed in the fire pit! And it is apparent what it is.*

*On that sunny day (as I guessed), Uncle Zhou officially became a soldier with the help of a relative. His life then was filled with harsh training: 200 sit-ups, 200 push-ups, 200 squats carrying his fellow soldier, running the mountain trails in the mornings and all kinds of inhumane punishments. Geez, maybe I'd hold on for three days? Two days I'd be satisfied... He said although he was exhausted every day, he always had an ideal to take the military academy entrance exam.*

*Then he finally clicked. It wasn't a place for anyone with a normal mind. On another sunny day (which I think was), Uncle Zhou was officially transferred to another place with the help of the same relative, but still was a soldier. What do they even do in a peaceful era though? It turned out that it was just planting and farming. Was this what Uncle Zhou did? He took care of pigs... The inhumane part got better, but only for a bit. Maybe raising the fat four-legged creatures was something cruel. Anyway, he was still tired every day even after the transfer. But he always had an ideal to take the military academy exam.*

*Later, by chance and through his own efforts, he went to work* as a security guard at a very, very good leader's house. After-wards, he was admitted to the military academy. After the lead-er's death, he is now a deputy battalion commander. So, if you want to climb out of this fire pit, you need some luck! Uncle Zhou said that having a few good teachers and friends in one's life is really lucky. I said, is this your way to escape from the fire pit? Of course, it's not about taking the military academy exam... A clear and unwavering goal is just too important!

Ps. I still wish to do some raids...

08 / 03

Ah Long woke up at 6:30 am, went back to sleep after breakfast, and then woke up again 12:00 at noon. Getting glasses in the afternoon, he said it was the first time for him to see the world so clearly, worked out with me in the evening which was enjoyable, and play Battlefield II.

08 / 04

Ah Long went to sleep at 1:30 am in the morning and woke up at 11:00 am. He went to his grandparents' for lunch, did laundry in the afternoon, worked out in the evening, and listened to me lecturing from 11:00 pm to 1:00 am. He was excited to go from lying down to sit up and then was listening actively. The topic of my speech: "On Contemporary Educa-tion and Class Struggle".

08 / 07

Ah Long and I planned a social investigation.

08 / 08

Ah Long decided to lose some weight by running.

Today, Mrs. Hao had surgery, and I, along with Ah Long and Ah Xi, were waiting in the hallway of the hospital as family members.

Taking this time, I said to them, "Let me take you to play a game called 'Looking Forward to the Future'. When it comes to human affairs, there is only one thing to say, not about misunderstandings, levels, or grudges. There is only one ultimate killer in life, and that is time. All regrets come from the concept—it's too late. You didn't have time to express yourself, and then the girl you liked got married to someone else and had a kid. The kid is already having his wedding, and you are there. You're there making a toast to his father.

"I want to show filial piety to my parents, but they seem young and busy with their careers. Before I can express my gratitude, they grew old. I never really talked to them properly, but they have passed away. If time could turn back, and if we could all go back to the past like Haonan's father said, would we be happier if we could turn back time? Will life be less regretful?"

"So, we started to worry, and worry is the most exhausting feeling. You watch your child born and grow up, carved from the same mold as you in the mirror when you were a child. Then you start to worry about what if he knows what you are like. You start to worry what if your mother tells everything to her daughter-in-law. What if your wife tells your son? Would he do the same to you as you did to your father? Or maybe he is sent by fate to retaliate against you from the moment he was born? You worry about turning old before you have the answers. You worry about your son turning into a problem child and cutting you off from his life. Think about the possibility of this outcome.

"The worst sorrow is being helpless. We never tell our offspring what our regrets are because they get ahead of us and think we know nothing.

We helplessly look at them taking the wrong paths like we did and ask ourselves "what's the point of our life if we can't guide them?"

"There's always a lot happening around us. We keep assuming that happiness is ahead of us, and we will no longer be lonely. But our loved ones leave us one by one as time flies, and the so-called happiness disappears and turns into scattered fireworks, and the warmth of the past rises in our minds, becoming memories.

"We are numbed by parting, like the ending of a song. We are like passersby, watching countless stories of ourselves and others flow by us. Love becomes a privilege, and all ideas turn into a dream."

My speech really shook him. Ah Long wrote in his diary that night:

> "Uncle Ye and I joked about Ah Xi's topic "Looking Forward to the Future". Five years, ten years, and fifty years after the end of the world in 2012, tragedies unfolded—Ah Xi suffered a crushing defeat at every stage of his life. Although it seems like I am discussing Ah Xi's story with Uncle Ye, I am well aware that it will also happen to me if I don't do anything about my life. If there really is one day, maybe I will be very successful in the future, but what's the use of that? Maybe it'll be like the movie. I only wish she finds someone who likes her like I do, but that must also be my prayer to God after death. Time flies by no matter what you do. So, what is everyone doing at every moment? I suddenly realize that I'm already 20 years old. I should take it more seriously even if I am doing something meaningful, I cannot be so leisurely.
>
> Looking back at the past five years, never being serious and not having a future were always the reasons for my breakups. I got to something so she could see that I changed."

*I don't know if my body and mind would still be the same after
not using them for so long.*

*I pray to the gods for a miracle.*
*God blesses me.*
*Not for a guaranteed success, but for not giving up mid-way.*

*Ps. While I was imagining my future. I saw my child. He was
in his adolescence. I was nervous, for he knew my history. I
needed to do much better, or my wife and I would be punished.*

08 / 20

Xiaomin came to visit me. Ah Long was excited to see him, and he was
moved after speaking to Xiaomin. His diary of the day described it well.

*The doorbell rang when I woke up in the morning. The three
of us were all confused by it. Who could it be at this hour? I had
many curiosities in my mind and opened the door. It turned out
to be Brother Xiaomin. I really wasn't expecting him! I always
wanted to visit him, for we were similar in many ways, and I
thought it'd be beneficial to hang out with him, too. I didn't
get to talk to him for very long, and I felt half asleep most of
the time, but it was still influential to me. Whether going to
college or not has been the biggest issue for me for the longest
time, and I told Brother Xiaomin that "college degrees are all
the same, but having one or not is completely different", which
was something that I figured out by myself a few days ago. I
feel that it will be less likely for me to go to college as time goes
by. So, does that mean I only get to aim at whatever doesn't
require a degree? Brother Xiaomin told me "Though a degree
is important, a life goal is more important." Uncle Ye joined the
conversation, "Why does it have to be either...or? Why can't
it be going to college and reaching for a goal at the same time?"*

*Then I realized what he said was the truth about everything! But one thing that I feel is important other than losing weight right now is to learn English. Dang, I didn't want to say it because I'm lazy and I didn't want to do it...*

*We had spring pancakes for lunch! It was delicious! I wrapped my own for the first two and they looked like Baozi, but after taking some advice from grandpa they looked a lot better. I like spring pancakes a lot... I like eating delicious food a lot... It's the biggest joy to eat delicious food.*

*Aunty Hao was released from the hospital today. She recovered fast. Her student visited her with so many flowers and prayers... we should all take after her. She'd probably be more active in a few days.*

*Ps. I learned to play "Left 4 Dead" with Uncle Ye and Ah Xi today. It was amazing!*

08 / 21

Ah Long and I have been doing this social investigation, where I asked him to circle out a random building on a map and then spent around two weeks investigating the backstory of the residents there. A man who started from nothing left a huge impact on Ah Long, and he started to understand how difficult it was for his father to make it.

"Uncle Ye, you always tell me to do things for others. I've made up my mind now. I'm going to get into politics like my father did."

"Oh yeah? Why?"

"Uncle Ye, I want to serve the people."

"I don't know, man. You'll have to have an under-graduation degree. How are you going to do that since you've never really studied since middle school?"

"Uncle Ye, I have never done before because I didn't know what it was for. But now I have a goal, do you think it'd be a problem for me?"

Done! Setting a goal was completed. On the morning of August 22, Ah Long went to Mrs. Hao and asked to learn English. My wife wasn't expecting Ah Long to be excited to study so soon. That was the purpose of helping kids find their life goals, as a prodigal who returns is more precious than gold.

On August 22, Ah Long started learning English. It was the first day of his journey. Later he took on literature, math, physics, chemistry, and biology one by one. He laid out the book and said, "Let's study! I want the best teachers out there!" I told him, "Teachers are for answering questions. You can start on your own, save the ones that you don't understand and ask later." He agreed.

On September 18, Ah Long called Mr. Ren in Beijing asking for instructions for the college entrance examination as well as tips on reviewing. He started learning all subjects.

On October 6, Ah Long became online friends with his mother, and confessed his mistakes to his parents, starting to believe that they are good parents. Instead of going down the wrong path, a man tends to need his family when he's achieved something. Due to the responsible nature of a man, he is set to break down when lack of ability meets responsibility. The only way to solve such an issue is to boost his confidence by letting him finish a few tasks, and naturally, he would need recognition from his family when he achieves the goals. Everyone has the dream of returning home after achieving something. And treating the family well like never before comes naturally after success.

On October 8, Ah Long unexpectedly got into a relationship with a ballerina after knowing each other for only one day. I was surprised.

On October 10, Ah Long started to understand his friend.

On October 11, Ah Long changed his computer wallpaper to the color green and changed into some bright-colored clothes. (He used to wearing black.)

On October 13, Ah Long helped his friend to prepare for a physics exam.

On October 14, Ah Long started helping me with education. All his teachers were surprised by his learning ability, and he mailed three certificates that he obtained in Olympic math competitions. I asked him what Olympic math was, he explained that it is high school level of math but taught in elementary school. I firmly believed that he was able to get into Tsinghua University with one more year of study.

On October 19, today something huge happened. Ah Long wrote about it in his diary.

*10 / 19 / 2011*

*All this studying day after day, year after year… next year is not going to be the same as this year, to hell with repeating the same year after year! It's alright though, I'm going to work hard and maybe I'll get into a third-tier university, or maybe a second-tier university, or maybe a top-tier university. Who knows? We'll see how it goes. I'm going to try my best to do what I can.*

*I spoke with Uncle Ye this evening because something shocking happened while everything was going so smoothly, which I hadn't noticed before. But after speaking with Uncle Ye, I real-*

*ized something crazy: a terrifying creature had crept up around me—my own mother. She was ready to really mess me up! The control from my parents is so terrifying to me, and it is so sneaky that I didn't even notice! But at least Uncle Ye saw it coming. It turned out that my mother said no matter how I did, my father had already got me into a top-tier university through his con-nections. Anyone with a normal mind would've stopped trying after hearing that, for having a guaranteed result beforehand, but after speaking with Uncle Ye, I've made up my mind to prove my worth through hard work! I've already wasted five years before, and in those years, everyone was telling me how smart I was, and academics wouldn't be a problem for me at all. Now I'd like to see what would happen if I really tried my best. Uncle Ye was right about Panjin being my last stop. I know that nowhere else can save me besides being with Uncle Ye at his home. Nowhere else enables me to realize who I am.*

What does it mean to hurt someone in the name of love? I always send out a survey to the parents before I meet them, and there is one question in it: Have the parents or grandparents stated the boundaries? For exam-ple, "As long as you stay in school, we can get you into a top-tier school even without taking the entrance exam." "We can arrange you a job even if you quit school." or "As long as you stay healthy and not messing around." If yes, what did you say exactly?

If they answered yes, I would consider refusing to take that child in, for working hard for something unworthy is something we strive to avoid throughout our lives. If the parents can be above the rules, then be it. Why bother wasting time with the children and teachers?

"Your father will get you into a top-tier university no matter how you do in the exam." This is how the parents lose their dignity as parents. How do they expect to earn their children's respect? They tell you to work hard, but also tell you that all your efforts cannot keep up with your father's words. It is so discouraging! It had me think that Ah Long's tragedy really is a coincidence?

I had to tell him that whatever happens, "They want you to stay calm, not to be stressed about it." I only knew afterward that his father had told his mother to say it. But they didn't understand that Ah Long was working hard for himself!

10 / 22

People who succeed in their careers are persistent.

Ah Long's father dropped by unexpectedly in Panjin a few days later. He was followed by an elderly gentleman, a master who was hired to provide pre-exam guidance for Ah Long. He was in his 60s, wearing traditional clothes and old-school glasses. He was well respected by many as he was a leading figure in the industry and was originally a member of the college entrance examination proposition group. He looked at me up and down, and then drove me away, saying he was going to give Ah Long some face-to-face advice.

I realized that his father was worried about not having a top-quality education in Panjin and hired an expert to investigate. Ah Long's father and his followers made random conversations with me, and I replied knowing what they were trying to do. The door opened after two hours. The expert walked out angrily as Ah Long smiled bitterly. I asked how it was, but Ah Long gave me a look, implying that we'd talk later, greeted everyone and left with me.

Ah Long was silent on our way home. I asked him, "What was that about?"

Ah Long said, "What? The smile?"

"Yeah, you smiled as if you didn't want to be there."

"Uncle Ye, do you know what we talked about there?"

"What?"

"That guy questioned me about every single detail of my life for two hours straight and gave me two pieces of advice in the last five minutes."

"Oh Yeah? What did he say?"

"Oh, he told me that I wasn't utilizing my time well. I can learn English while in the bathroom and memorize vocabulary while crossing the streets."

"How do you feel about that?"

"Oh, I feel sad."

"For you?"

"No, for him."

Sometime in 2012

It was time to go back to Beijing, and it was time to break up again. During our last meal together with all his teachers, Ah Long expressed his feelings, "I would like to express my special gratitude to all the teachers for your help over the past six months. The teachers have witnessed my journey from scoring 100 points in the six subjects to now scoring 500 points. Others said that I was a legend, and I believe all the teachers are a part of the legend. No one was able to push me or advise me, and everyone kept telling me how smart I was. I always thought that I'd understand no matter who the teacher was, but it turned out not to be true. I could only listen to the best teachers. I was picky about teachers, and I always thought that they were unworthy of teaching me for having the slightest flaw in them. Therefore, you are the best teacher. I'm so glad to have met you guys, thank you so much!"

Ah Long completed the entire six-year curriculum of high school in just eight months and was admitted to a prestigious top-tier university in 2012 college entrance examination.

My student Ah Long, people got close to him for his wealthy family, as well as his natural noble characteristics. But he lacked realistic attitude and didn't know how to live life quietly. It was causing the people around him to be tired of his lifestyle. He was emotionally unstable and making him follow a set path was the ultimate challenge for a teacher.

He had a strong personality. He dreamed of the purest connections but refused to be bonded by them. He couldn't stand any type of restrictions, and he would not force himself to follow rules. He would work extremely hard for something that he was interested in. A boring life would make him upset or even generate a sick mindset. He was difficult to get along with, for sometimes he had jumpy thoughts and was funnier than most. Other times he was cold and distant.

He was unable to live in lies, and sometimes was considered weird for being too straightforward by someone who didn't know him well. He was like a wandering martial artist who was always ready to support the suffering ones. Sometimes he'd even go as far as putting himself in danger. He would always receive support from his family and friends, even from strangers when he encountered hardships. He didn't care about being rich or poor as he was able to adjust to simple life.

His inner world was complicated, which was difficult for others to understand. He appeared to be simple and straightforward, but deep within he was contradictory. For most of the time, he was friendly and willing to help others. But in other circumstances he was cold-hearted.

In fact, he preferred friendships based on spiritual connections instead of physical connections.

Ah Long, one would not be in this world if connections were not important. Uncle Ye wishes you to have a great journey ahead.

# Chapter 4

# How to Educate Children with Depression

On August 7, 2011, my student Ah Long wrote in his diary:

*I don't understand why there are two Valentine's Days in a year now, but it's finally over.*

*The legendary typhoon Meihua came right after the Chinese Valentine's Day. From a Level 7 wind with no risk at all, to a Level 14 wind with eerie winds, there were various rumors that made us feel a bit at a loss. Should we hide or bravely rush out? Anyway, it was drizzling down the ground. We'll wait inside the house, watching pedestrians fly into the sky.*

*This new guy came today. He was 16 years old, from Beijing. Beijing kids love to play Dota, so I guessed we had something to talk about. But he was good at it according to this guy himself. Who knows? He has only been playing it for six months…and he talked to himself. Maybe that's how we were. This got me feel like I was from another city.*

*Though I didn't get to raid tonight, I played a few matches of Dota with this dude. He was in a well-known clan or something. They played two sets, still 5 against 4… In the end, they still lost. I also noticed one of their players opposite me was a noob… too easy…*

*It was fun, though. I felt young again. Dang, I'm old now. All of a sudden, I was 20.*

On the second day of Chinese Valentine's Day in 2011, I met 16-year-old Ah Xi. His father gave me a Handbook of Student Growth, with the cover reading: School education—the bridge of family education. Mrs. Leng, homeroom teacher, angrily wrote in it during the first week of school: You can't be tired at the starting point; and none of your knowledge meet the standards.

The comments of the second week were full of the teacher's good thoughts: The seat was moved to the first row, and I wanted to pay more attention to you, but it seemed that you didn't adjust well to it. You lost focus several times during class, and there was a significant difference in writing compared with others.

In the fourth week's comments, Mrs. Leng cautiously wrote: After returning to school, the mental state was not good! On Thursday you didn't even finish math homework until 11:40 pm, and you fell asleep in in physics, English, math, and evening self-study classes. Please have a good sleep at home before you return to school.

The teacher was devastated in the fifth week: He has been doing the homework the entire week but has not still finished it yet! There was only a line of words in the ninth week's comments: Just keep working hard! I was touched, as I saw the efforts and helplessness of a frontline teacher.

In the twelfth week, things went for a change: what would you do if the teacher simply stopped paying attention to you? Before the final exam, the parents received a hint from the teacher: transfer to another school!

Ah Xi's mother thought he was sick and took him to the hospital. The doctor only asked him five questions and immediately concluded that Ah

Xi was suffering from depression. He prescribed a lot of medicines and reminded Ah Xi's mother to supervise her child to take it on time.

Ah Xi stayed home to play video games all day, and only ate takeouts. His mother decided to call me.

In a sense, the story of Ah Xi being with me was like Defoe's *Robinson Crusoe*, both of which tell the story of a person being suddenly thrown back into an unfamiliar and often hostile environment and having to adjust to it and survive relying entirely on wisdom, energy, and resilience to regain success.

I have been observing Ah Xi for five months and found that he only had the following 18 shortcomings.

1. He kept explaining himself.

"Uncle Ye, hear me out. Please let me explain!"

2. He kept making promises.

"This is the last time I swear, Uncle Ye."

3. He had selective amnesia.

He always forgot about the methods of learning and the key points of homework, but when to play games and what to eat for lunch tomorrow would never be forgotten.

4. He liked being sarcastic.

He had a thick Shanxi accent when he spoke sarcastically. Ah Long and I were carrying a huge metal box when we first met, and he was making fun of us and was yelled at.

5. He liked to procrastinate.

He always left things for the next day, saying "Just one moment; Wait a little longer" when it comes to things he should do immediately.

John Dewey said that procrastination became a habit when the motive was for the future instead of the present.

6. He never reviewed what he's learned.

Dewey had his own explanation for this phenomenon: the innate power of children and their desire to fulfill their impulses could not be suppressed. If external conditions prevent children from using their activities for the work they need to do, they have surprisingly learned to pay only appropriate attention to external textbooks to meet the teacher's requirements, while leaving the remaining strength to delve into associative things that interest them.

7. He dozed off.

There's an idiom in Chinese called "dumb as a wooden chicken". I don't know what a wooden chicken looks like, but I surely know it means to be as numb as Ah Xi.

8. He snacked a lot.

When he first got here, he was only found next to the computer, or in the kitchen.

In the computer room, Ah Xi just played games silently while in the kitchen, he stole food like a mouse.

9. He promised a lot but did nothing.

10. He was subjective and emotional.

11. He was pessimistic.

12. He was paranoid a lot.

13. He complained a lot.

14. He was opportunistic.

15. He always wanted others to pay for the bill.

16. He never opened up his heart.

17. He spoke poorly of others behind their backs. It was the worst sin in the Chinese tradition.

18. He looked down on his parents. It was something his parents really freaked out about:

Usually, Ah Xi was polite and friendly, but he showed abnormal mania and didn't like anything when his parents were present. He would pick a crowded place purposely to yell at them.

Both of his parents serve as CEOs in Fortune Global 500 companies, and both graduated from the prestigious universities and resigned from state-owned enterprises in the early 1990s to Shenzhen, gradually establishing the economic foundation they had today. In his father's words, he relied on strong self-control and a strong sense of struggle. And they've been married and had a profound partnership for 20 years.

In Ah Xi's eyes, his parents valued money too much. But they thought it was just something that could measure their success, maybe also a means to overcome boredom in life. Anyway, they each achieved success in their careers and were very satisfied.

But on a certain day in a certain year or month, their child was born, and as Liao Yimei said, under their noses, the most ordinary miracle in the world happened every day, transforming them from a carefree couple to worried parents.

They were cautious and full of extravagant expectations. They never gave the child any unfortunate news or story. Unrealistic, they wished to shelter him from everything ugly and sad. They hoped him to be a lucky child.

They protected him when he needed to be tested. They punished him when he needed to be encouraged. They weren't present when he needed their company, like many Chinese family. He was raised by his grandmother.

They failed at being parents, and they felt powerless when facing him. The only thing that was left was the dignity of being parents. With onions, there will be tears. Quickly, angry Ah Xi turned the last bit of dignity from his parents into a luxury.

If you ask me what these parents wanted the most, it could be communication and respect. Many con artists made a living off these parents! They were good at making children realize their mistakes within half an hour, having them hug their parents in tears. Instantly the parents got what they always wanted the most, and everything seemed perfect in that instant. The only flaw in it was the short-lived change of the child. They went back to the old patterns as soon as they arrived home, for they noticed that the parents were still the same as before. Then the parents noticed the old patterns of the child and went back to the so-called experts. They kept feeding coins into the slot machine, wanting that touching moment back like an addiction. The child then refused to go to the experts knowing it'd just be the same, and this is when the experts would suggest: to go with the flow.

There's one thing that the parents couldn't deny: all of your experiences, mistakes that you had made and the suffering you had endured were of no use to your child. They would not learn from them. You could forcefully instill in him, but they would fall many times and still shout "I want to live my own life!" What does his own life exactly mean? It means they want to experience life as a blank piece of paper, rather than have the experiences pre-installed. Parents put their hope on the offspring before living their lives to the fullest. We dip our toes in the water but always want to guide like we know how to swim. The children don't reject you as parents. Instead, they reject a life that's arranged. To them, it is as boring as it could be.

Someone might ask, "Is this still advantageous or charming?" Yes, this is the most charming advantage. In my eyes, repeatedly teaching without improvement fully demonstrates Ah Xi's tenacity, resilience, and perseverance.

Are there any strong points of him? Yes, Ah Xi's strongest point was he never changed the 18 shortcomings stated above. To me, this represented persistence and toughness. All the shortcomings were a sign of a right person doing the wrong things. The tougher to correct right now, the more successful he will be once he is guided to the right path.

Xiaomin was online for 16 hours a day, which represented that he was capable of focusing on one task for 16 hours. He was a tough guy!

Ah Xi also had many other strong points:

1. He was honest. This was the highest quality of someone, as nothing else could outshine honesty. He might speak poorly of the others behind their backs, but he spoke the truth.

2. Though he explained himself quite a lot, he had the patience to explain a problem to others. It was a quality of an educator.

3. He paid attention to the details when making plans, and he was good at making designs.

4. He was good with people when he needed to be. He was not afraid of strangers.

5. He had good hygiene and a personal image, and elegant temperament. This could not be achieved without the inheritance and constraints of parents.

6. He had good physical health.

7. He had a clear concept of money.

8. He was more intelligent than the rule makers for he saw the loopholes.

9. He dozed off, indicating he was good at taking breaks, which was important for someone successful.

Five months passed by. Ah Xi's parents kept calling me asking when their child could study normally. I only answered with "I don't know. We'll have to wait! We'll have to wait for his own will to emerge." They believed that I had already failed but kept it to themselves due to my reputation and their usual dignity.

It was surprising to me that the parents wanted so little. They only wanted their child to start studying, to follow their path towards success. What they failed to realize was that they had completely different starting points. Ah Xi had the potential of a decent manager. But, from my understanding, success was to move up in the social class. His destiny was not to follow his parents and become a manager. Instead, he was to be

CHAPTER 4

a leader and an innovator. Did he have enough good qualities? If not, what was missing? I was not quite sure what was missed. I only judged a man by his ambitions. He was going to find his own path once he was ambitious, and that's when his potentials got fulfilled.

How to inspire ambition? First, verify that he is indeed a boy, then let him witness a miracle, work together with him to create a miracle, and finally let him witness a bigger miracle. At the scene of the miracle, tell him personally that you can do it too!

It was time to start.

I walked in on him taking a shower and asked him such a question. "Are you in a relationship?"

"Not right now."

"Was it with a guy or a girl?"

"Of course, a girl, Uncle Ye."

It seemed like he surely was a man.

### Witness the first miracle.

After he came out of the bathroom, I kept asking. "What do you think is least possible to happen right now?" He thought about it and his face blushed. "To have Xiaolin's phone number."

"Why?"

"She has too many pursuers, and no one knows her number since she got a new one."

"Ask her friends."

"I did, but they didn't say. Uncle Ye, I've tried it all and spent a great amount of money, too."

"So, this is the lease possible to you?"

"Yep." He nodded.

I paused a second, "What are you going to do with the scholarship?"

"What do you think?"

"I heard your grandma was sick?"

"Yes, I think her throat doesn't feel good."

"You should get her some honey."

"I understand."

"Go now. I'll wait for you."

Soon after, Ah Xi returned with the honey.

"Ah Xi, I'll show you a miracle right now." I took out my phone and called the mail carrier and said I had something to mail to Beijing. After the carrier took over the honey, I tried to borrow his work clothes.

"Can I borrow your clothes for a few days?"

"Stop joking, Mr. Ye. They are too dirty for you." The carrier smiled and left as Ah Xi stared at me.

I took out my phone and made another call. The carrier put the honey on the handlebar of the bike he came with and went to another building. A man came out of nowhere, sliced open the bag that was holding the honey and left without a trace.

Soon my phone rang, it was the mail carrier. "Mr. Ye, I'm so sorry the honey bottle fell on the floor and broke."

"It's okay. Come by again. I have some more." I told Ah Xi to get more beforehand.

I heard the knock on the door and opened it. "I'm so sorry, Mr. Ye. It was all my fault."

"Did it all break?"

"Yes. Was it kind of expensive?"

"Yes, my student bought them for his grandmother."

"I'll pay you back for it, though it might be two days worthy of my paycheck."

"Don't even worry about it, man! I'm not going to ask you to do that."

"Are these the new ones you just bought?"

"Yes, I asked him to get them. He just got back too."

"Sorry kid, it was all my fault. I'll see you guys around then." He took the honey and was about to leave, then stopped, took off his work clothes and handed them to me. "Just give me a call after you're done with them, Mr. Ye."

I turned to Ah Xi, and he was shaking.

I made a phone call, took out a cardboard box, put a crystal ball in it and sealed it. "Let's go to Beijing, Ah Xi. Let me show you what 'anything is possible' means."

I remembered there was snow on the highway, so it was partially blocked off. We took some regular roads and finally arrived at the hotel in Beijing at around 11:00 pm at night.

We were both exhausted. Ah Xi fell asleep quickly after checking in, but I had to make out the plans.

We drove to Ah Xi's school the next day. The closer we got, the more stressed he was. I felt his fear of school. I changed into the mail carrier's clothes and walked over to the school gate. Soon after, Ah Xi saw his crush write down her number on the package I was holding.

I got back to the car. Ah Xi was shaking, "That was amazing, Uncle Ye."

"It's time to redefine 'impossible'."

Ah Xi was speechless.

I took him to go-karting after lunch and he drove lap after lap until dark. It seemed that he was thinking about something.

After returning to the hotel, Ah Xi came over to me as I was resting, "Uncle Ye, I'm going to tell you a secret."

### Make a miracle together.

Ah Xi spilled his heart to me that evening. I finally understood his tragic life.

He went to a boarding school and was bullied by his classmate Xiaowei. Whether it was in the classroom or cafeteria, Xiaowei bullied him at will, even making him strip down naked in the dorm while others laughed. Ah Xi was too weak to fight back, and never told anyone about it due to Xiaowei's family being powerful. That had left him with low self-esteem and barely any confidence.

That was his main conflict. Everything we did before was for that moment. Nothing would work unless we solve it.

"Let's get some sleep. We'll deal with Xiaowei together, the first thing we will do when we wake up."

Ah Xi jumped up with excitement. I was godlike to him in that instant. Suddenly his happiness turned into worry, "His father is a powerful figure, Uncle Ye. He's probably going to mess us up if we do anything to him."

"Don't worry! We take off and run after we deal with him, and it'll be our turf once we pass Shanhaiguan. Then you can transfer to another school." I tried to calm him.

He thought it was reasonable, and then went to sleep.

What happened next was described very well in the *Beijing Evening News* on August 27, 2013:

> The next day, Ye Zhigang took Ah Xi back to school. "How dare you to come back here?" Xiaowei got aggressive once he saw us.
>
> "Get him!" Ye shouted, and Ah Xi charged. But Ye Zhigang stood still. Ah Xi only wanted to fight because he thought it was going to be a two-on-one, but he found himself alone in

*the fight once it broke out. It was too late for him to pull back, and all the rage in his heart transferred into power at that moment. He fought back for his dignity for the first time in his life. He then realized the meaning of all the running, push-ups and pull-ups he was told to do. Ah Xi dominated Xiaowei with unexpected power.*

*"We're staying at the hotel. Come find us if you want more!" Ah Xi wanted to leave afterward, but Ye Zhigang gave Xiaowei their address. Ye knew that Ah Xi was only afraid of Xiaowei's parents for their power.*

*"We're so done! His parents are definitely coming for us!' Ah Xi couldn't stay still after returning to the hotel, shaking in bed with a flashlight in hand waiting for their revenge. Three days passed and nothing happened. Ye made Ah Xi understand that Xiaowei was only a paper tiger, and his parents still lived under the law.*

### Witness a larger miracle.

What happened next was even more surprising to Ah Xi. The hotel we stayed in often hosted foreign guests, and I had earned the opportunity for him to dine with the British Royal Family through my connection. Ah Xi was completely in shock by the scene—the Royal Family dined in the splendid hall with confidence emerging from every single movement. Ah Xi made up his mind after shoving the last bite of bacon in his mouth, "I decided, Uncle Ye, that I'm going to work hard. I hate the lonely, negative loser as I was. I'm going to build a business empire as my father did!"

It was time to go back to the Northeast. Ah Xi hopped in the car excited. He kept looking around while on the highway, for fear that someone might come for us. But nothing happened. Once we passed Shanhaiguan, he seemed to remember what I'd said, finally relieved and fell asleep in the backseat.

On his trip to Beijing, Ah Xi witnessed miracles. He opened up to me willingly, showed me his main conflict and solved it with my help, and even found his life goal of building a business empire.

We arrived home in the evening. Ah Xi took out a stack of cash and handed it to me, "Uncle Ye, you've done so much for me, but I didn't even offer to buy you a bottle of water or anything. I resent how selfish my family is. This is all the savings that I have been keeping with me. Please accept it for helping me become better."

Plato once said that slaves are slaves because their actions do not represent their own thoughts but represent others'. Ah Xi broke the chains on him, retrieved his dignity, found his direction and started a responsible life for himself.

Later, Ah Xi witnessed his friend Ah Long restoring the relationship with his parents and started to reflect on his relationship with his parents. I asked his parents to write about their own growth process and the development history of their family in their spare time. After a slight adaptation, I read to Ah Xi half an hour before bedtime every day. Not long after, Ah Xi understood his parents and began to face up to his past behavior towards them, apologizing for his rudeness over the phone.

Shortly thereafter, Ah Xi took the initiative to improve his learning methods, and his grades got better day by day.

Once after Ah Xi returned from an exam in Beijing, he excitedly told me, "Xiaowei and his classmates seemed to respect me a lot more once I showed up at school. My classmates said I had a certain style, but they couldn't say exactly what it was."

"That's a confident expression. You got it from having knowledge. Wisdom in hold, elegance in mold." I summarized for him. The biggest problem for him was essay writing, but it was solved now. When Ah Xi first came to me, writing was his worst aspect. He was only able to write a few words in a whole morning.

After the trip to Beijing, he wrote in his diary:

> After washing up every morning, I would symbolically sit at my study desk, daydreaming with a book to kill time. When Uncle Ye walked past me, I would suddenly wake up from my dream and take a deep glance towards him, while Uncle Ye was always looking at me. When avoidance clashes with discipline, the atmosphere between us becomes lively like lightning flint.

> I remembered Uncle Ye once led me to make a comparison:

> Morning for Ah Long: wake up, brush his teeth, make bed, use the restroom, send text, space out, restroom again and then study, eat, read.

> Morning for me: wake up, space out, observe him, brush my teeth, use the restroom, space out, space out more, check the kitchen, eat, space out, get yelled out and space out more.

Above, Ah Xi vividly reminisced about the mornings back in 2011. Dewey explained this progress (as early as 1919):

Literature is a reflection and elucidation of social experience. Therefore, it must emerge after experience rather than before. It cannot serve as the foundation of the unity, although it can become the sum of the unity.

Ah Xi later wrote a letter to his father. His father replied excitedly:

CHAPTER 4

*I have read what Ah Xi had written, and I almost couldn't be-
lieve it was written by him. The style was so different! What's
important is that he's learned to think about certain things, have
standards and make changes. Thank you for your hard work and
help! I'm also trying to understand your methods for treating
Ah Xi, and we parents, especially I, surely do need to make
changes, too. I understand that it is not easier than having Ah Xi
make changes. I would love to have your options and advice.*

Ah Long, Ah Xi's friend, wrote down in his diary after returning to Beijing:

*I've started my life here in Panjin. I've met Uncle Ye's friends
here: one of them went to school abroad and came back. One
of them joined the military army after high school. One of them
sold cars after university. One of them did photography, and so
on. One day Ah Xi showed up, and we became a crew.*

*We lived together, ate together, exercised together, played
together, studied together, and got crazy together. We broke
walls and carried bricks, but what I'm most proud of is beating
professional mode in Left 4 Dead 2! Or you can call it impossible mode. Even though it took us about two months, and we
were weak in the beginning, eventually we became decent at
it and the crew was unbeatable! We even ran it again without
using guns! Too bad we can't stay together anymore...*

*We were always trying to make the home better: feeling un-
comfortable with using a computer desk, we looked for one all
over Shenyang to buy materials and assemble one by ourselves.
The lights in the hall were not domineering, so we decided to
install the crystal lights on Taobao by ourselves. The hanger was
too small, so we installed a two meter one on the exterior wall
of the house and put a sticker saying "Guard Dogs Inside" on*

*the window edge, haha! We made changes to wherever that made us uncomfortable, and we were happy to do it.*

*We picked on Ah Xi when he first got here, maybe because he was from the south. He kept talking about random stuff. It was so annoying. My memory wasn't that good, and Ah Xi would always space out, or be snaking. Anyways, Ah Xi changed eventually. I'm happy that we are friends, and I'm happy that you have friends other than LZY...*

It is said that some lives are linked across time.
Connected by an ancient calling that echoes through the ages.

Later, I delivered two consecutive speeches, "The Most Important Word in Life is 'Do'" and "Vanity is the Favorite Sin of Devils".

Ah Xi leaned on the corner of my bed and said loudly: "Uncle Ye, I came here for not having good grades, but I know that my classmates aren't better than me just because they have better grades. Their grades actually prevented them from learning actual knowledge. I really wish they could come and listen to your teachings."

One more month flew by, and Ah Xi had already become someone new. We became a family in six months. It was time for him to leave. Tears came to my eyes once again. His mother sent a text message to us:

*Mrs. Hao and Mr. Ye,*

*Thank you from the bottom of my heart! My heart has changed recently. When I bid farewell, tears flow down my face. You must be filled with sadness after experiencing this kind of separation time and time again, right? Thank the heaven that you guys showed up in our lives when it was difficult. It must have been fate. I firmly believe that our son has become someone ex-*

*cellent for spending the six months with you. And I also believe*
*that it'll be the most precious memory of his life too. Panjin will*
*be the harbor of his soul, where there is a lighthouse that always*
*lights up for him. Thank you once again! And hope you have*
*a good holiday.*

*02:36 pm, 02 / 05 / 2012*

Ah Xi returned to school, and he started respecting his father's achievements and understanding the shortcomings of the family members. He
was strict with himself but being tolerant of his family. Currently, Ah Xi
is preparing for admission to Ivy League universities in the United States
in the future.

Do not question one's nature by one's history. Ah Xi is kind and honest.
He is empathetic and always considerate of others, which makes him look
indecisive. He monitors what he does and says carefully, and it makes
him lack candidness. He loves making life enjoyable, and he gets over his
head when happy. He doesn't like to live in an environment that lacks
warmth and passion, and he needs respect and praise from others. Ah Xi
desires a romantic life that is full of positivity and beauty. He avoids conflicts and hardships. Indecency scares him, and violence traumatizes him.

Ah Xi acts with class and speaks with elegance. He is charismatic to
women, likes to predict their inner voice, listens to them and understands
them. He is a good friend and an ideal partner. Marriage will impact his
life way more than others.

One might ask how a kid with such a personality is going to build a business empire. It is not important. What I seek is for him to find himself
and like himself.

Ah Xi likes taking walking in the garden, which is more beneficial to the
physical-mental balance than exercising.

Ah Xi is a perfectionist. He often feels guilty for not doing things perfectly.

The friends that he spent every day with are significant to his life. He has eyes for beauty, and he resents ugliness and violence. Forcing things onto him makes him clueless. You can only get what you want from him through patience and encouragement.

Ah Xi, life is too long if you don't do anything, but it is too short when you focus on one thing. We might be both old when we meet next time, for life is unpredictable. Uncle Ye would like to tell you that building a family is also an incredible achievement, for more and more men see having a happy family as success, even their greater achievement. I hope you are happy in the future.

# Chapter 5
# How to Educate Children
# from Wealthy Families

## A funeral at Babaoshan Cemetery

In May 2012, Chen passed away in the Chinese PLA General Hospital. He held his grandchild's hand and didn't let him go.

The funeral was held at the Babaoshan Cemetery. It was a large funeral with an attendance of more than 2000 people. He lay in the casket peacefully.

The final moment came. "Goodbye, father." Qiming' uncle led the entire family to bow deeply three times to the coffin. I stood behind Qiming and bid farewell to the old man quietly while wiping away my tears.

The old man often said during his lifetime that a happy ending in life was something he had never imagined before.

## The defeat of a successful family

In March 2011, a father of a child invited me to meet at his grandmother's house and said that the grandfather wanted to meet me and also talk about an education plan.

On the afternoon of March 19th, I was taken to the child's grandmother's house. Inside the room, eight family members were waiting for me in the living room.

The atmosphere of the room was solemn. There were inscriptions of several generations of leaders hung on the walls, and sitting opposite me was the grandfather of the child, whom the family called "gramps". He remained silent and sat beside me, looking at me. I could feel that he was the alpha of the pack.

After a brief exchange of greetings, the grandmother leaned over to me and pulled my hand with tears in her eyes, saying, "Mr. Ye, you are the only hope for our family! You should save our child!" The gramps sitting beside frowned.

The child's mother told me about their family history. The gramps had two sons and one daughter. They had successful careers, but the eldest son and his wife were unable to procreate, and only the younger son had a boy named Qiming.

Qiming's parents were successful individuals, and the couple had the child at an old age. Qiming was 15 years old and was in the third grade of junior high school. He enjoyed playing the violin and singing. He was weak and often got sick when he was young, and only got better once he entered elementary school. His mother, who often took his child to the hospital, mocked herself that she had almost become a pediatrician.

After going to school, Qiming still fell ill every year. Despite this, his performance and academic grades in school had always been good, and he was often rated as Excellent Student. This situation persisted until Qiming entered junior high school.

In fifth grade of elementary school, Qiming's father was appointed to a local government and could only return to Beijing on weekends, and there were also many social activities on weekends. His mother was responsible for administrative work in the office, and she returned home late on a daily base. Slowly Qiming's academic performance dropped, and by the first semester of the third year of junior high school, he ranked the last in the class. In the second semester of the second year of junior high school, he got addicted to video games and stopped obeying his parents. Due to the rapid decline in academic performance, Qiming lost many friends and became avoidant to the outside world. He was indifferent to family matters. Sometimes he would pretend to be happy when there were guests around, but it made them uncomfortable to be around him. When encountering setbacks in life, Qiming often feels disheartened or suddenly becomes angry and leaves by slamming the door.

He became weak and was persuaded by the school to temporarily absent from school for a month prior to my arrival. Ever since then, Qiming started playing video games all day and would only get up from the desk to watch TV, and then rinse and repeat. He would yell at his parents for just a little dissuasion from them.

His parents held their anger, but it was unacceptable for them to be yelled at by their child. His father said, "The kid doesn't care about any of us, and we do not have any family activities. We were working for nothing, and my job became my escape." His mother said, "I've reached my peak. I admit that we aren't good parents and I have failed as a mother. I wanted a happy family in the beginning, but now returning home is a punishment for myself." Qiming's grandfather was a man from the north. The elderly man said in despair, "Qiming is the only child of our Chen family, but now his spirit and body have collapsed, and our Chen family is done." In his parents' eyes, Qiming had a decent nature, but refused to study. Having Internet addiction and insulting parents were the main problems. He would be a good child again once these problems were solved. But was it really the case? We should not draw hasty conclusions but identify the main contradiction through investigation. Qiming's parents asked me what the best strategies are to solve the three problems. I said I needed to meet with the child first.

I asked his mother what he was doing at home. She said that he might be playing video games. I asked his father and grandfather to take me to him, but the family had their concerns. It turned out that they had brought many experts to the kid but he refused to see them and even shouted insults at them. The family were embarrassed.

I said that it'd be alright, just take me to them.

**On the mission alone—Uncle Ye who came out of nowhere.**

We arrived at his home shortly after. A sound of door slamming came out of the front door as soon as the key touched the keyhole. His father told me quietly that he went back to his room knowing someone was coming.

We stayed in the living room for a while. His father told him to open the bedroom door, but it was ignored. The family said that it was unhelpful sitting there, and it might piss him off even more.

I told them, "It's okay. Your guy can leave, and I'll stay alone." His father said quietly, "I don't think it'd be wise, Mr. Ye. It'd be difficult to move forward if he got mad at you right now." I told him, "Don't worry! Just do as I said".

"Qiming, we are leaving. Come to your grandmother's house for dinner if you get hungry!" They got up and left after speaking to the child through the door.

I closed my eyes sitting on the couch. The room was so quiet that I could only hear the clock ticking. There were some used tissues lying on the tea table. Ten minutes had passed. The bedroom door opened gradually, and a small head stuck out. I dashed to the door and jammed it with my foot. Qiming was spooked and fell down on the bed.

The curtains were shut in the bedroom. It was extremely messy with a smell of sneakers in the air. The computer was on, and there was a used bowl on the floor.

This child sat on the bed. His hair was long and messy, and his face looked tired. However, I could tell he was handsome even with the nose hair sticking out. We looked at each other and he was shy. I went over to him as he fell back down to the bed.

I leaned my mouth towards his ear, let out a sigh, and mysteriously asked, "Are you in a relationship?" He nodded and looked confused. "Is it a guy or a girl?" He paused and said, "a girl." After speaking, Qiming's right hand suddenly clenched the bedsheet with force, and a stream of snot flowed out of one of his nostrils.

There were two layers of meaning behind it:

Firstly, the parents couldn't handle the child, for the child already knew their game plans. However, the parents did not understand the child enough, which gave the child the advantage in the battle. Saying things like that first time meeting him would confuse him and crash his defense.

Secondly, the ambition of a man is the key to any kind of success, and it is directly linked with the male hormone level. He was able to attract the opposite sex at such a young age, indicating that he had the biological foundation for success in the future.

"You're Qiming, right? I'm your Uncle Ye, from the Northeast region. I really miss you for not seeing you for so long. Let's go to the living room!" The child was confused but still went with me and poured a glass of water.

Then it was a long silence. None of us talked until dark.

Qiming broke the awkwardness, "Are you hungry, Uncle Ye?"

The process above was to gain "the revolutionary leadership"—whoever spoke the last has the upper hand. I call the constant battle for such leadership "Emotional Judo".

Qiming asked me, "Are you hungry, Uncle Ye?"

I replied, "Let's get some KFC."

Then I took out a coupon, but Qiming turned away. I asked him what was wrong. He replied that he didn't eat junk food (He was trying to weaken my position through refusal.). I thought the firmer you refused, the more you wanted it. I told him that we should let ourselves go once in a while. He thought about it and said that he needed to call his mother.

Qiming showed care through the phone and said that he was going to take me out for dinner.

I thought to myself that he wanted to be a caring kid. After hanging up, he suggested that I get the food to go and eat at home with him (Ask me to do the work the first time meeting me. It was a gamble certainly). I said, "No way. We are going together. Or people will think of you lowly." He saw there was no room for haggling, got up and went with me.

While having dinner, I asked him, "Why didn't you go to school today?"

"It's Saturday."

"No after-school classes?"

"I didn't feel well so I stayed home."

"How's school?"

"It's alright."

"What's your ranking?"

"I used to be Excellent Student every year before." (Later I was told that it was during elementary school.)

"You don't look happy."

"Oh, it's just how I am. What do you do, Uncle Ye?" (Change the subject quickly)

"Oh, I do kids."

"Huh?"

"Ha, I'm in business concerning children."

"You must be smart then!"

"How so?"

"I once read in a book about the intelligence of the Jewish people. It says that it is the easiest to make money from women and children."

"It depends on the women and children."

Qiming was speechless.

"I came to Beijing just to walk around the city, but I don't know it well. Can you be my guide since you don't have much going on?"

It triggered him. He hated people saying that he doesn't have anything to do.

He argued, "I'll see if I've got time tomorrow, probably not though since I've got classes."

Was it really wise to ask those questions the first time? To make children like Qiming accept you, you need to make them understand the following two points:

The first one is to make them know that you understand them, and you are very clear about the problems they are facing.

The second is to make children believe that you have the ability to help them solve their problems.

The relationship is built once the child accepts you based on these two aspects. Trusting someone should include these five basic elements: integrity, ability, responsibility, communication, and restraint. The reason why Qiming didn't trust his parents, was that he believed that they lacked ability and restraint. They couldn't solve the problems even though they would find them constantly.

Qiming lost all his moods, and I sent him to his grandfather's 15 minutes later.

Everyone was surprised that I got to meet with Qiming. Suddenly they had high hopes for me. Everyone was excited. Gramps even poured a pot of tea for me. His grandmother sighed, "My grandson is saved!"

## A day of being my little guide

At 10 o'clock the next morning, I arrived at Qiming's home. He was still in bed. His mother said that he watched TV till early morning.

At 10:30, his mother woke him up. I walked over and said, "Let's go, be my guide for the day!"

"I got classes today!" His face was red.

"Don't worry," his mother said, "We'll skip today. Take your uncle out and buy whatever you fancy!"

We left 20 minutes later. He asked me: "Where to go first?"

"The mall."

He put on headphones and started walking. We took the bus to the mall, and he didn't say a word on the way there. Once we arrived, he asked, "Do you want to go from the bottom floor to the top or the other way around?"

"From the bottom to the top is good." (I thought, this kid made plans.)

Carl Menger described excellency like this: Outstanding individuals always recognize their own desires and the wealth they can control and make preparations to satisfy their current or future desires.

I believe that having a life goal and having plans are the best quality for middle school students.

Every time we went inside a store, Qiming went straight to the couch. I asked him why and he explained that he never liked shopping, and he was there only for me.

I asked him what he liked to do. He replied studying.

I looked at him, knowing he meant what he said, but why did he act the opposite of it? Anyway, I was happy that he had plans and goals.

Qiming asked me at lunch, "Do you like Chinese or Western meals?"

"Chinese."

"Do you have a budget?" (His thought process surprised me.)

"50 Yuan."

"Let's go to the Yoshinoya. We could get two combo meals."

"Alright."

No one said a word during lunch. I drove him home in the evening and he seemed exhausted. I asked him about the plans for the next day before I left. He told me that he really needed to go to school. I told him that I was going back home the next day. He wished me a safe journey. I called his parents after we parted and told them to tell Qiming who I was exactly. They were anxious about telling him the truth, but I insisted. Qiming learned about my identity that night, replied with a simple okay and went back to his room. At the same time, I stayed in a hotel not far from his place and stayed up late thinking. I went to say goodbye the next day. His mother knocked on his bedroom door hoping he'd go outside. Some time had passed, the bedroom door was still shut. We couldn't hear any sound of movements at all. His mother gave me a worried look, sighed and cried.

"Please don't cry. It's not the end yet." I told her. I sent her to the grandmother's house and started my plan as soon as the front door shut.

### There is always another day after tomorrow.

I took out a pen and wrote down a poem on the wall of the living room. Then I put a CD in the player and set it to loop. The song was called Dream Catcher by Bandari, and the poem was entitled *There Is Always Another Day After Tomorrow*.

# CHAPTER 5

Life has two clear states:
Asleep and awake.
It is a confrontation in spirit,
It is a reversal in time.

Some go to sleep at a set time,
Some go to sleep late at night or dawn.
They have two completely different types of eyes:
Bewildered, sleepy, and scattered,
Clear, sharp, and wise.

Life also has two vague states:
Alive and dead.
Some try to figure out how to stay alive,
Some try to think about how to die.

Some never give up,
They feel like sunshine.
Some are aloof and lonely,
They organize their thoughts in the dazzling night.
They live quietly,
In the noisy city.
They growl yet still exhausted.

Their lives were covered in bruises,
But those years,
Were never stopped,
And never returned.

The wasted time is dragged into slender shadows by the hour hand,
Drifting heavily behind you.
But if you can see it,
Do not forget:

*There is always another day after tomorrow,*
*So be brave and live it.*

## Pouring rain, a phone call from Beijing

I arrived at Qiming's grandmother's 20 minutes later. Everyone looked lost. I tried to comfort them and made the following plans. Firstly, the next few days were extremely important. Everyone had to act like nothing happened and couldn't show any strong emotions. Secondly, I left the poem on the wall. The parents had to pretend that it wasn't there.

I predicted that the child would call me within three days, but everyone was unsure about it. I knew that Qiming loved to learn, and he also had a clear goal. He must have some difficulties in his heart, and he would surely ask for help from me!

At 7:30 in the evening, there was pouring rain outside. I got a call from Beijing when I was on my way back to Liaoning.

"Where are you, Uncle Ye?"

"I'm going back to the Northeast."

"When are you coming to Beijing again?"

"I'll call you when I do."

"And when is that?"

"I'm not sure, but I'll call you!"

The phone rang an hour later. Qiming's mother sounded excited on the other end. She knew that the kid had called me. She told me while she cried that she was happy that her son still wanted to be better, and still had the will to ask for help. They didn't waste their time worrying.

I told her not to be too happy too early, but to stick to our plan of not showing obvious emotional changes in front of Qiming. She asked me if I could come to Beijing earlier because she wanted me to intervene early when the child wanted help the most.

I said no. For Qiming, the later I went back, the stronger his desire is for help. The unknown is way more desirable than the guaranteed. It powers the will to understand. It is called the "Waiting Effect" in psychology.

## Qiming's nightmare

A week later, at 8:30 pm on March 26, 2011, more than 130 countries, thousands of cities, and over one billion people worldwide participated in the Earth Hour event. The red lights surrounding the National Stadium—Bird's Nest—went out from the top to the bottom. At the same time, the National Aquatics Center located on the west side of the Bird's Nest, the Water Cube, and the Linglong Tower on the north side of the Bird's Nest both turned off their outdoor lighting. The three iconic buildings of the Olympic Central Park have shed their glamorous lighting and stood still in the darkness.

In the darkness, Qiming spilled his heart to me:

During his elementary school years, Qiming had occasional colds and fever, but he never delayed his study. He wanted to succeed in his study like his father (Qiming's father held a Ph.D from China University of Geosciences). He studied very hard and was an excellent student every year. In order to keep his body strong, he often participated in sports activities.

But after entering junior high school, he moved to the house he is currently living in. In the second semester of the first year of junior high school, a strange phenomenon gradually appeared: He caught a cold and had a fever more and more frequently, and it was easier for him to have a fever during weekends off. In the end, a vicious cycle formed: after having a fever at home on weekends, he had to receive intravenous fluids at the hospital on Monday and Tuesday. By the time the fever subsided on Wednesday, he had already missed three days of classes when he returned to school, and he had to make up for the missed classes on Thursday and Friday. After returning home on Saturday and Sunday, his cold and fever further worsened. This vicious cycle continued until the third year of junior high school, when the difficulty of the courses increased and the amount of knowledge increased, making it difficult for Qiming to return. In addition, he was a strong child, and if his grades did not rank at the top of the class, he would feel ashamed and unwilling to go to school. He had to pass the time and anesthetize himself by surfing on the Internet and watching TV.

He told me that his goal was to attend the University of Geosciences like his father did and get into politics eventually (I was relieved and didn't have to find a life goal for him anymore.).

"But Uncle Ye, there's no way that I can do it if I get sick every week!"

"What do I do? I don't know why it's happening to me!"

The truth has surfaced. Regular illness was like an unforgettable nightmare, which was the main contradiction in Qiming's heart.

Online games and television were safe havens for children to avoid insurmountable problems in real life. Children insulting their parents were only to transfer responsibility, which made them feel better. This was different from those who immediately shift responsibility to others when they fail in life. Qiming does not intentionally shirk responsibility, but performs a self-defense behavior of human beings, known in psychology as the "Defense Mechanism". Qiming's actions express his inner despair and disappointment towards himself!

I told him frankly that I had no idea neither, but we would get closer and closer to the truth so long as we observe and analyze carefully.

"Let's go straight to the point and figure out why it is so easy for you to get sick on the weekends."

I said the first step is to stay at your house for a weekend. If I, like Qiming, also had a cold and fever, it meant there was a problem with the living environment. If I was okay, it meant it was his physical problem, and then we would go to the hospital for checking up. He nodded.

### Investigation—truth in the bedroom

April 2nd and 3rd were a weekend, and I stayed in his home alone.

During the day, everything was fine. However, I started sneezing after I got into his bed at night and got a runny nose the next day. I started getting headaches soon after. Could it really be the room?

On Monday, I hired some professionals to test the radiation and formaldehyde levels of the room, but the results were fine!

On the evening of the 4th, as I was sick, I sat on Qiming's bed pondering the cause of the problem. Looking at the high piles of gifts and thick dust around the bedroom, I couldn't help but wonder. In the latter half of the night, I unconsciously fell asleep.

The next day around noon, I woke up but didn't rush to get up and take medicine. I looked at everything in the room, including the computer desk, bookshelf, wardrobe, piled up gifts, and the dust covering everywhere. I also saw the sunlight shining into the room through the cracks in the thick curtains, and the dust under the sunlight was dancing gracefully.

Why does dust fly in a fixed direction from the windowsill into the house?

There's wind! This window is leaking air!

And Qiming's bedside was right under the window!

The wind was so subtle, and it was almost impossible for anyone to detect. It turned out that the window was held open by the dust due to lack of cleaning. He lived on the 8th floor, and there were no other buildings in front to block the wind at night. Qiming would rest in bed after exercising on the weekends, which dramatically increased the chance of getting sick.

His parents were too busy to notice anything at home, which caused him to resent them for not getting any help at all. He started to spend the majority of his time online as the reality was so disappointing.

To test my theory, I asked him to sleep in another room from April 6th to 11th for five days in total, and the 9th and the 10th were a weekend. On the 11th, he woke up healthy. The entire family hugged together and celebrated.

The following week passed, two weeks passed, and Qiming never caught a cold again.

Actions speak louder than words. Qiming no longer needs to worry about his study being dragged down by his body. Qiming started to catch up in academics. Our slogan was "Where you fall, get up from the next door!"

# CHAPTER 5

## Waking up from the dream

I walked around the rooms. There was dust covering everywhere, which my eyes could see. The souvenirs from all over the country were piled up against the walls. Qiming's bedsheet was so dirty. It turned yellow. Dishes were also in piles in the kitchen sink. They were only rinsed on the spot when needed.

Qiming's parents stood outside his bedroom conflicted knowing everything was avoidable.

When he was sick before, they would only take him to the hospital when they were free. They were moved by their own sacrifices then, only to realize that they neglected him for so long, and the family had to pay the price!

I gave them the following suggestions: Firstly, keep the room clean. Secondly, be better listeners and stop giving advice unless they were asked. Thirdly, they need to be on the same page. Fourthly, dine with the whole family. Fifthly, spend the weekend with the whole family on something other than studying. Sixthly, move the computer from the bedroom to the living room.

I told them, "To teach a child well is the top priority of parents. It's a good opportunity to get to know the child to accompany his growth, but you guys ignored it. His Internet addiction was not because of the computer. Rather, it was because of the unsolved issues inside.

I've seen broken children. Don't wait till he grows up and realizes that he's had a lonely childhood.

And if you do not change, what was done was for nothing.

This is a home without happiness. You guys were just avoiding it by being busy, but you can't avoid it for your whole life.

You ran away from it because you did not understand it, but now you do, and both of you and the child are going to change for the better."

I told Qiming's father, "A father figure has a tremendous impact on the child. You should spend as much time with him as possible. I know that it might be difficult to make changes, but you might lose the chance to talk to him if you don't do it now.

Nearly all mothers would be fixated on small problems while the fathers take care of the family. The child would become rebellious and shift his focus to fighting against the mother."

Qiming's mother cried to me, "I really think that I'm a bad mother! I'm going to cherish the time left to us, because I feel like he would want to stay away from us when he's older.

I used to think the atmosphere at home was weird, and I didn't do enough for him, but I was ashamed to admit it!'

I told her, "We need to do what's right, and keep doing it till the end. You'll be a good mother, and I'm sure he will tell you in the future that you're a great mother and he loves you."

## The life of the leader

One day in May, Qiming's father called and said the gramps wanted to invite me to his home for a meal. The gramps told me his life story. He had a rough life. When he was a child, the country was unstable. His parents died when he was young, and he joined the revolution after only two years of schooling in 1947. He had been the leader in many fields such as military, agriculture, finance, health, and industry. He gave his life to help the people and the Party.

He kept his head down at work, and never asked for anything in return even though his family had problems in health and work.

For many years he had chronic diseases, but he kept working for the Party even after retirement. He expected a large family from his sons but was only granted one grandchild who was unhealthy both physically and mentally, which had broken his spirit. He told me, "Mr. Ye, your appearance gave my family hope. I thank you dearly on behalf of the entire family!"

I raised my cup, "There is one more thing to do earlier."

"Please enlighten me, Mr. Ye."

"To define the mission of Qiming."

## Teaching moment from the gramps

The lights in Chen's family were well-lit on the weekend evening. The entire family gathered around the grandparents. Qiming stood by his grandfather, and I stood right behind him.

Gramps told Qiming, "It is only because of our faith in the Party and our own hard work that we have what we have today. We all have great responsibilities as men in our family. Mine was to move from the village to the city. Your father's was to become wealthy from poor, and yours, Qiming, is to become intelligent from ignorant.

I never dared to expect a fulfilled life like this, and I'm sure it was because of four decisions that I'd made: Firstly, follow the Party firmly. My life was granted by the Party. There wouldn't be any of us here if it weren't because of the Party. Secondly, marry your grandmother. I wouldn't make it to this day without her. Thirdly, serve the people when the revolution started. Fourthly, hire Mr. Ye as Qiming's mentor, to help us in the dire moment of our family. We are forever in his debts." I wrote a book, The Origin of the Chens, based on the family history that he had told. It has been Qiming's favorite.

Gramps expressed, "There're a lot of details in the book that I've told Qiming about, but he wasn't a fan of it. But, Mr. Ye, the same things in your writing had become his favorite. I believe that your talent is to make the kids fall in love with what they resent."

Maybe education is to pass down information and the spirit of it to the kids.

After Hermann Goring's speech, the audience said, "What a great speech!" But after Hitler's speech, the audience said, "Let's attach France!" Though Hitler was as evil as he could be. I'm with him on this one.

### The sadness of parting—the never fading Chen family

On April 12, 2011, Qiming started private lessons. His grades went straight up. I finished my task before it was due, so it was time for me to part with Qiming.

Before leaving, the gramps gave me a piece of calligraphy to commemorate.

On June 23, 2011, Qiming's mother called, "I no longer believe that I failed as a mother. I know that my family is going to be better!"

In 2012, Qiming started his academic journey in the US as a representative of outstanding students. His goal was Yale University.

Qiming was a selfless person. He recognized family and career, and he had an unmatchable attitude towards work. He inherited the spirit of hard work, as well as the intelligence of his grandfather, and he never relied on fate or luck. One would understand what "heroes emerge from the youth since ancient times" means. He was serious, wise, honest, and reliable, just like his grandfather. He was somewhat sentimental, and only showed his true self when he sensed trust. Or he'd rather be silent, only to listen and observe.

He is a hard worker, and he cherishes the outcomes of his handwork. One of his favorites is a bench he made in middle school. He makes plans on spending money, and he doesn't like to waste it. It is how the Chens are.

Just like his parents, Qiming will become a man who focuses on his career instead of his personal life. I believe that his happiness in the future comes with a woman who loves him and can carry the responsibilities of the family. Though he is difficult to get close to, he is easily concurred by passionate emotions.

Qiming had a rough childhood, which gave him the motivation to work towards a better future. He desires success, maybe to fill some needs or the loneliness deep inside his heart. His logic and organizing skills can lead him to social or political work.

In 2013, the entire family cried at the funeral of the gramps. Qiming put a Chinese flag in front of the tombstone after he returned from the US. A flock of pigeons flew by. Qiming raised his head and looked at them sadly, starting singing St. Matthew Passion by Johann Bach:

> We sit down in tears,
> And call to thee in the tomb:
> Rest softly, softly rest!
> Rest, ye exhausted limbs!

*Your grave and tombstone*
*Shall for the unquiet conscience,*
*Be a comfortable pillow,*
*And the soul's resting place.*
*In utmost bliss, the eyes slumber there.*

## The inheriting crisis of the family

Above is the story of me and the family from Beijing. I'd like to talk about the crisis of families in the market economy. Qiming's parents are excellent. They are dedicated to their careers, and they have great achievements in their respective fields. They are the most important parts of the market economy. The market economy also made them lose themselves. They forgot what was the most important to them and they had to pay a price. The market economy made them who they were in exchange for their futures. As the ancient saying goes, "the key to one's success is also one's undoing."

As a biological being on this lonely planet, we spend our entire lives preparing for our death, and there is only one goal behind all the hard work. That is to keep the family legacy. The family legacy is how to determine whether we are successful or not. Do you have a strong family? How to determine the strength of your family? Below is The Strength of Clan Scale:

1. Same values between the father and the son.

2. There is inherent sense of duty on the family legacy.

3. Inherently understanding the importance of the next generation and is willing to procreate.

4. The family has a core belief.

5. The family has a story to explain their core belief.

6. The young generation fully understand the story and recognize the spirit that it represents as well as the sacrifices that the older generation have made.

7. Having a dedicated location and ceremony for honoring the ancestors.

8. Holding family activities regularly that involve all the members.

9. Having literature that explains the family spirit.

10. Having relics that motive.

11. Having a family tree.

12. The family leader is on good terms with the wives of the sons.

13. Not having any cases of death due to genetic disease within three generations.

14. Having fixed assets that generate stable cash flow.

There are 14 questions in total and 1 point per question. If the score is lower than 10, that means you need to work harder.

The basis of the national culture is family. The success of an individual is the success of the family. The moral system throughout thousands of years was prolonged by the power of bloodlines and families.

We all have the dream to continue the bloodline, and we hope to hold on to what we have forever. However, the dreams of families are being forgotten in the ever-growing population, the process of urbanization and the arrival of the digital age. At the same time, the strength of the families is fading away.

Family is the obstacle that hinders the growth of the market economy. The presence of the families handicaps the free flow of products, services, and labor.

No matter what era we are in, someone has to pay the price of the changing societies. I think the highest price would be the fading away of the family, having all the hard work of the ancestors jeopardized at once and having the Y chromosome defeated by the concept of society.

If you were trapped and could only take one out of the 12 family members with you to escape, who would you take? This was the problem my great-grandfather had to face back in 1948. He chose his oldest son.

The most important trait for a leader is vision. For family leaders, it is shown in the preparations for the legacy inheritance. Passing down the family spirit is the premise of passing down the family business, and it is only done when the inheritor understands the family history and recognizes the family culture.

Former Prime Minister of Singapore Lee Kwan Yew once said, "It is only when you know your roots and understand what your ancestors had gone through can you find basis and know when to advance or retreat." The reason why children stray to the wrong paths is that the culture of the cliques is stronger than their family culture. Of all the families that I've encountered, none had a core belief or intriguing family culture before they met me, let alone having the knowledge on passing down the family spirit.

A well-known entrepreneur once told me, "It doesn't even matter if the son is a disappointment. I'd just pass down the company to the board and take interests from my share."

Is it really that simple? From my understanding, the wise families all have one thing in common. That is, they always keep the power of decision to themselves.

Elizabeth Arden, Helena Rubinstein, Estée Lauder and Charles Revson, who were the founders of Revlon, created the cosmetics industry. They each dedicated their lives to their own companies. However, only the ones with vision were granted a decent ending. After Rubinstein passed away, her company was taken over by L'Oreal. After Arden passed away, her company was taken over by Unilever. And Charles Revson lost his company, which he had spent his lifetime building, to someone else for not giving his children the controlling interest. So, who was the real winner here? Salome wrote in The Three Queens of the Beauty Empire: Esther Lauder:

In 2003, not long before Estée Lauder left the world, she was very satisfied to see that the family workshop style small company of simple face cream and lipstick developed by her and her uncle Shauzi 60 years ago had become one of the largest cosmetics companies in the world: all brands under the company, except the original Estee Lauder, Clinique, Alamis, prescription, etc. Through product research and acquisition, a large number of new brands have been added, such as the natural and environmentally friendly Origins and Aveda skincare brands, independent makeup artist brands M.A.C and Bobbi Brown Essentials, etc., controlling nearly half of the high-end beauty product market in the United States. The company employs over 210000 employees worldwide, and its products are sold to 130 countries and regions including the UK, Australia, Switzerland, South Africa, Belgium, Canada, Spain, Venezuela, etc. The company's annual profit reached 4.744 billion US dollars, making it a truly powerful beauty empire that none of Estée Lauder's competitors could dream of and surpass before her death.

Only Esther Lauder lived to witness the deaths of all her opponents, and more importantly, the Estée Lauder Company remains the "Lauder family" of Estée Lauder. The Lauder family not only has absolute control, but also the third generation of the Lauder family—the children of Leonardo and Ronald, William, Gary, Erin, and Jane—have all joined the Estée Lauder company and taken over the family business.

Many would consider it a miracle that the wealth of the Rothschild family was not impacted by the subprime mortgage crisis. Let's take a look at what the Rothschild left for us:

So long as you are united, you are invincible. The day you break apart will be the beginning of losing prosperity.

Let's take a look at the slogan of the Toyoda family:

With hundreds of patience and thousands of efforts, everything will come true. Father pass down to son. Son passes down to grandson. From generation to generation, it continues endlessly.

The social competition is not only the competition between one another. We should see both the huge wave and the stream. The social competition is between DNAs, personalities, and families. Generations of visionary leaders and excellent teachers are needed to pass down the family spirit and to keep the business flourish.

A client of mine hired me to mentor his son to have a child, but unfortunately his only son decided not to do that until his 40s.

The families without strong cultures will be destroyed at a certain unfortunate moment. The legacy in the dust that they left behind would be used as lessons by others. And once they are gone, their story will only be something people talk about between meals.

This painting is called "Ivan the Terrible and His Son". The Russian artist Ilya Repin depicted the grief-stricken Russian tsar Ivan the terrible cradling his dying son shortly after the elder Ivan had dealt a fatal blow to his son's head in a fit of anger.

To successfully raise an heir requires a competent team and parents who can work with the team well. Families with visions understand the meaning of life. They work with professionals to keep the family alive. No matter in the East or the West, family leaders with visions always leave splendid culture behind for the children. The family genes are encoded in the stories, relics, and rituals. They become the protagonist in the spiritual world of the children, calling them to pass down their spirit.

# Chapter 6

# How to Educate Children from Underprivileged Families

## A desperate mother cannot be refused

A desperate mother came to me in 2013. She brought me a difficult problem alongside a reason for me not to turn her down.

Three years before, the mother took her only son from her hometown to a high school in the city center to study in. They rented a 15 square meter apartment near the school, without a separate bathroom, and with a shared kitchen for three households. That was their home in the city. The mother didn't go to work, and spent three years full-time accompanying her son, taking care of his daily life. She hoped that her son would become successful soon and take over the responsibilities of a man.

Her son's name is Xiaowu. Xiaowu's family represents the survival status of the vast majority of families, with four siblings in his father's family. Only Xiaowu's father is an oilfield worker while the rest are farmers. There are seven siblings in his mother's family, and except for Xiaowu's mother who was married to an oilfield worker, all the other siblings are also farmers. The whole family's life is solely borne by his father. To support his son in high school and university, the father rarely visits them.

The son would spend 16 hours of review and exams every day, and his mother cooked different dishes for him. In order to save a bit, she would go to the wholesale market that was far away to buy fresh vegetables and meat for her son. She wouldn't spend any money on herself to ensure her son's food and clothing. Seeing her son devoted all his energy to studying every day, the mother felt that no matter how hard or tired she was, it was worth it.

Nine months before the college entrance examination, Xiaowu suddenly went home and told his mother that he decided to drop out of school. His mother thought it was temporary, but Xiaowu stayed at home for six months playing computer games day and night and even contradicted his mother.

Xiaowu's mother cried and said to me, "For him, I may be a good mother, but for the whole family, I have put in too little effort. I am not a good daughter, for I didn't even visit his grandmother when she was seriously ill. I'm not a good wife neither for not taking care of my husband. And I even failed the only task of taking care of my son. I'm such a failure for not fulfilling any obligation, and I often feel like there's no hope in life. I can't sleep every day.

Only three months was left before the exam, and it seemed that we needed a miracle.

What's the point of blaming the parent? What's the point of figuring out which parent to blame? Was there enough time left to pray to the gods? What gods would show their power in such short period of time? What should we do then?

To put elephants in the refrigerator, there are three steps in total: firstly, to obtain revolutionary leadership. Secondly, identify the main contradiction through investigation. Thirdly, resolve major conflicts and establish life goals in social activities.

Firstly, to obtain "the revolutionary leadership".

One night, Xiaowu and I chatted for ten minutes in my castle. Before parting, he expressed his longing for my life and the curiosity about me, and also showed fondness of my keyboard and mouse. When I invited him to go to Beijing with me, Xiaowu agreed right away.

There are two types of teachers, one being the teacher for subjects and the other the spiritual leader. Teachers might have authority. It is only the spiritual leaders who can inspire the children. We follow the ones with dream, not because we have to, but because we want to. We follow the spiritual leaders, not for them, but for ourselves. Only the ones who aim to change the world can inspire the ones around them.

Second, identify the main contradiction through investigation.

Why did Xiaowu leave school? His mother couldn't explain, but Xiaowu did have a hobby of writing novels. She suggested that I read Xiaowu's 200-thousand-word novel from the beginning to the end, looking for clues from it. Xiaowu's father said he is addicted to the Internet and tired of learning. Xiaowu's teacher said he failed his early love and was rejected by the girl. Xiaowu's classmate said he injured someone in a fight and fled in fear of guilt. Could Uncle Ye of Xiaowu, I thought, know him better than himself? I asked him directly, why did he drop out of school?

Xiaowu replied, "I couldn't see any possible reward for the constant hard work."

"I have a question for you."

"Sure."

"What do you want the most?"

"Money and social statues."

"What if you could only pick one?"

"Money."

"How do you want to make money?"

"I don't know."

"Do you know what's the best way for a man to make money?"

"What?"

"To make money with his hobby."

"That sounds nice."

"What's your hobby?"

"Biology, chemistry and playing computer games."

"Can computer games make money?"

"Yeah, but they can only make small money."

"Can't it make big money?"

"The chances are slim."

"Well, let's go to Beijing, to see if we can make big money by mastering biology or chemistry."

"Great!"

Third, solve the conflict and find a life purpose through social activities.

Before we left for Beijing, we needed to investigate who would be the best to answer the question of whether biology or chemistry can make big money.

This question was the most convincing for Xiaowu. This person must be someone with some kind of connection and persuasive. Xiaowu's parents shook their heads and there was no suitable candidate. I picked up the phone. My team immediately started searching, and shortly after, one person showed up in my sight. After investigation, it was found that the female top scorer in the 2000 college entrance examination at Xiaowu's high school was admitted to the biopharmaceutical major of China Pharmaceutical University with a score of 600. She was in Tianjin at that moment. Xiaowu said he had heard of such a major a long time ago and was very eager for it, but he didn't know the actual situation. Let's go as soon as we say!

The female top scorer hosted us at her home in Tianjin. She said that there were two ways to make money through biology and chemistry: One is to become a pharmaceutical sales representative, even without having to graduate from university. As long as you are good at communication and can be a good person, it doesn't matter whether you have a degree or not. The second is being the head of the new drug R&D (research and development) team in a large pharmaceutical factory.

Great! He was excited, "Let's do the representative, and we can even skip the studying part."

"Uncle Ye, I want to do R&D. I really like biology and chemistry. I have even won the first prize in the Liaoning Province Biology Competition and the second prize in the National High School Chemistry Competition. Also, I'm an introvert, and I'm not good at interacting with people. Sales is not suitable for me."

"Alright." I pretend to feel sorry.

"Sister, what are the requirements for me to become the head of the new drug development team in a large pharmaceutical factory?"

"You need to go to university first. You may have two choices: Southern Med (China Pharmaceutical University) and Northern Med (Shenyang Pharmaceutical University). Southern Med needs a higher score of around 600 points, while Northern Med needs around 560 points."

"And then what?"

"Then I'm not sure. I joined the civil servants after I graduated from the biopharmaceutical department. It's been so many years, and you can ask someone else for that."

"Thank you, sister."

I asked Xiaowu a question on our way back to the hotel.

"Which country do you like the most, Xiaowu?"

"Germany."

"Which pharmaceutical factory in Germany have you heard of?"

"Bayer."

I picked up the phone. My team started searching immediately, contacting Bayer Pharmaceuticals' international research and development center, meeting with the R&D team leader and the financial personnel at Bayer. Soon, Dr. Xu met us in his office. Dr. Xu was a Ph.D in biology from MIT in the United States, and the team leader of Bayer Pharmaceuticals. Xiaowu was extremely excited, and his eyes fixed on Dr. Xu, heading straight to the topic.

"Uncle, my name is Xiaowu, and I'd like to know how to become a team leader at Bayer Pharmaceuticals like you do?"

"To have learning experience abroad, and to be good at foreign languages because we need to read a lot of English materials. We are usually Ph.Ds. In addition, being proficient in professional business alone is not enough. I am also the team leader and need to manage the team well."

"Dang, his English is not good, and he does not really enjoy communicating with people." I stepped in.

"Well, it was because I didn't know what learning English was for. And now I do, and the same goes for communication skills. Just watch me."

Afterwards, Dr. Xu answered Xiaowu's questions one by one. Time passed by quickly, Dr. Xu escorted us to the elevator before he doved into his work. He said something to Xiaowu that I'd never forget: "Xiaowu, I sense your passion towards biomedical science, but please remember that whether science is beautiful depends on who handles it. To love biological science, you must first love life, love humanity, love our family and friends, and love every grass and tree around you. I wish you success!"

Excellent! Xiaowu was shocked and remained silent. We came to the finance department of Bayer Pharmaceuticals, and I came straight to the point:

"May I ask what the annual salary for Dr. Xu's position is?" The accountant in finance department wrote two sets of numbers on paper, stating that it fluctuated within this range. Xiaowu leaned his face closer, with an incredulous expression on his flushed face.

"That's too little. It's not even worth the efforts." I said to him.

"Uncle Ye, it's quite a lot. My dad won't even earn that much in his lifetime." Xiaowu said seriously.

"Is this amount worth striving for?"

"Yes!"

What is something we cherish called "effort"? Striving for the sake of effort is something we must strive to avoid throughout our lives. Leaving the goal to be achieved, effort is just a series of brief moments of tension.

Dewey believed, "Although the theory of hard work always shows us a strong and vibrant character as a result of its educational methods, in fact, we have not obtained such a character. What we obtain is either a stubborn, irresponsible, narrow-minded person who appears to be stubborn, irresponsible, narrow-minded except for things related to his own expected goals and beliefs. Otherwise, it is a dull, mechanical, and clumsy character."

When the result is uncertain, hard work only inspires us to constantly stop and consider: is the goal worth the time? Is it worth continuing to work hard? Is there any other better way?

A person's life is a life of resource capitalization. Before putting in effort, a man's mind is quite serious, just like a housewife filling her shopping basket step by step. The most effective weapon that influences human judgment is the benefits outweigh the drawbacks. But what caused the vastly different lives of childhood partners in orphanages? Vision. Arthur Schopenhauer said, "Everyone takes the limits of their own vision for the limits of the world." Only through imagination and action can they cross the barriers of reality.

CHAPTER 6

On the fourth and fifth days, I took Xiaowu to communicate with out-standing people from all walks of life in Beijing: professors from the Central Party School, hosts from CCTV, presidents of chambers of commerce, Olympic ambassadors and well-known collectors, which broadened Xiaowu's horizons and made him filled with emotions.

At night, exhausted as we drove back to the hotel, the flickering lights and blooming flowers on Tiananmen Square complemented each other.

"What's your next move?" I asked Xiaowu.

"Go back and study hard, pass the exam with a score of 560, and go to Shenyang Pharmaceutical University!"

"Who said Shenyang Pharmaceutical University needs a score of 560?"

"The senior sister said. Didn't you also be present, Uncle Ye?"

"Have you learned about the enrollment changes this year? Did the di-rector of the admissions office personally tell you about the 560 points?"

"Oh, I understand."

"What do you think we should do, Xiaowu?"

"Go to Shenyang Pharmaceutical University to ask for more informa-tion!"

"Can't we just call them?"

"No, Uncle Ye. I think seeing is believing."

Some people say that schools should cultivate three things for students: knowledge, skills, and character. I focus on cultivating three things for students: reading, online searching, and identifying authenticity.

On the sixth day, we drove to Shenyang Pharmaceutical University, and the teacher from the admissions office said that we were the first students and parents to come for consultation this year. The school predicted a 550-score requirement.

"Dang, Uncle Ye, I don't even need as much as I thought." Xiaowu grabbed my hand excitedly.

"Xiaowu, how many points can you get right now?" I asked Xiaowu in the back seat of the car.

"About 520."

"There's less than three months left. Is it enough?"

"I can do it." Xiaowu tightened his lips.

Suddenly, he noticed an allergic reaction in the arm of my assistant while driving. Xiaowu leaned over to take a closer look and said, "Allergy is an allergic reaction in the body, and the oxidative damage of large amounts of free radicals to mast cells and eosinophils is the internal cause of allergic reactions. This is the first time I have seen such a spectacular allergic phenomenon, and I suggest taking loratadine as soon as possible." It was truly shocking! Looking at the excited expression on his face, I thought to myself, a person's success depends on love and research like Xiaowu. Finally, when we returned to our hometown, Xiaowu's parents hosted a feast to welcome us. Xiaowu's mother asked him about the experience those days, but Xiaowu felt a bit embarrassed.

"Tell us what you think."

"Alright, Uncle Ye. After returning home, I will study hard and aim for Shenyang Pharmaceutical University. I'm going to score at least 560, an extra 10 points just in case. Then after I get in, I'm going to keep working hard while learning English and working on my own skills, and hopefully to get in the Students' Union so that I can practice my leadership and managing skills. I'm going to save money because I'd like to study abroad one day for a doctor's degree, which might cost a lot of money, but I'll take part-time jobs. After returning from my studies, my goal is to become the head of the pharmaceutical team at Bayer, striving to develop new drugs to benefit the society." After hearing him, his mother was in shock, and his father couldn't stop nodding.

It was time to have the last glass of wine when Xiaowu suddenly stood up and offered me a toast with tears in his eyes. "Uncle Ye, I will never forget you in my life. Wait for my good news!" Then he emptied the glass at once.

## The present

This is the story that happened in the spring of 2013. I gave the plan of mentoring Xiaowu as a birthday present to my wife, Mrs. Hao. Her sympathy for Xiaowu's mother was the reason that I could not refuse her.

Afterwards, I have never seen Xiaowu again. I heard that Xiaowu had gone back to school, and his Internet addiction had suddenly disappeared. Later I heard that Xiaowu's mother had a new problem: urging Xiaowu to sleep. A parent asked me after seeing a sample of this book, why all the children I educated have had Internet addiction at some point? Why is it so addictive? I was shocked to hear this question, and to my surprise, I had never thought about it! After thinking for a moment, I realized that there was only one answer: It is fun. The online world is not a flood of beasts, but a sanctuary full of fun where people soothe each other. Do you want the Internet addicts to turn their focus from the screen to the reality? Tell them that the reality is more interesting and valuable, and make sure to prove it.

Oh, by the way, let's get down to business: Later on, Xiaowu fulfilled his wish.

# Chapter 7
# How to Convince a Child to Go to Yale University

I don't like educational cases full of preaching. I resent boring stuff. Ladies and Gentlemen, please allow me to use Northeastern dialect to talk about another classic case of "From Success to Excellence—Challenging the Limits of Education with Pragmatic Philosophy": A wealthy child's journey to Yale University.

The child came from a wealthy and versatile family. He had excellent grades, and being admitted to a top-tier domestic university was not a problem. He was adept at learning but had never given it his best for a simple reason that he was satisfied with what he had. His parents thought, though, that he was able to go to Yale University if he tried hard enough, but he didn't think so. He thought that his parents didn't understand the essence of life—To feel comfortable, the first thing to do is to preserve his strength!

I took action immediately!

I tried to make friend with the child and make him like me. It was the most difficult part, so I had to plan it out carefully. The place of meeting was important, and I had to make him feel out of place.

Then I walked towards him from a distance, which was also part of the plan. I had to have a refined appearance, and my outfit had to be tasteful yet young enough. It was no wonder that nobody likes to have a heart-to-heart talk with a middle-aged man.

I needed to act similarly to him to fit it. Speaking was also crucial. I needed to find his basic language, which was the vocabulary that he liked, but the way I explained things had to be completely different. Speak in a way that surprised him, make him interested in you, and attract his full attention.

The conversation needed to be on point as well. I needed to be knowledgeable, witty and humorous, but only a little bit more than what he was. It was best to casually point out a tiny flaw from what he said within ten minutes of the conversation, and things could be done!

I did just that and became his idol within 30 minutes. He definitely would text his "best friends" about our meeting on WeChat before going to bed: "Dude, I met this friend of my dad's tonight, and he's pretty fun and really dope!"

The prisoners were silent, but you have to see what kind of prisoners they were. The wealthy kids would talk endlessly and spend a lot of money after you earned his respect. He would talk endlessly about his past while desperately ordering you drinks. And all you had to do was to have a smile on your face, keep nodding and drinking!

As you listen, I suddenly exclaimed, "Dude, you are a genius! I wish we could've met earlier! We had a deep bond. How did we meet in this life? Uh… may I ask what university you can get into now?" Don't be afraid of messing up, and don't be afraid of sharp questions. If he doesn't like you, whatever you do is a mess-up, but you can kick him to the floor if he likes you. He'd act like it's no big deal after hearing you and tell you with a big smile, "Top-tiers for sure." "That's it? What a waste of talent, man!"

Upon hearing this, his pupils would contract, and his legs would tighten, and a few top-notch ones would even cross their legs and their feet would shake violently. After a while, three words would be squeezed out of his mouth: "Whatever, I guess?" It would be an easy case if he showed uncertainty.

That's when you wink at the door, and a tall man in suits would show up. "May I help you, sir?" He'd have an authentic London accent that exudes a sense of prestige. You would ask him to help you carry your laptop, and don't mess with the HP, Lenovo IMB or Apple. These are reserved for school kids. We needed the Alien 18 series. Tell the man in suits to carry the laptop out of the trunk for you, before you put the key to the Bentley on the table.

Take out the laptop from the backpack, without a single word. You just earned even more respect when the logo "human skeleton" lighted up. Then you ask him to open his eyes to see how pathetic he really is.

What's the laptop for? It's for the Directory of Alumni! Let him see the alumni list of Yale and the university he wanted to attend in the year he was born. Why? Do you know Nv'er Hong (the wine for daughter's wedding)? Because people only care about the years that are relevant to themselves.

The alumni record includes a lot of group photos of people when they were in college, or when they started working, photos of getting married, photos of their children, and photos of going abroad, all of which are various highlight moments of life's appearance. The living conditions of graduates from the same major in these two institutions are absolutely different. Where the difference lies, you need to ask the child to point them out! It's simply clear at a glance! And The differences are easily located from the visual cues.

However, just looking at it for a moment wouldn't make the child change his mind. The effect is equivalent to putting a single sand into his shoes. It was not a big deal, but that discomfort would continue bothering him all day and night.

But please note that the difference you have shown him must be real, and the path you have pointed out to him must be smooth! Practice is the only criterion for testing truth, and truth will always appear. It's only a matter of time!

In the market economy and business society, everyone has several names of big companies in their minds. Ask him which company he think is the best and arrange a meeting with the HR director of this company. Once they meet, he will understand the difference between Yale and his university in the eyes of these directors. This ironclad fact will deeply hurt his self-esteem and inspire his ambition to attend Yale University.

What if he never had that kind of self-esteem in the first place? Rest easy, for the wealthy kids wouldn't waste anytime walking the right path if he didn't have self-esteem, because there is so much hardship there. Once self-esteem is hurting, and the trauma has arisen, you must start calculating right away, including mental, written, and mixed calculations. Protein lives by reaping more than giving! Wealthy kid belongs to high-quality protein and definitely does not engage in loss making transactions. His genes determine everything.

The key to this step is to let him understand, through calculating, that it is not only possible for him to getting admitted to Yale University, but also it would be so easy for him.

Through calculating, he'll need to understand that as long as he puts in a little extra effort, there would be a huge return. This reward is not about how much more money you will earn in the future. Remember, never mention money. It's never been a problem for them. This group of people wants to be better than others! What they want is a sense of superiority! What they want is the envy, jealousy, and hatred of others!

You have to paint the picture of how surprised their friends will be when they hear he gets into Yale University. Describe the jealousy and hatred. It's best to describe the scenario that someone asks where he went and he said with a helpless expression, "Oh, Yale University was the only option. I had no other choices, for my father doesn't recognize Harvard University." Haha, it's too Versailles.

If he already has a girlfriend when you meet, then it's even more fool-proof. Describe how much his girlfriend would admire him if he got into Yale University. Remember that men change the world and women change men's worldviews.

Some might ask, is this even education? You should guide him in a positive way. The purpose of attending Yale University is to seek knowledge and research! Well, children engaged in scientific research don't need guidance. Besides, education? Parents didn't even give you the chance to choose education. Parents only provide the kind of education they know.

Speaking of this, after experiencing these things, he'd feel ashamed of being late to enlightenment. You'll have to prove it to him that going to Yale University is his own idea. By swearing, making a vow, and adjusting surveillance, whatever it takes! Why? So that he doesn't hate you later. People like him wouldn't tolerate having taken help from others on something so important. The moment he shows gratitude is the moment he's ready to ditch you.

Once these are done, it is time for the parents, and you'll see the most touching scene in the world: everyone will have a huge smile on his face, the father is like a father, the son is like a son, and the family is happy and harmonious. Contradiction? It disappeared long ago, as if it had never appeared before. What's going on here? Mr. Lu Xun provided a good explanation: "The lack of unity in the front line is due to inconsistent goals." Once the goals are aligned, there is no revenge.

Hard work? That's a guarantee now! Staying focused is a kind of piety that people show when facing profits!

Watching over him? Stop kidding. It is not necessary at all! Just wait quietly for him to get admitted. His intelligence is so much higher than the average Joe.

By the way, don't forget to call him before the exam. Not to wish him luck but to let him know that you'll be gone for a while after the exam, not dead, but going on a trip to Antarctica, which will take six months or a year, so that he doesn't bother you afterwards.

Orson Wells said: A perfect ending depends on where the story ends.

# Chapter 8
## How to Educate Children with Autism

Children in adolescence love one thing the most: exploring the edge of the world. They always want to figure out how deep the river is, or will one definitely catch a cold for not wearing many clothes in winter, or will my parents get crazy at me?

Samuel Ullman said that "Youth is not a time of life, but a state of mind." I once asked myself, "Where is the boundary of education? Is there a limit to education? Is education effective for mental illnesses? The arrival of Wenxi gave me the answer.

"Mr. Ye knows what to do!"

"Could you please think of a way for our child?"

Too many parents came to me because of my reputation, and they all wanted me to solve their issues in one move.

Good education is about saying something refreshing and doing something unforgettable at the right moment, in the most perfect place. However, parents cannot imagine how much waiting and observation are behind the subtleties of that moment, place, sentence, and event.

Wenxi, the child with autism, used his 180 diaries to document the ordinary years behind the educational miracle.

My name is Wenxi, and I'm from Shanghai. My parents have been very successful in their careers, and I have always been proud of them. My academic performance is not good, and my behavior is strange. Unfortunately, my classmates are not friendly to me. They often laugh at me and call me "stupid X".

When I was a child, I was diagnosed with autism by the Sixth Hospital of Beijing Medical University. I couldn't remember from back in the days anymore. My mother said that I ignored people all day, and when others talked to me, I hardly cared. At that time, I always stared at the ceiling, and when I wanted something, I'd just grab it.

From childhood to adulthood, my parents have shed tears due to school matters. My father told me that the kindergarten was closed three times due to my own reasons. The parents of other kids united to boycott me, saying that as long as there was me in the kindergarten, their children wouldn't come.

My parents have led me constantly to try various methods to cure me, though the effect was limited, and I'm very grateful to my parents for not giving up on me now. I couldn't remember much about myself, but I remembered the classmates that I had. Whenever I was with someone, I felt pain from time to time, and sometimes it was too much so that I had to scream in pain, so I was very scared at school every day. Those days went on day after day, year after year, until I heard that voice.

"Wenxi, Wenxi…" The voice was soft and warm. It sounded like it was calling me, or maybe not. It's close at hand and as if far away in the sky. For several days, this voice had been calling me, and every time I heard it, I felt warm. Gradually I was addicted to it.

My body was shaking, and I was being hugged by someone, and it was so warm. Was it Mom? It was Mom. It felt like Mom. It was so warm! Then the voice started calling me, "Wenxi, Wenxi…" I was curious in

my heart. I wanted to see who was talking, and who was hugging me...
it felt like Mom. It must be Mom! No, it was warmer than Mom. Let me
just take a look and take a quick peek. Oh, it's not Mom. Isn't it really
Mom? Let me take another peek. I saw her eyes... She is not really Mom,
but I wish she were.

"Mom" kept hugging me, calling out to me, and asking me to look into
her eyes. I was willing to speak in her eyes, just looking at her.

Later father told me that my teacher Miss Jiang hugged me and called out
to me for several days. Gradually I woke up from my autism and began
occasionally making eye contact with them. I also started pestering Miss
Jiang and calling her "mom".

Dad also said that during the days when I was at Teacher Jiang's house,
she was exhausted by me every day, but my situation was getting better
and better.

Finally, Miss Jiang suggested that my father send me to stay with someone in Panjin, Liaoning Province, for the first half of the year. My father
said this person once helped a young Internet addict who hadn't studied
since he was in the third grade of elementary school get into a top-tier
high school and even made the leader of a youth gang turn around and
reform. What's surprising is that he helped a primary school student with
an IQ of only 63 pass the Beijing Middle School Entrance Examination!

On January 24th, 2010, my father and I arrived in a small town in Northeast China called Panjin. We got off the high-speed train and took a bus
for the city. It was windy outside the window, and there were few people
on the street. It was rare to see a few tall buildings, and everything looked
gloomy. I regretted coming here, doubting what I could learn in such
a place! Can I return to Shanghai earlier? At that moment, I felt I had
been struck by lightning when I saw a person with black gloves standing
opposite me. He gestured for me to go over and said to me, "Call me

Uncle Ye."

I started my 180-day life in Panjin, in the words of Uncle Ye. It was the transition from an ape to a modern man. Before my father left, he asked me to write a diary every day to record my life with Uncle Ye.

The full text of Wenxi's diary.

07 / 30 / 2011

I am about to leave. This diary records the details of my life at Uncle Ye's house in Panjin for six months. I'd like to dedicate this diary to Uncle Ye for his education career, hoping it brings hope and confidence to whoever reads it.

**Comment**: *Thank you Wenxi. If you have read this book, Uncle Ye wants to tell you that I have learned a lot from you as well. If, as Haonan's father said, time can be turned back, and we can all go back to the past, Uncle Ye could even do better.*

01 / 28

I've made the following achievements:
1. I only picked up the food from my side of the dish.
2. I kept quiet when chewing.
3. I regulated my eating habits.

**Comment**: *From this day on, Wenxi made his transition from a planta-tion to a primitive life form, as well as from a purely physiological stage to a self-awareness stage. Character is the attitude and behavior that the society needs. The daily norms of adolescent behavior are of great signif-icance for the cultivation of character.*

01 / 29

1. Uncle Ye taught me to study for 40 minutes and review for 10 minutes during the 50-minute class.

2. Xiaojian (another student of Uncle Ye) gave me a hamburger, which was very delicious.

3. Uncle Ye asked me to face everyone with a smile.

01 / 30

1. Everyone helped me get rid of the bad habit of farting and burping casually.

2. Aunty Liu made delicious dishes, and she helped me with taking the food!

01 / 31

1. Aunty Hao (Uncle Ye's wife) taught me the principles of being a good person, telling me to remember the good of others more, face everyone with sincerity, and always have a grateful heart.

2. Grandma (Uncle Ye's mother) cooks a lot of delicious dishes for me every morning. Grandma always makes me eat more.

Comment: *At this stage, Wenxi, from January 28 to March 14, the first day in Panjin, mostly focused on eating, drinking, and going to the bathroom. This is the starting point of his education. A good education is to sit together and eat a lot of meals.*

02 / 01

1. Uncle Ye took us out to dinner. At the dining table, I saw a dish that I had never eaten before. What was it? It is Double Cooked Pork!

2. I have a lot of bad habits in the daily life. Uncle Ye reminded me at noon that I should keep my mouth closed when walking, for it is how we differ from the apes. I also think this is more appropriate.

3. Uncle Ye taught me to make my bed.

4. I am becoming more and more honest when speaking.

02 / 02

1. In the reading class, everyone praised the article that I read was deep, had connotations and was philosophical.

2. Xiaoyu (another student of Uncle Ye) took me for a run every day, running a total of 4.4 kilometers. He was really diligent and responsible. During this stage of running, my physical coordination and stamina had improved dramatically.

02 / 03 – 02 / 08

1. Uncle Ye helped me develop a good habit of reviewing in the first class every morning.

2. Aunty Hao saw that I hadn't had a bowel movement for a long time, so she gave me honey water every morning, and Uncle Ye urged me to drink more Runchang Tea, and finally I pooped.

3. Xiaoyu taught me how to mop the floor, and my grandmother taught me how to wash my clothes.

4. Lele (Uncle Ye's daughter) and Aunty Liu taught me how to wash dishes.

5. Everyone praised me for mastering many idioms.

6. I received a 12 Yuan scholarship for helping others in my study and daily life.

7. I helped colleague at Aunty Hao's school move oil, flour, and seasoning.

8. Uncle Ye and Aunty Hao made me eat spring cakes during the Minor Lunar New Year. The taste was excellent, and it was very warm to be with everyone.

9. Today, I went to the Minor Spring Festival Gala with Lele, Xiaobo (another student of Uncle Ye) at Xiaobo's house. Uncle Ye taught me that I should have a shallow taste of food and treat people and things according to the host's preferences. After learning these two points, I wouldn't embarrass myself when I visit someone in the future.

10. Xiaojian gave me an egg tart, but my reaction made him sad. Uncle Ye taught me how to receive gifts from others, so I did what he said, and Xiaojian was happy.

11. After tonight's reading class, everyone identified my strengths. I was very happy and determined to do better.

**Comment**: *In a big family, there are multiple perspectives of care, and the children's emotions improve dramatically in the frequent giving and taking.*

02 / 09

1. Brother Min bought Aunty Hao an egg tart, and Aunty Hao shared half of it with me. I forgot to say thank you, and Aunty Hao taught me to say "thank you".

2. In the evening, Aunty Liu made delicious rice noodles, and I was responsible for bringing the rice noodles to the table. I set the first bowl at Aunty Hao's position unconsciously. Uncle Ye saw it and hugged me. He said that it was the first time that I thought about others before myself, and that I really meant it. It was remarkable, so Uncle Ye gave me a fried dough as an award.

**Comment**: *This was the first time that Wenxi prioritized others before himself and cared for others willingly. An open-minded family has a clear attitude towards the vast majority of behaviors, encouraging and negating everything for children. In terms of behavioral norms, the children do not need to guess what they should do, and any acts of kindness are immediately rewarded.*

3. I was very happy to receive a reward of 12 Yuan from Uncle Ye and Aunty Hao for helping my friend, which made me think that a drop of water should be repaid by a gushing spring.

**Comment**: *Reward immediately after praise. You can refer to Ivan Pavlov's conditioned reflex experiment.*

02 / 10

1. Xiaoyu and I helped Aunty Hao move things together, feeling so happy in our hearts.

2. Today, Xiaojian brought a mangosteen to Uncle Ye, I wanted to eat it, but Uncle Ye refused. At noon, Aunty Hao bought a bottle of canned

yellow peaches. After eating my own portion, I also wanted to eat the one left for Xiaobo. Aunty Hao taught me, "You can't have other people's share, for it is not yours."

**Comment:** *Parents in the family should have consistent requirements for their children, ensuring that there is no leakage. Only in this way can rules be established.*

3. From childhood to adulthood, I have been bullied and did not dare to resist. Today, Xiaoyu bullied me. I endured it, too, and didn't dare to fight back. Uncle Ye asked me if Xiaoyu had bullied me and I kept lying and said no. Uncle Ye encouraged me to counterattack, so I bravely began to counterattack. Xiaoyu was surprised and couldn't believe I dared to fight back. In the end, Xiaoyu was beaten to tears by me. Afterwards, Xiaoyu apologized to me, and said that we would become a family from now on, and he even cleaned my shoes to make up for me.

From this incident, I have summarized the following two points:

1. Dad hitting me and Xiaoyu hitting me are not of the same nature. Dad hit me to educate me when I was naughty, but Xiaoyu hit me to vent on me.

2. When encountering bad people, patience alone cannot solve the problem. Uncle Ye said, "Sometimes when dealing with unreasonable people, we need to fight back hard because fighting back can defend dignity. It is only when the bad people are overthrown that can they possibly respect us."

**Comment:** *It is powerful to educate children through real-life events, and the best education is lively and on-site. Teach them the philosophy of men in a timely manner. What is philosophy? Philosophy is the contemplation of getting rid of difficulties.*

02 / 11

1. I got a hair cut today, and I felt very happy.

2. Today, Uncle Ye invited me to have Korean barbecue, and I thought it the most wonderful meal of my life. During the meal, Uncle Ye and Aunty Hao wished me to make more progress, and I wished Uncle Ye to be more handsome, and Aunty Hao to be more beautiful. I had also learned a lot of social etiquette.

**Comment**: *There are two ways to get closer to children: eat and play. If we can't play together, it doesn't matter. Let's eat!*

3. Uncle Ye told me, "If you fall behind, you'll be beaten." This is a famous quote from Chairman Mao. To change the situation of being behind, one should make progress with determination and make changes actively! I'm going to challenge myself and defeat myself in life.

**Comment**: *On this day, Wenxi realized for the first time in his life that the true enemy was himself. He was determined to challenge himself, make changes actively and defeat himself in life.*

This is the first time Wenxi had a big realization in his life, and also the first time he felt he needed to make a big change. It marks Wenxi's psychological transition from a purely physiological stage to a self-awareness stage, which took him 15 days.

02 / 12 – 02 / 16

Spending the Chinese New Year Holiday in Shanghai.

02 / 17

1. I returned to Panjin. I calculated that I have 70.6 Yuan of allowance.

**Comment**: *Seeing Wenxi's calculation of his allowance, I remembered two relics that were left to me by my great-grandfather: a knife he used to carry with him and a palm-sized abacus he carried with him. To my understanding, they represented bravery and frugality. And in years of educational experience, I have also found that if a young man has economic concepts in his mind and the idea of changing his life through hard work, even if his adolescence is turbulent, he will generally return to a regular life track in the end.*

2. Brother Min gave me an egg tart, and I thanked him.

**Comment**: *From this day on, Wenxi started the transformation from a primitive life form to an ape, from a stage of self-awareness to a stage of passive change. During this period, through letting him watch movies, do household chores, reason, and experience unexpected life events, I was pushing him to think about his life. The existence of Xiaoyu also exposed the weaknesses in Wenxi's personality. Wenxi gained friendship and support from Xiaoyi and Xiaojian by teaching them to do laundry and helping them with their English.*

3. I recalled what happened during the Chinese New Year.

02 / 13

On Chinese New Year's Eve, I paid New Year's greetings to my grandparents, who were happy for my progress in Panjin. My grandparents gave me 300 Yuan for the new year. I thanked them and had a New Year's Eve dinner at home. I watched the Spring Festival Gala at my own home and was very happy.

02 / 14

In the morning, I went to Miss Jiang's house to pay New Year's greetings. Miss Jiang was happy with my progress.

02 / 15

In the afternoon, I went to the Ditan Temple Fair with my whole family, and we had lots of fun!

02 / 16

In the afternoon, I went swimming with my family. I felt great! In the evening, we went to Grandma Bi's house and paid her New Year's greetings.

**Comment**: *Afterwards I only learned that Wenxi's performance during Chinese New Year impressed the entire family with my education. They had never thought that Wenxi could have made such significant changes in half a month. Wenxi's family are all professors from famous universities and rocket satellite experts from the Aerospace Group. Previously they believed that Panjin, Liaoning was only a place where rice was produced. What expert would live on the edge of the reed marshes in the swamp?*

02 / 18 – 02 / 24

During these few days, the following events left a great impression on me:

1. Aunty Liu cooked very well and took great care of me by serving me dishes during meals.

2. Uncle Ye had always been very concerned about my bowel movements, and he reminded me to drink Runchang Tea every day, which made me poop on the second day.

3. Uncle Ye taught me how to respond correctly to others. When someone says something that I've already known, I reply with "Yes". When someone says something that I don't know, I should say "is that right?"

4. Xiaojian bought me a tiny dessert, and I was very grateful to him.

5. We run 4.4 kilometers every day under the guidance of Xiaoyu, so my physical fitness has greatly improved again, and my strength and physical coordination ability have also improved significantly.

6. Uncle Ye taught me how to apologize to others for their forgiveness after I make a mistake.

7. Uncle Ye told me to not soak my rice with soup when eating with others, because that would make everyone think I was very childish.

8. Uncle Ye told me to look into the eyes of others when speaking. This is not only for politeness, but also for the convenience of communication with others, as 80% of the information is reflected in their expressions and actions.

Comment: *I'm really surprised that Wenxi is probably the only one who can remember everything I taught him like a video recorder.*

9. Aunty Hao often talks to me. She told me, "Your progress here is not only to repay your parents, but also to make yourself have a better future."

02 / 25

Today Uncle Ye and Aunty Hao guided Aunty Liu to make fried sweet dumplings. I thought it was delicious!

Comment: *Sister Liu has been the most excellent life assistant who has served Zhigang Education for many years, but my mother is the best one to make fried sweet dumplings.*

This afternoon, we boys were playing basketball, and we passed the ball around. But just as I was grabbing the last ball, I tripped Xiaoyu and he fell into the ice pond, wetting his clothes. At that time, I was immersed in the joy of success... Later Aunty Hao taught me to be empathetic when others are in difficulty.

**Comment**: *From a business and management perspective, I am very reluctant to let my family participate in my career, but their participation is so affective, and they are also well-trained. We work along very well, although what I do is education. I often feel lucky for having a hobby as my job, and my family members and friends as my colleagues, and I work from my own home.*

02 / 26

1. Today, Lele taught me to eat by watching the dishes.

2. Uncle Ye taught me to boil water every morning.

02 / 27 – 02 / 28

1. Yesterday, Uncle Ye told me not to always pout because it's impolite.

2. Today, we were on vacation, and I watched an animated film called Meet the Rob at Uncle Ye's house. From there I understood one thing: be brave and walk forward in times of difficulty.

**Comment**: *I often feel the powerlessness of human language. Educators should make good use of various art forms to help students gain insights.*

3. Grandmother spent a whole day making me a mattress, which was comfortable to lie on.

**Comment**: *Mother doesn't live with us. One day, she came over and* touched Wenxi's mattress with her hand, and she thought it was a bit thin, so she sewed a new one with her hand for Wenxi. Mother's compassion moved us.

4. Today was the Lantern Festival. Aunty Liu made fried sweet dumplings.

03 / 01

1. Today, grandfather, grandmother, and great-grandmother came over to visit Uncle Ye's house, and I poured them tea.

**Comment**: *The great-grandmother that Wenxi mentioned was my grandmother, a daughter of the aristocratic family of the Qing Dynasty. She's proud and ambitious, with a royal aura in her every move. After visiting my home, the elderly person nodded lightly at the door and looked into my eyes, saying, "Not bad. Keep up the good work, my great-grandson."*

2. When studying in the evening, I helped Xiaobo tutor ENGLISH.

**Comment**: *Pay attention to the last word here. Wenxi's tone was slightly naughty.*

03 / 02

1. Today, I helped Uncle Ye and Aunty Hao move the curtain cloth. Although it took a lot of effort, I felt very happy.

2. Today, I helped Xiaojian review Chinese. Xiaojian was very touched, so I felt the joy of helping others.

03 / 03 – 03 / 04

1. These past few days, the Runchang Tea has helped me successfully poop twice.

2. Uncle Ye told me that, sometimes in life, I might not get the thing that I want the most, so I need to have a good mindset.

3. Uncle Ye told me to think it through before doing something.

4. Aunty Liu made mashed potatoes and chicken nuggets, which I found very delicious. However, because I really wanted to eat the last piece, I asked everyone at the table, "Don't you want it, do you?" Aunty Hao didn't give me the last piece. Therefore, I understood that being a person should not be too greedy.

**Comment**: *Wenxi was analyzing his own mental activity.*

5. I was praised for helping my classmate study.

03 / 05

1. Today was Learn from Leifeng Day. I remembered Leifeng's spirit of being helpful. I also wanted to learn from him.

2. I had my first basketball lesson today. Mr. Ren told us to be bold in shooting.

**Comment**: *We should enable students to have more exposure to real society. The basketball classes helped Wenxi interact with more than 20 peers. Compared with being at home, the environment in the basketball court was more realistic and closer to the real society. All the challenges that Wenxi would face from his peers when returning to school in the future would appear here. Mr. Ren's basketball court was a controlla-*

ble environment, and we repeated this practice until Wenxi was able to calmly tackle these challenges.

03 / 06

1. Today, Uncle Ye, Grandpa, and Grandma went to Liaoyang to visit relatives, and I learned some table manners.

2. I started to become interested in basketball today while playing basketball.

03 / 07

Aunty Liu made fried sweet dumplings today, and I was so excited.

03 / 08

1. I made a long-distance trip this morning.

2. It was March 8th, International Women's Day, and I expressed my sincere wishes to my mother. Uncle Ye taught me to be grateful, and I felt my mother always caring for me. When I was sick, she took care of me and even chatted with me. I love my mother!

**Comment**: *On the eve of International Women's Day, I investigated and learned many details on how Wenxi's mother cared for him, and vividly described scenarios to him at that time, and he was deeply moved.*

03 / 09 – 03 / 10

1. In the past few days, I have been playing basketball with great enthusiasm.

2. Uncle Ye told me to use a polite form of speaking when talking to

someone who is older than me, and in some cases, to speak softly.

3. Uncle Ye has been guiding me on how to be a decent human, and he told me to memorize Di Zi Gui (Disciple Rules). He said I had a strong memory for accurately memorizing the passages.

**Comment**: *Wenxi's strength is not ordinary. It is super strong! What is super strong? It is a photocopier; it is a scanner. If you don't accept genetics, it won't work.*

4. Uncle Ye told me to learn to start with small things and overcome my shortcomings.

03 / 11

1. Today, I found that I can't help but giggle for no reason, and there have been many times.

**Comment**: *It is exciting that Wenxi started self-awareness.*

2. Grandmother's dog always pooped outside, so Uncle Ye arranged for me to pick up dog manure to prevent pedestrians from stepping on it.

3. Grandfather was going to Anshan today. I helped him move stuff, and I was happy about it.

4. I played basketball today and learned how to do layups and crossovers.

**Comment**: *All of these are a part of the Sensory Integration Training. It is a set of training methods based on Dr. Ayres' Sensory Integration Theory at the University of Southern California in 1972. This method is very effective for teenagers like Wenxi who have inconsistent movements and sensory disorders.*

# CHAPTER 8

03 / 12

1. Today, I was praised by my classmates in all aspects, and received a "Helpful Award" of 10 Yuan, which filled my heart with a wave of honor.

**Comment**: *I like Wenxi's simple way of expression.*

2. Today, I video chatted with my parents, and was extremely happy.

03 / 13

1. Uncle Ye was playing pop songs today, and I quickly covered my ears. I told him that from childhood to adulthood, I only listened to foreign symphonies, and I found other music very unpleasant. Uncle Ye told me that pop music is as beautiful as the symphony.

2. Today I was doing laundry at Grandmother's house.

3. I always come forward to guide others when I see they are doing something wrong. Uncle Ye told me that I can't casually guide others. Comment: Geez! From childhood to adulthood, I only listen to symphonies. What kind of family is this!

**Comment**: *This is what Wenxi usually does when he tries to guide others: his body would twitch as soon as he realizes they have done something wrong and makes the sound "umm" in his mouth. The size of the sound is proportional to the degree of absurdity of the other person's mistake. Then he'd take a deep breath and walk to the unfortunate person rapidly, grabbing him tightly by the arms with both hands, making a smiling expression on his face, and whispering to the guy: "Umm, this uncle (or this old comrade), what you just did... I think you should..."*

4. My parents came to visit me today, and we had a pleasant time to-

gether.

5. Aunty Liu made delicious dumplings for us.

03 / 14

1. Today, Aunty Hao gave me a Taiwanese mochi, and I thanked her.

2. Today, I found a table lamp was broken. I thought it was caused by a short circuit and helped Uncle Ye fix it. I was glad to apply my knowledge to life.

**Comment**: *I knew it was caused by a short circuit. What's important was that you helped me fix it.*

03 / 15 − 03 / 16

1. Uncle Ye told me to remind him when someone among us makes a mistake.

**Comment**: *It seems that Xiaoyu had his pants unzipped at that time.*

2. Uncle Ye discovered that I intentionally poured "thousands of boiling water" for others to drink, and I knew very well in my heart that "thousands of boiling water" was toxic. I found myself keep doing something even if I knew I wasn't supposed to. When writing my apology, I wrote that happiness consumes will and I resent happiness. However, Uncle Ye said that people need happiness. I thought I couldn't get to eat for doing it, but Uncle Ye said that even prisoners on death row get to eat their last meal before they die.

**Comment**: *Wenxi has seen all the uglies of various human nature. Before coming to Zhigang Education, his classmates would humiliate him casually, and his female desk-mate would slap him in front of everyone.*

*Wenxi's growth path was full of tears, and he used this type of petty vil-
lain to retaliate against others. Gradually this kind of petty villain became
a habit. Repetitive behavior shapes our vastly different lives.*

3. Aunty Hao told me to keep my smile after showing my gratitude.

4. Aunty Liu made delicious fried sweet dumplings.

03 / 17

1. I helped Uncle Ye hang the curtains and felt the joy of physical labor.

2. We had spring pancakes today, because it was 2 February on the lunar
calendar.

3. I bought spring rolls with my scholarship to express my gratitude to
Uncle Ye and Aunty Hao.

**Comment**: *Thank you, Wenxi. Aunty Hao and I will never forget it.*

4. I received a pomegranate from Lele as a reward for helping Xiaojian
review math.

**Comment**: *Wenxi's sense of humor has returned.*

03 / 18 – 03 / 20

1. Aunty Hao told me to make choices based on my own situation.

2. My posture was a lot better when playing basketball, and I even made
a shot during a game.

3. Uncle Ye has been correcting my lifestyle constantly, such as, not being too full when eating, and not using too much water when washing

dishes, feet, or socks.

**Comment**: *Every student needs to learn something different; teachers need to put their heart into it. There's always someone telling me that my education can't be replicated. This is simply nonsense! What cannot be replicated if you do it with your heart?*

03 / 21

Around 132 days before going home

**Comment**: *I'm deeply gratified to see this countdown. As I mentioned before, teachers are people who make themselves increasingly redundant. Others love their children for gathering, while our love for our children is for parting. Children are like birds. They'd want to fly away once their wings are fully grown. The countdown is the reflection of the growth of their abilities and self-identities.*

1. Xiaoyu said that as long as I am willing to work hard, I will quickly correct my shortcomings.

2. Grandmother made noodles for us today. It was delicious.

3. Today, my parents and I had a happy time through video chat.

03 / 22

Around 131 days before going home

1. Uncle Ye told me that in order to change my indifference, he wanted me to learn to prioritize helping others.

2. I'm falling in love with basketball.

3. Uncle Ye noticed that I was rigorous in my study, so he asked me to form a study group with Xiaojian. I helped him with his study, and he helped me correct my bad behaviors.

**Comment**: *No one can replace their peers.*

03 / 23

Around 130 days before going home

1. Uncle Ye told me that in order to train my attention to others, when someone sneezes, I should say, "God bless you!"

2. Aunty Liu made spring rolls today. It was delicious!

03 / 24

1. Today in basketball class, someone said I was stupid, so I wanted to commit suicide. But later on, I realized that I should "not be afraid of difficulties", so in order to change my foolish current situation and have a beautiful future, I'm going to:

    1) Keep working hard and moving forward!
    2) Strive for progress!

We will definitely make progress!

**Comment**: *People are not born great but become great in the process of growth. This is Wenxi's first great determination in his life: "In order to have a better future, I will work hard! Move forward! Strive for progress! I will definitely make progress!"*

2. Today I read an article entitled "I'll wait for you after the show ends", which reminded me that maternal love is always great.

03 / 25

Xiaoyu hit me today, and I endured it until Uncle Ye exposed the incident where I was hit by him. Uncle Ye told me to fight him, but I
couldn't fight him. So, Uncle Ye asked me to fight against Xiaoyu, and
Xiaoyu eventually gave in to me. I scared Xiaoyu, "If you dare to bully
me again, I will kill you." Xiaoyu then reconciled with me and swore not
to hit anyone again in the future.

**Comment**: *I have a famous saying—All power is the result of struggle.
Also, thanks to Xiaojian's father for providing me with the intelligence.
Your help and reminder will be remembered by Zhigang.*

Through this incident, I learned that when bullied, one should learn to
defend oneself in self-defense to maintain their dignity.

**Comment**: *"Legitimate defense to maintain one's dignity." "Rise of a
great power." This is what came to my mind when I saw what Wenxi
wrote.*

03 / 26

1. Fortunately, the refreshing and bowel-cleansing Runchang Tea allowed me to travel a long distance.

2. I got a Sachima as a reward for helping Uncle Ye move the couch.

3. Uncle Zhang came to visit Uncle Ye. I poured tea for him and got a
piece of chocolate as a reward. The taste was so rich, and the crispy hazel-
nut and malty shells reminded me of the birthday party of my classmate
in the past.

**Comment**: *Thanks to brother Zhang and your wife for all the help
throughout the years. I've learned so much from you.*

03 / 27

1. Uncle Ye told me that providing happiness to others is a kind of happiness itself.

2. Aunty Liu made shrimp pancakes and peanuts today. They were so delicious!

03 / 28

1. Uncle Ye told me not to overeat when eating.

2. Today I received a reply from my parents and felt very happy.

03 / 29

Uncle Ye showed us a movie named Forrest Gump. After watching it, I learned that life is like a box of chocolate, with different flavors, and one needs to take responsibility for one's own life.

03 / 30

1. Today, I learned how to defend when playing basketball.

2. In today's reading class, an article taught me how to take responsibility.

03 / 31

1. Today, Grandmother made fried doughs and Aunty Liu made egg custard. These foods reminded me of the dessert snacks I had in Heguyuan. They were delicious and attractive.

2. Uncle Ye taught me to interact with girls appropriately.

04 / 01

1. Today, I poured tea for the guests, and Aunt Hao rewarded me with a big red apple and a sticky sweet banana.

2. Aunty Hao gave me a piece of dried tofu today. It was delicious! The delicious taste reminded me of the dried tofu my father used to buy for me.

3. Today I read an article called "Haima Dad", which taught me the greatness of fatherly love.

**Comment**: *Parents of rebellious children should not be overly anxious. Love requires strength. Children will treat their parents well once they solve their main conflict and feel their own abilities by achieving something remarkable to themselves.*

04 / 02 – 04 / 03

These days, Uncle Ye went on a business trip to Beijing. I was at my grandmother's house and these things happened:

1. Xiaoyu said that he wanted to teach me wrestling, but actually he wanted to bully me. Grandma scolded him. Xiaoyu regretted it very much, apologized to me, and helped me wash my pants to make amends.

2. Grandma made sweet potatoes, and they were so delicious. That reminded me of the pumpkins that I had with my parents.

3. My vest broke, and Xiaoyu gave his vest to me. I didn't expect him to be so generous.

4. When we were resting and playing cards, Grandma gave us candy to eat.

P.S

1. Today, Aunty Hao made seafood noodles. It was so delicious!

2. Uncle Ye gave me a small notebook, asking me to develop the habit of doing things in a planned manner.

3. It was Easter today. Lele gave me a piece of Easter chocolate.

04 / 05

1. Today, I watched a movie called The Independent, which taught me the meaning of hard work.

2. I helped Aunty Hao move rice.

3. Brother Xiaoyi came to our house and bought us grilled meat. It was so delicious, which reminded me of the scene when I was eating barbecue at Xidan Super Cool.

4. Aunty Liu gave us potato chips.

5. Uncle Ye told me to learn how to manage time.

**Comment**: *"Having a plan for doing things"* and *"learning to control time"*, with the growth of Wenxi's abilities, the requirements for him have also risen to a higher level.

04 / 06

1. I took a shower and had my hair cut today, and it felt so refreshing!

2. I gave a piece of apple to Aunty Hao, and she was very happy and even told my father about it.

04 / 07

1. Uncle Ye and I went to buy a TV today.

2. Today, Brother Xiaoyi came over and we celebrated by eating delicious cake.

3. New friends are here!

**Comment**: *"So refreshing!" and "New friends!", Wenxi's emotional expression is increasing.*

04 / 08

1. Uncle Ye told me to remember to take out the trash after dinner every day.

2. Aunty Hao told me to gather up all my mistakes in English and have an overall- review.

**Comment**: *Haha, the language in Northeast China is always so friendly and interesting. Wenxi has learned a lot of powerful expressions in Northeast China. After he returned to school, his enthusiasm, kindness, and his style of Northeastern people's speaking, as well as his muscle, made his classmates respect him as "Big Brother".*

3. Grandmother made us delicious sweet and sour ribs today, and they are really palatable! I even learned the recipe (blanching pork ribs, then adding salt, sugar, vinegar, and soy sauce to stir fry).

04 / 09

Today, Uncle Ye asked everyone to write down their evaluations of me, and I was much encouraged.

*Brother Wenxi is doing things more seriously, much better than before. He is more detailed when he speaks, instead of speaking in riddles. This is what a man looks like. He is more caring for the others. Should we have a charity ambassador event to let Wenxi participate in, he's definitely getting first place.*

—Asian man (Xiaojian)

*Brother Wenxi has learned to speak normally now, and he doesn't eat fast anymore. This is what a man looks like.*
*He is more serious and caring, even helping us study.*

—Happy Boy (Xiaoyu)

*Wenxi has made great progress, such as "daring to point out Xiaoyu's shortcomings" "not using other's belongings" "not staring at the dishes while eating" and so on. Hope you can keep working on yourself!*

—Lele

**Comment**: *One sentence from peers is worth 100 sentences from elders.*

04 / 10

1. Grandmother made pancakes. It was extremely delicious!

2. I taught Brother Xiaoyi to do laundry.

3. Today, Aunty Hao and I went for a walk.

4. Dad came over today, and we had a great time. Dad told me to speak like an adult, and quickly to fulfill what I promised Uncle Ye.

5. Aunty Liu taught me to make doughs.

**Comment**: *Sweet and sour pork ribs two days ago, we'll start making noodles today. He might start making roast duck the day after tomorrow! Wenxi's culinary skills are getting much better.*

04 / 11

1. Uncle Ye took me and Xiaoyu to have some Rougamo. It was so delicious!

2. Uncle Ye told me to learn to do everything seriously, and not go to extremes.

3. Aunty Liu made delicious steamed buns today, which reminded me of the bamboo shoots buns and roasted pork buns that my mother and I ate in Chenghuang Temple.

4. Aunty Liu taught me to make stir-fried garlic sprouts.

5. Today, Xiaobo's family made grilled chicken wings. After I had a delicious meal, I said thank you to Xiaobo's father, and Uncle Ye praised me.

**Comment**: *The real situation is that after Wenxi finished eating grilled chicken wings, he shouted and ran to Xiaobo's house, asking loudly, "Who baked such delicious chicken wings?" Then he held Xiaobo's father's hand hard and kept saying thank you, making Xiaobo's whole family burst into laughter.*

04 / 12

1. Today, I watched a movie called The Legend of 1900, and the music in it was so touching.

2. Aunty Liu made chive omelettes and fennel peanuts today. They were so delicious.

04 / 13

Today, we went to a distant city to see the ocean. I also met brother Xiaomin. It was really fun.

**Comment**: *Xiaomin is like a flag, whose experiences inspire the younger brothers.*

04 / 14

Today, I read an article called "A ticket for Eighty Years", and I learned to cherish the present.

04 / 15

1. Today I saw Xiaoyu stealing food and told Uncle Ye. Uncle Ye praised me and pointed out that I should have stopped Xiaoyu first. If he didn't listen, then I needed to tell Uncle Ye.

2. Today I was too greedy for my meal. Uncle Ye told me to consider the others when eating. He also told me that making mistakes is not a bad thing; what's bad is repeating the same mistakes.

**Comment**: *The greatness of God lies in giving people opportunities and hope. Teachers are the messengers of God.*

1. Today, Aunty Liu made delicious eggplant cakes.

2. Uncle Ye taught me to focus on the present and grasp the future, which gave me confidence.

**Comment**: *What? Is that what I said? Sounds like an empty talk.*

04 / 16

1. I played basketball with Brother Xiaoyi today, and it was fun.

2. Today, my stomach felt weird after I ate some chive omelettes and drank cold water. Ouch!

**Comment**: *Brother Xiaoyi is a gift from God to Wenxi. Xiaoyi's tolerance and patience towards Wenxi in life are touching, and his appearance has greatly accelerated Wenxi's progress.*

04 / 17

1. Today, Uncle Ye and I went to attend his friend's wedding ceremony, and on the way back, I vomited for a while.

2. I went to see an art exhibition with Uncle Ye, Aunty Hao and Xiaoyu.

**Comment**: *Wenxi did not handle the delicacies all over the table well.*

04 / 18

1. It was Aunty Hao's birthday today, and we had delicious chocolate cake and Guobaorou (Double Cooked Pork).

**Comment**: *Guobaorou is the favorite food of all my students. And we only eat Guobaorou at Taoyuan Xincun Main Store in Panjin City. Highly recommended!*

2. Aunty Hao gave me strawberries today.

3. Today, I had a happy video chat with my parents.

04 / 19

Today, I watched a movie called Small Shoes (also: Children of Heaven) at Uncle Ye's house. It was about a boy with a rough upbringing, and once he accidentally lost his sister's shoes (which were just repaired). So, he lent his sports shoes to his sister and would wear them back after school. He was so kind!

The school held a long-distance running competition, and only third place can get a pair of sports shoes as an award. So, he decided to take third place and get sports shoes for his sister to wear (because he promised her), but he didn't get them because he ran first.

My heart was incredibly shocked. An ordinary child, in order to get sports shoes for his sister, was incredibly persistent! This is worth learning from. In life, we have all promised others to do things, but how many people have fulfilled their promises?

This little boy can help his family at the age of only nine. How many children with wealthy upbringings can do it? So, we not only have to work hard and endure hardships, but also make every effort to fulfill what we promised others to do.

**Comment**: *Geez! This is the longest thinking record of Wenxi so far.*

04 / 20

1. Today, Xiaojian scored 84 in the English exam, and he is very grateful to me because I have been helping him learn English.

**Comment**: *Wenxi received respect by helping others, and as a result, he found his position at home. In his subsequent diaries, we will find everywhere that he treats himself as the owner of the family.*

2. Uncle Ye told me to pay attention to the feelings of others when doing things.

04 / 21

1. Today I can eat the saucy noodles made by Grandmother. They are so delicious!

2. Uncle Ye told me that if one wants to manage others well, first manage himself well.

3. Uncle Ye also told me that for us teenagers, sex and learning are equally important. I should try to get close to females and enhance my understanding of them, but never completely engage with them.

**Comment**: *I have a longer-term perspective for Wenxi's education, which will be discussed in detail later.*

04 / 22

1. Grandmother made us bean buns today. Although they were delicious, I restrained myself in order to help my stomach and intestines recover quickly. At the same time, I took the initiative to wash the dishes, and Uncle Ye praised me for that.

**Comment**: *Wenxi is getting more and more confident in expression. It was all because he found his position in my home. Finding one's own position is such an important thing. Setting life goals for students is to find a career they want to pursue in the future, to find their ways to serve society, to find their position in society through serving society, and ultimately, gain a sense of happiness.*

2. Uncle Ye gave me a task today: to set questions and take exams for Brother Xiaoyi.

04 / 23 – 04 / 24

1. I bought myself toothpaste and did something within my ability. After learning about it, Uncle Ye told me that the ingredients of toothpaste in the market are similar, but in daily life, we should be frugal in spending money. A 13.8 Yuan toothpaste was too luxurious. A toothpaste worth 5 Yuan in the market was good enough, so he reimbursed me 5 Yuan, and the rest was on me. This is really a necessary lesson to learn!

2. Uncle Ye told me, "In life, there will be many people criticizing you, even insulting you. We should focus our attention on what others are criticizing, carefully understand what others are criticizing, correct any mistakes, instead of focusing on the words of criticism, which will take a long time to let go." At that time, I wanted all students in Shanghai to listen to this sentence.

**Comment**: *Ha, thanks.*

04 / 25 – 04 / 26

1. I am very cowardly and was often bullied in Shanghai, which is indeed worrying. So, one time, while playing basketball, I was scolded by a primary school student. I tried my best to refute it. In the end, Uncle Ye praised me, and my parents were happy because of it, too.

**Comment**: *This was a historical event, as it was the first time that Wenxi counterattacked against outsiders.*

2. When playing basketball, Mr. Ren taught me to have my arms raised up when defending.

3. Thanks to the Runchang Tea, I pooped.

4. Aunty Liu made delicious stewed beef with potatoes.

Recipe: Boil beef ribs with spices for 15 minutes, and then add carrots, scallions, and potatoes to taste.

**Comment**: *I think Wenxi has been reading recipes a lot. Otherwise, how could this recipe be written so professionally!*

04 / 27

Today, Aunty Hao and I went to Wafangdian to visit grandma. Grandma made egg fried rice for lunch, and then Auntie taught me to make pimple soup… What a wonderful day!

04 / 28

1. In the morning, Uncle Ye, Brother Xiaoyi and I ate steamed stuffed buns and drank porridge together.

2. I washed clothes at grandma's house.

04 / 29

1. In the morning, Uncle Ye, Brother Xiaoyi and I had deep-fried dough sticks, deep-fried dough cake, soybean milk for breakfast together.

2. I bought Xiaoyu some snacks because he's about to leave.

3. We had a farewell party for Xiaoyu's departure.

4. Uncle Zhang praised me for making rapid progress.

5. I went to visit Aunty Hao's house at the logging station.

# CHAPTER 8

04 / 30

1. Today, Uncle Ye, Aunty Hao and I escorted Xiaoyu to the train station together.

2. Uncle Ye told me to learn from Xiaoyu his qualities of diligence, hard work, and selflessness.

3. Aunty Hao made noodles for us in the morning, with rice kernel dumpling inside, and she made us delicious purple rice porridge and chicken soup for dinner in the evening (and the lamb brought by Brother Xiaoyi).

4. In the evening, we watched the opening ceremony of the World Expo.

05 / 01

1. This morning, I led Xiaojian to run 4.4 kilometers.

2. Today, Uncle Ye taught me how to use a radio.

3. I cleaned the table quite well today.

4. I helped grandfather move the box today, and grandmother rewarded me with an orange.

5. Today, I helped Uncle Ye dry some mats and dropped one by accident. I jumped down bravely to pick it up, and Uncle Ye praised me for it.

6. I pooped once today.

7. Uncle Ye told me not to get too addicted to certain things.

8. Today I received a reply from my parents, and we spent a happy 30-minute video chat together tonight.

05 / 02

1. I helped Aunty Hao move things today.

2. Uncle Ye told me to learn to accept others' opinions. For example, Aunty Hao asked me to write down the answers in an English exercise book.

05 / 03

1. Grandmother's brother and his wife came over this morning and made us a lot of delicious food, such as triangular steamed bun stuffed with sugar, raisin porridge... They were delicious. We took them to the train station at noon, and I helped them carry their luggage.

2. I watched a comedy show New Humor Jokes at noon today, and I felt happiness is everywhere in life.

05 / 04

1. Today, Uncle Ye and I went to buy breakfast, and Uncle Ye told me to check the price when shopping.

2. I went shopping with Uncle Ye and Aunty Hao, and I helped carry watermelons.

05 / 05

1. I shared a cake with Aunty Hao.

2. Uncle Ye told me that when others point out shortcomings, I need to

be optimistic and correct them in order to make progress.

3. Uncle Ye told me that there are some things that need to be practiced personally.

4. Aunty Hao told me to calm down and study.

5. I helped Uncle Ye brew cucumber seed powder.

6. Aunty Liu not only taught me to make Wonton today, but also made delicious sugar cakes at noon, which reminded me of the baked cake that my mom bought for me on the weekend morning.

7. Brother Xiaoyi returned from attending the opening ceremony of the World Expo. It is said that he saw the national leader and brought us back delicious cake.

05 / 06

1. Today, Uncle Ye and I went out for breakfast together. Uncle Ye told me to share the delicious food with others, and to stop chewing like a camel during meals.

2. Aunty Liu made delicious Wonton today, which reminded me of the Wonton that I had with my mother.

3. Brother Xiaoyi and I went to visit grandmother today. We chatted together.

05 / 07

1. At breakfast today, Uncle Ye told me not to take advantage of others.

2. Today, Brother Xiaoyi and I went to Aunty Hao's house at the log–

ging station to learn English. On our way back, we bought scallion fla-vored Nang (a kind of crusty pancake), pumpkin bread, and rice. We had bread at noon, which was so delicious.

05 / 08

1. I scored 105 on an IQ test today.

**Comment**: *Wenxi was pretty confident before the test and getting a 105 actually made him very sad. My score at the time was 128.*

2. My parents came to visit me today, and they were happy about my progress. Then we went to a supermarket together, where I bought sweet potato chips and jujube cake for my mother. Because it is Mother's Day tomorrow. My father told me to act like an adult and to have confi-dence. My mother said that academic performance depends not only on intelligence, but also on diligence.

05 / 09

Today was the most heart-wrenching day for me. Uncle Ye and I went to my grandmother's house, but I only remembered reading and didn't remember taking care of her. Later it started raining. I had my own um-brella, but Brother Xiaoyi didn't have one. He wanted to share mine, but I refused. Uncle Ye harshly criticized me when he found out. After-wards, I lay down on the bed and calmed down. In my sleep, I saw the sad expression of my parents, the ridicule from my classmates, and the criticism from my teachers... I suddenly realized that I was incredibly selfish, and I felt extremely guilty about it. How could I make such a mistake on Mother's Day!

At this moment, Uncle Ye came over to comfort me and said, "Think more of others." Moreover, because it was the first time that I had made such a mistake, Uncle Ye said that making a mistake might not be a bad thing but try not to make the same mistake.

**Comment**: *How can a child make progress without making mistakes? Should he make mistakes in adulthood instead of in childhood?*

05 / 10

Today I took care of my grandmother. Grandmother was sick and she couldn't move as well as usual. At noon, I brought her lunch and watched a comedy show New Humor Jokes with her. In the evening, I fed her and gave her a foot bath. What a meaningful day!

05 / 11

1. Brother Xiaoyi and I helped Uncle Ye move the gas can today, and Uncle Ye gave me a white chocolate bar. It was delicious.

2. Brother Xiaoyi and I bought sweet potato chips and shared them with Uncle Ye.

05 / 12

1. Today, Uncle Ye, Aunty Hao, Brother Xiaoyi and I went to the suburb to pick up wild vegetables together, and we got a lot. We were really happy.

2. Aunty Liu made hand-rolled noodles today, which reminded me of the noodles that I used to have with my mother.

05 / 13

1. Aunty Hao made rice soybean milk for us today. It was delicious.

2. Today, while playing basketball, I was provoked by a primary school

205

student, and he was kicked off the stadium.

**Comment**: *What a strange expression. I thought that Wenxi was kicked out of the stadium.*

Today, in order to change my stingy habit, Uncle Ye intentionally used my backpack to hold things. I felt sad at that time, but later Aunty Hao told me that if someone doesn't give, he will be very selfish and difficult to establish himself in society. Some changes in life are inevitable, and we should accept them. However, I heard that Uncle Ye was going to buy me another backpack.

**Comment**: *I've been trying to figure out who leaked my action plan. He wasn't supposed to know until a few days later.*

05 / 14

1. Uncle Ye told Brother Xiaoyi and me to learn from and help each other.

2. Uncle Ye took Brother Xiaoyi and me to visit grandmother today. I gave her a pear and she was happy. I then gave Uncle Ye a pear. His tongue had been blistering recently. I wanted him to eat pears to reduce heat.

**Comment**: *Thank you Wenxi! I'm very touched.*

05 / 15

Today, I went shopping in Shenyang with Uncle Ye and Aunty Hao. I saw many clothing products, and I also helped them carry stuff. Uncle Ye praised me for my capability, and Aunty Hao rewarded me with a sausage and a corn cob. I know from this matter that as long as you are willing to work hard, you can get what you want.

**Comment**: *Wenxi summarized his experience for the second time: as long as he is willing to work hard, he can get what he wants!*

05 / 16

1. Uncle Ye told me that when interacting with people, do not make strange noises. Do not talk to myself or talk nonsense. Do not use certain type of phrases such as "I do" or "I also…"

2. Uncle Ye gave me a set of nail clippers as a reward for my progress.

3. Today, my parents and I spent a happy hour on the video.

05 / 17

1. Today, Uncle Ye told me that whenever I'm addressed as a kid, I should tell them to address me as an adult.

**Comment**: *Whoever others think you are will make you also think you are, and whoever you think you are, you will become. Many children's dreams have been ruined by the negation of those around them. I refuse to let others around me treat Wenxi as an autistic and weak person, which may deprive him of the right to become a normal person.*

2. Aunty Hao cooked delicious egg fried rice today, which reminded me of the fried rice that I had at a restaurant with my parents.

05 / 18

1. Uncle Ye told me to greet others based on their statuses.

2. This morning, Aunty Hao got delicious fancy bread for breakfast, which reminded me of the fancy bread my mother bought me. In the evening, Aunty Hao gave us a watermelon and litchis to eat.

3. Uncle Ye detected that I had low blood sugar and low blood pressure, so he made me drink water with egg and brown sugar and eat a few dates every day.

05 / 19

1. Uncle Ye, Aunty Hao, Brother Xiaoyi and I went for a walk by the dam. The scenery over there cleared away the tension in my heart.

2. I set an application question for Brother Xiaoyi, and Uncle Ye thought I was working hard and gave me a piece of chocolate.

**Comment**: *Since May 19, he stopped documenting about food as that much.*

05 / 20

1. Today, I gave my spot to Brother Xiaoyi in the English lesson, and Aunty Hao was very happy.

2. Uncle Ye, Brother Xiaoyi and I went to visit grandmother today. She was very happy.

3. Aunty Hao cooked delicious kimchi fried rice today, and we shared some taro strips in the evening. It was both salty and sweet, and very delicious.

05 / 21

1. Uncle Ye told me not to do things that harm others but benefit myself.

2. Aunty Liu made Chinese toon scrambled eggs for lunch. It was delicious, which reminded me of the Chinese toon scrambled eggs that I had with my parents at a farmhouse restaurant.

05 / 22

1. I was setting some questions for Brother Xiaoyi. Uncle Ye appreciated my enthusiastic and helpful qualities.

2. Uncle Ye told me not to speak childish language.

3. Today, I washed clothes at Aunty Hao's house, and learned how to use the washing machine. I also took the initiative to wash Uncle Ye's pants, which made Aunty Hao very happy.

Comment: *Since May 22, Wenxi started caring and helping others actively.*

4. Uncle Ye and Aunty Hao gave me and Lele, Niuniu some sweet potatoes, which were really delicious.

5. Auntie Ye and Niuniu's parents came to our house as guests, and I poured water for them.

Comment: *Proactively caring for and helping others marks the complete end of Wenxi's self-awareness stage, and self-awareness begins to be transformed into action! From February 11th to May 22nd, Wenxi spent altogether 100 days in this stage! These 100 days are the distance between wanting and doing.*

05 / 23

1. This morning, Aunty Hao gave me a sweetened baked wheaten cake, which reminded me of the sweetened baked wheaten cake my mother gave me. Afterwards, I was concerned about whether Uncle Ye had breakfast, and Uncle Ye praised me.

2. Today, my parents and I had a happy time through video.

**Comment**: *Starting from May 23rd, Wenxi began his transition from a humanoid ape to a human, transitioning from a passive change phase to an active change phase. During this period, I promoted Wenxi's growth by giving him nicknames, having his friends remind him, watching movies, reasoning, giving him guidance by his grandparents, uncles, aunts, and other relatives, replaying videos of Wenxi playing basketball to encourage him to reflect on himself, and so on.*

05 / 24

1. Today, Uncle Ye had a successful lecture at Experimental High School, and I was happy for him.

2. Aunty Hao provided me with seasonal side dishes to help me digest, which were really delicious and tasted like salad.

05 / 25

1. Uncle Ye told me not to nag endlessly about a small matter.

2. Uncle Ye told me that if you want someone to do something, first ask if he can do it.

3. We went to visit grandma today. We helped her with eating and read her a newspaper. Grandma was very happy.

05 / 26 – 05 / 28

1. Uncle Ye told me that the tragedy of the vast majority of men is to think too much and do too little!

2. Uncle Ye told me to be a relaxed person and pay attention to my personal behaviors.

3. Uncle Ye told me during dinner today:

1) Don't open my mouth too wide when eating, and don't lift the bowl too high.

2) Don't extend my upper lip long into the bowl when drinking soup.

4. I gave the engine oil to Uncle Zhang, and he was very happy.

5. Uncle Ye told me: if any elementary school students provoke or curse in person, immediately counterattack and don't listen to their orders to pick up the ball!

05 / 29

1. Aunty Hao made noodles for us this morning, each with a poached egg. She had something going on, so she was to eat after us, but when I was served the second bowl, I saw that there was still a poached egg in the pot. Even though I knew it was Aunty Hao's, I couldn't help taking the poached egg, and when Uncle Ye asked me, I didn't admit it.

In the evening, Uncle Ye took us to the restaurant and ordered a lot of dishes, but he told me to watch them eat for an hour. Later on, I realized that if one deprives others of their rights due to greed, not only will their own interests be compromised, but they will also be looked down upon by others.

2. If a person does not pay attention to his own behavior, he will be despised. I understand that I should think more about others.

**Comment**: *Every time Wenxi touches the bottom line, it's the same outcome. He will come to the same conclusion, and the conclusion will continue to strengthen, eventually forming his own behavioral norms. Throughout late May, Wenxi was regressing, and based on my years of* *experience, this rebound is a precursor to major events that are about to occur. Only when major events occur can there be significant progress.*

05 / 30

1. Uncle Ye, Aunty Hao, her student Han Xue and I ate dumplings together today. I gave my sister Han Xue many dumplings, and I'm getting used to caring for others.

2. I got a reply from my parents and had a video chat with them tonight. It was delightful!

3. I took a shower and had my hair cut today. It's so enjoyable!

**Comment**: *On 05 / 29 he realized his mistake and started correcting it right away on 05 / 30. In addition, Wenxi's handwriting has become increasingly neat and organized as his situation improves.*

05 / 31

1. I went to visit grandmother with Brother Xiaoyi, and she was very happy.

2. Mr. Li gave us a math lesson, and I learned many techniques.

06 / 01

1. It was Children's Day today. When I saw children happily spending time with their families, I remembered my childhood and felt very uncomfortable.

2. When doing sit-ups, Uncle Ye told me to keep a smile after finishing, for many athletes had this kind of expression after their matches, and I thought it'd be good to do so.

3. I scored 100 in the English quiz these days, and Aunty Hao was very happy. She told me to keep working hard.

06 / 02

1. Uncle Ye told me not to keep making mistakes recklessly, and to speak logically.

2. In the evening, we watched a movie called The Shallshank's Redemption, and I learned that there is hope so long as we work hard.

3. Aunty Liu made steamed rolls today, which reminded me of the ones my mother bought for me.

**Comment**: *This was the last time that Wenxi mentioned the feeling of eating in his diary.*

06 / 03

1. Today, I went out with Uncle Ye and Aunty Hao to watch the sunset, and it was very enjoyable.

2. Aunty Hao asked me to drink diluted salted water every day to help with my bowel movement.

3. Uncle Ye told me to greet acquaintances on the street, and I could ask them if they have eaten, or what they are up to.

06 / 04

Today, I went to a wedding ceremony with Brother Xiaoyi and Aunty Hao. At the wedding ceremony, I saw the groom and the bride paying their respect to their parents when they got married, and I was touched by it. During the meal afterwards, Aunty Hao told me not to make noises when eating in public, and I thought it was more civilized that way as well.

06 / 05

1. Today, I washed clothes in Aunty Hao's house at the logging station. I felt the joy of physical labor.

2. Father came to visit me today, and he was pleased to see my progress. At dinner, Aunty Liu made fish with tofu, and I picked the caviar for my father, and he was very happy. Then I bought a jujube cake for my father. Uncle Ye praised me for having a conscience.

**Comment**: *Wenxi's father had him at an old age. His hair turned gray when he entrusted Wenxi to me. As a son, Wenxi has this filial piety, and I'm so happy for him.*

3. Father hoped that I could improve faster and return to my parents as soon as possible.

06 / 06

Today, Aunty Hao and I went to Wafangdian to see grandma. At noon, we had lunch together. I felt very happy because I hadn't been together for a long time. In the afternoon, Aunty Hao and I went to visit Aunty Hao's elder sister. Although her house was a bit messy, Aunty Hao told me not to say that. In the evening, I told grandmother (Aunty Hao's mother) health stories and chatted, and she was really happy.

**Comment**: *Imagine a young man sitting cross-legged, telling an elderly person across from him about health preservation. Can you believe it? This is what actually happened. Wenxi talked about my mother's philosophy of health preservation, which I regarded as nagging. However, Wenxi never lost a word and could memorize everything.*

06 / 07

Today, I went to the supermarket to pick up baking sodas for Uncle Ye. I encountered some difficulties along the way, but eventually I managed to retrieve it successfully.

06 / 08

Today, Uncle Ye and I went to visit grandmother, and we chatted, and I poured water for her. I also told her stories of health preservation... she was happy.

**Comment**: *My disciple taught my master about health preservation, and the Grandma was still very happy. LOL.*

06 / 09

1. Uncle Ye told me to try to stay silent for half a day, allowing me to experience a life of being "mute" and observe life in a silent world.

2. I shared my cookies with Uncle Ye, and he said no, thanks! But I insisted and kept shoving the cookie to him. Uncle Ye told me that doing so would only annoy others, and I also think politeness should be moderate.

06 / 10 – 06 / 12

1. Today, I went to buy noodles for Aunty Hao. Although I made some mistakes in the process, I still managed to buy them successfully.

2. Uncle Ye told me not to do things that make people feel uncomfortable in social situations.

3. After I helped Aunty Hao's colleagues move oil, sugar, and tea, I went

to grandmother's house to collect a fax, poured water for her, and fed her tomatoes. Although it was very difficult, I think it was necessary for a capable person to do so.

06 / 13

1. Uncle Ye has always been concerned about my work habits. He asked me to watch how the characters in the TV drama Drawing Sword behave.

2. Uncle Ye told me that the toilet seat should be placed gently.

06 / 14 – 06 / 16

These days, it's the Dragon Boat Festival holiday. We've had a lot of Zongzi. Someone unexpectedly sent meat zongzi to Uncle Ye from Shaoxing, Zhejiang! At the same time, these few things happened that made me really happy:

Firstly, I took Zongzi to Uncle Zhang, who said that I acted more like a man now. Then I took Zongzi to my grandparents and they were very happy. After hearing this, Uncle Ye praised me and rewarded me with a popsicle.

Secondly, my sister Han Xue came to our house, and we had a very pleasant time.
Thirdly, I wrote a letter to my parents and sent it out.

06 / 17

I ate the Zongzi that Uncle Zhang made for me, and then I called him on the phone to show my gratitude. Uncle Zhang praised me and said I acted like a man. Finally, I waited for him to hang up the phone first before I hung up, and Uncle Ye praised me.

# CHAPTER 8

06 / 18

1. Today, at the dining table, Uncle Ye praised me for speaking and doing things more appropriately.

2. Today while playing basketball, I learned a pitching method from sports advertisements. When others are defending, leave space, make a fake pitching posture, wrap the ball behind, and take advantage of the opportunity to throw the ball. Learning these four points will make playing more exciting in the future.

3. Today was Uncle Ye's birthday, and I made him a greeting card to show my gratitude for what he's done for me in the past four months.

**Comment**: *Thank you for Wenxi's greeting card! Uncle Ye has been keeping it.*

06 / 19

1. I went shopping with Aunty Hao, and she told me that, during shopping I need to:

1) Take a good look at the price and pay attention to thrift.

2) When buying goods, it is important to distinguish the quality of the product in order to use it with peace of mind.

2. Today, many relatives went to visit my grandmother. Afterwards, Uncle Ye and I went for a walk with them in the forest by the dam. I saw how beautiful the gold there is! It reminded me of the scenery of my home in Hanbi Bay, Qingpu. Afterwards, we went shopping together.

At the mall, my grandfather asked me how tall I was. I said I was 1.67 meters tall, and my grandfather said he was 1.74 meters tall. But we were surprised to find that I was taller than my grandfather. Grandfather touched my head and said I had grown taller. He said that I'm more like a man from the way I act and look at others. After returning home, Uncle Ye measured me at 1.76 meters. I was only 1.67 meters when I first got here. It's almost unbelievable that I've grown 10 cm in the past six months!

Aunty Hao helped me analyze the reasons. There are two reasons. First is that my diet is now more reasonable than before. The food at Uncle Ye's house is very delicious, and with the help of Uncle Ye and Aunty Hao, my appetite is well controlled. The second is that I engage in a variety of outdoor and indoor activities every day. For example, I run 1 kilometer each morning and 1 kilometer each afternoon, and my best record is 3 minutes and 55 seconds. I also do push-ups and sit-ups every morning in my spare time. I can do 30 of each in a row.

06 / 20

Today was Father's Day. On this day, I remembered the little moments my dad and I spent together from childhood to adulthood, feeling incredibly moved in my heart.

I was tasked with household chores at Uncle Ye's house. In the morning, I boiled water, poured water for Uncle Ye and Aunty Hao, woke Brother Xiaoyi up, took him for a run, picked up bowls, cleaned the table, set up chairs, took out the garbage, controlled everyone's schedule, washed my clothes, helped Aunty Hao with groceries, and took care of my grandmother...

**Comment**: *Since June 19th, his diary has gotten longer and longer as he pays more attention to the details in life. He also analyzed his thoughts clearer and even started summarizing the key points of the letters from his parents.*

06 / 21

I don't know why there has been a rebound in many aspects recently. For example, being absent-minded during meals, not in a good state of playing basketball, having slow reactions when doing things, missing stuff, and so on.

**Comment**: *Wenxi himself has felt the problems as well. At that time, the problem was already very serious, but it was not reflected clearly in his diary.*

06 / 22

Father wrote a letter in which he said, "Only by knowing oneself can one have the ability to meet others and society.

—Every single detail in the communication process dictates where the conversation goes, as well as the result of it.

—To respect others is to respect yourself. I think there is still room for improvement in the following aspects:

1. Articulation can be clearer when speaking.

2. When food and other desired items arrive, be calm and composed.

3. When working with Uncle Ye, be more proactive.

4. Thinking and doing things in daily life can be more thoughtful.

After reading my dad's letter, I realized that no matter where I am, my parents are always caring for me. I feel sad because I cannot spend the holiday with my family, which makes me more determined to repay my parents with progress.

**Comment**: *Wenxi began to understand the love of his parents. In addition, Wenxi's handwriting is more refined and his brain's ability to control muscles is enhanced.*

06 / 23

In recent days, Uncle Ye has changed his way of educating me. Every day, he allows me to watch the TV drama Drawing Sword, and the protagonist Li Yunlong has left a great impression on me. When he talks to his superiors, he is very respectful and sometimes argues with reason. When talking to comrades, he is humorous, witty, and reasonable. When talking to the soldiers, he is enthusiastic and inspiring. When talking to fellow villagers, he is approachable. When talking to his wife, he is gentle and considerate.

Uncle Ye told me, "The highest state of conversing is to speak according to the audience!" Upon hearing this, I was deeply moved.

**Comment**: *I have noticed that after watching the TV drama Drawing Sword, the men around me have significantly increased their voices when speaking, and they also appear more energetic. This is the influence of good films on people, and after watching this film, Wenxi has also undergone significant changes.*

06 / 24

1. Today was the high school entrance exam for my classmates in Shanghai, and I feel a bit disappointed. I thought to myself that on the same day next year I would also be taking on such a challenge just like them, which has given me confidence to work even harder.

**Comment**: *Wenxi has a spirit of hard work and progress in his bones, which is not what I brought to him, but comes from genes. His father's legendary experience of becoming a top scientist from a farmer in the* *mountains with this spirit fills me with excitement.*

2. Today, Xiaoyu had a video chat with us. Xiaoyu passed his entrance exam, and I am truly happy for him. When Xiaoyu first came to Uncle Ye's house, he performed very poorly in all aspects. His study was at the bottom of his class. Now that he can pass the entrance exam, I am truly happy for the progress he has made.

People always think that I'm childish because of the way I talk. Uncle Ye said that this is because I have a problem with my use of breath when speaking. So, Uncle Ye asked me to speak only with the falling tone out of the four tones from 7:00 in the morning to 7:30 in the evening. I have a resistance to Uncle Ye's suggestion because:

Firstly, I have recently regressed and lacked confidence. Secondly, I think Uncle Ye's suggestion is a bit strange and I can't accept it. Uncle Ye noticed my resistance and told me that progress does not refer to constant improvement, but to macro-level improvement. From a microscopic perspective, it is often two steps forward and one step back, and then three steps forward and one step back. On hearing his words, I was very shocked. I thought that even though the path to human change is winding, as long as I have confidence, I can definitely pass!

**Comment**: *My dose of medicine worked!*

06 / 25

1. Aunty Hao had dedicated so much in my English that I have scored 100 points in English many times in a row. I thought to myself that if I could maintain such good English grades when I returned to school, my English would definitely be at the forefront of the class.

2. Brother Xiaoyi recorded the basketball game today. After playing basketball, Uncle Ye and I watched together. From here, Uncle Ye pointed

out that there are areas where I need to improve when playing basketball games:

1) I always follow others for a slow jog during competitions.

2) I pass the ball to others right after I get it.

3) I don't jump high enough when shooting.

We also found some areas of improvement:

1) I'm able to distinguish between teammates and opponents.

2) I know when to pass the ball to my teammates.

**Comment**: *Xiaoyi, who pays great attention to details, is a good friend of Wenxi's. He provides many observations of Wenxi from the perspective of peers.*

06 / 26

Recently, I kept making mistakes on tasks that Uncle Ye gave me. Uncle Ye asked me what my classmates called me when I was in Shanghai before, and I said they called me Silly X. Uncle Ye asked me why. Was it because of my low IQ or not paying attention? I said it's because I didn't pay attention.

**Comment**: *Actually, it still stems from the effect of autism.*

Uncle Ye asked me what is the most important word in life? I know the answer to that. Uncle Ye once told me before that the most important word in life is "do". Uncle Ye asked me again: "Do you know what to do in the first half of your life?" I said, "I don't know." Uncle Ye said, "Don't be afraid." I asked Uncle Ye again: "What should I do in the latter half of my life?" Uncle Ye smiled and told me, "I'll tell you when you call me after you're 40 years old!"

06 / 27

This morning, Lele's elder auntie made delicious dumpling soup. I quickly finished a bowl and took my empty bowl to the edge of the pot and I filled a large bowl full of dumpling noodles when no one was paying attention. Looking at the thin soup left in the pot, I feel guilty. But the attraction of the delicious food made me doing so anyway, although I really hoped that it didn't happen.

**Comment**: *Wenxi can make a deeper analysis of his thoughts and actions, which is one more step closer to actively changing. I summarize that a person's journey from being driven by primitive desires to being driven by reason involves five stages: repeated awareness, self-deprecation, accidental change, continuous reinforcement, and habit formation.*

Aunty Hao told me that men should learn to take care of others. Uncle Ye said that taking care of others is a virtue, and the foundation of all virtues is not to harm others for personal gain. I'm shocked after hearing them.

Aunty Hao also said that I should mature as soon as possible. I understand in my heart, after all, that a young man who is almost 16 years old and cannot resist the temptation of food is very childish. Another thing is that many people are very greedy, but they will not do anything unpleasant because of it.

**Comment**: *"Many people are greedy" is powerful. "I used to be just like you", or "I was not as good as you back then", to start lecturing with statements like these would really leave an impression. Legend has it that the most powerful spy organization in the world is Mossad in Israel. When training new recruits, they hire those who were previously* eliminated as instructors because they are more empathetic, tolerant, and encouraging. I think this is impossible. Mossad is not an educational institution, and harshness seems to be more beneficial for agents to survive in the future than tolerance and encouragement. This legend illustrates the enormous value of empathy.

06 / 28

Lele had the high school entrance exam today. Everyone encouraged her to succeed in the exam. At the same time, I made my mind to study harder and strive to achieve better results on the same day next year.

06 / 29

Lele finally completed the high school entrance exams tonight, and I feel really happy in my heart. Thinking to myself: in this last month, Lele will have a lot of time to tutor me in my study.

**Comment**: *What a wishful thinking! Lele went traveling with her classmates the next day, and Wenxi got excited for nothing.*

06 / 30

1. Every time I go to play basketball, Uncle Ye asks Brother Xiaoyi to record it for me. After returning home, we sit down together and analyze the problems and progress I have made while playing basketball.

Today when I came back from playing basketball, Uncle Ye said that I had a few shortcomings:

1) I didn't stand on the opposite side from where my teammates were shooting.

2) I should defend in front of them when the opposing team member is

shooting.

Uncle Ye said that I've made the following improvements:

1) I have a sense of ball control and no longer rush to pass the ball to others as soon as I get it.

2) I have an attacking mindset and I can dribble to get around the defenders and put the ball into the hoop by using techniques.

3) My shooting motion is smoother, and I can make jump shots now.

4) For the first time in a confrontation, I tried to "block the ball" when someone shot it (that is, when someone is shooting, try to fly his ball without committing a foul).

**Comment**: *Wenxi's blocking action is extremely handsome, and this is also his first time successfully blocking someone in a competitive sports event.*

2. Ever since elementary school, whenever I was bullied, I would put something nasty (such as tartar) in the cup of the person who bullied me. Gradually, things changed, and putting tartar in someone else's cup became a habit for me. I gradually got used to putting tartar in the cups of all the people I came into contact with.

Eventually when I was putting tartar into Uncle Ye's cup again, he discovered it. I am ready to accept punishment, but Uncle Ye did not punish me. Instead, he reminded me that it is impolite to do so, and it puts everyone's health at risk, my parents, Mrs. Jiang, my classmates, Uncle Ye, Aunty Hao, grandparents, Xiaoyu, Xiaoyi, Lele, Aunty Liu... Uncle Ye said that I would be alienated if I didn't stop doing it. I really wanted to make changes at that time.

**Comment**: *Everyone in the family was disgusted by it for a week.*

In the evening, I couldn't help but put tartar in Brother Xiaoyi's cup. Uncle Ye was very angry when he discovered it and taught me a lesson. I cried and confessed all the mistakes that had been buried in my heart for many years. At that time, my heart was bleeding, as if hearing my former classmates scolding me. I thought to myself, "Never make such a mistake again."

Before I went to bed, Uncle Ye came to me and once again told me the importance of getting rid of this bad habit and told me: taking advantage of others never benefits ourselves! Safeguarding the interests of others is safeguarding our own interests!

I felt a warmth in my heart after hearing him, and I slowly fell asleep holding Uncle Ye's hand.

**Comment**: *This is the most epoch-making event in the entire educational process of Wenxi. It is known as the "tartar tragedy" in history. I firmly believe that there are a considerable number of people in mental hospitals who are not sick. They just dare not tell others that "I have recovered", because once they lose the label of "patient", their behavior needs to be reinterpreted. The term "mental illness", which is often avoided by ordinary people, has become a privilege for this particular group because it brings them privileges.*

*Some might say that I'm joking, but being called a psycho is humiliating. What are the privileges? Are the two words "mental illness" insulting or privileged? Don't be dissatisfied. Don't believe me. Put tartar in my cup and try it out. See what I do to you? Or let out farts in classes and see how the classmates treat you. "He's a psycho." A simple statement can solve all the problems, and that is the privilege. It is impossible for the "mentally ill privileged class" to voluntarily give up their privileges. Reasoning is useless, and all power is the result of struggle. There are only two paths in front of Wenxi: one is to admit that he is no longer the Wenxi with autism. That is the past and he needs to live a normal life. Okay, Wenxi, Uncle Ye has patience. The second is to continue pretending to be autistic. Alright, every time you make a mistake as an autistic person in the future, I will punish you in the strictest way in society! Because you are no longer Wenxi with autism. Heaven knows, earth knows, you know, and I know. Disguising yourself is useless.*

*So, without any hesitation, I used the most common way of teaching an ordinary person a lesson in society to deal with the "tartar tragedy"—I whooped his ass and told him that maybe he used to be autistic, but I can't remember well. All I know is that Wenxi is not sick now. If it ever happens again, the result will only be worse than this time.*

Wenxi laid in bed for the entire day the next day. After getting up, he pushed open my door and hugged me tightly, taking a deep breath. I understood right then, that Wenxi has made his choice. In fact, I also felt very sorry for Wenxi. I understand that it is not an easy task even for an adult to make a complete decision to bid farewell to the past, let alone for a teenager. It is better to suffer short term than long term. Let the inevitable come.

What was the result? Let's take a look at Wenxi's next series of progress! Let's take a look at the huge rewards of facing your own inner self in reality!

07 / 01

I used to sweat a lot every time I played basketball before, and when I got home, I could rub a lot of mud balls. I would intentionally or unintentionally throw these mud balls onto the carpet. Although Uncle Ye didn't notice, today I vacuumed all the carpets at home, hoping to make up for my mistake. I was so dedicated that I cleaned every inch of the carpets. I thought I could use a vacuum now, and I felt very happy in my heart.

**Comment**: *What a remarkable day! Wenxi took the initiative to identify a problem and solve it. This marked the complete end of Wenxi's passive changing and the beginning of his proactive changing, which took 39 days!*

07 / 02

In order to further improve my basketball skills, Uncle Ye supervises me to watch Zhang Weiping's basketball teaching course videos every day. I've learned a few things that I couldn't have learned in class. Uncle Ye has so many ways! Coach Ren was also surprised by my tremendous progress.

**Comment**: *This is called "A thought makes a world". When Wenxi chooses his own life again, he can make huge progress as a normal person. It was also from this day on that Wenxi began his transformation from a human being to a highly capable man, and from a stage of active change to a stage of mature mentality.*

07 / 03

Today, I went to the Liaoning Provincial Museum with Uncle Ye, Aunty Hao, and Lele to see the exhibition of ancient Shu exploration— the exquisite cultural relics unearthed from the Sanxingdui and Jinsha sites. I was extremely shocked by the bronze masks! Looking at them, I felt as if I had returned to the Yin and Shang Dynasties thousands of years ago. On the high altar were placed sacrificial cows and sheep, and two bonfires were blazing brightly. A priest danced beside the fire, reciting words. Under these masks, the king led his officials and presented gifts to the gods on behalf of the people, hoping that the gods would bless his country with prosperity and strength.

After watching the exhibition, Uncle Ye took us to Zhuozhan Shopping Center. I have seen many famous brands like Dior, Cartier... and so on. In the Louis Vuitton specialty store, I saw a keychain designed very exquisitely, and said to Uncle Ye: "That's probably gonna be over 400 Yuan." After hearing this, Uncle Ye smiled and asked the salesperson for the price. The salesperson said it was over 4700 Yuan. I thought, geez! I'm going to buy such good things for my parents and my future wife.

**Comment**: *Attention! Attention! I really wanted to use the biggest font size to write this paragraph! This was the first time that Wenxi mentioned the word "wife". A month ago, his relatives wanted him back to Shanghai as soon as they saw his learning ability recover. However, I asked them a question: What's the point of raising Wenxi? His mother said she'd be satisfied if Wenxi could take care of himself and study normally. I said that a man has the responsibility to prolong the family bloodline, and our education is a failure if he lacks sexual awareness towards women. Give me some more time! Wenxi's father walked forward excitedly upon hearing this and held my hand tightly. Accepting the old self, as well as having the concept of a "wife", marked that Wenxi's soul had grown to the level of outstanding peers, and he could return to Shanghai.*

Coming out of the shopping center at night, we set out on our way home. Although I was very hungry, I didn't say a word. I noticed that I had made some progress and stopped chattering about food. Later, Aunt Hao realized that I might be hungry and suggested eating. We drove back and forth on the streets of Shenyang and finally arrived at a place called "Chen Ji Dumpling King". We ate all kinds of dumplings, and I thought to myself: I haven't eaten dumplings like this for a long time.

After dinner, Uncle Ye told me to ask for the receipt and I only gave it to him when we were waiting at a traffic light. Uncle Ye said it was great progress for me. I am now able to seize the opportunity to do things. I thought to myself that I want to maintain this good habit.

**Comment**: *This is the longest diary he has written. He has no secrets anymore from the way he thinks in his diary, and he has unloaded all his burdens and is embracing the world as a brand-new self. At Zhuozhan Shopping Center, he began to show ambitions for things beyond food, feeling obligated to take care of his parents, wanting to buy good things for his future wife, and seizing the opportunity to do things on his way back.*

07 / 04

Uncle Ye has changed his way of educating me again. He asked me to watch a show called Brother's Happiness, and often replays some clips to analyze them, helping me understand the complex interpersonal relationships in the show. I think Uncle Ye's education is very effective for me.

**Comment**: *The society is formed by people, and the people live in the society. After Wenxi was determined to become a normal person, the most important lesson was to understand basic interpersonal relationships.*

07 / 05

1. Uncle Ye dismantled the combination trash can at home into parts, and I tried every means possible, but still couldn't fit it. Later, Uncle Ye helped me figure out the root cause of the problem, and told me to pay more attention to details, and I also believed that I should use my brain more when doing things.

**Comment**: *This was to train reverse thinking and meticulous hands-on skills.*

2. In the evening, Uncle Ye took me to see a fountain. I asked Uncle Ye if salt could undergo a double decomposition reaction with stomach acid. Uncle Ye stopped and said to me: "In daily life, we can have con-

versations about certain things in everyday life such as the weather, the scenery around us, what's happening in life, and even dietary habits, etc. Do not always talk about academic topics." After hearing him, I remembered a time in Shanghai when I was ridiculed by my classmates for not discussing knowledge in different situations.

3. Lele's high school entrance exam results came out. She got more than 20 points higher than the score line top tier high school. I was happy for her and decided to learn from her.

Comment: *Lele is my obedient daughter, who excels in both skits and learning, and has a wide range of hobbies.*

07 / 06

1. Uncle Ye has adjusted my educational plan. In daily life, I am constantly required to complete complex tasks and make plans before completing them, and then proceed according to the plan. My ability in this area is still very weak, often falling behind and making mistakes in my busy schedule. However, Uncle Ye has been encouraging me frequently these days, and my ability has improved very quickly. I think I can do even better.

Uncle Ye said that in the future, he would evaluate my performance every time I completed the tasks that he gave me. Calculated on a 5-point scale, the maximum score is 5 points. I feel that Uncle Ye's method is very intuitive, and I really like it.

Comment: *Wenxi is making progress extremely fast, and I need to adjust my educational methods almost every day according to his new state. I like change.*

2. Aunty Hao said that I have made a qualitative leap in my interpersonal skills, and I am very happy. Thinking to myself: In the future, new class-

mates will like to be friends with me.

**Comment**: *My wife has questioned the way I handled "the tartar incident", but now Wenxi's tremendous change has impressed her.*

3. Before, I farted a lot in Panjin, and the whole room smells bad of me, so Uncle Ye gave me a nickname, "Weird-smell Xi". The day before yesterday, he gave me a new nickname, "Man-eating Panda" to encourage my kind heart, adorable looking and diligent and courageous style.

07 / 07

I've been doing things on my own every day without any supervision. In the past few days, I haven't woken up on time and gone for a run downstairs, and Uncle Ye discovered it like a detective. I often wonder how Uncle Ye discovered it? Uncle Ye told me that he has radar in his mind. I know Uncle Ye doesn't have a radar in his mind, but he has a strong observation ability. I should learn from him.

07 / 08

Today, Brother Xiaoyi bought a big and sweet melon. He cut the melon into thick pieces and served it up. I gave the largest piece to Lele, which was praised by Aunty Hao. I also feel I can naturally leave good things for others to eat, unlike in the past when I would swallow them alone or endlessly pass them on to others.

07 / 09

1. Lately I have been forgetting to turn off the lights. Aunty Hao often reminds me to save electricity, and I do feel guilty about it. I should know how to save energy.

2. Ever since the "tartar incident", I have been washing my hands fre-

quently. Uncle Ye told me to wash my hands before meals, after using the toilet, and after taking out the trash, but not too frequently. Uncle Ye also reminded me that, "Don't pick your teeth, nostrils, or ears…"

3. My parents are coming to visit tomorrow, which will be their last time visiting me. There are about more than 20 days left, and I will end my six-month study life in Panjin. I feel like I'm not the same Wenxi who used to be timid and childish anymore. I'm a capable man now.

**Comment**: *Take a look at his words! Upon seeing Wenxi's words again, tears covered my eyes, and memories flashed back to my mind. Who would've thought that the loud noise of "I am a tall and capable man" came from the chest of an autistic child who was once despised and abused by classmates? What's the unforgettable moment in life? A moment to witness a miracle!*

07 / 10

Today my parents came to see me, and they were very happy about my progress. We were together yearning for a beautiful future. Then we went shopping together in New Mart, and I bought them a lot of delicious food using the scholarship I received at Uncle Ye's house. When they were eating the food I bought for them, I saw the relief on their faces. I heard from my parents that many people were greeting me, and my heart seemed to have suddenly returned to Shanghai.

07 / 11

I didn't sleep well last night. I tossed and turned all night for two reasons:

1. I may not be able to attend school temporarily after returning to Shanghai, and my dad said he was still making connections.

**Comment**: *Note that Wenxi began to refer to his father as his dad.*

2. I will be leaving Uncle Ye in a while, and I cannot bear to leave him. Uncle Ye told me not to be too sad, and that life is full of getting together and parting ways, and all we can do is to cherish the present.

**Comment**: *Wenxi, Uncle Ye is reluctant for you to leave, and I have been tossing and turning. Next door.*

07 / 12

The days before I return home are getting closer and closer. I have gradually increased my study load so that I could have a better performance after returning to Shanghai.

**Comment**: *Increasing the amount of learning is not what I requested. It was initiated by Wenxi. This is Wenxi's first automatic adjustment of learning intensity, gradually increasing his study load! This indicates that he has successfully stepped into the phase of proactive change, approaching excellent peers in mentality and steadily advancing towards the mature stage of mentality!*

07 / 13

In the near future, I will be able to meet my parents and dear Mrs. Jiang, and I miss them more and more by the day. Aunty Hao told me: "Progress is the best reward for family."

**Comment**: *From my diary, it seems that I have done all the work, but in fact, my wife Jianhua has done a lot of guidance and communication work on the side. We are like Fault Young and Miss Dragon, helping each other and wandering the world.*

07 / 14

1. Today Lele returned to school, and her school was going to hold a

red-carpet ceremony. Students who are admitted to key high schools should walk along a red carpet and go to the podium to receive awards. Seeing Lele standing on the podium with a certificate in hand, I thought to myself: one day I will have such an honor as long as I work hard.

**Comment**: *If one day I had resources at a world level, I would definitely take children like Wenxi to observe the Nobel Prize ceremony to let my students see the big picture and inspire their ambition to move forward.*

2. I spent nearly the entire day writing my literature exam, but when Uncle Ye noticed it, he asked me to stop and told me that it was only meaningful if only the task was completed within the time limit. He asked me to change my learning methods based on this principle. After listening to Uncle Ye's words, I thought I should do it quickly and well within the time limit.

07 / 15

Today, Uncle Ye asked me to go to the dry-cleaning shop to pick up the ironed pillowcases and bed sheets. However, I first remembered the address of the dry-cleaning shop incorrectly, and then remembered the items and quantity to be picked up. When Uncle Ye asked me to hand my phone to the dry-cleaning shop owner next to me, I instinctively hung up the phone. Uncle Ye criticized me, and I felt ashamed in my heart. I thought to myself, "How can we do big things if we can't do such a small thing well?"

Through this experience, I've learned:

1. In the future, we should pay special attention to time, place, things to be done, and the quantity and characteristics of things.

2. Be calm when doing things. Although there is still a gap in my ability to do things compared with my peers, I have made my mind to do it well.

**Comment**: *In this state, self-improvement has reached the most terrifying state among robots—writing programs and clearing bugs on your own.*

07 / 16

1. Today, Uncle Ye asked me to go to New Mart to buy toilet paper. When I arrived at the supermarket, I was overwhelmed by the various brands, so I casually bought two large bags of toilet paper. After I got home, Uncle Ye told me: "There is a concept called cost-effectiveness, which refers to the ratio of a product's performance to its price. When it comes to buying toilet paper, it refers to the weight and quality of paper that you can buy for every penny." Upon hearing that, I picked up the toilet paper and rushed back to the supermarket, only to find that I had forgotten to bring the shopping receipt again. I felt very regretful at that time. I hated my own incompetence. I went back for the receipt and bought two packs of tissue that have a high-cost performance ratio.

After returning home, I told Uncle Ye about my regret in my heart. Uncle Ye said to me, "Think more about what else we can do in the face of difficulties." He told me to be brave and strong, and quickly helped me improve my personal abilities through practice. After listening to Uncle Ye's words, I felt empowered and knew how to work hard. I must do well and make my parents proud of me.

**Comment**: *Oh, I'm touched.*

07 / 17

Today I went to visit my grandmother. I brought her food, poured water for her, and watched TV with her… Grandmother was very happy, and she praised me for being capable.

**Comment**: *Wenxi is very filial and shows great respect to the elderly. In* *this regard, my parents have played an indispensable role in educating and encouraging Wenxi.*

The teacher from the second high school provided high school tutoring for their children who were admitted to high school, and I also participated in this class as an observer. In English class, Aunty Hao asked some complex questions, and I received a reward of green tea from Aunty Hao for answering very well.

07 / 18

1. I said two inappropriate things today. Firstly, I pointed out that Lu Mingyu spoke impolitely, and secondly, I said that Niu Niu's father's car was too small. Uncle Ye found out and told me that there are three principles when speaking: "kindness, necessity, and truthfulness!" After listening to Uncle Ye's words, I thought to myself, "If only I had known earlier." Uncle Ye told me, "Pay more attention to the strengths of others." He also asked me to praise another person from four different perspectives. Uncle Ye has so many ways. If only he could promote it!

**Comment**: *That's exactly what I'm doing right now, Wenxi.*

2. I asked Uncle Ye: "How can a person be considered successful?" Uncle Ye said: "Everyone has his own job and responsibilities, and when a person does his job well, it is a kind of success for him. Wenxi, your current identity is a student, and the student's job is learning. Although we need to improve in many aspects, we are very strong in terms of enthusiasm, focus, and interest in learning. As students, it is important to learn well." Uncle Ye said he greatly appreciated me and appreciated the courage I had shown in overcoming difficulties. Uncle Ye gave me a new nickname, "Study machine-gun", which means "learning machine guns". I like this nickname.

07 / 19

1. I apologized to Lu Mingyu, and at that moment, I remembered the three principles of "kindness, necessity, and truthfulness" that Uncle Ye told me about. I thought to myself: if only I had known these three principles earlier! Sometimes I feel like Uncle Ye is like a spring, bringing hope to those who are close to him.

**Comment**: *Thank you for your praise, Wenxi.*

2. Today, I went to class at Second High School again. In class, the math teacher praised my strong understanding of mathematical problems. The physics teacher praised me for being diligent and able to learn, and I was very happy. I thought to myself: if I keep doing that, my teachers will be surprised when I return to school. Although I am only in junior high school now, I have developed a strong interest in senior high school life and am full of longing for it.

3. My parents replied to my letter, and they were very happy to see me writing to them in English.

*Dear Wenxi,*

*After reading your English, we feel that your writing has made great progress. Although there are some errors in writing and syntax, your expression of meaning is very clear. We are happy for you.*

*Whether it is an exam or completing an exam question or practice paper by oneself, it must be completed within the specified time. If it cannot be completed within the specified time, the purpose and effect required by the paper will not be achieved. If a person cannot complete the course within the specified time, they must also stop in order to measure their understanding* of the course. Moreover, if you don't understand a problem, spending too much time won't have any effect. Only through further review and understanding with classmates or teachers can these problems be solved. From another perspective, long-term use of the brain to consider the same thing can make a person's thinking stiff, lack flexibility, lose innovative motivation, and hinder a person's ability to think and solve problems. Uncle Ye is right. The time spent doing the same thing should not be too long, as it may be in vain.

Uncle Ye's request for you to go to the laundry to pick up something is a good test of what you are doing. No matter what you do, you must be fully prepared. Taking Uncle Ye's request for you to go to the laundry to pick up items as an example, first of all, you must bring a receipt or voucher (receipt) for picking up items, ask for the address and operating hours of the laundry, remember the name, characteristics, and quantity of items to be picked up, and figure out how many buses can be taken to the laundry. If necessary, you should use a pen to record these things one by one for future reference. Although this is a small matter, big things start from small things, and if small things are not done well, there is no opportunity to do big things. At Uncle Ye's house, you have received training that you did not receive at your own home in Shanghai. You should cherish every opportunity to exercise and gradually become mature. The success of doing something can make you feel happy, fulfilled, strong, brave, and confident.

In two weeks, you will return to Shanghai after half a year of living in Panjin. We look forward to your arrival and hope that you can make greater progress in the remaining two weeks, so that you will better adapt to future high school life, and that you can have the abilities to face the challenges in life and study, dare to challenge society, and eventually you can reach for a bright *future of your own.*

*Miss you*
*Father and mother*
*Jul.18, 2010*

In the letter, dad said:
—The time spent doing the same thing should not be too long, as it may be in vain.
—Be well prepared for anything you do.

I think that I should:
—Do one thing well within the set time limit.
—Cherish the precious opportunities of self-challenge.

07 / 20

1. During the literature class today, the teacher walked over to me and reviewed my classroom notes carefully. The teacher said that my notes were very detailed, and that I understood how to listen in class.

2. Today, there was a heavy rainstorm in Panjin, and the water in the river flooded the dam, leaving a vast ocean on the road. Uncle Ye took me to Brother Xiaoyi's house, and I helped him carry stuff on our way back. He saw me shivering from the rain and said: "Thank you for your hard work, Wenxi." He was proud of my performance tonight. Aunty Hao said that I'm a man now, and I thought that it was something I needed to do. I feel like that I'm already a member of Uncle Ye's family. This is what I should do as a member of the family. Arriving home, I took a hot shower and went to bed. I was so exhausted and soon fell right asleep.

07 / 21

Uncle Ye treated me to a sumptuous breakfast as a reward for my brave performance yesterday. Later, while moving the car mat, I accidentally dropped one of the mats into the water. Uncle Ye looked at me in frustration and said: "Don't blame yourself, Wenxi. Let's keep working on it."

07 / 22

Aunty Hao was going to Shanghai to study tomorrow, and I invited her to stay in my home. She was really happy and thanked me for it.

07 / 23

1. Mom's birthday is coming up, and I want to wish her a happy birthday in person.

2. According to Aunty Hao, dad is going to take me to the World Expo on August 1st. I'm really excited for it.

3. My parents and I video-chatted tonight. They told me to study hard in my last week at Uncle Ye's house, and I'm going to take the entrance exam to the middle school when I go back.

My parents also said, "Your relatives, former classmates, and teachers have all said hello to you." I was very happy. I felt like a different person from staying with Uncle Ye for the past six months. I am ready to go back to them.

07 / 25

I went to see grandmother today because I'm leaving in a few days. My heart is heavy, since I don't want to leave grandfather, grandmother, Uncle Ye, Aunty Hao, Lele, Brother Xiaoyi, Xiaojian, Xiaobo and everything here in Panjin. I have been cherishing my life in Panjin these days.

Tonight, I gave grandmother a foot bath and swept the floor for her. I was very happy to see her face getting better and better. Grandmother told me that Uncle Ye's entrepreneurial experience and years of education had benefited many students, and I felt Uncle Ye's greatness at that time.

**Comment**: *At that time, my mother had a bone fracture in her waist and was bedridden for recovery. Wenxi volunteered to give her foot baths every time when he visited. I was touched by him.*

07 / 26

During breakfast today, I asked Uncle Ye, "What are the nicknames I have in the past six months in Panjin?" Uncle Ye pointed them out to me in chronological order.

1. "Weird-smell Xi"

Before I went to Uncle Ye's house, I often casually farted and hiccupped. My fart was particularly smelly and often made my relatives and classmates unhappy. After arriving at Uncle Ye's house, I still casually farted, so Uncle Ye and his friends gave me a nickname, "Weird-smell Xi".

Later, with the help of Uncle Ye and my friends, I corrected this bad habit. During the Chinese New Year, when I returned home, my relatives and friends noticed that I didn't fart casually anymore.

2. "Shark Gang Leader"

When I first arrived in Panjin, I felt that it was a small city, and the people of Panjin were from small cities. So, when others gave me valuable advice, I often disdained it and sometimes even stared at the person who gave me the advice. Uncle Ye said that I looked like the leader of the shark gang. Later on, I realized that my attitude towards mistakes was my biggest enemy, so I humbly accepted criticism and suggestions from others. I found that since my attitude changed, my progress rate has been exceptionally fast. Gradually, everyone stopped calling me "Shark Gang Leader".

3. "Wen Bing Bing"

My movements were always uncoordinated, sometimes even reaching the point of femininity. Uncle Ye and friends corrected my posture in a timely manner. On the other hand, Uncle Ye started taking me to exercise.

Uncle Ye said that if my body lacks muscles, my movements must be uncoordinated. We had to run 4.4 kilometers every day. After completing the attention training every morning, I had to do 30 push-ups and 30 sit-ups. I went to the basketball court every other day to play basketball. I did all the physical work at home, such as moving the liquefied gas tank, helping grandfather load goods, sweeping the floor, washing dishes, wiping the table, and so on.

When I first arrived at Panjin, I looked weak and powerless when I walked, but now I am always in a state of excitement wherever I go. The last time it was hot and sweaty. I accidentally took off my shirt when I suddenly heard someone next to me exclaiming. It turned out that they had seen my two pecs and my six abs, and I was also surprised by the progress I had made. I didn't expect to become so strong under Uncle Ye's guidance. I think Uncle Ye's methods are really effective.

4. "Man-eating Panda"

This is a positive nickname given to me by Uncle Ye in Panjin. Uncle Ye gave me this nickname to commend my kind heart, adorable looking and bold style.

## 5. "Study Machine-gun"

This is my last nickname in Panjin. One night, while studying, Uncle Ye walked over to me at a certain moment. Uncle Ye touched my head and said to me, "A man should do his job well." Uncle Ye appreciated my progress in all other aspects while still focusing on and dedicated to learning. Uncle Ye said I will definitely succeed in the future.

These are the five nicknames I received during my time in Panjin, and I think the changes in nicknames reflect my progress along the way.

07 / 28

As I am leaving on the 31st, my grandparents are reluctant to let me go. Grandfather invited me to Xinglong 400 for lunch today. He ordered six dishes for me, representing grandmother in thanking me for everything I had done for her. He hoped that I could continue to improve upon returning home, achieve academic success upon returning to school, and get along well with my classmates.

Listening to grandfather's instructions and remembering how many people in Panjin treat me so well, I feel extremely grateful in my heart. Looking back on the six months I spent in Panjin, my grandparents helped me, and I couldn't forget their kindness. In the future, when I succeed in my study, I will come back to visit them.

07 / 29

Today was Xiaobo's birthday, and I wished him a happy birthday. I was about to leave the day after tomorrow, and I couldn't bear to part with Xiaobo. However, seeing that with the help of Uncle Ye, Xiaobo had found his life goal and was studying hard every day. I was happy for him from the bottom of my heart. At this moment, I remembered the time when I helped Xiaobo with his study. Every evening after dinner, in front of the desk lamp, he would humbly ask me questions. At that time, my language expression ability was very limited. I dumped all my thoughts out all at once, and Xiaobo was confused by me. It is so funny thinking about it now.

**Comment**: *On July 29th, Wenxi witnessed Xiaobo's transformation and began to accept his former self.*

07 / 30

1. After finishing basketball class in the morning, I bid farewell to Coach Ren.

2. Uncle Daliang came to Uncle Ye's house this morning and gave me a small wooden piggy bank as a souvenir.

**Comment**: *"Uncle Daliang" is my close friend. As my assistant, he went to the property management company in the noble community to investigate and successfully uncovered the insider information of the walking school. It was also because he was ambushed by Xiaomin at midnight and kissed six times, swearing not to engage in education again.*

3. In the afternoon, I took a shower and got a haircut. Then I went to Xinglong 400 to buy gifts for my dad, mom, Mrs. Jiang, and Mrs. Xiao. In the evening, Uncle Ye, Aunty Hao, Lele, Niuniu, Xiaojian, Xiaobo, and Xiaomin hosted a farewell party for me. The farewell party was great, and we took pictures together as a souvenir. I thought to myself, "goodbye, my dear friends!" I will keep you guys deep in my heart. After all, parting is for a better reunion.

4. After the farewell party, it was already late at night, and I couldn't wait to visit my grandparents with Uncle Ye. Grandfather bought me a shirt and a pen as a gift. Grandparents said they appreciated what I had done for them and for the family, and asked me to study hard, and apply what

I have learned here to my life in Shanghai.

5. Today is my last day in Panjin, and there are many "last times" today. Last morning exercise. Last basketball class with Coach Ren on the basketball court. Last time I ate the dishes made by Aunty Liu. Listening to Uncle Ye's teachings for the last time… My life here in Panjin came to an end like this. This end is not the end, but the beginning.

I'm going back to Shanghai tomorrow and start a new life there. I'm not afraid of what's coming. Because I have gained so much in Panjin, and I know that I'm walking steadily, and my future is bright!

**Comment**: *Wenxi, I hope everything goes smoothly with you in the future!*

09 / 01 / 2010
Wenxi returned to his original school.

09 / 15 / 2010
Wenxi achieved the fifth place in the class in the first monthly exam.

09 / 16 / 2010
Wenxi charged forward for the top three.

07 / 2011
Wenxi was admitted to a Middle School Affiliated to a Normal University.

06 / 02 / 2014
Five days before the college entrance examination, and in the world's largest exam, Wenxi will compete with 9.39 million peers, like a normal child.

# Chapter 9

## Can Anyone Find
## His Goals in Life?

### 1. Twilight of the Idols.

Autumn. Late autumn.

Old temple, sunset, and sickbed.

An elder, and a youth.

Bell rings die away, and people are about to part.

"Let's get going."

"But who's the enemy?"

"It's not a person."

"What is it?"

"It's a kind of feeling."

"Is it loneliness?"

"Loneliness makes one self-sufficient."

"Is it pain?"

"One cannot have happiness without pain."

"So, what kind of feeling is it then?"

"Anxiety!"

What's there to be anxious about?"

"What's your being taken away, and not having what's not."

"So, no one can escape it?"

"Sure."

"Who?"

"The wholehearted ones."

"The wholehearted ones?"

"Yep."

"What are they like?"

"Let me tell you a story that you've never heard about. It all started from that one night."

## 2. Give me back my life.

When Youqing's mom came back through the front door, Youqing's dad had already made four dishes.

"Came back so early today, huh?"

"I made some of your favorite dishes. I think we should have a talk."

Youqing's dad pulled out the chairs and poured two glasses of wine. The wine's color was rich, and it looked like blood through the glass.

"Let's finish this bottle."

"I thought you wanted to talk."

"I want a divorce…"

Youqing's mom was about to pass out, while five-year-old Youqing shouted with a smile: "Kangxi!"

Mr. Jia*: "What's that about?"

One month before, Youqing's mom took him to the children's hospital for a common cold. She had no idea that fate was going to laugh in their faces.

The pulmonologist suggested that they should go to a psychiatrist. 30 minutes later, Youqing's mom rushed out of the hospital.

A few weeks later, the whole family went to see a top psychologist at the Peking University No. 6 Hospital.

Youqing's mom held his hand when they left the hospital but couldn't say a word.

---

*Mr. Jia, Ph.D in Education and Psychology, Harvard University, first assistant of Mr. Ye's, known as the "Yang Talent".

Youqing's parents had no idea what had happened to him, which has become a myth to them since that day.

Arriving at home, Youqing's mom sighed while staring at her son, thinking about the life ahead.

"Whose fault was it?"

"Mine." said Youqing's dad, whose voice was heavy with guilt.

Last meal together, clinking the glasses only made a sound of heartbreaking.

"I want a divorce." Youqing's dad said, "You can start another family while you're still young. I'll take care of the kid alone."

The heart only showed itself when it was broken. Youqing's mom couldn't hold her tears back anymore. She hugged her husband and burst out crying.

The next day, the two of them locked fingers. The bond was as strong as ever.

The next year, Youqing started school. He was in the most prestigious school, with the best teachers. They taught him everything he should learn. Every morning, he went to school, same as usual. At noon, he went to his auntie's for lunch and napping, as usual. He got out of school in the evening, as usual. His mom would help him with the homework while his dad read a book next to them after dinner, as usual. And during weekends, he would have one on one tutoring, all as usual.

A decade passed by in the blink of an eye. Youqing's parents gave it their all, in order to maintain the situation of "same as usual".

In these 10 years, Youqing's mom became riddled with wounds in her heart. She felt helpless. She was not weak, although her resistance became her tragedy. She didn't fail like a rationalist because she never acted on reasons, but rather on emotions. However, she would become clueless when things were above her intuitions. She often asked herself late at night, "Why did I give birth to a child like this? Why me?"

In these 10 years, Youqing's dad became a workaholic. He had love because he believed that blood is thicker than water. But he also felt the bitterness because of his egotistic pride. If one loses hope and faith, one can only keep pushing, wholeheartedly.

One only finds comfort and compromise behind love and bitterness.

Though, the nature is always cruel. Whether it was in the classroom, the school field or restroom, Youqing was always bullied. He had never tried to hide away. Instead, he always faced it calmly with a smile.

The education he had received proved unsuccessful. He had only learned to read a few characters, mostly on his own.

It was a dead end after the nine-year compulsory education. Through connection, Youqing's mom found Principal Jiang, who was fishing on the Qinhuai River of Nanjing and was well known for seeking out paths.

Principal Jiang had developed an instinct to handle dire situations through his experiences. He always had advice right to the point. Even though Youqing's mom tried to pretend things weren't as bad as they were, the principal gave his advice with seriousness, "it seemed that only Ye Zhigang could handle your situation."

———————

"Why did she pretend things were alright?" Mr. Jia asks.

"The society judges based on whether you're successful or not," says Mr. Ye, "success paints over an action with the brightness of kindness but failure only shows the shadow of guilt even when it is an honorable act. She had her reasons."

"So were you reliable back in the day?"

### 3. Sadly, even you have fallen by the side of fame and fortune. Even you are an outcast.

He was reliable back in the day.

He entered the education field at the age of 21 and was considered one of the best even when he first started.

Confidence was developed through experience. Besides confidence, he had also built integrity through 10 years of dedication.

However, loneliness was nearly unbearable to him.

Frederick the great once said, "A title is a decoration on the head of a fool. A great man needs nothing but a name."

Ye didn't understand it back then. He came to Beijing and managed to become a head teacher of Young Business Leaders Class at School of Economics, Peking University, merely for the title.

All his students had a pent-up fire in them. However, he saw it as scenery in the wild even if they acted not that good.

But the students that he had now were like lost sheep requiring guidance from him.

He thought they were humbling.

And he felt more lonely than ever before being amongst them.

Life is the present and the past. One is meant to experience it again and again, without exception, in the same order.

However, one can only see the results of a few things.

To him, life was abstract, and everything felt the same.

His mental health was in crisis.

The others thought he was picky. Though he had a great career and friendships, they were not what he wanted. He felt empty inside.

He was also considered immature. But he thought maturing was simply a label given by people to the ones that followed the norms and rules.

That's when one truly loses oneself.

To him, maturing is when someone finds the true self, and develops his own character.

He couldn't leave the position because it was too difficult to let go of the fame.

After all you fell for wealth and fame, he thought.

After all you were surpassed. Such a tragedy.

A prisoner would only have the courage to tear down the cage once he realizes that it was he who built it in the first place.

He was waiting for a sign.

———————

"Any advice for me to earn money?" Mr. Jia asks.

"The money you earn should include the appreciation of your ability, your worth and your innovation. Not one less." Says Ye, "To me, missing any part would make me feel guilty of receiving it, and I'd do anything, even tearing down what I've built, to avoid the guilt, without any hesitation."

"So what kind of person were you trying to turn someone into?" Mr. Jia asks.

"I wanted to help someone to become useful for the society." Says Ye, "Someone who can help the society move forward. That person should have the courage to challenge himself and would always look forward and never give up."

"Did you ever see the sign you were waiting for?"

"Yes, that I did."

## 4. Re-evaluating the incurable

One day I received a call from Principal Jiang, inviting me to meet with a family of three at Meizhou Dongpo Restaurant.

My life was divided into two halves—before I met Youqing and after, ever since that day.

Three years later, Youqing's mom remembered that day. "On our way home from the restaurant, Youqing's dad said he'd like you to help the child because you looked wholehearted to him."

"How was he so sure about it?" Asks Ye.

"He said you were observing Youqing all the time and didn't even eat much." Says Youqing's mom, "He thought you were reliable."

"But what did you think at the moment?"

"I was shocked when he said it. I didn't know you at all, so I didn't want to make the decision."

"So, who did?"

"He said he trusted you, and it was settled right then. I didn't understand but who would've thought it turned out like this. It's always the man who makes the big decisions. I wonder what he was thinking."

"It's difficult to truly understand someone. He trusted me because he was willing to."

———————

"What do you mean by that?" Asks Mr. Jia.

"Human nature is as complicated as a maze. She thought she understood but in fact she only felt familiar. We often mistake familiarity with understanding, but understanding something familiar is the most difficult."

"She said you were observing?"

"Yes, I was trying to see if I really liked the kid."

"Did you?"

"Not really, but he wasn't annoying."

"Was it really important whether you liked him or not?"

"I think it's necessary to only teach the kids that you like, even when it's only schoolwork. The results might be disappointing if you can't accept each other." Says Ye, "A lawyer can defend someone who's guilty of a crime, or a surgeon can operate on someone that he or she doesn't like. But if a teacher wants to be effective on the student, the student should be gravitated to the teacher at some level."

"You mean instinctually?"

"Yeah, or more like if he has what I am seeking in a student."

"I thought his mother did a great job introducing the situation."

"I never let other's opinion get between a student and me." Says Ye, "I always try to learn about them on my own during the first meet."

"So, what now?" Asks Mr. Jia.

I tended to start the process by investigation, so I went to visit Youqing at his home.

I was surprised to see he was having tutoring when I arrived.

He was playing with his arm hair, while giggling and murmuring some gibberish. The tutor looked awkward.

After a while, he suddenly stood up and rushed to the restroom.

CHAPTER 9

He glanced at me when he walked past, so I decided to investigate further.

---

"What got you interested?" Asks Mr. Jia.

"I saw him having some mental activities from his eyes."

I asked Youqing's dad to arrange a visit at Youqing's school in order to check on him.

Next day he introduced me to his teacher. I went up to the teacher, bowed and shook her hand, "I'm Youqing's uncle. It's nice to meet you, Mrs. Mo."

She pulled back her hand as she was about to shake mine once she heard Youqing's name, "I'm pregnant, please excuse me."

"You will not get hurt shaking my hand."

"I have to leave now. Go wait in the room straight down the hall. I'm quite busy."

I went down the hall and found out the room was a water room. The humidity invaded my nasal cavity aggressively. As I was in a daze, I heard music playing. Thousands of students left their seats and started moving. It was the Monday flag raising ceremony.

I stayed in the building, saw everyone gazing at the flag with respect as it was raised, and thought how I was supposed to find Youqing in such a crowd?

I didn't need to.

A naughty boy stood out from the entire school. He put his palms together while facing the sun and mumbled with a mystery smile. The sun cast a shadow behind him.

I saw unparalleled freedom within this incomparable awkwardness, as if there was a new hope in the unprecedented darkness. That was when I knew I was going to take him in as a student.

"Why did you make up your mind only from that instant?" Asks Mr. Jia.

"You could give your students everything, Mr. Jia, except for one."

"And that is?"

"Courage."

"How come?'

"Because it is inherited."

"What's this courage? It is how someone is willing to fight against the world for something one cherishes."

Youqing is unique. He's unparalleled, since he's self-transcendent.

Standing upstairs, I observed Yongqing in the distance. He's so original but somehow purer, more passionate. It is his nature, while it is the nature that consumes him, preventing him from becoming who he was meant to be. It's an illusion unless I help him to rid of his chains.

I'm the wind to a dandelion like him.

"Is courage the most important to you for a student?" Asks Mr. Jia.

"Yes. Or bravery."

"And what do you think about when you meet a student whom you like?"

"I think about their future."

After I went back to Beijing, I began to expect Youqing's arrival. But I didn't hear from him or his family in two weeks of time. I was deviated and lost all appetite. I asked Principal Jiang to get in touch with him, and it turned out that he was preparing for the Zhong Kao, the entrance exam for senior high school.

"Is that even necessary?" I asked the principal.

He laughed, "you'll have to wait for another two weeks."

Three years later, Youqing's mom asked me during a phone call, "Mr. Ye, can you guess how many points he got in the Zhong Kao?"

"How many points did he get?"

"20 points in total, seven subjects."

"Any thoughts on that?"

"My son had wasted nine years in school. The whole nine years!"

Eventually he came. In the evening, 16-year-old Youqing sat with crossed legs and bare feet, and wrote in his diary:

*Last night dad took me to a bath house. I got into my red slip-
pers and went into the dressing room with dad. I took off my
pants, put on my watch and went to the shower. Before shower
I weighed myself. I weighed 100 kg and dad weighed 300 kg. I
went into the shower room, turned on the shower, and then I
rinsed my head, which wasn't itchy. I also rinsed my butt, and
my butt felt tight.*

*Then, I held a towel and got on a tiny bed. After I laid flat,
some uncles came to scrub my back. I got out of the tiny bed
and soaked in a big water bucket. At that moment, lots of men
came to the big water bucket for a bath while holding some
cold bracelets. I watched the news while bathing. Surprisingly,
the water in the bathhouse was kinda murky. I did that.*

*Then I went to brush my teeth in the sink. I used blue Colgate
toothpaste, and I felt my teeth got whiter. And I shaved with a
razor today, and dad got angry at me.*

*Then I put some Q-tips in my ear, and there was earwax on the
cotton ball. I couldn't hear the voice of the Kangxi Emperor, so
I tossed them in the trash, then I went home.*

*This morning, I and dad and mom took a car to the station to
wait for the train. When we got inside the security used a device
to check my height, then I turned around, the security used
the device to check my back. There were a lot of people on
the train. We were all pushed against each other. It was lively.
What a hassle!*

*Then, I went to pee. While peeing, I locked the door, so that
others couldn't see me. After peeing, mom went. I stayed on
the side and didn't wander off.*

*Going to Beijing, I felt happy. There was a lot of people watching TV on the train. I closed my eyes, without looking at anything. I was scared of the timestamps. There were three ad signs outside of the train. They were "China Petroleum" (CNPC) "Tesla Cars" "Panasonic". These ad signs were interesting and left a deep impression on me.*

*There was a wanderer lying on the floor. He's poor, getting nowhere to live, whom I should take after.*

*We got to Wanquan Xinxin Jiayuan. I listened the adults talking carefully and didn't cut them off. I was pretty humble.*

*Uncle Ye's apartment was really big, way bigger than mine. Kangxi!*

*Then I went to eat. I had a bowl of congee. It's even better than soy milk. I think congees are nutritious.*

*Then I cleaned the silver bowl. I turned on the faucet to rinse the dirty stuff of the bowl with water, and then the bowl became clean.*

*I didn't know I had silver bowls. I went to look for them when I read this part. I didn't find any.*

Anyone would be concerned about questions like, what's happened to the child, who can diagnose without bias or who can I trust, if they ever find their 16-year-old child writing like this in the diary.

Based on this I went back to the doctor whom Youqing's mom visited 10 years ago. After a 51-minute consultation, we made three conclusions:

Firstly, Youqing has the following nine characteristics:

1. He doesn't listen when spoken to.
2. Talks like an infant.
3. Spaces out alone.
4. Talks to himself, and repeats names and advertisements.
5. Repeats actions even when they lead to punishments.
6. Doesn't obey or hold a grudge when he does.
7. Can't maintain friendships.
8. Gets lost in unfamiliar environments.
9. Obsession over certain things.

Secondly, he has attention issue.

This is treatable with medications. However, at the age of 16, it'd be extremely difficult to return to a normal level.

Thirdly, Youqing's IQ is lower than 46, and it's not necessary to use medications.

Other parents came over to comfort me: "I'm sorry man, but your situation... it's untreatable. This is science. Our kids are done for."

———————

"What were you thinking when you heard that?" Asks Mr. Jia.

"I was like so what is untreatable? It doesn't guarantee a tragic life, doesn't mean he can't live, can't have a job, can't find love or have kids. It doesn't mean his life is worthless."

I'm going to redefine "untreatable".

I stood in the hospital lobby, taking a look at Youqing. He was giggling and murmuring next to me. I have never thought what an exciting life we were about to experience together.

"What would you say to me if I had met a kid like him?" Asks Mr. Jia.

"We all lose if the next generation loses. Take your love and creativity to your loneliness, Mr. Jia, and happiness will find you on the way."

**Day 18**

It was already dark when I got back from the hospital. I had made my own conclusion for the past 18 days:

Youqing's failures are all vital failures because he is unable to learn any lessons from them.

Also, he has no will power, since his will power is his habit. But he lacks what most people have, namely inconsistency.

Habits are his worst enemies.

We had to start right away. So most of our impactful trainings started at that night.

At that night we initiated the fundamental training, since fundamentals are essential to each one of us on this earth. The chief ones include sleeping, eating, bathing and excretion.

At that night we initiated attention exercises. He was able to keep a high level of concentration by Day 439.

At that night we initiated posture exercises: standing against the wall for 30 minutes each day. He stood tall with confidence after being consistent for five years.

At that night we initiated physical exercises: doing push-ups and running. His mental health and physical health were improving at a similar pace. By Day 549 he was able to do 20 perfect push-ups.

At that night we initiated exercises on promptness: cleaning the bedroom and the restroom, shadowing me, shopping and paying bills, taking out the trash, taking the mail, greeting guests, getting hot water to soak feet before going to bed, massaging, checking the door lock, turning off the stove and lights before going to bed, and so on so forth.

Also at that night I initiated nightly investigations. I was able to achieve more at night when we lived together. I've made surprising discoveries from three years of nightly investigations.

My abilities are reflected by my creation, as well as my destruction. That night, his "four treasures of study", including a tiny white cap, a flashlight, a fan with the portrait of the ten founding marshals of the PLA and a children's keyboard, were all thrown in the trash. So were the medication bottles for his rhinitis and the simple luggage that he came with. I wanted him to have a complete fresh start. Later on, his tiny watch was also nowhere to be found.

From that night, I was dedicated to keeping the rules, even if by force. I was alone in it, but I knew I was correct.

If I couldn't enter his world, may as well bring him into mine. Make the most basic rules and run with it. It was surely challenging to our will power, but we'd make through if we believed.

I had only one simple rule in my world:

Reward and punish according to the right-wrongs.

And all of my actions were based on these four principles:

1. To fight against any wrong thoughts or actions with consistency;

2. To create hard-earned success constantly;

3. To be a role model;

4. To change someone with action and criticism.

Since then, Youqing started a life revolving mine. I gave him a purpose in life. I rewarded and punished accordingly. Every right and wrong was answered by me.

5. From incompetence to mediocrity

The most troublesome characteristic of Youqing was that it seemed like he didn't listen when spoken to.

What do I do?

At first, I thought it was an attitude issue. Maybe he didn't want to respond. But he remained the same when we fixed his attitude. It had to be his attention span, I thought. Then, after he was able to keep his attention, I found that he was actually having trouble in understanding.

It's impossible to for him be like the regular kids if he doesn't improve on his intelligence.

**Day 69**

I decided to start intelligence exercises.

I asked other family members of mine to go on a vacation and turned off my cellphone. It felt like a lab of loneliness within my 4m by 5m home library, isolated from the rest of the world. Any deficiency became free from blame or guilt due to the lack of comparison.

We sat in front of the desk in our new shirts and shorts, looking at each other. I realized we didn't even have any textbooks.

Looking at Youqing, I remembered a stage comedy.

Zhao Benshan: "I'm to give a brain teaser for the three-year-old."

Fan Wei: "Not the three-year-old ones. I dare you to give me some for the four-year-old."

I took out my phone and bought the following children's book.

1. *Baby Fun to Find Difference (3–6 years old)*, published by New Century Press
2. *Baby Fun to Navigate a Maze (3–6 years old)*, published by New Century Press
3. *Brain Potential Development (5–6 years old)*, published by New Century Press
4. *Left Brain Development (5–6 years old)*, published by New Century Press
5. *Whole Brain Upgrading Training (5–6 years old)*, published by China Population Press

The books arrived three days later. Then officially we started the intelligence training.

———————

"This is so fantastic, Mr. Ye." Says Mr. Jia.

"I cultivated students by using my own method, and I also learned from all of them." Says Ye.

"Thinking back now, I remembered a quote from Walt Unsworth's Everest:

One of the great benefits of having no experience is that you are not bound by tradition or precedent.

To the novice, everything seems simple, and he will choose the most direct way to solve the difficulties he faces. Of course, this usually keeps him from success, and sometimes causes tragedy... However, it is because they are not limited by any limits that firm faith drives them far, far away.

But I would never have thought about how difficult it was going to be."

It took Youqing an entire day to solve a simple math problem from 10 am to the evening. My head was completely blank. Every second of the intelligent training was suffering to both my mind and body.

It took us two days to solve a Sudoku puzzle that was meant for preschool children.

We sat at the desk for two whole days. It felt like I was losing my mind, and I was desperately in need of two tools commonly used in animal research: a radio collar and a sedation shot.

Then we spent another three days on a parent–child pattern puzzle.

"He finally did it, Youqing's mom. It took him three days."

"Nice job, Mr. Ye!"

"That was nothing. Even the bees understand the concept of zero, and monkeys can count to Four. It's not a problem for Youqing."

Youqing's mom was speechless.

"Are you still there, Youqing's mom?"

"Yeah... did he figure it out on his own?"

"Yes."

"I was wondering, Mr. Ye, what if he didn't solve it after three days?'

"Well, then we would spend another three."

"What if he still can't?"

"Then we would spend three more days, until he does."

"How are you so sure that he was going to solve it?"

"I chose to believe."

Suddenly Youqing's mom started crying over the phone.

A pattern puzzle designed to boost kindergartners' confidence glued us to the desk for five whole days.

> The air around us is getting thinner, and it must be remembered that it is impossible to be conscious at 8,848 meters above sea level.

> —Jon Krakauer*

———————

*Into Thin Air, Zhejiang People's Press, 2013.

Finding the pattern based on a few simple graphs took us seven days. In these days it felt like my chest was under heavy weights. Then it was seven more days on a maze.

> *I was in extreme pain and had never been so exhausted in my life. My throat burns, I can't feel my breath at all... I can hardly go on.*

> *No despair, no happiness, no anxiety. I have not lost control of my feelings, in fact, I no longer have feelings. All I have is the will.*

> —*Transparent Horizon*, by Reinhold Messner

**Day 101**

The intelligence test results came back from the hospital: IQ 58.

Youqing's mom sent an E-mail to my wife:

> Mrs. Hao,

> ... *This result is so exciting, amazing as well. I don't even know where to start. Mr. Ye is such a great teacher, and I'd never thought that his teaching was able to change a kid in such an incredible way. Thank God, thank you! Youqing can be saved...*

Saved? Not yet.

"Finding Differences" "looking at pictures to find rights and wrongs" "Ordering the pictures and making stories" ... 16-year-old Youqing was stumped by these Pre-school puzzle games.

> *The sun is setting, the feeling of loneliness arises, and I seem to*

*have put life and death on the line. I knew I had to do my best to fulfill my mission. But sometimes I wonder if the trek is just to confirm the fact that I can find something I've lost.*

—*Everest: The West Ridge*, by Thomas Hornbein

Finally in that instant, Youqing backed down.

During the night on Day 117, Youqing was playing dumb and was not taking it seriously. Day 118, Youqing said casually but firmly, "I found it!"

But I insisted on staying disciplined. Mrs. Hao was feeling depressed during these dreadful days.

As the day passed, Youqing needed to make the answers after understanding the rules of the questions. The exercises were proved to be a dead end when math mixed with literature.

*The higher I climbed, the less important the goal seemed to me, and the more indifferent I became to myself. My concentration was slipping, my memory was failing, and my mental fatigue was far greater than my physical fatigue. How pleasant it is to sit still by yourself. Even if the life is taken now, it is very pleasant.*

—*The Transparent Horizon*, by Reinhold Messner

**Day 156**

The intelligence test results from the hospital: IQ 108.

I got a message from Youqing's mom:

Mr. Ye, I can't thank you enough. I've had countless heartbreaks because of Youqing's situation. So much scorning, but I'd never thought of giving up, since something tells me that the kid would get better. That's why we met. I knew you could make it, and I knew there existed hope for him.

Details of the grueling training can be found in Appendix 1 of the Chinese version of *Salvation Lies Within*, published by Tsinghua University Press. One has to exert his best to look like making a light work of it.

———————

Mr. Jia: "That's amazing. Any more intelligence exercises after his I.Q. reaches 108?"

Mr. Ye: "No."

Mr. Jia: "Why not?"

Mr. Ye: "Being smart alone is not enough. He should have enough wisdom not to be too smart. According to my observation, once passing the average ratings, the higher the intelligence gets, the lower the leadership goes."

Mr. Jia: "He has leadership?"

Mr. Ye: "Yeah. A series of events proved it. But they happened after that unfortunate evening."

Mr. Jia: "Unfortunate evening?"

Mr. Ye: "Yeah. It was known as the Waldorf Stormy night."

## 6. The Waldorf Storm Night

I should've been proud to see his intelligence recovered. After all, over-coming the obstacles, we've done the impossible. But the performance he was putting on wiped it all out for me.

After knowing her son's intelligence recovering to a normal rating, You-qing's mom rushed to Beijing. I made the following plans:

We had lunch together at a hotpot restaurant at the Apm Mall, and then I showed off my achievement to the parent at a steaming atmosphere. We checked in at the Waldorf Astoria Hotel, and Principal Jia and I would take in all the praises from Youqing's mom in the Peacock Ally.

But what I didn't know was that Youqing, like a coin, had two sides.

**Day 157**

After staring at his mom for five seconds, Youqing started giggling and talking nonsense like a clown. He started picking his nose and plucking his arm hair very seriously, and then started moving as slowly as possible and asked a bottle of liquor to liven things up.

Youqing's mom was starting to look like a red rabbit and desperately wanting to see the improvements on his son.

The steam from the hotpot flowed in the air. Youqing tilted his head and gave me the side eyes, as if saying, "My mom's here. What are you going to do with me?"

After lunch, we met Principal Jiang at the Peacock Ally. Youqing got even worse. He kept repeating, "KANGXI" "ZERO SEVEN", and at-tracted all the attention of the guests. The face of Youqing's mom turned pale as Principal Jiang had all sorts of doubts and conjectures in his mind.

Eventually, Youqing's mom stood up, "I'm very disappointed", and left.

What she didn't know was that being disappointed was far from enough.

I walked her out. By the time I went back inside the hotel, Principal Jiang was barely sitting still.

It was getting late, so I suggested that we have dinner together.

While on the way to dinner, Youqing became even more unorthodox.

He bumped and pushed a petite lady right against the siding of the elevator. Her shoulders were shaking but couldn't make a word. As she fought her way out of the elevator, she turned around and shouted, "I know exactly who you are! How did you stoop so low! What a shame!" Principal Jiang and I stepped to the sides as she spoke, making sure to be distant from such a monster.

The door of the elevator closed. Youqing giggled sinisterly, as if he was laughing at the world that he had just pranked.

After we got to the restaurant, Youqing sat down while murmuring to himself. He did that only to keep his mouth busy. Principal Jiang didn't want to look at him anymore, and my mind was only focusing on the food.

When we were leaving, Principal Jiang said casually. "Alright, Youqing, keep up the good work."

"Good bye, Uncle Jiang." Youqing answered with his child's tone.

"Alright, whatever…" the principal gave me a complicated look, turned around and left.

Things had already happened. I thought I could still do something about it.

Getting back to the room of the hotel, I took off my shoes, and set them on the floor. Then took off my belt and rolled it. Having hung my shirt and pants and put on Mozart's "Canzonetta Sull'Aria", I tapped a towel around my right hand.

"Come and check this out, Youqing."

Man can only remember the endings.

"My bad, Uncle Ye, I'll change." Youqing breathed heavily, like a fish on the shore.

If one returns from death, one must have friends in high places.

Later that evening I received a text message from his "friend".

> Don't be sad, Mr. Ye. You've already made a miracle. It's not easy for Youqing either. Your emotions are important to him. Although the devils are mighty, we'll have to infiltrate little by little, and it's impossible to defeat them instantly. It's cracking, and we have to be optimistic.
>
> When I said I was disappointed in front of him, I only wanted to push him. Actually, I was optimistic, especially after reading your work diary and seeing the kid's improvements.

Looking at the text, I asked Youqing:

"Whose fault was it?"

"Mine."

"What was the problem?"

"I needed to be disciplined."

"It had to be my fault."

"Nothing was your fault."

"Then whose?"

"It was all mine."

"What's next then?"

"We will take things seriously."

---

Mr. Jia: "Why did he change back to the old ways only after looking at his mom for five seconds?"

Mr. Ye: "Because her bottom line for him is that she loves him unconditionally no matter what he is. And one is only strong when it's vitally necessary. That's why he went back to it right after seeing his mom.

You know the differences of his actions between being with me and being with his mom were dramatic. Every time he became depressed for a long time when coming back to me from home, also because of this reason.

But don't forget that his mom was remarkable. She's gradually waking up. She was also maturing in the course of our battle. She went from "Mom and dad love you no matter what you are" to "Being disappointed". She felt like "Youqing was getting picked on" and then "Youqing needed to be disciplined". Finally, she felt like "Don't ever come back if you keep acting this way". Youqing was also growing rapidly alongside his mom's growth, and eventually overcame the shortcomings in front of his mom.

Since that day, Youqing would tell me before going to bed: "Good night, Uncle Ye… it's not your fault."

Mr. Jia: "Is it so important for him to say that?"

Mr. Ye: "Yes, it is. Remember No. 6 of the nine characteristics of his that I concluded before?

He doesn't like to obey or hold a grudge when he does.

They are friends of the earth, and they believe that family and friends are supposed to ignore your shortcomings. So their resentfulness towards the critics is inherited. This is their commonality.

That's why I want them to make the statement out loud, making sure to hold themselves responsible, without grudges."

Mr. Jia: "Dang…"

Mr. Ye: "It's not only him, Mr. Jia. Please remember that people always are strong when it's vitally necessary. Let's use our intelligence to create such necessity, in order to create success."

Mr. Jia: "Do we really have to go head to head?"

Mr. Ye: "Tt is an old misconception that it is said to be a more effective way to rely solely on rewards than any other therapy in treating exceptional children. Indeed, one might not make any mistakes that way, and someone likes me might go down the wrong path being harsh and strict, but I'm more honest and sincere, and my attitude towards life is correct. Those who rely entirely on rewards may not make mistakes, but their attitude towards life itself may be a mistake."

Mr. Jia: "What did Youqing's mom mean when she said devils?"
Mr. Ye: "She thought that the devils were messing with Youqing. She entitled me of 'devil fighter' four years later."

Mr. Jia laughs, "What do you think of a parent of faith like her?"

Mr. Ye: "If one doesn't believe in anything, one might not believe in everything."

Mr. Jia: "What do you believe in?"

Mr. Ye: "I believe in myself. Believe in yourself as the strongest shackle, the harshest lash, and the hardest wing."

Three weeks after the Waldorf Stormy night, Youqing sent a letter to his parents:

> Father, I'm well in Beijing. Uncle Ye has sacrificed a lot for me, but I still babbled names when I saw mom. These were my enemies. I wanted these people to become my friends, but also caused other people's disgust. They didn't want to make friends with me, so I will stop babbling names. I will earn mom's respect, thank you mom.

> Father, you stayed in Stanford for 11 days. Did you study hard?

> Mother, I want to change. I want to be better. I want to make improvements. I want to be better. I want to make improvements.

Youqing's mom wrote back:

> Remember, son, you are the master of your own life. Don't feel
> sorry for Dad and mom whenever you make a mistake. We love
> you, and we hope you do the best of yourself. We love you no
> matter how you are. Anyway, you are Dad and Mom's good
> boy we love.

------------

Mr. Jia: "She loves her son unconditionally for sure."

Mr. Ye: "To love a child is something even a hen can do, and to educate
a child well is the art of getting love right. It is true that this love makes
Youqing love in his heart, but Youqing uses this love, unconditionally
instead of necessartly. But one is only strong when it's necessary.

Not only in Youqing, ancient human and animal nature, and even the
whole prehistoric era, still exist in modern human, making their influences. We're still taking tiny steps along the evolutionary path from ape
to man. Willfulness makes one happy more than any profit."

Mr. Jia: "What's your plan after the intelligence exercises?"

Mr. Ye: "There are some capabilities that I find vitally important:

Planning capability: the ability to make step-by-step plans to achieve a
goal or complete a task.

Organizing capability: the ability to place items in an orderly and organized manner.

Time management: assessing the remaining time of a task and how to al-
locate it, as well as the ability to complete a task within a limited amount

of time, including the understanding of the importance of time.

Work memory: the ability to memorize information while finishing complicated tasks, including using previous experience to complete current tasks or develop solutions to future problems.

Reflective cognition: the ability to understand one's own situation in a bird's eye view, or the ability to evaluate and solve problems alone, including self-monitoring and self-evaluating.

Reaction inhibition: the ability to think before acting. It makes us able to control our impulsive behaviors, taking the time to evaluate the current situation, as well as evaluate the impact of our actions.

Emotional self-regulate: the ability to regulate emotions to complete complicated tasks or take control of guiding behaviors.

Task initiation: the ability to start completing a task alone, no procrastination.

Adaptability: the ability to adapt and modify plans when facing setbacks, obstacles and new information, including the ability to adapt to the ever-changing environment.

Purposeful persistence: the ability to persist in completing a task or reaching a goal without being distracted by other things."

Mr. Jia: "Oh my god, that's lot of abilities to train."

Mr. Ye: "The above abilities have a collective name: executive power. Youqing likes to daze and fantasize, so improving execution is the key."

Mr. Jia: "How long is it going to take? It seems like a lot of work."

Mr. Ye: "Not really, don't trip over these fancy words of psychology. One simple activity is good enough to improve his execution."

Mr. Jia: "Which one?"

Mr. Ye: "Mopping the floor."

Mr. Jia: "How is mopping going to help? Is it that magical?"

Mr. Ye: "Because it requires him cleaning the tiles one by one, from the first one at the south-east corner to the very last one at the north-west corner, which is a great planning ability exercise.

He has to move the things out of the way, like the pots, chairs, iron, vacuum cleaner and so on, and then put them all back to where they were once he finished, and he has to put the mop and the soap back to where they were once he cleaned the mop. It is intended to train the organizing skill.

He has to finish cleaning the entire 400 square meters within the set time, which is to train his time management skill.

He has to figure out the mistakes he has made from the last session, find solutions to make improvements and to avoid the same mistakes, which is to train his work memory.

When he finishes mopping every day, he has to check on the floor and evaluate how he did. Whether he spaced out or daydreamed, he then reflected on the result of his work, which is to train the self-reflection ability.

And he can't just pick up the mop without thinking, but he has to consider what mistake to avoid beforehand, as well as take control of the bad habits to make the best work, which is to train his reaction control.

When he makes a mistake and is criticized, he can't have negative emotions. Instead, he has to approach with a positive attitude and keep pushing towards the goal. He has to finish the task within 150 minutes, which is to train his emotion-regulating skills.

He has to start mopping willingly at the same time every day, without procrastination. He does what needs to be done when it needs to be done, which is to train the initiation skills.

When any unexpected event interrupts the task, like when the doorbell rings and a package arrives he has to go back to where he left after signing for the package. He even needs to improve his efficiency to make up for the lost time, which is to train his adaptability.

While mopping, he needs to ignore the chattering of the others, and sometimes save the fruits given by the elderly until after the task is done. He has to think about nothing other than finishing the task as well as possible to the best degree, which is to train his purposeful persistence.

All these exercises concluded collectively are known as the executive power training."

Mr. Jia: "What are the considerations behind your design?"

Mr. Ye: "People build and restore themselves by doing physical work. Youqing's upper limbs became tools to conquer the environment That's how he built his confidence. He used his bare hands and dug himself out from the illusions and nonsense.

People are not born with value but exist based on the value we can provide to others. The others can live in a clean environment because of Youqing, which grants a meaning to his life.

Squatting and bending constantly while sweeping is the best way to overcome arrogance and let go of one's ego. Touching the dirt and dust on a daily basis, the differences between beauty and ugly, clean and dirty, self and others gradually lose their meanings. That is how he's truly able to shine."

## 7. People eventually die, and the sun eventually cools down.

We start to ask a question no matter what type of training is conducted:

What's the ultimate goal of training Youqing?

The answer has to be for him to fit in the society.

But somehow people always falsely believe that children can be made into adults simply by teaching them indoors.

Society is the real school. The education of Youqing cannot be isolated indoors, but to lead him to temper in the society.

So, I led this ignorant boy with an IQ of 108 to carry out a long-term social practice, which I called "social education". We spent totally 649 days in five phases. (See Appendices 2-6 of the Chinese version of *Salvation Lies Within* published by Tsinghua University Press.)

Day after day, I kept using our hard-earned success to stop Youqing from going back to his comfort zone in daily contact with the society, leaving him no other choice but to suffer in the difficult situation. The only way out was to rush towards the unknown.

People are only strong when it is necessary.

He had nowhere to go.

It was too hard. The problem with Youqing was that every single day was brand new to him. My happiness was rooted deep within my disappointments. When I sought, he ignored. When I found it, he got lost. When we succeeded, I failed. Right when we built a little confidence, I lost it right away. I wanted improvements, but right after we made a little progress, he went right back to the origin the next morning.

The only highlight was the occasional flash of inspiration. Otherwise, it was completely darkness.

But who's to blame?

If anyone was at fault, then anyone was as innocent as Youqing.

I had a feeling, though, that in the midst of all this, there was a big educational opportunity brewing.

And the opportunity showed itself eventually on that morning.

**Day 409**

I'd go to Youqing's bedroom to wake him up every morning, and he'd reply: "Good morning, Uncle Ye."

But he didn't respond to me this morning, his eyes lost.

In my mind, an insight burst out like a lightning.

I dashed out of the room, feeling the joy and the immense tension that could be relieved by deep breathing. I made a rule: from that moment on, I wouldn't speak if Youqing didn't. No more telling him to eat, no more telling him to drink water. I quickly emptied the house, shut off the phone and changed the mails to other addresses. There were only two of us in the house.

Youqing got out of the bed and walked to a chair sluggishly and sat there for the whole day until 21 o'clock. He couldn't stop yawning, got up and went to his room, and slept deeply.

I moved the chair he was sitting on to the lobby for easy observations at night.

## Day 410

He got up without anyone waking him up and walked out from the bedroom, found the chair and sat on it until 21 o'clock again. He started yawning wildly, then got up and went back to his room to rest. There were occasional tosses and turns at night.

## Day 411

He sat on the same chair all day once again.

It had been three days. Neither of us had a drop of water or a grain of rice. The weather was so hot, and Youqing almost stank for sitting on the chair for so long. (It was a top-tier item in my collection.)

Later that night I made a call to a doctor.

"What's the longest limit someone can survive without food or water?"

"Are you trying to challenge the human limits, Mr. Ye? In this hot weather, it might be okay without food, but it'd be easy to get heat strokes without water. And it'd be hard to predict the outcome once you get a heat stroke."

I was almost dying of thirst and started to worry. So, I made a huge decision:

Officially I would surrender to Youqing the next morning.

But what if he surrendered first? While observing him in the dark of the night, I found him tossing and turning so much that his back was getting scratches. So, I made four pictures overnight.

**Day 412**   In the morning

I came to Youqing's bedroom door quietly and listened, but it was only quiet inside. The door unexpectedly opened as I was pushing on it. You-qing leaned against the door frame, his face pale and lips dry. He spoke to me softly:

"Uncle Ye...le...let's ea.... eat the desserts on the table..." he pointed at the dining table with his finger half curled.

I felt a daze with excitement.

"Oh, you want to eat? No rush. Let's take a look at a few pictures."

Youqing smelled rancid and stinky, walking to the computer desk with me.

"How long has it been since you last ate?"

"Three days."

"Do you know how long you can survive without food?"

"No."

"Three day and a half. That is to say, once the clock hit 12 at noon, you'll drop dead with a 'clang' sound, and this is science. And it has been three days, right?"

"Yes, I don't want to…"

"Don't worry. You still have a few more hours. Just hold on a second. Let me show you what happens when you die."

"I don't want to die…" Youqing shook his head.

"No so quick. Let's look at the first picture of you after you die. Your body would be loaded in a body bag and get taken away by an ambulance."

"I don't want to die." Youqing kept shaking his head.

"This is the second picture of you. You would be tossed into a freezer in the morgue until you're frozen solid." I tapped on the table with my knuckles, and Youqing gasped, shaking his head desperately.

"And this is the third picture, where your parents come from home to see you off for the last time and send you on your way, crying over your dead body. You see that tag that's hanging on your left big toe, with your name on it."

"Dad and mom… send me on my way…" Youqing murmured affectionately.

"Your parents will definitely blame me for not taking good care of you, but is it my fault? There's food on the table, but you don't eat it. There's water in the bottle but you don't drink. You kill yourself. How will it be my fault?"

"It's not your fault!" Youqing was getting a little emotional.

"Giving birth to you is a mistake, which will take your parents their lifetime to correct.

Everyone is trying to get rid of you, but we're all too nice to kill you, so we have to take care of you in the spirit of humanity. It's such a relief that you committed suicide. Thanks to the heavens, we're all saved.

Your parents are in their mid-40s, with great careers and healthy bodies. A year and something later, they will get another baby boy, and the whole family are so happy that they cannot stop smiling. Now take a good look at the fourth picture. It's everyone having a party to celebrate the Full Moon for the baby's one-month-old at your grandma's."

"…" Youqing was in complete shock.

"What's more, the baby is also named Youqing, and he plays your piano, sleeps in your bed, wears your suits, and he's growing up strong and healthy with the love of your parents, your grandma and the whole family.

Oh by the way, he's not an idiot. Actually, he's incredibly smart. He goes to the same school as you did, his grades are so good, and your former class teacher Mrs. Mo likes him very much. He's made so many friends in school, and he goes to your auntie's for a nap every day after lunch, and the family read and play piano happily every night after he finishes homework.

Uncle Ye is also saved, though I might be sad for a little while, but you committed suicide so it's not my fault, and finally I get to teach normal kids instead of dummies, and Uncle Ye lives a happy life ever after.

But you, you died for nothing. Nobody remembers you because there is a boy called Youqing who is living happily. You're like a grammar mistake that is quietly erased by everyone."

"…" Youqing didn't say a word, his fists clenched.

"Don't worry! There are still a few hours left. Goodbye, Youqing, go ahead to die."

"I don't want to die!" Suddenly Youqing became furious and pushed the keyboard off the desk. He stumbled to the dinning-table and desperately shoveled bread into his mouth.

I did it.

I felt a sudden rush of blood in my head, and quickly lay down.

After calming down for a moment, I walked to the dining table. Youqing looked up at me, tears in his eye. I asked him:

"Do you want to live or die?"

"I want to live."

"It's your choice to live, Youqing. However, it is not the purpose of life. The purpose of life is to live confidently, live nobly, and live courageously.

We don't want to live passively but want to take the initiative to do things and become strong.

But how do we do it? We should try our absolute best to do every single thing in life, from morning till night, thinking of nothing but doing it well, and to the best. Do you understand?"

"Yes, I understand."

"You need to memorize what I just said."

"... I just did."

"Then say it."

"We should try our absolute best to do every single thing in life, from morning till night, thinking of nothing but doing it well, and to the best." Youqing said with a dry voice, sounding almost miserable. He looked at me with full attention, a drop of tear slipping down from his eye.

"I'll tell you one more thing, and you need to memorize it as well."

"Okay!"

"Say it now."

"The best things all belong to my generation and myself. If they're not given to us, then we'll take them by ourselves: the most exquisite food, the clearest sky, the strongest will and the most beautiful woman."

Youqing's voice trembled, and he expressed the pain and desire buried deep within him that he'd never revealed to anyone before. Once these words came out of his mouth, he burst out crying.

I stretched my back and found myself covered in sweat because of the excitement and fatigue. I decided to weigh myself and found out I was four kilograms lighter than before. The person in the mirror in front of me looked strange. Thinking back on the past few days, I suddenly remembered something Malcom X said:

If you're not ready to pay that price, don't use the word freedom in your vocabulary.

———————

Mr. Jia: "That was such a great educational timing, but how do you look for them?"

Mr. Ye: "You use your intuition."

Mr. Jia: "And how do you develop such intuition?"

Mr. Ye: "It originates from addiction.

When you live with your student, try not to let him leave your sight when awake. The way the student breathes, and acts will leave their mark in your head day by day, until you develop the educational intuition.

It's only developed through long-term distress, and the meaning of its existence only reveals occasionally to the ones who seek regardless of the difficulties."

Mr. Jia: "So what exactly is the timing we're talking about?"

Mr. Ye: "It's abnormality. When things go into an abnormal state, that's the very time when we make the abnormal helpful for the education.

All secrets lie within taking hold of this timing."

Mr. Jia: "Why wouldn't you speak if he didn't speak?"

Mr. Ye: "The premise of the existence of life is that all lives strive to survive. He'd die if he didn't speak to the others. And if that couldn't push him to change himself, then nothing could. And if so, he should've been fed like an animal instead of having been educated."

Mr. Jia: "Why did you push him using death?"

Mr. Ye: "Death is the highest awareness. The root of the tragedy for Youqing and, even the entire humanity is that they live like they're immortals.

Death is extreme. And when one is put in an extreme situation, it accelerates the speed of the self-awareness development. The depth of the awareness is proportional to the extremeness of the situation.

On the surface, it seems that Youqing struggled with abilities, but the nature of lack of ability is lack of attitude, the attitude towards death, which directly determines the attitude towards life.

As a teacher, the primary task is to help students understand that people eventually die, and the sun eventually turns cool."

This was what happened from Day 409 to Day 412. In those days, the two protagonists of the story suffered from hunger and thirst, and their minds were in a trance. So, I call those days "the days above the cloud".

"The days above the cloud" is a turning point for Youqing. The soul of Youqing has been deeply imprinted, and the energy emitted is endless for his lifetime.

"The days above the cloud" brings out two traits in Youqing's nature: initiative and persistence. And there is an idiom in Chinese that corresponds to it:

One should strive continuously to strengthen oneself.

Its spirit is the essence of all virtues. With such spirit, in the next 649 days and nights of social education, Youqing has made great progress in society.

Youqing's mom concluded:

Youqing was willing to learn new things. "I demonstrated once, and then he did it on his own, but pressed the wrong button, so he started over and did it correctly the next time." (Day 470)

He also volunteered to do housework. "After dinner, he'd actively gather the chopsticks, wash the dishes and wipe the table." (Day 471)

His ability to form cogitations improved. "He's even making jokes with us now." (Day 475)

He saw kinship more importantly now. "Youqing actively prepared hot water for his parents for foot bathes, even massaged my feet…he wanted his dad to stay home… he'd ask if we wanted to eat anything before he eats…" (Day 477)

He's willing to challenge himself now. "For the first time he took the bullet train alone from Panjin, Liaoning Province to Taiyuan, Shanxi Province to visit his parents."

He had social morality now. "… he gave his seat to other people on a bus." (Day 534)

On Day 659, Youqing's mom wrote in her journal: "His dad and I believe that he has become someone who's beneficial to the family."

Youqing's parents were also changing. They're no longer the parents that only knew how to love Youqing unconditionally, knowing nothing when it came to other details. They grew with Youqing and eventually became the master of their lives.

Over 600 days and nights, winters and summers, the weak, lost child became a strong handsome young adult.


## Day 640

Youqing sent a WeChat message to his parents on his 18th birthday:·

Uncle Ye told me that my birthday is mother's suffering day. Thank you for raising me for the past 18 years. I'm going to keep working on myself with Uncle Ye, so I can become a real man.

Youqing's mom cried out of joy.

What a beautiful moment. People hate the unpredictability of life, and we all wish the beautiful moments in life could last to the end, to the very last second of life. However, compared with the unpredictability, people hate how life always catch us off guard and how things would happen out of the blue.

## 8. There are three powers above the horizon that can conquer the hearts.

**Day 806**

I received a phone call from Youqing's mom: it's time for Youqing to return home.

Later a letter from Youqing's dad:

Mr. Ye, Mrs. Hao,

You have invested so much effort in Youqing in the past two years, which helped him make such a dramatic change in himself and benefited a lot for his lifetime. Youqing's mom and I will be forever grateful, and I believe that Youqing will regard you as a family member for the rest of his life.

**Day 807** 9:00 am

The final moment was here.

At the entrance of the train station, Youqing said to me:

"Goodbye, Uncle Ye." Then he turned around and started walking into the station. Suddenly he turned back around and reached out his right hand, grabbed my left hand and said respectfully while looking at me in the eyes:

"Uncle Ye, let me shake your hands!"

Two men hugged each other tightly without a word, the way soldiers hugged each other before a battle and before they died. The hug means much more than any emotion, speech or tear.

**Day 808**

For Youqing, my conscience was clear.

**Day 809**

For Youqing's parents, my conscience was clear.

**Day 810**

My gut told me: "Stop lying to yourself. If the letter from Youqing's dad meant that you did something right, then Youqing's leaving all out of a sudden meant you did something wrong."

My ego told me: "So what?"

**Day 811**

You know the feeling that the people are there, you could've called or messaged, but you just can't help deleting whatever you type out, only because of the lack of a decent reason?

# CHAPTER 9

**Day 812**

Never mind. Getting to meet and know someone always happens when we least expect it, and parting is always long planned. Too many stories finish without an ending. It is what it is.

**Day 813**

I heard a voice saying: Youqing's parents are idiots.

And another voice saying: How could they be idiots?

**Day 814**

I wrote a poem for Youqing.

**Day 815**

Don't bother them. It'd be embarrassing giving an emotional speech.

**Day 816**

I was able to let go of anyone during the day, but not at night.

While lying in bed, I kept thinking about the unfinished educational blueprint of mine. The regret was so strong, like ever-expanding bubbles emerging along my spine from somewhere deep in my heart.

**Day 817**

People always become rigorous and solemn only after the catastrophe happens.

Early in the morning, I bounced off my bed, sat in front of the desk and tried to retrieve every single detail from being with Youqing's parents from my memory.

I looked through the journal and kept asking myself: What needs of theirs were neglected?

I couldn't find an answer.

I kept thinking until the sun came out. Then I had another doubt: What did they say that made me feel the most repulsed?

I remembered this very quickly:

"In the days to come, would it be possible for Mr. Ye to consider letting him continue to learn the piano?"

For details, see Appendix 2 of the Chinese version of *Salvation Lies Within* published by Tsinghua University Press: Training is important, but that's only half the story.

## Day 818

11 days after Youqing's departure, I picked up the phone and called his mother.

"Hello, Youqing mom, is it a good time to talk?"

"Sure, Mr. Ye. Actually, I've been wanting to call you..."

"I think Youqing is a genius." I interrupted her.

She went silent for a second.

"I think so too. But, Mr. Ye, which subject do you think he's gifted in?"

Youqing's mom was excited.

"What's your thoughts on it?"

"I think he's a gifted piano player."

She was serious. She sincerely believed that her son was a piano prodigy, because Youqing was able to make out some simple melodies on the piano for his favorite songs heard on TV. With this, she firmly believed that her son was a prodigy.

I gazed out of the window, the disappointing image of Youqing playing a children's keyboard came to my mind. I gathered myself and said:

"Oh, that's exactly what I thought. He is a piano prodigy."

"Do you really think so?"

"Yes," I gulped, "and I'd love to have the opportunity to show you that your son is truly gifted."

"Great, I'll send him back tomorrow."

---

Mr. Jia: "What was your motive there?"

Mr. Ye: "I remembered this. One year, Zhang Jianhua, the assistant to the president from Hong Kong Sunwah Group, sent me the draft proposal from his friend Lei Tianliang, a deputy to the National People's Congress at the time, hoping that I could help improve the proposal by combining my understanding in the process of educating special children and certain social investigations.

So, I took Youqing to a special need facility next to a village for the survey.

I asked him before we entered the village:

'Do you remember what you looked like before?'

'Yeah.'

'Show me.'

He thought about it for a second and then hunched his back and started giggling, while murmuring nonsense with his elbows flared out and fingers curled, walking as a turtle.

"Good job, keep at it, and from now on I'm your uncle and you're my elder sister's child. Got it?"

"Got it, you're my uncle." He poked me with his finger.

"Let's go."

I started shouting once we had entered the village:

"I need to rent a room!"

All kinds of landlords showed me different rooms passionately, and also grandly presented me with the privacy of their tenants'.

I couldn't help but notice that they were full of gloomy, lifeless self-depreciation and self-denial in their personalities.

# CHAPTER 9

There were anxious parents everywhere, waiting for the training. They scattered in every corner of the village.

A lot of parents stayed in the village and wouldn't go home even after the training. I asked them why, and they said that they're treated as outcasts in their hometown for giving birth to children like that. They were sinners in the past life. While in the village everyone had a child like that, they were considered normal.

They had to leave home to be considered normal. What a shame! Hopefully the peace seeking hearts were able to find it there.

They stopped putting their strength and intelligence into development and improvement. Rather, they lived on numbly, even unconcerned.

I walked among those people, but I felt like I was walking in between human fragments and limps. There were only broken pieces, limp and dreadful misfortunes as far as the eyes could see, not a single human in sight.

Early morning, an old lady was making breakfast in the kitchen with old style stoves emotionlessly, her grandson sat on the bed and the mom sat next to the child hopelessly. The dad was a truck driver who would only be home on the first day of the lunar new year, and then left the next morning after dropping off some money. I asked this old lady about her head space, and I'd never forget her answer:

"I'm dying with a huge regret."

How could someone feel that way when they were still alive!

The ones who were favored by the heaven should do good deed for the heaven.

From that moment on, I made up my mind to find a way out for the people who felt the same as the old lady.

Also from that moment, whether Youqing succeed or not was not meant for himself anymore. Instead, it became a great adventure.

The goal of the struggle was not for an individual. Rather, it was for the entire human. There's no other instinct that's older, stronger, colder and more uncontrollable than this.

'I think your son is a genius.'—such a lie existed because of love, which made people have something to look forward to, only to finish the adventure without shame."

Mr. Jia: "Did you think Youqing's mom was going to believe you before the phone call?"

Mr. Ye: "Yes."

Mr. Jia: "Why?"

Mr. Ye: "One always tended to believe whatever he/she desired."

**Day 819**

13:22, Youqing appeared in my sight.

He ran over to me, saying: "Hello, Uncle Ye. I'm Youqing! I'm back!"

As I was about to start a new adventure with Youqing, another incident happened.

I was able to resist anything but temptation.

The wife of a chairman of a listed company contacted me. They were willing to pay me 16 million Yuan each year, alongside of a luxury apartment on Chang'an Street, a vacation house in the suburban area with a housekeeper and a Mercedes SUV with chauffeur available, as long as I would agree to be the mentor of their son.

The sole reason that she chose me was that I had helped their "little prince" steal an airplane from a military base in a video game after he failed for months. He took me as his idol.

However, this elegant lady implied that she had one single condition: I had to get rid of Youqing.

She said that they understood the connection between Youqing and me, but she wouldn't be able to sleep well knowing her son had to grow up with someone like Youqing.

She also said that she knew I wouldn't send Youqing away for money, but money could solve all problems of inequality. Money was freedom in physical form, and she believed that it'd be well enough in the name of freedom and equality.

I respectfully refused her, because she didn't know that Youqing's parents were able to provide more.

––––––––––––

Mr. Jia: "Were they really able to give you more money?"

Mr. Ye: "No, but they could give me things that others couldn't."

Mr. Jia: "And what's that?"

Mr. Ye: "The first thing in the morning for them was they prayed for my health towards the direction of my home. I mean, every day.

Mr. Jia: "I feel like there's something else."

Mr. Ye: "You're right, Mr. Jia, I wouldn't expect less from a Ph.D in Psychology, Harvard. There were our truths, fears, fatigue and selfishness in the justice that we believed in.

The main reason I chose Youqing was that I wanted to change the world and find a way out for the ones who believed that they were dying with regrets.

I've already made my mind, and nothing could make me change.

Mr. Jia: "Do you pity them?"

Mr. Ye: "If you are truly strong, there would be no doubt that you had endured hardships, and there would be no doubt that you know about the value of the hardships. Then you hope the others wouldn't run away from such hardships, so, out of respect for others, you don't show empathy easily.

Indeed, human suffer from the most extreme hardships. The deeper the suffering gets, the more someone understands life, and one experiences and enjoys life to the fullest during the hardships. So, the secret to achieving greatest happiness in life is to live in hardships and the battles fought against life itself.

The best way to comfort a sufferer is to let them know that their suffering is inconsolable, and such respect towards them will push them to solve the problems on their own.

Therefore, the greatest help is not to sympathize, but to arouse the heart of self-respect and self-improvement of the sufferer.

Mr. Jia, we don't want to be sympathizers, we want to be creators, and solve problems creatively."

## Day 823

Youqing and I started our journey once again. This time we aimed to prove that he's truly a piano prodigy.

## Day 824

14:30, I turned off the computer.

15:01, I picked up the phone and made a call.

15:30, I met Mr. Hu at a warehouse behind an activity center for the elderly near the Longtai Oil Extraction Plant in Panjin, Liaoning Province.

Mr. Hu had a pair of clear eyes. He moved agilely and neatly, and he spoke straight to the point like a sharp edge.

I told him that Youqing wanted to go for the piano 10th level test.

"Do you like playing the piano?" Mr. Hu asked while he was playing on the keys.

"I do." Youqing smiled.

Mr. Hu: "Can you play any songs that qualify for the 10th level?"

"Nope, never learned." Youqing spoke straight to the point, like a sharp edge as well.

Mr. Hu: "Can you play something that you're good at for me?"

"Sure!" Youqing then sat in front of the piano with excitement.

Suddenly he started singing loudly: "The wandering man is missing you from far away from home, dear mother!" Then he stuck out his right hand and played, la so la la, four chords without hesitation. That was, and I gave him a high-five to celebrate.

Mr. Hu was confused, with all sorts of doubts and conjectures in his mind.

"Is that it?" Mr. Hu frowned his eyebrows, flicked away a dandelion seed that landed on his arm.

Mr. Ye: "Yep."

Mr. Hu: "You wanted to pass the 10th level test with that? This is an art form, and it takes years and years of practice..."

Mr. Ye: "I humbly recommend that you buy one of my books and maybe we can talk after you read it."

**Day 829**

Mr. Hu called.

Mr. Hu: "I finished the book that you recommended, Mr. Ye."

Mr. Ye: "Can you describe it using one word?"

Mr. Hu: "Miracle."

Mr. Ye: "Do you want to create your own miracle?"

Mr. Hu: "Sure."

Mr. Ye: "You, together with Youqing, would be that miracle."

Mr. Hu: "I'll see you guys at the piano room."

Two hours later, Mr. Hu came to believe that Youqing actually was capable of passing the 10th level.

Mr. Hu: "Are you confident that you'll pass the test, Youqing?"

Youqing: "Yeah!"

Mr. Ye: "Never underestimate those who overestimate themselves, Mr. Hu."

Mr. Hu laughed: "Haha, I see, Mr. Ye."

---

Mr. Jia: "You found him a teacher in such a short time! That was a legend Mr. Hu, right?"

Mr. Ye: "Yeah, any advantage was advantage in efficiency."

Mr. Jia: "Tell me, how did you find him?"

Mr. Ye: "There were around 102 piano teachers within the city limit that I found online, and I was about to call all of them one by one, and Mr. Hu was the 8th on the list."

Mr. Jia: "What's the difference between Mr. Hu and the first seven?"

Mr. Ye: "All of the first seven talked about money first when picking up the phone."

Mr. Jia: "And what about Mr. Hu?"

Mr. Ye: "The first thing he asked was whether the kid truly loved playing the piano."

Mr. Jia: "What's the reason of going for the 10th level directly?"

Mr. Ye: "Because I wanted to prove that Youqing was a genius, and only geniuses had the privilege of reaching the limit in one go."

Mr. Jia: "How did you know that you were able to convince Mr. Hu?"

Mr. Ye: "Most people live ordinary lives but they always want to go beyond that, believe me."

Mr. Jia: "And how did he even believe what you said about him and Youqing could be the miracle?"

Mr. Ye: "I can give you an answer with Mr. Hu's words: Mr. Ye has the spirit to drive others to follow his grand ideas. He's able to keep an irrational belief in the goals that are against the common sense, and to cling to them almost crazily. Facing him, people would say, "oh, he's crazy. We cannot ignore him."

One of his characteristics is that he doesn't care about the outcome and turns a blind eye to the oppositions of others. And that was why I admired him so much that I chose to join him on this journey."

Mr. Jia: "Why were you so confident in Mr. Hu?"

Mr. Ye: "Because he was ready."

One night 30 years ago, a female teacher at a county middle school in Heilongjiang Province, came home and told her husband that she was pregnant. The husband was nervous and said that they'd already had one child, and according to the policy, one was the limit. They had planned to go to the hospital and have an (induced) abortion the next morning, or they'd be fired from work.

The next morning, once the bedroom door opened, Mr. Hu's parents saw their daughter holding a bright kitchen knife around her neck and said, "Mom, if you get an abortion, I'll end myself right here."

Mr. Hu used to say that it was his elder sister who gave him his life.

Hu's mom gave birth to Mr. Hu secretly in a village at his second uncle's, where he was. None of the relatives liked him, since they all thought he was troublesome.

Five years later, his aunt said to his uncle: "It's him or me. One has to go."

So, he was secretly sent to a Shaolin martial arts school that was freshly established in Heilongjiang, and a decade passed by in a blink of an eye.

One day, Mr. Hu heard sound of a piano by chance on the street and fell in love with it right away. He wanted a piano, but his parents made so little money and couldn't afford it. He was so lost in the thought of learning to play the piano that he walked nine kilometers on the back country road to visit a piano teacher. His grandfather felt sorry for him and bought an antique piano from a warehouse of an elementary school. It had 88 keys, but 48 of them didn't bounce back when pressed. He moved the piano to the room on the street, though it was cold in winter and hot in summer, surrounded by mosquitoes and flies, during which Mr. Hu was bitten too much. But love was love. He was obsessed with no regret.

One day, in the martial arts school, he was practicing standing on a log.

The teacher called him over and asked about his plans for future. He didn't have an answer and the teacher told him to ask his mother.

His mother said: "Let's take the high school entrance exam. (Zhong Kao)"

Mr. Hu was surprised to hear that, "Mother, for the past decade I had only learned martial arts. How am I supposed to take the exam?"

His mother said: "We'll try to find some connections."

And he thought his life was going to change for the better.

On the first day of high school, everyone had to take a placement exam. The teacher handed out the paper to everyone in the class but Mr. Hu. When he asked why, the teacher said: "What do you even know?"

"You should give me the paper whether I know anything or not."

"Why would I give it to you if you don't know anything?"

"And how exactly do you know that I don't know anything?"

"If people like you can make it to college, I'd let you ride me like a donkey across the school field!"

Mr. Hu was so pissed that he slammed the desk and jumped up. The corner of the desk fell.

"I'll let you ride me like a donkey if I don't make it!"

That night when Mr. Hu went back home, he kneeled before his mother and vowed to study hard and go to college. His mother couldn't help crying and got up in the middle of the night and covered all his textbooks to keep them like new.

Three years later, Mr. Hu was five points away from the Harbin Institute of Technology. Instead, he was admitted to the Daqing Petroleum Institute.

And he thought his life was going to change for the better.

The son of a college leader was in the same age as Mr. Hu. He was arrogant in any way possible. He had heard that Mr. Hu came from a martial arts background and decided to challenge Hu on a daily basis. Mr. Hu had to endure the continual bullying for the entire four years of university for a smooth graduation.

Hu also practiced playing the piano during his free time, and eventually earned a decent place in one of the national piano competitions. He was granted to visit Germany for further study.

And he thought his life was going to change for the better.

He called his mother, saying the plane ticket would only cost about 2000 Yuan if he took connecting flights through a few other countries. He wondered if he could borrow the money from her to pay it back once he started making money on a work-study basis in Germany, but his mother said: "Son, the purpose you attend the college is to get a nice job and live a better life after you graduate, isn't it? You should focus on study right now."

Mr. Hu almost couldn't hold back the impulse. He had sighed in his dormitory bed all night long until the sun rose.

At the mid-autumn party, Mr. Hu first demonstrated his Shaolin Boxing technique, and then changed into the suits and played one of the Nocturnes by Frederic Chopin. He had won over the heart of a female student in the lower grade.

After their marriage, his father-in-law bought them an apartment, and helped him to get a decent job in the Liaohe Oil Fields.

And once again, he thought his life was going to change for the better.

Most of his colleagues went in late and left early most of the time, and Mr. Hu had to be the one who actually did the work.

Others were credited when the job was done nicely, but he was the one to blame when the job was done poorly.

"I wasn't there, boss! It was Hu." They said to him.

Mr. Hu was frustrated at work, and thought his happiness was at home.

Some of the relatives from his wife's family trusted him very much, to the point that they made him do every little thing possible without showing appreciations. At a Chinese New Year's Eve dinner party, after one of his wife's elders publicly compared the careers of the two grandsons-in-law, Mr. Hu was so embarrassed that he stumbled back outside the house, punched the door, and left with a broken hand.

Yet, he thought that his son would bring him happiness.

The baby liked being cradled and rocked when sleeping, and he would lash out crying when the rocking stopped. It's so loud that the entire building was able to hear him. The maternal grandparents were in another city for medical treatment, and the paternal grandparents didn't retire at that time. The young couple were left to take care of the child without any help. Mr. Hu had to work during the day and look after the baby at night.

# CHAPTER 9

What a life…

Mr. Hu got himself a small warehouse and turned it into two rooms. A punching bag on the right, and a piano on the left. Every day after work, he'd release his energy on the bag for around half an hour, and then calm himself down by playing the piano before he tidied himself up and went home.

Mr. Hu was born with an ego, and when his ego was hurt, something else more powerful was created. He'd never accept handouts if he had the power to take. Having the spirit of a competitor, being disciplined, never backing away from a fight and chasing improvements were what he strived for in life.

People like him want to be recognized for their values. They want to prove to the world that they are geniuses.

Just like me years ago, he was waiting for an opportunity, a proper opportunity like Youqing.

One month later, Mr. Hu witnessed a miracle. Youqing played three level 10 songs without any preparations.

I had just finished shopping for vegetables, and I was standing by the four wells outside the warehouse, green onion and broccoli in my hand, teaching Mr. Hu my prejudices about career, love, men, women, family, work, respect, equality, and money, which is my philosophy.

After listening to me, Mr. Hu made an important decision in the stench of the well: From now on, instead of going home, working, or taking care of his child, he was going to stay in the piano room and teach Youqing full time.

**Day 977**

Youqing passed the level 10 exam in piano.

The memory of those eventful days, see Appendix 7: Genius comes from perseverance, the Chinese version of *Salvation Lies Within* published by Tsinghua University Press.

According to data statistics:

Youqing had studied playing the piano for 17 weeks. In the 122 days, he rested for seven days only, and went back to Shanxi for one day. Totally he attended 114 days.

Mr. Hu gave instructions for 159 hours and 56 minutes.

Youqing practiced playing the piano after class for 385 hours and 47 minutes.

Music appreciation practice for 33 hours and 20 minutes.

Finger strength training for 36 hours and 10 minutes.

———————

Mr. Jia: "It's surprising that you had time to record all of that."

Mr. Ye: "Maimonides, the greatest Jewish philosopher after Moses, produced all of his works after ten hours' medical work during the day."

Mr. Jia: "Why did you record them?"

Mr. Ye: "You can't make improvements without the records."

Professor Li Xiaodong from the Central Conservatory of Music made the following comment on Youqing:

> Passing the exam after three years of practice would be considered a miracle, let alone a year or six months. I believed that Youqing was truly gifted to play at such a level, but the gift was not the most important aspect. What's important was his passion for the piano, for music. It's really touching.
>
> I would recommend children who are learning playing the piano not to aim at gradings or competitions, rather aim for mastering the piano, mastering a song. Don't even think about how much money you can make from playing it. What is the most important was the attitude rather than the technique.

**Youqing and Professor Li Xiaodong**

**Day 978**

I had written a short passage to commemorate this event:

I never believed that Youqing was musically gifted. However, I was touched by his parents' sincerity after they had expressed their expectation towards Youqing as well as their trust in me, and I made up my mind to give it a try.

The heaven recognizes the effort. I found this incredible dude named Hu in a warehouse behind activity center for the elderly of the oil extraction plant. His rebellious spirit was influencing, and the way he practiced Muay Thai and plays the piano was flashy. I quickly brainwashed him into joining our journey, and after I tried to open his eyes a few times, he and Youqing became a good pair. They were like a band or a team, always staying together.

A month and something later, Youqing played three songs of level ten on the piano, Mr. Hu shouted from inside the warehouse: "I gotta say, Mr. Ye, it might have only taken two weeks if I had given it my all."

Later on, in order to fully unlock his potential, Mr. Hu decided to leave his family and work behind, and invest in teaching Youqing all the way. His whole family went into chaos, and his wife had to save the day by expressing her support for Mr. Hu.

The grandparents didn't hold back their love, either. They made Youqing dumplings and spring pancakes, and even delivered on their own. Although Youqing had to walk miles on a daily basis, he gained about five kg in weight.

I delivered the great news to Youqing's mom. I said that she didn't waste her efforts on Youqing, who had made such a miracle. And she didn't get looked down on for nothing. It wasn't Youqing's problem at all. Rather, it was the teachers who didn't recognize a prodigy. She started crying again.

Our protagonist Youqing was not an energetic boy until he met Mr. Ye. His personality changed dramatically and became wise and confident. He was unmovable when challenged; and walking around the capital city, he always kept his composure when he met with great scholars and magnates who were famous in their fields.

Wow. How many people are truly able to keep the same passion after thousands of battles on this earth? And how many can truly stay young at heart after traveling thousands of miles? One for sure! It is Youqing.

Youqing's dad expressed all sorts of his emotions:

All kinds of strange people and events were recorded in strange passages. The one who wrote this passage was hard to find nowadays in the society. I could tell the amount of hard work and passion from such an emotional writing. Through your consistency and innovation, Mr. Ye, you've created another chance at life for Youqing and made dramatic changes for his world. You are truly incredible!

Youqing's mom replied with tears in her eye:

Oh, my son! It hurt me so much that you had to endure being looked down on for all these years. Mom and Dad gave you your life, my son, but it was Mr. Ye who brought you to nirvana. We'll be grateful for the rest of our lives.

Mr. Hu recalled on the journey of Youqing's learning the piano, saying with deep emotion:

Youqing would eagerly re-do the questions that he'd gotten wrong in the practice exam every time, and he'd rush to me for comments after finishing playing a song. What's more impressive was that once you made a higher standard for him in one aspect, he'd make it the standard for all the other aspects on his own. I've never seen any student who's as passionate as him.

I've heard and seen people who were pushed to make miracles, but when it happened before my eyes, even I became part of it as well. I wanted to cry because I felt so alive.

You'll get addicted to the feeling of being alive once you have experienced it.

After passing the level 10 exam, the tuition that Mr. Hu charges went up 10 folds. People went to him for lessons to the point that the traffic outside his studio was in an endless stream.

But he wasn't the little Hu like he was before. He put his pointer aside and shouted: Never mind this, my passion lies in writing novels!

Everyone was well–content and pleased.

He put himself in isolation and wrote with no stops. A few months later, he finished a novel*, whose royalty reached up to 400 thousand Yuan.

Everyone was impressed.

Mr. Hu was not the little Hu like before, and Youqing became someone new as well.

Youqing wrote to his mother on her birthday:

> Mother, it is your birthday today. Uncle Ye asked what I felt when I closed my eyes and thought of you. He asked me to describe it with one word, and all I could think about was love.

Youqing's mom cried out of joy.

Remember the third characteristic that Youqing had? Where he would sit alone and daze blankly.

He was allowed periods of time to daze while he was learning the piano every day. But as he was getting better in the piano skills, he became more and more resentful towards it, until that one evening.

**Day 926**   at dusk

Youqing walked by the door of the study and said to me:

"Uncle Ye, I'm very lonely right now. I'd like to talk to you."

---

*Mr. Hu had published his novel *The Doctor of Soul* on Blackrock under the screen name Wen Xiaoxiao.

That one moment to me, was worth a lifetime.

**Day 958**

It was in the Chinese New Year, and we three gathered in the warehouse studio once again.

Mr. Ye: "It's in the New Year's Eve, Mr. Hu. You have the day off from work, but do you feel the grief of the day being wasted?"

Mr. Hu: "Yeah."

Mr. Ye: "Do you think there is a masterpiece that can express such a feeling?"

Mr. Hu: "Yeah, let's hit it."

He then played La Campanella by Franz Liszt, with some grief fused into it. It was to commemorate the days that we worked together.

No one lives life to the fullest, unless rebellious.

We enjoyed our time in the studio that night while fireworks went off outside.

---

Mr. Jia: "I thought you were going to make it a point to stop him from dazing off. Why was he allowed to do so?"

Mr. Ye: "Because you can't stop the life instinct."

It'd weaken the physical form when human nature is suppressed, while letting it go wild produces the spirit of guilt.

As a matter of fact, suppressing the instinct can cause some pain inside because holding the desire doesn't make the desire disappear, and the spirit of guilt would still be there too. Complying to it also leads to physical harm because complying with guilt wouldn't satisfy the true desire. It was harmful either way, and there was no point losing the joy of life. Therefore, I made a rule that he tries hard to learn the piano during the daytime and focus on dazing off at night.

And if one day he stopped dazing off, it would mean that he decided not to do so on his own."

Mr. Jia: "I'm sure that other parents won't be able to find teachers as good as you and Mr. Hu."

Mr. Ye: "Back in the Ming Dynasty when they were fighting against the Wakoku, Governor Hu Zongxian said: 'I would've gone to do if people from Zhejiang had been trained. I wouldn't have waited for your arrival.'

General Qi Jiguang then replied: 'There would be loyal people even in the place with only ten families, so it was impossible not to have courageous people in the entire Zhejiang.' Later he had found the people of Yiwu, and from whom he hand-picked the Army of Qi and seriously injured the Wakoku Army."

Youqing became the so-called piano prodigy. All his hardworking proved to be ignored when he was called gifted or talented, or the prodigy.

Whatever. The next problem I was eager to solve was huge to me. Or more accurately, it was difficult for me to speak about. The reason went back to the second night after I met Youqing.

## 9. If you lower your foothold,
## you will make up for all the misery.

**Day 986**

I took Youqing to the First Affiliated Hospital of China Medical University for examination.

> *Semen volume: 0.5ml*
> *Grade A forward motile sperm: 3*

With examination report we came to the doctor's office, and saw an elderly man was pulling up his pants. His face couldn't be more red. The doctor turned to look at me, and said:

"What's wrong with you?"

"Oh, not me, doctor. It's for my nephew. Could you please take a look at the report?" I handed the report over respectfully.

"What do you think of him?"

"Asthenospermia."

"Does it make any difference?"

"Future sexual dysfunction, infertility."

"How can you tell?"

"Normal semen volume would be 2ml; he has only 0.5ml. That's too little. And grade A sperms only 3."

The following questions were for Youqing's mom.

"How many sperms does it take to get a woman pregnant?"

No one would be ready for questions like that.

"One." The doctor knew he was in for some arguing.

"We've got three. Isn't it enough?"

"What matters is the probability?"

"So, we've still got some probability?"

"It's next to zero."

"Is it because he's still young? Would it get better when he's older?"

"How old is he?"

"19." Youqing stepped up.

"You're already 19. Do you really think it'll get better in the future?"

Youqing shook and stepped back.

"So how do we treat it?" I asked.

"You can start by taking medicine. Be mentally prepared, though. It takes a long time."

We left.

**Day 987**

Aunty Liu wrote:

"Are you mentoring a kid who's a little slow?"

"Yes."

"There is an old saying, which goes like "to cultivate the forest with old clothes and broken carts." It only gets more difficult further down the road, but it is your calling. Keep at it!"

**Day 988**

Sure enough, it was getting more difficult.

I came to Youqing's home alone to discuss what the next step was with Youqing's parents.

Youqing's mom: "It was really inspiring that you made him take the level 10 exam directly, Mr. Ye. We need to dream bigger in the future, or we'd never achieve anything big."

Mr. Ye: "We are getting there."

Youqing's dad: "Indeed, we are. Now, we all dream bigger than before. I think we should aim to become professional."

Mr. Ye: "Do you mean going to school for music or another teacher?"

Youqing's mom: "I think a university would be the best choice, or an art school abroad. Or maybe we could find a teacher to take him in for his potential. And if it doesn't work, maybe we can ask Mr. Hu to teach him another 20 to 40 songs, so he could play at a hotel."

Mr. Ye: "It's a matter of direction. We're talking about the next step here."

Youqing's dad: "We could probably look into it and see how far he's able to go down this route. He's surely talented for passing grade 10. And it'd be something to look forward to if he had great potential. But if his potential is limited, I think we should think about how he'd make a living with it."

Youqing's mom: "I asked him if he could write a pop song last night, you know, like a simple one. I mean he's able to play a song accurately on the piano only from listening to it. So, I prefer that he should go to become a composer in the future."

Mr. Ye: "Yeah, sure. I mean I saw a bunch of people, writing original songs. You know, they stand in the street with a guitar and such, and people would give them two yuan, sometimes five."

Youqing's mom: "Dang."

Youqing's dad leaned into the couch and stared at the ceiling.

We all got quiet.

I thought the parents paid me to make the right decision for Youqing. I was wrong. They paid me to achieve their dreams instead. Youqing's mom fell in love with her illusion at that moment, even though she was suffering emotionally, and the road ahead was hopeless.

Our disagreement was on the route that Youqing should take. It was unable to be resolved. Youqing has already got the ability to learn on his own. I wasn't irreplaceable anymore, and I would step away if we couldn't agree on one direction. And all the work that Youqing had done would be for nothing. Only 10 seconds left, and I could almost hear the clock ticking.

I tried for the last time.

"Youqing's mom, you know I had a dream last night."

"Tell me about it, Mr. Ye." She was eager to break the awkward silence as well.

"In my dream, I was 89 years old already. And it was the New Year's Day. During the day, my students visited me with their families. Some brought their children, and that made me very happy. Then we had dumplings in the evening. As I was about to go to sleep for the night, hoping I could make it to 90 the next year, my phone started to ring. I looked at it and it was Youqing. I waited a second. Why was this name so familiar. Then I remembered now, he was the one that I mentored back when I was in my 30s. So, I picked it up.

'Hello, Youqing.'

'Uncle Ye, it's me, Youqing.'

'Where are you?'

'I'm in a retirement home right now.'

'Oh wow, Youqing, how old are you now? 70 something? I heard that your parents asked your younger brother (son of your uncle's) to take care of you before they died. Why aren't you with them?'

'No, they have gone to the U.S. to visit their grandchildren and left me in a retirement home.'

'Oh, how have you been lately?'

'Not well.'

'How come?'

'I kept wetting the bed, Uncle Ye, and the nurse always hit me.'

I felt the rage in my heart after hearing that, so I wanted to ask him which retirement home he was at so I could pick him up, but then I woke up."

The room went strangely quiet.

Youqing's mom shouted, with tears in her eyes:

"I wouldn't rest in peace if it would be real. I would've died with so much regret.

…

Sigh… You're right, Mr. Ye, I've been thinking about these as well, and I get so anxious whenever I do. It's like a fear, you know. Sometimes I wake up in the midnight and can't fall back asleep. I feel so anxious and insecure whenever I think about my son's future. It's torturing." You-qing's dad kept nodding once he heard what she said.

Mr. Ye: "Well, for most of the time, Youqing's mom, what we have got are substitutes. His grade 10 certificate is a treasure now, as it's the proof of his being a genius. But it'd just be a piece of paper that you wouldn't bother to look at in 10 years.

All time sitting playing the piano is not good for men's health. He's not going to be able to recover from it if he kept going. Here, this is the report that we got yesterday from the hospital, semen volume is only at 0.5ml, with only 3 grade A forward motile sperm. The doctor said it's asthenospermia, which means he has sexual dysfunction, and that would cause infertility."

Youqing's mom: "Wait, what?"

Mr. Ye: "If we split up today, I'll go home and start mentoring other family's heir until I'm 90. I wouldn't need anything else, but what about your guy? You're young and wealthy, with great careers. Maybe you think it doesn't matter if you have grandchildren or not, and you're giving all your resources to Youqing, just to make him a little more normal. But have you thought about what other kids at his age are doing? They fall in love, and maybe get married and have children in a couple of years. By the time you two retire, Youqing might have learned about 40 songs by then, but he'd need you to find gigs for him. When you come home and open the front door, your 40-year-old son say to you:

'Mom, where am I going to play tonight?'

Then you hear the voice of grandchildren running around, laughing and playing from your upstairs neighbor.

All you feel would just be loneliness.

I would go to him whenever he called, but I'd be 89, and seeing him like that I'd realized how big a failure I was. I'd probably die with regret not long after."

Youqing's mom: "I fully understand, Mr. Ye. We understand that you've done so much for him. I'd love to hear what you planed for him."

Mr. Ye: "You should raise your standing point, Youqing mom. We heighten everything by raising the standing point. But if you lower it, you will complete all the miseries.

You'll have to see and think from a clan innovator's point of view, instead of only a mother's.

Let me take him and resolve the physical issue, so that he could fit in the society, get a job that he truly loves, find a woman who loves him and start a family of his own.

What makes someone great is being a bridge, instead of the end goal.

Youqing is not the end. Make the transition to the next generation through Youqing as early as possible and spend your resources on them.

Every other route leads to a dead end, except this one."

Youqing's dad: "I recognize the efforts you put into mentoring Youqing for the past more than two years. I want to say that we approve your understanding and vision on the future, as well as the steps that you believe are necessary. You think further than us, and your thoughts are more detailed and more purposeful. Therefore, I understand what you just said. I support you no matter what you want to do."

Youqing's mom: "Knowing that there are tigers in the mountain, yet willingly go towards the tigers' mountain. Only Mr. Ye has such courage."

Half an hour later, I left Youqing's home to the airport, with the trust on me being extended for another 3 years.

During that era, I might have been the first teacher who was included for designing a student's life blueprint.

After boarding the plane, I changed into slippers. Then I remembered something important. I took out my phone and sent a text:

Dear Youqing's dad, Youqing's mom, the airplane is about to take off. I thank you thousands of times, like before I'd like to shake your hands and thank you for trusting me…

It started snowing right when the plane was taking off, and the entire city was covered in white.

———————

Mr. Jia: "It was impressive of you to keep calm, Mr. Ye."

Mr. Ye: "It doesn't matter what happened, Mr. Jia. What matters is how you react to it."

Mr. Jia: "Why couldn't Youqing go for art?"

Mr. Ye: "Art is not based on emotions. Rather it is based on understandings."

Mr. Jia: "That was a thrilling exchange."

Mr. Ye: "It surely was. I got 3 more years of time from that one dream.

My biggest advantage is that I can get close to the parents, and I would suggest treating it like a long-term companionship. For me, long term is my biggest advantage. Thinking back, the service that I provided was the most parent-driven in the market. I always set my standard for special parents who make difficult demands, you know, the weird ones. All their demands were strange, and I stubbornly thought that it was my privilege to satisfy these parents. It was also these strange parents who pushed me to keep bettering myself, while working with easy going parents kept me from real success in my career.

I always do it this way: I listen to what the parent wants, and then respond by meeting or exceeding the parent's needs."

Mr. Jia: "Looking for a job, looking for a life partner and even having kids, every one of these is a huge life event. How did you have the confidence to complete such difficult tasks?"

Mr. Ye: "From misunderstanding one's origin, uniqueness and mission, one is truly able to better and even surpass oneself.

I'm the me in my eyes. I knew I could do it."

Mr. Jia: "I think you're really humble when you speak to parents, Mr. Ye. Not like when you're with us. Why were you that humble in the text?"

Mr. Ye: "The one who's braver than a ruler is in danger. The one who claims credit over the entire world is unrewarded."

## Day 993

Back to home, I asked Mr. Sun Hongzhuo, a famous doctor, to check Youqing's pulse and prescribe medicines. Then I pulled Youqing to a map.

"I'll take you on a vacation in a few days, Youqing. We can go anywhere you want. This is a map. Point out where you want to go."

He pointed at the map.

"Isn't this the Changbai Mountains?"

"Yes, let's go there."

## Day 997

We arrived at the Changbai Mountains, and I quickly started working. There are 360 industries. One is considered capable for doing well in any industry. But in my eyes, one capability is superior to all the 360 of them combined.

And that is, to recognize someone's potential.

**Day 998**

Mr. Li appeared in my sight.

**Day 1003**

We came to the Center for Reproductive Medicine of Yanbian University Affiliated Hospital for examination, and the results were:

> *Semen volume: 0.8ml*
> *Grade A forward motile sperm: 137*

The ancestors said that the universe is full of mystery. Intangible and elusive, it is the origin of all things. I wrote a passage named The Adventure at Changbai Mountain based on this outing, which was collected in the Kaizong Museum.

Youqing's mom sent a congratulation after seeing the report:

> *Congratulations to Mr. Ye for completing another challenging task! And congratulations to Youqing for becoming Mr. Mighty. You're awesome, Mr. Ye! It is so memorable that Youqing became Mr. Mighty three days before his 19th birthday. Thank you so much, Mr. Ye! The weight has finally fallen off my mind.*

Youqing's dad said emotionally:

> *Even a father couldn't do what you have done! I do appreciate your innovation and achievements in your work!*

I wouldn't exchange the happiness that I got in that moment for anything in the world.

At lunch, Youqing raised his glass:

"Uncle Ye, can I make a toast to you?"

I raised my glass to him.

Youqing said sincerely:

"Uncle Ye, I wish you kept up the good work with cautiousness and conscientiousness!"

"What are you even talking about?"

"Uncle Ye, I wish you success."

"What do you mean?"

"I mean you could help me improve more quickly."

"You're welcome. Just stop." I chugged my drink.

Afterwards, on Day 1041, Youqing went back to the First Affiliated Hospital of China Medical University for examination, and the results told: Semen volume: 2.0ml, and the Grade A forward motile sperm: 103.

His sexual function recovered to a normal level, which surprised the doctor that Youqing had met during the first visit.

———————

Mr. Jia: "When did you come up with going to the Changbai Mountains?"

Mr. Ye: "Within the two seconds after hearing the doctor from the First Affiliated Hospital of China Medical University say that Youqing was sexually dysfunctional."

Mr. Jia: "What made you let him point out anywhere he wanted to go on the map?"

Mr. Ye: "What you can see is manipulated by what you cannot see. I wanted to prove my philosophy, which had nothing to do with the location."

It's time to go home. Looking out of the window, a red glare in the horizon, the sun was half hidden behind the clouds. An indescribable pleasure flooded into the heart. Looking at the "Mr. Mighty" next to me, I suddenly wanted to find out what he had learned from me. So, I took out the phone and made a call to someone.

**Day 1045 – Day 1063**  Late Spring, Panjin

Mr. Zhang was an experienced businessman, a friend of mine for many years, and Youqing called him Uncle Zhang. Mr. Zhang had witnessed the miracles that I had created, but he had one different opinion on my approach. He thought the principles and rules that I had made were like glasses, which didn't fix the near-sightedness.

He thought that children should be allowed to grow freely, instead of punishing them, and we should encourage and trust them.

So, I decided to let Youqing have an experience that's completely opposite to everything we had done at that point, by living with Mr. Zhang, as an experiment.

There were no more rules and principles, with everything being a good thing and everywhere birds singing and flowers blooming. The chief pedagogy that Mr. Zhang used was advice. What he's never thought about was that advice was rarely valuable, destined to be forgotten, and never practiced.

After eleven days, Mr. Zhang called and said:

"I think Youqing definitely needs to be disciplined."

Therefore, a decent parenting style does not cultivate decent children. Instead, decent children make the parenting style decent.

I met Youqing 18 days later. He had nothing left but his self-improving spirit.

## Day 1085

In the evening, I asked Mrs. Hao which memories of Youqing and me had made an impression on her in the past three years. She laid them out like treasures:

First, walking away from the past. Throwing away the four items that he brought with: a fan with the portrait of the ten founding marshals of the PLA, a tiny white cap, a children's keyboard and a flashlight. Sadly he said goodbye to his past. In your words, "taking it all away so I can give you even more."

Secondly, the physical exercises. Youqing had become an attractive young man from his bad, turtle-like posture, especially when he wasn't speaking. You tapped into his confidence.

Thirdly, you spent a large amount of money on his personal items. You got rid of his old tank top and shoes and turned him into a charismatic person. In your words, "the outside looks as beautiful as the inside".

Fourthly, a large amount of mental exercises. In the beginning, he was not able to understand the others and communicate. By using your educational philosophy of "suffering is the only cause of consciousness", you helped Youqing become someone with logic from a babbling silly child. You put a lot of effort into just answering whatever you're asked. It made people particularly angry when they wouldn't answer when asked, or even answer with something completely out of context. It was kind of depressing when anyone asked him about anything.

Fifthly, the change of his voice. He used to sound like a girl, with his high-pitch voice. It really made people uncomfortable. But now he has a stable, pleasant voice, and it was all because of the training you have done. You were available to him anytime of the day, from morning to evening. Think about how much you've done for him! You were correcting him even before sleeping. You probably corrected him all except when he talked in his sleep.

Sixthly, the shopping exercises. It started with paying the bills in restaurants. He somehow always got it wrong on the things that he was asked to buy. But what's valuable about you was that other people would just let it go because they wouldn't want to deal with the hassle. They would be like "Whatever, let's get it next time." But you would insist that he return whatever he got wrong. And what's more, you would ask him to do it on his own. That was pushing him to the brim. He couldn't get any help at all besides relying on himself. And he probably wouldn't make so much progress if you babysat him step by step like every other teacher. There was so much buying and returning back in those days. Eventually the returning process became smooth. Later, he wouldn't even need to return anything anymore because he could get the correct items.

The seventh point was paying the bills. When he was given 10 Yuan to spend 5, and asked how much the changes should be, he had learned to divided 10 by 5 and answered 2. He would take 50 Yuan for a 200 Yuan purchase and expect changes back. The waiters would get so confused by him that I could tell that they were miserable from their expressions. To target that, you made Youqing do all the cash deals whenever possible. Through doing it little by little, day by day, you guys finally did it. According to your philosophy, "The more you use it, the better it gets; the less you use it, the worse it gets." Later on, at the highway toll station, not only did he use the correct amount of cash, but also organized the changes from small to large.

Eighthly, the exercises on his speech. Everyone knows that in order to express a spoon's worth of stuff you have to have a bucket's worth of stuff inside. He has never made much of observations on life, and he didn't have a library of accumulated material for speech. He was not able to express himself or speak on anything for the lack of social contact, but you started making him speak in any circumstances little by little. I don't know if it was the limitation on logic or on speech, but it took him a really long time just to learn a single sentence, unlike other kids who would've learned from repeating a few times. He would remember a bit but then completely forget, as if it was never taught to him, and that took a while too. I think the most difficult part of teaching him was that he was not a blank piece of paper like everyone thought he was, you couldn't just start drawing on it. Instead, he was a piece of paper with random lines and doodles already drawn, so you had to erase them before making any progress. And they weren't just pencil lines that you could erase easily. Some of them were done by pens, even carved with knives. It was a complicated process to erase the carvings.

Ninthly, you weren't afraid of innovations. You kept trying new things with him, which was an example of teaching according to his abilities. You have reached the extreme of individualized instructions. I remember when you asked him to mop the floor, but he had no confidence in himself, and made the floor even dirtier from messing around. But you helped him find the confidence and technique by asking him to clean up a single tile, which then helped him with the rest of the floor. It took a while for him to get floor mopping as well. Later he was able to do it well on his own, but that process took about two years.

Tenthly, the way you encouraged him was memorable. He either wouldn't care too much when the others encouraged him, or he would've done a worse job from being too excited. However, you always encouraged him in a way that he was able to understand. It wasn't anything like "Great job! You did well" and so on. It was built on top of a deep understanding. You even started doing signs that only you two would know, and every time you encouraged him after he did something well, he would work even harder. You wouldn't hold back when he was lacking, but instead you pointed out where he didn't do well and helped him make improvements. That kept your encouragement unbiased and gave him the reason to be confident. That's probably why he only wanted to be your assistant instead of anyone else. He wouldn't follow anything even if he liked it, and he eventually went back to you no matter where he was because of the confidence that you gave him. In his words, "Uncle Ye can help me improve!" Others would question what's so special about mopping the floor, but floor-mopping was where he started to gain confidence and expanded such confidence into all the other aspects in life. He even became humbler with the improved abilities, rather than egotistic like when he first started. He wouldn't even take advice.

Eleventhly, the communication and coordination with the parents was elevated to a new level in the past three years. You focused more on the student's growth before, and you would do things on your own terms. But now you stand by the parents, and you aren't afraid to execute every wish of the parents even when it seems impossible. To my surprise, you actually fulfilled their unrealistic wishes through practice. Later on, you even granted the parents things they wouldn't even dream of. For example, Youqing, you didn't promise his parents anything and only said that you would give it a try. But while trying, the achievements you guys have made were totally unexpected and unimaginable. His parents probably only wanted him to be a little more normal at the beginning so that he wouldn't embarrass them. But look at him now, a handsome young adult, a piano prodigy, and even his physiological indicators returned to a normal level. He's already a child who made his parents proud of, but he was definitely an embarrassment a few years ago. Now they openly talk about him in any circumstances. For the first time Youqing's mom showed his status in her social media, and his dad even used his photo as a WeChat cover. All of these are proofs.

Twelfthly, it is a huge relief to have Youqing with you for his parents. They were able to live back life freely again.

Thirteenthly, you fully utilized your resources. For example, you took him to the fire fighters for a fire drill. He was always avoiding human contact, and at the fire station he even didn't speak to anyone. He liked listening to the others while sitting in between the fire fighters when they were telling stories about protecting people and properties. He told me by himself that it was the first time that he had expressed the will of being with the others. He went to the cafeteria with others when I realized that he started to be willing to have contact with other people. That was a huge breakthrough which had never happened before. Since then, I was also more willing to take him to places. It was embarrassing before because he was murmuring all the time and would push people intentionally in the elevators because he didn't have control over the distance with other people. Now he acts accordingly, and he knows what to say and what not to say, and always leaves a good impression on others. He's smooth at shallow conversations now, but still having trouble connecting deeply.

Later, you asked grandparents to teach him all the functions of the Casio electric watch. You urged him to master all of it, like the alarm, the stopwatch, charging and so on. That was when he started managing time on his own. And it was the first time I was impressed by him. I thought, "Oh, Mr. Ye is awesome!" Because I truly think that watch was complicated to use. And I thought to myself, "everything was really possible!" Then it took him only four months to pass the Grade 10 piano exam, and then he learned to ride a bicycle with his grandparents. These were things that I thought were impossible to do.

Fourteenthly, your connection was based on your caring about him deeply. For example, you took him for an examination when he first came here, and you found out that he had penile adhesion, which was something that his parents didn't even know about. It was cured afterwards, though. Other than that, his rhinitis was cured too. He also had all the spots on his skin from scratching himself, and he'd bite his nails instead of using a clipper. And you got rid of all of them, which was difficult too. Remember that one time his mom got super excited when she saw him using the nail clipper. When people talk about you and the way you taught, people imagine you would simply speak about something once and it would work. Actually, not at all. It was all because of the hard work you put in off the stage, and that one move you use when things get critical. That's how you made fundamental changes. I think you really know when to say what needs to be said.

Fifteenthly, you did that experiment of "complete opposite". Mr. Zhang called and said you were right only after about two weeks, because his family were almost mentally abused. He thought what you did was easy until he experienced it himself. His wife said: "We only learned about how much you have been through and how much hard work you put in, only after taking Youqing in."

Sixteenthly, you're the only one who knows what Youqing is really thinking about, and you know when he's lying. You truly became telepathic with him. I remember one thing that struck me. One day I came home, and you told me how you had a deep conversation with him about the whole event of his breaking the eye glass of a grandma's, as well as his mental activity during it. Wow, I thought, that was the first time I heard about his mental state. I thought he was dumb, but in fact he had thoughts and logic! And you did that! You helped him find it! It made me think about the other student who you mentored before. Everyone thought he was dumb, but you also had deep conversations with him and helped him get rid of some bad habits. And I think these are the reasons why your teaching can be considered legendary.

———————

Mr. Jia: "I would've assumed that it was your talent that created these miracles if it was not Mrs. Hao."

Mr. Ye: "You should give your maximum effort to look effortless. Don't believe it if anyone tells you only Mr. Ye is capable of something.

The parents who put their trust on me were innovators who were able to discover the full potential of a teacher. They were visionaries. They predicted that my method would help their children achieve happiness and help their families achieve happiness.

Countless families in China are hoping for someone like me to help them create their own miracles."

### 10. The rubble paved the way to the ends of the earth, wielding a sword without fear of taking the wrong path.

Alright, the intelligence is normal, and the physiological function is normal. Youqing has been proven to be a piano prodigy, and he will find a life partner and have children in the future. But if our mission is to give honor, beauty and treasure to someone unemployed, are our efforts meaningless?

Is Youqing able to keep himself alive? Can he justify his existence in a court of survival competition?

We had to do some preparations to find the answer to these questions. It was still going to be a journey, a brand-new journey which I called it an "independence journey".

The "independence journey" had 4 stops in total, and every one of them had a unique goal.

### ✦ First Stop

**Day 1065 − Day 1115** Panjin, Liaoning Province

Staying with Grandpa Ye, Grandma Dai for 51 days in total

Goal: Become a person who wouldn't starve to death.

Result: Learn to make scrambled eggs with tomatoes, fried tofu and steamed rice. Learn grocery shopping by bicycle.

These are the most basic in cooking. How difficult was it for Youqing? Please keep reading my diary below.

**Day 1115**

Today was the inspection. Youqing went out to buy food at 9:00 am, and came back from the vegetable supermarket at the gate of the community at 9:24 am

He did everything by himself from shopping to presenting the dishes, and the flavor was 9 out of 10.

It was difficult. The entire process took 51 days, and the difficulties included: 10 days of getting started. For some reason he just couldn't do it in those 10 days. It took everything for him to learn step one, but he'd forget about it the next day. And he couldn't form the concept of certain steps, so he wasn't able to learn no matter how he was demonstrated to. The details would just linger around for a bit and then disappear in the void. Sometimes, the pan was turning black from the heat, but he was still at ease and couldn't realize the situation… it was endless hopelessness. The pan was overheated totally 89 times in four days. In the next 22 days, we had scrambled eggs with tomatoes twice a day, and by accepting the overcooked dishes again and again, we finally succeeded.

It was risky. Imagine letting Youqing use the gas stove. Gosh, I wouldn't dare. I was about to quit imagining him holding the vegetables with one hand while holding a knife in the other. Those were the easy part. The most difficult was controlling if the ingredients were raw or cooked, how much of heat to use and how much salt to add. All of these were just like the rhythms when playing the piano. He was nearly unable to overcome. But we spent 51 days and dealt with it.

The survival radius. The important part of expanding the survival radius was using tools. Are bicycles tools or a habit? Of course, tools. He spent 14 days wiggling on a bike, learning how to ride it within the community's gates. On the 15th day, grandpa took him to practice on the road with heavy traffic and practiced for a whole day.

Now he is very agile on a bike, from going grocery shopping to picking up files from the University for the aged, and he was given the nickname "lightning".

Purpose. Nowadays, it only takes 98 minutes for Youqing to make two dishes with rice, and that includes grocery shopping. This is incredible. The purpose of the whole event for us was that we spent two years and three months figuring out if he was a genius or an idiot. It turned out he's a genius. Then we spent 51 days figuring out that he wouldn't starve if he had money. We should push for more in the future, to achieve the following goals: to live a great life if he had money, and then to make money and to live a great life. And the final goal is to meet someone who loves him and start a family.

Style. I praised my mother to her face: "You're truly amazing, mother." The old lady in front of me said calmly: "It was nothing, just like how I raised you."

We were leaving the next day. During the last day Youqing wouldn't let grandma leave his sight, and he followed her no matter where she was. She asked him:

"Why are you following me, Youqing?"

"I'm leaving tomorrow, grandma. I'd like to give you a hug."

✦ Second Stop

**Day 1116 – Day 1152**  Shenyang, Liaoning Province

Staying with grandpa Zhou for 37 days.

Goal: To master two dishes: braised pork ribs with green beans in sauce, and dried tofu with chili pepper.

Grandpa Zhou picked up cooking as a hobby after his retirement, and Youqing was to improve with him.

It was mid-summer. The sun was blazing, a breeze of wind was rare. They spent all their time together from morning to sunset in front of the stove.

On Day 37, within only 59 minutes, braised pork ribs with green beans in sauce, dried tofu-green with chili pepper, stir-fried cucumber as well as white rice were ready. Youqing cooked all by himself, and the color, smell and taste were at the top level.

Grandpa Zhou had canker sores in his mouth for worrying about Youqing. Though he said it was well worth it, as it was pleasant seeing Youqing make progress.

Granda Zhou didn't only teach Youqing about cooking, but also wrote him a poem before he left:

Between the sky and the earth, we see time brings a great change to the world.

See you off for a thousand miles but finally farewell, without knowing when to meet again.

Staying in Shenyang for dozens of days, you and grandpa have been deeply in love.

If we meet again in the future, you must be an indomitable real man.

The sun was setting, with the shadow of the tower in the park, the grandpa and the grandson parted in tears.

**Day 1158**  Summer, at Youqing's

A mother probably wouldn't remember the first time when she cooked for her son, but she'd surely remember the first time when her son cooked for her.

Youqing made braised pork ribs with green beans in sauce, and dried tofu with chili pepper for his mother, two dishes.

"How do they taste?" I asked Youqing's mom.

"Delicious."

"How do you feel?"

"I feel like crying."

✧ Third Stop

**Day 1165 – Day 1196**  Liaoyang, Liaoning Province

Stay with the maternal grandpa for 32 days.

Goal: Learn how to take care the elderly.

**Day 1165**

Youqing arrived in Liaoyang and met with two elderlies who were not able to take care of themselves at all. They'd been lying in bed for 10 years at that point. The room was clean, the sunlight shined through the clear window and made it smell really nice. The nurses were the sons of the two elders—my uncle, Youqing's new teacher.

Youqing got into a groove as soon as he arrived at the room, with a happy smile all over his face.

My uncle wrote in his diary: Today, my nephew Zhigang brought his student Youqing to my home. He saw the potential in me to help Youqing learn how to take care of the elderly. This work includes all aspects of life, and is detail orientated, so I need to repeatedly instruct him with seriousness, without missing any detail.

Youqing was accepted by my maternal grandfather on the first day. He pointed at Youqing who was wiping the table: "I like his effort!" That night, Youqing fed and massaged him.

---

Mr. Jia: "What made him start taking care of the elderly?"

Mr. Ye: "The answer is in his blood and bone. On Day 246, when he saw Mrs. Hao massaging the legs for her mother, he showed excitement like never before.

Day 270, he saw this senior gentleman with an injured hand, and it seemed like he wanted to help.

Through a long time living together, I discovered that he was really interested in anything that had connection with the elderly. And the essence of an interest is the ability to attract someone to a job or task.

From these observations I realized that Youqing was meant for the senior care industry."

## Day 1174

In the morning, the room was 23 degrees Celsius. My 90-year-old maternal grandfather was tossed around naked for about half an hour by Youqing who only wanted to change his diaper. Grandfather hadn't spoken for one week, but he did right then:

"What are you even doing? Are you done, kid?"

Youqing bite down his lip and finished the battle with the diaper quickly.

In the afternoon, my uncle asked Youqing:

"What are you going to name your son?"

"Wang Qiang, Qiang for self-improvements."

## Day 1179

In the morning, Youqing "helped" my grandfather sit on the floor by accident. The man spent about an hour sitting before he had the energy to stand up. My uncle wanted to punish Youqing but was stopped by my grandfather. He spoke quietly: "Give the kid a chance..." He let Youqing keep serving him.

Giving the kid a chance is something that the weak souls would've never said. The love behind such a line is deeper than the ocean, indicating the sacrifice that he made to help the next generation grow. This love is wholehearted, and it is beyond life.

**Day 1195**

My uncle made the following conclusion on Youqing:

> *"He is now able to independently put on and take off clothes, shoes and socks, and change clothes, do laundry, change diapers and clean up the waste. He can also chat with them.*
>
> *Youqing learned to make stir-fried shredded potato and stewed tofu with cabbage. It was not very easy to cut the potatoes into thin strips. He usually did it for three hours a day, and his hands were usually cut four times in a month. He was not afraid of working hard, and no matter how much he bled, he would put on a band-aid and kept practicing cutting.*
>
> *Cleaning the floor. Teaching him how to use the broom cost me three days, and sweeping the yard took another three days. He took it seriously and he could manage time well. He would clean wherever he found dirty, and I wouldn't have to ask him, as he did everything great.*
>
> *Flexibility. Take serving rice as an example, half a bowl or a full bowl, dry or wet, all these took me three days.*
>
> *From living with Youqing I saw his pure heart. Though he was*

*not flexible, he was eager to do things, he was not afraid of hard work, and not afraid of getting his hands dirty. And he really meant to do things well with all his heart."*

## Day 1208

Today was the Mid-autumn Festival, Youqing went home to visit his parents. His parents were happy from seeing the changes on him brought by the "journey to independence".

Youqing's mom concluded:

*We can easily see Youqing's improvement during this visit. His communication skills improved dramatically, and his vocabulary broadened as well. He had more patience during a conversation and would wait for others to finish before he starts to speak. And he could answer questions about his daily life now. His improvements were shown during a call to his grandma and auntie. Grandma said he's a lot better at having ask-answer conversations now, instead of pouring out what he wanted to say and hanging up the phone. The great part is that you can tell he thinks of others now and is very filial to the elders.*

*... Youqing also showed a strong will to learn. He took out a book to read on his own, and it was about the science on the earth's rotation...*

———————

Mr. Jia: "Why did he change so much?"

Mr. Ye: "It is not the teacher and textbook that benefit someone. It is the relationship between the teacher and the student.

The teachers he met during the journey to independence really treated him like a son.

As the ancestors said, masters and apprentices are like father and son. There might be 100 students learning English in a class in front of a teacher, but a master can't have 10 apprentices by their side because the fatherly love cannot be divided into 10 pieces."

Knowing his son was stepping into the senior care industry, Youqing's dad wrote him a poem at a farewell dinner:

*To My Son*

*Stately and handsomely the evergreen trees in the wind,*
*My son has grown up and become well-cultivated.*

*Wholeheartedly efforts paid for eight years, and you have made*
*a break-through,*
*With a mastermind you may have reached out for the stars in*
*the Ninth Heaven.*

*Though it is difficult to seek career into the first level industry,*
*you can also bow down to the marketplace.*

*The rubble paved the way to the ends of the earth, while wield-*
*ing a sword without fear of taking the wrong path.*

There is an old fable:

A person asked gods if a person really agrees with his own path?

The god said, it depends on if he would let his favorite son go this way. It'd be extremely easy for Youqing's dad to get him a job with his connection, but he didn't. Instead, he blessed his son for giving back to the others, to the society. This is the type of parent that I respect. And it is worthwhile to strive for someone like him.

#### ✧ Fourth Stop

**Day 1223 – Day 1229**   Shanghai, Seven days in total

In these seven days, Youqing participated in training to improve his skills in elderly care and passed the exams to obtain a certificate in the elderly care industry.

Youqing also learned to give massage during the independence journey and passed the skills appraisal exam as well*.

**Day 1267**

I asked Steven Yu to make a resume for Youqing.

In the self-introduction section, Youqing wrote:

> *I'm not the smartest, but I work hard. Uncle Ye said that I'm the hardest worker he's ever seen. I don't like having spare time. I love serving the elderly, giving them massages, preparing for*
>
> *the foot baths, feeding them, cleaning them, cleaning up their waste, as well as playing the piano for them. I also love mopping the floor, cooking, doing the laundry and chatting with the elderly. I love the retirement home, and I feel happy whenever I see the grandpas and grandmas. My dream is to serve the people.*

---

*He had built a good foundation on elderly caring and massaging while practicing with Mr. Ning Haiquan and my uncle. Therefore, he passed the exams smoothly.

Mr. Jia: "Who would've thought that Youqing's dream was to serve the people! Mr. Ye, how did he find his dream?"

Mr. Ye: "A loyal soul is not forged in a day.

In his childhood, on his way to the kindergarten, he saw 'to serve the people' written on the wall.

When he was seven, he saw the five characters in a notebook of his father's, 'to serve the people'.

When he was in 6th grade of primary school, he learned a text in class, entitled To Serve the People.

Later, he heard the host of Heart-to-Heart Artistic Troupe of CCTV said, 'to serve the people.'

Then, he saw the carvings on the stone tablet outside of the Party School of the CPC Central Committee, to serve the people.

And finally, when we drove by Zhongnanhai, outside of the Xinhua Gate, he saw the calligraphy on the wall—to serve the people."

An example is better than a precept. Youqing's father is an excellent Chinese Communist Party member, and he had fused this sentence into his own life. From being exposed to the examples with words of the teachers and combined with their love towards the elderly, Youqing took 'to serve the people' as his dream in life.

If one wants to solve the problem of the meaning of existence, one must seek the unity between the individual and a certain wholeness beyond the individual, the unity between the individual and the collective, and the finite and the infinite. And it is these four simple words that give people the greatest satisfaction in life: to serve the people.

Youqing was about to enter the stage of the society. I wanted to gift him something for protection."

Mr. Jia: "Protection?"

Mr. Ye: "Yeah. Do you know what is the scarcest in the world?"

Mr. Jia: "What?"

Mr. Ye: "It's the understanding of someone."

On a moonlit night, I picked up a pen and wrote an entire page.

## A Recommendation Letter

*Youqing came to me three years ago. He took over the responsibilities of cleaning the house and cooking as well. Living under the same roof, I've found that Youqing had the following unique features:*

*1. There were two things he loved best: playing the piano and taking care of the elderly. He took care of my maternal grandfather, who was not able to take care of himself, like his own family members. Youqing wiped shit and urine every day, holding filthy hands like holding gold, and always kept the same smile. Back in the day when Zixia asked about how to honor the parents, Confucius answered: "It's difficult to keep a cheerful spirit." It could be seen that young people like this have been rare since ancient times.*

*2. He even loved the elderly who refused to cooperate. My grandmother moaned loudly from pain constantly, and my un–*

cle and Youqing did not sleep enough every day, but Youqing kept his smile, loyalty, and respect.

3. He was willing to admit his mistakes and correct them. Sincere criticisms only inspired him to be better.

4. He was generous. When criticized, even for no reason, he never talked back.

5. He never talked about others behind their backs.

6. He didn't care about personal gain or loss. To serve the people had been the motto of his family for three generations.

7. He didn't smoke.

8. He didn't drink.

9. He didn't leave his post to go out during work.

10. He didn't argue or get into physical altercations. That is his nobility.

11. He didn't take others' belongings.

12. He didn't like to be on his phone, even when he's on break.

13. He didn't like to waste.

14. He wouldn't take anyone in to spend the night, nor did he spend the night elsewhere.

15. He didn't take holiday breaks. He believed he should work even during the New Year's Holidays.

*16. He loved his job. He only did work or study related things when he's working or studying, and never left today's task to tomorrow. Relying on this spirit, he passed the piano grade examination of the China Conservatory of Music in only four months, and Professor Li Xiaodong of the Aesthetics Laboratory of the Central Conservatory of Music made the following comments on him:*

*To pass the exam in three years would be considered a miracle, let alone four months. His gift is not the most important. Rather, it is his consistency that's the most important. It is really touching.*

*Compared with the 16 points above, the most respectful aspect of Youqing's is that he is loyal and honest through and through.*

*Any organization that hires such a youth would doubtlessly grow in prosper.*

*The referrer:*
*Ye Zhigang*

I read this letter to Youqing's parents through video chat. Tears came to his father's eyes, and his mother burst out crying.

Later she sent a message to Youqing:

*Hello Youqing. I saw the recommendation letter that Uncle Ye wrote for you, for which I am touched. I've never noticed that you had all these qualities. I should look up to you now. Mom is proud of you, Youqing.*

With the resume and recommendation letter in hand, Youqing prepared for the departure to Shanghai excitedly.

Auntie Liu, who was highly respected, sent a text message from thousands of miles away, which made my heart sink.

On it were eight words:
Wan shui qian shan, cuo tuo wu nian (The Chinese Pinyin)
Which means: Ten thousand of rivers and mountains, five years wasted.

We would see about that. I grabbed my luggage and took Youqing, walked through a river of people and boarded the train to Shanghai.

## Day 1332

We landed in Shanghai, and Youqing got his health certificate and a debit card. He also took a shower and got a haircut. With full confidence we handed in the resume and the recommendation letter to a housekeeping agency. The manager saw them and promised that he'd find Youqing a job with no problem once the registration fee was paid.

Nobody could have thought that it all started going downhill three days later.

## Day 1334

I had this conversation with Youqing in a cold, humid six-square-meter room next to a highway:

"When did we get here?"

"The 5th."

"What's the date today?"

"It's the 7th."

"What have we been eating?"

"Boiled cabbages."

"Every day, right?"

"Sometimes there were potatoes in there." Youqing thought I should've been a little more precise.

"How did we sleep in the past two days?"

"In this tiny room."

"We didn't even undress, did we?"

"Nope."

"And we used the down blanket that we brought here, right?"

"Yeah!"

"And what's on top of it?"

"Two down jackets and scarves."

"And we were still cold, right?"

"Yeah!"

"The manager told us clearly that there wasn't any job for you, right?"

"Yeah."

"So, we suffered for nothing?"

"We did suffer for nothing."

"We were told to leave here, when?'

"Now."

"Why?"

"Because someone else is moving in."

"So what now? You still want to look for jobs here in Shanghai?"

"Yeah."

"Where exactly?"

"Shenyuan, Taikang Home."

"Even the housekeeping agency didn't want you. Do you think Shenyuan will take you in?"

"Yeah."

"When are we going?"

"This afternoon!"

"What if they don't want you?"

"Then we go somewhere else."

"Where exactly?"

"Another Taikang Home."

"Which one?"

"Yueyuan."

"Let's go."

---

Mr. Jia: "Did you believe what Youqing said, Mr. Ye?"

Mr. Ye: "Yes, I did."

Three hours later, Mr. Deng, the manager of Shenyuan, agreed to have Youqing as a volunteer there.

For details of the bizarre job search, see Appendix 9: too easy to be cherished, the Chinese version of *Salvation Lies Within* published by Tsinghua University Press.

**Day 1335**

Youqing and I left Shanghai.

---

Mr. Jia: "Didn't the manager agree to hire him be a volunteer? Why did you guys leave?"

Mr. Ye: "The ease of obtaining a certain resource isn't equal to its significance. I choose to ignore any mediocrity. What we need is a real job."

## 11. Give the kid a chance.

*The west wind hunts and cannot disperse the desolation of the world.*

*A thousand miles of flying snow cannot conceal a thousand years of regret.*

*The snow is about to settle, and the wind is uncertain, in front of the ancient city.*

*Two figures, a past story.*

**Day 1371**  Wuguocheng, Heilongjiang Province

Mr. Ye: "It is your 20th birthday today, Youqing. There was an emperor who ascended to the throne when he was 20. I took you here to tell you about his story. His name was Zhao Ji, known as Emperor Huizong of the Song Dynasty in history. You might ask who he was.

He pioneered thin gold calligraphy. The handwritings of Emperor Huizong were elegant, from which you could see his personality.

He founded the Hanlin Calligraphy and Painting Academy, officially incorporating painting into the imperial examination, and exploring and cultivating painting talents, and changed the features of Chinese painting art.

The innate artistic talent, diligent practice day after day, and his explration and development of aesthetic techniques have made future generations sigh with admiration that the Song Dynasty was the pinnacle of ancient Chinese artistic achievements, and Emperor Huizong of the Song Dynasty can be regarded as a representative of the entire Song Dynasty art.

During the reign of Emperor Huizong of the Song Dynasty for 25 years, although he created an incredibly splendid culture, it wasn't an emperor's job to be an artist. He was not a good emperor and was ultimately captured by the State of Jin, and imprisoned here in Wuguocheng, which was known as the "Shame of Jingkang" in history.

On that day, Emperor Huizong of Song was tied up on a horseback and escorted together with more than 3000 people, including his son, royal family, concubines, and ministers, from Kaifeng, Henan to the north. When they arrived here, there were only 140 of them left. Behind him, the capital city of Kaifeng was looted, and his Empress Zhu committed suicide by drowning, his daughter Princess Maode was raped, and 83 concubines, 24 princesses, and 22 princesses were sold, resulting in a loss of 18 million people nationwide.

He lived here for eight years before he died tragically. He once wrote tragically during his lifetime:

> *All night long, the west wind shattered the door, and the lamp in the desolate hall was faint.*

> *Looking back three thousand miles at Jiashan, there are no wild geese flying south in the sky.*

I'm telling you all these today because there's a principle of being a person in the story:

A man must do his job well. Otherwise, he'll face tragic death even if he is the son of the heaven.

Starting from today, we will begin to practice in society until you can stand strong on your own.

The ancients said: ten people are called heroes, a hundred people are called greats, and a thousand people are called talents.

This journey is what I call "the Journey of Talent Whetting".

"Which retirement homes have we inspected so far?"

"We have visited Shenyuan, Yanyuan, Yueyuan of Taikang Home, and Hezhong Younian in Wuhan."

"Which is your favorite one?"

"I like Shenyuan the most."

"Is there anything different between the elderly in Shenyuan and those in other places?"

"They are all elderly people."

"Are you trying to take care of the elderly in Shenyuan or the elderly in general?"

"In general!"

"That means we will serve any elderly when they need us, right?"

"Yes."

"You must first recognize whom we're doing for, Youqing. The road to serving the people is a wide one, and life is only difficult for those who are picky."

"I understood!"

"Where are your favorite elderly?"

"Sitting downstairs in my hometown, basking in the sun."

"So where are we going?"

"Go home!"

---

Mr. Jia: "I noticed that you always give students a mental mobilization before you act."

Mr. Ye: "We must first change the motivation before changing the action."

Eventually, we returned to Youqing's hometown. There was the land that nurtured him, with an unchanging local accent, and the fellow villagers who were more willing to put their trust on him.

During the 87 days of Talent Whetting Journey, we interviewed at 54 retirement homes, traveled over 1000 kilometers, and experienced one car accident, and finally, Director Li's elderly apartment opened to Youqing.

The intricate and funny details can be found in "It is too easy to cherish" of Appendix 9 of the Chinese version of *Salvation Lies Within* published by Tsinghua University Press.

---

Mr. Jia: "What was the purpose of the journey?"

Mr. Ye: "One must stand strong on their own legs. Otherwise, they cannot love at all. And only those who love themselves can love others. Likewise, only the wealthy can give back.

Education, on the other hand, can no longer ignore the pain and itching of life. As a cold and dry training cannot provide a ready-made answer to the mysteries of life that should never change. Education should care about people and their inner world, with rich personality colors, and embark on a path of exploration with lost people, which is uncertain about good or bad."

Mr. Jia: "Why did you choose to stay at Mr. Li's elderly apartment in the end?"

Mr. Ye: "On the evening of my job search, Mr. Li sent me a text message, 'Everything is for children to adapt independently to society and become useful people.'

Before we left for the journey, Aunt Liu predicted that it would take Youqing five years to find a job, but it only took us 87 days. Later when we met, I was about to start questioning, but Aunt Liu spoke first:

"It wasn't that I was not accurate, but that your mind has changed."

Your purpose was not simple before you set out with Youqing. You wanted to show people your talents. 'Look! I did what you all couldn't.' So, you were aiming for famous institutions in big cities. But you got rid of your selfishness and dedicated your heart to serving others, and that's why it only took you 87 days.

However, the place where he works is not just a retirement home."

"What else is it?"

"It's also a big forge."

"For what?"

"For forging characters."

On the loess land stood a mottled high wall, with several rows of bungalows running from north to south. In front of the houses were vegetable fields, with over 50 elderly people, some planting, some basking in the sun, and others chatting.

20-year-old Youqing appeared in the sight of the elderly, wearing a white coat, and holding four thermos flasks in his hand. He had a refined temperament, and every single movement was so different compared with the locals. The way he walked was so carefree, like a walk in a park.

## Day 1389

Mr. Li had asked Mrs. Du, who was the associate dean of the organization, to lead Youqing to practice on the front line all day, mastering the three skills of changing diapers, feeding, and moving the elderly as soon as possible.

Mrs. Du's understanding of Youqing was increasing throughout the day.

At the morning meeting, Vice President Du said that Youqing would need at least six months to reach his goals.

During the afternoon break, Vice President Du said that Youqing needed at least one month to achieve his goals.

At the end of the evening, Vice President Du said that it would take at least two weeks to achieve the goal.

I said to him that I did't want to overestimate his abilities, but also didn't want to underestimate his willpower. Strengthening discipline and strict requirements might just take him one week.

Mrs. Du smiled confidently.

Vice Dean Du had a rough upbringing. She went to work in an elderly apartment because of her mother.

Vice Dean Du lost her father at a young age. Her mother had a strong character and demanded that her children improve themselves. Vice Dean Du inherited her mother's straightforward personality.

Her marriage was arranged when she was 20. After marriage, her husband succeeded in his career, and he despised her. He wanted a divorce, but soon he regretted it because his career went downhill. His family also advised Vice Dean Du to take a long-term view. At the age of 21, Vice Dean Du rebelled for the first time in her life: Why did you get me here and there? I must divorce! After the divorce, she was criticized by her fellow villagers.

In the next year, Vice Dean Du rebelled to the end and met a handsome man from a neighboring village. She fell in love at first sight, got married, and had a son.

She loved her mother. Her mother lived with her elder brother, but she was treated poorly. Her sister-in-law asked her mother to go out for a stroll on a windy day but locked the door. Her mother curled up on the stone steps outside the door, and coincidentally, Vice President Du came to visit her. Seeing this scene, she was furious and kicked the door open. Entering the room, she argued, and her sister-in-law choked back:

"You're amazed. Then you can take her away."

"Let's go!" She took her mother in to stay with her for three months before her brother took her mother back. And the old lady suddenly passed away 20 days later.

Vice President Du couldn't believe it and was convinced that her sister in-law had something to do with it. After an autopsy, it was found that her mother had died naturally. Vice President Du asked the heaven in silence:

"How did my mother die suddenly for no reason?" She thought.
She cried like a baby on the night of her mother's death.

She fell seriously ill, and a month later, with doubts about the cause of her mother's death, she went to work in an elderly apartment and witnessed the fragility of life with her own eyes. Four elderly people who were still chatting and laughing at dinner passed away on the same night, and Vice President Du forgave her brother and sister-in-law.

That night, she missed her mother, suppressed herself from crying, and suddenly became an adult.

Youqing's dedication touched Vice President Du. She said that she'd rather teach 10 Youqing than one college student.

I asked her why, and Vice President Du said nowadays college graduates wanted to start from management as soon as they graduated, unwilling to start from the ground floor level. More importantly, when they worked, they didn't prioritize the elderly. Youqing's priorities were all on the elderly, even if he made a mistake, which was the fundamental difference.

**Day 1391**

Mr. Li praised Youqing for feeding the elderly. He said that Youqing did a great job for being calm and patient.

Compared with the elder's room, the employee dormitory was tougher. The room was at 11.9 Celsius degree, making Youqing's hands tremble with cold.

**Day 1398**

"Go take a break." Vice President Du said to Youqing.

# CHAPTER 9

"Vice President Du, I can't stand not working!"

Mrs. Du smiled.

**Day 1400**

In the evening, an electric tricycle came out from the forest which was located on the side of the dam. It was carrying twigs. As it staggered into through the front gate of the apartment, four elderly people rushed over to help transport firewood into the shed.

Soon after, a sensational smell of food with the steam created from the cooking spread out all around the dam from the kitchen.

After dinner, Mr. Li and Mrs. Du made a decision to entrust Youqing to take care of Grandpa Feng who was in the VIP room.

Youqing was excited on hearing this, though he didn't know the secret of the VIP room, where "the four heavenly kings" lived, and everyone in the apartment got nervous even when talking about them.

While they were dining, the moon hung low in the hazy night sky, and a truck drove by the gravel road in front of the apartment. Its headlights pierced through the darkness of the night.

In the retirement home, all the elderly had gone to sleep. The wind blew open a door, making a squeaking noise against the door frame, and a sign "VIP" was nailed to the lintel. There were four iron beds laid out before the four walls.

The person sleeping in bed number one was Qian Xiong, with a grinding sound in his mouth. It wasn't hard to tell, with the help of the moonlight, that he was not an old man. He was only 37 years old, wearing a blue boxing helmet, bare-armed, and wearing diapers underneath.

He was the only child. Though he had epilepsy, his mother still made the arrangement for him to marry a woman. His mother demanded that his wife stay by his side all day and not leave half a step. Whatever does his wife like, his mother would say, "It's okay, Mom will buy it for you."

Qian Xiong was able to take care of himself, but every night he would excrete in bed on purpose. He would wake up in his waste every morning and spread his legs for the caregiver to clean it up. He would stare and insult the caregiver for not meeting his demands, known as "the beast".

In Bed 2 was Grandpa Feng mentioned by Mr. Li.

He was 81 years old, with a dignified face. A quartz watch with no numbers on the dial was worn on the wrist.

Ten years ago, he had a motorcycle accident without a license. After lying in bed for half a year, he got venous thrombosis and diabetes.

At this moment, his lower body was covered with decubitus ulcers and he was barely awake.

In Bed 3 was Old Lin, 77 years old. He slept with his mouth wide open, with only a few teeth left in there. He snored loudly. He believed that camo-shirts could have grand power to him, so he would wear them all year round, even when sleeping.

Old Lin was strong in the village in his earlier years and could do the work of two people. He was a warm-hearted person and was always asked for help by his neighbors.

Later, he did something wrong and went to prison.

He came to the retirement home after he was released. He would bow to anyone who was in a uniform but showed a cold shoulder to the elderly in the retirement home. He had a negative evaluation of anyone and everything.

You can see Bed 4 without turning on the lights. This was a colorless old man with a cold face, wearing a beige shirt with black spots. There was an aluminum alloy cane by the bed, shining cold at night. Everyone called him "Lao Geng".

According to the village chief who brought him here, Lao Geng was a bully of Tiangang Village when he was young.

Lao Geng had a cerebral thrombosis in his head, half of his body was not obedient, and he liked to drool. Whatever he wanted you to do, he would just shout at you, like "Hey you!" But he wouldn't speak. Instead he would command with his sights. And if he didn't like it, he would lift a crutch and hit someone.

These were the people that Youqing was going to deal with tomorrow. I was lying next to him, unable to fall asleep.

**Day 1401**

At 5:30 in the morning, at the door of the VIP room, there stood a young man, wearing a pair of round-framed tortoiseshell glasses and a white coat. He should be a regular person, looking even a bit too honest, but the reality was far from what it had seemed. Youqing's eyes were congested, his hair was messy, and he held paper diapers in one hand and a trash in the other. His eyes fixed on Grandpa Feng in Bed 2.

Youqing was there to change Grandpa Feng's diapers. Qian Xiong was waiting with his legs spread out for the caregiver to serve him. He looked at Youqing up and down, with a disdainful look in his eyes.

Youqing took a few quick steps to Feng's bed and bent over to him:

"Grandpa Feng, I'm here to change your diaper."

No response.

Youqing smiled, then skillfully lifted the blanket and took off the cushion, unbuckled the strap on Grandpa Feng's wrists and tore open the stickers on his diapers... These essentials were something he practiced for half a night last night.

Qian Xiong looked coldly at Youqing's busy figure and taunted, "What a beggar!"

Lao Geng burst out laughing from across the room as he walked to the restroom.

Master Zhao, the chef, called everyone in the yard to have breakfast. Youqing washed his hands and rushed to the kitchen. He filled his white coat pockets with half a bun, a spoon of soup, a bag of sheep milk, a banana, and a tiny bag of daily nuts. Master Zhao was surprised to see that Youqing poured all of that into a mixer. He squatted on the ground and blew with his mouth for 10 minutes, and then ran back to the VIP room.

Youqing took spoonfuls and calmly fed Grandpa Feng. Every time Feng opened his mouth, Youqing also followed suit, as if he was eating. A small bowl of paste, Youqing fed it for half an hour.

After feeding, Youqing wiped Feng's mouth and said: "Rest well now, Grandpa Feng."

Youqing stood up and walked out. A person on crutches stumbled and hit Youqing, causing the basin to fall to the ground. The bowl fell on the ground. The person snorted, took a step with his left foot, followed by his right foot, and moved step by step towards the windowsill. His eyes were fixed on a yellow and black beetle on the window, which flew out with all its might, hitting the glass repeatedly. It was flying against the clear window, making a noise every time it hit the glass. In the end, it became angry and rolled aimlessly on the glass, making a sizzling sound.

Ka, suddenly it all went quiet. A cane squeezed it into a puddle, and the owner of the cane was the colorless face. Yes, Lao Geng came all the way to do this.

This beetle was by no means an ordinary one. It had its own name, called "Stinky Sister", which meant that whoever made it die would be smoked to death. The pungent stench spread, and Lao Geng looked regretful. He let out a vicious "Hey you" and spatted out a mouthful of sticky phlegm at Youqing's feet, urging him to quickly clean up everything.

After tidying up everything, Youqing realized that he had missed the employee's meal. He took Grandpa Feng's rice bowl back to the kitchen and picked up a mop to continue working.

At 10:00 am, Youqing came to the VIP room to give Grandpa Feng a massage. Opening the blanket, a salty smell rushed over Feng's face. Grandpa Feng's two rugged black legs were covered in large pieces of dead skin, and every joint in his lower limbs had bed sores. These bed sores were like eyes that had been burning for many nights, looking red and lifeless.

Youqing, smiling slightly and enthusiastically, started to massage using the techniques taught by his master before.

Whenever Youqing massaged, it was more than just a service. He really put his heart into doing it as he covered every acupoint, every joint, and every inch of skin.

In a moment, the yellow scabs, black dead skin, and red blood were all mixed together, like sticky honey, sticking to Youqing's hands.

An imperceptible sound emanated from Grandpa Feng's throat, as if someone was shouting at you from a distant mountain peak.

According to Mr. Li's analysis, Youqing was probably rubbing his flesh against his bones.

What Grandpa Feng didn't know was that Youqing had planned to give him a massage like that for half an hour in the morning and half an hour in the afternoon, all year round.

In the afternoon, in the hallway, you could hear Feng's shout out of breath, "Oh man... please... it's too much..."

Suffering was the only reason for consciousness. Youqing used his hand to pull Grandpa Feng away from the void.

The rapid progress truly surprised Mrs. Du. Mr. Li emphasized again at night: "Mr. Feng is completely entrusted to Youqing."

**Day 1402**

Grandpa Feng had gained more consciousness under Youqing's detailed care these days. His pale face was getting rosy.

I showed Grandpa Feng a video of the lively spring, and he expressed his strong desire to go outside and bask in the sun.

**Day 1403**

The ground of the first row of a retirement home in Youqing's charge was cleaned flawlessly, and Vice Dean Du called on all employees to learn from Youqing. Upon hearing the praise from the dean, Youqing nodded and said, "They surely need to."

I reported to Youqing's mom:

"Youqing mom, do you remember Grandpa Feng? The one with all the ulcers all over his body that made you couldn't bear even looking at him?"

"Yeah, I thought about him today."

"The previous caregiver poured out the food midway feeding him, and the old man was all ulcered and probably wasn't far from death. After Youqing took over the job, with three meals a day he got so much better under Youqing's care, and you could see the light in his eyes and his face was rosy. Once he gets a little better, he can go outside in a wheelchair to bask in the sun."

"Nice! Congratulations to him."

"The old man shouted "thanks" behind Youqing as he was walking out of the room. Today, Grandpa Lin saw Youqing giving massages and said that someone like Youqing was hard to find even with much money."

"Congratulations to Youqing as well!"

---

Mr. Jia: "Do you talk to his mother often?"

Mr. Ye: "I did some calculations at that time, and it turned out that I talked with her for about 600 hours in the first four years."

Mr. Jia: "Why?"

Mr. Ye: "Her life was kind of empty after Youqing left home. No more helping with homework, no more preparing dinner, no more Youqing's laughter, no more heartaches and no more piano sounds.

After 16 years she finally had time to spend alone with her husband, away from all the noises and worries. But they were not able to find the feelings that they had before.

The feeling of walking hand in hand on the street back then was no longer there, and all that was left was exhaustion. She only wanted to be quiet and to relax. The person next to her was the same person that she loved at the beginning, and the only thing that changed was time. Accompanying Youqing all the way, she realized in the end that some things had gone forever.

Her entire life was about Youqing. Youqing was all that she talked about, thought about, cared about and worried about. She hid her tears in front of others and quietly dried them with dissatisfaction towards herself.

Only Youqing's dad and I would understand all these things. He was always busy with work, and as a wife, she didn't want to give him extra pressure by telling him her worries. Therefore, listening to her had become part of my job.

I reported to her about Youqing, or talked about philosophy, discussed Youqing's progress, and sometimes even took on the responsibility of interpreting her dreams. But more than anything, I was listening to her and comforting her.

Mr. Jia, you and the young people following my steps, need to make the parents feel how popular they are from the sound of you answering the phone. All they need is love."

Mr. Jia: "Understood, Mr. Ye. But how?"

Mr. Ye: "You decorate what they like and get rid of what they don't."

Mr. Jia: "How many times did Youqing's dad call you in the four years?"

Mr. Ye: "Two."

Mr. Jia: "How came?"

Mr. Ye: "The less one understands, the more he worries; the less one trusts, the more he speaks."

**Day 1404**

During the dinner, Mrs. Du said that the entire elderly and hygiene work in the first row of the retirement home had been entrusted to Youqing in the afternoon. He did such a great job, and she didn't have to worry about him.

**Day 1407**

People grow up three times in their lives.

The first time is when you realize that you can't make the person you love turn around.

Youqing's mom came to visit out of the blue and arrived at the retirement home. She headed straight to Youqing's dormitory, where the windows were bright and clean, and the internal affairs were in order.

"Is that all?" Youqing's mom asked while sitting by the bed, pulling up her son's hand with a smile.

"Yes."

"Don't you want to do something else?"

"No."

"Don't you want to work in an office?"

"No."

"Huh?"

"Don't you want to be a flight attendant?"

"I don't like it."

"You can deliver coffee or drinks to guests on an airplane. Wouldn't that be nice?" The mother and the son's voices grew louder and louder.

"I don't like it."

"Why not?"

"I like taking care of the elderly here."

"And this is what you want to do for the rest of your life?" She became angry.

"Yes." Youqing said quietly.

"Can't you play the piano somewhere?"

"I want to play the piano here to the elders."

"It's not necessarily just for the elderly, but for people like Mom?"

"No!" Youqing shouted. His mom was startled and leaned back.

"Why not?" She grabbed his hands.

"I want to play for the elderly." He pulled his hands back.

"You don't want to play in a theater for others?"

"Which one?" Is that even important at this point? I thought to myself.

"Anyone, you know, as a part of a band."

"No, I want to play for the elderly."

"I don't understand you. Did Uncle Ye brainwash you?" She smiled at me awkwardly.

"He chose to do it." I squeezed out a smile, reminding myself not to lose my temper when feeling down.

"No, he didn't. Uncle Ye has been great." Youqing raised his hand and gestured to me.

"Umm. I was thinking on the way here, don't you have any other hobbies?"

"This is what I like to do!"

"I just want to know if this is truly what he wants to do. I don't want to go against his will. Neither do I want him to think that this is his only way out."

Oh, that's what's going on. "Do you feel happy doing this, Youqing?" I asked.

"I'm happy!"

"You're so noble, aren't you? You're so noble that I can't even believe it." Youqing's mom stood up and walked outside, without saying hello when she saw Dean Li.

After Youqing's mother left, Youqing lost his level of work and was in a daze.

---

Mr. Jia: "What happened?"

Mr. Ye: "His mother exposed the hook, got some nibbles.

Ordinary people work for wages and social status, satisfied with the basic labor and amusements. But Youqing would rather die than do something he's not interested in.

Compared with ordinary people, he's not smart at all, but driven by emotions, he never cares about gains and losses.

He's wholehearted.

But the secret of life is to do only one thing at a time. When you do it, nothing else is worth mentioning."

## Day 1408

In the morning, Youqing came to the kitchen to prepare breakfast for Grandpa Feng. He took out a bag of sheep milk, a banana, and a bag of daily nuts from his white coat pocket and prepared to pour them into a blender as usual.

Mrs. Du came over curiously, "Where did you get all these?"

Youqing: "Sheep milk was given to me by Director Li (Mrs. Li), and bananas and daily nuts were brought to me by my mother from home."

Once again, Youqing missed the meal after feeding Grandpa Feng. He sent the bowls back to the kitchen and as he was about to start mopping the floor, he was stopped by Chef Zhao, "Keep up the good work, child. There will be always warm meals for you whenever you're here." He took out some food from the pot.

In the afternoon, I was surprised to find that Grandpa Feng's bed sores had healed, and the original skin lesions had turned into white patterns that looked like castor seeds.

Mrs. Du asserted that if Youqing could dress the elderly and move them onto a wheelchair, he would be an excellent elderly care worker.

After Mrs. Du left, Grandpa Lin came over to me quietly and whispered: "That woman is not something! But Mr. Ye, you're awesome," He raised his thumb, "The kid works hard whether you're here or not."

Looking at Youqing's busy figure, I realized that even life goals have density. He was so pure to the point that giving without taking credit was all that he was. He devoted himself, remained silent and worked hard day and night, for the happiness of others.

**Day 1409 – Day 1410**

People grow up three times.

The second time was when I found myself powerless in the face of laws. My maternal Grandpa passed away, and I went to offer condolences.

## Day 1411

When Youqing got up in the morning, he said that after Labor Day he was going to the retirement homes that rejected him before, to show them that he could do all the work well.

In the morning, Youqing was sweeping the floor in the VIP room. Qian Xiong, standing in the middle of the ground, suddenly remembered something. He fixed his headgear, turned around and sat back down in his bed, as if he was waiting for something (He realized that his epilepsy was about to break out again).

With a convulsion, he fell onto the bed. It seemed that he was trying to resist 4–5 different forces simultaneously from pulling him apart. The muscles on his arms and legs were tightened like a brake line. His head twisted to one side, foam gushed out from mouth, and a strong tremor followed the wave. The headgear was grinding on the wall making a buzzing noise. He tucked in his arms and raised them up, looking like surrendering—surrendering to fate.

Lao Geng glanced at Qian, spat on the floor, and walked out of the room to bask in the sun.

Old Lin, lying in bed, turned around and turned up the radio to its maximum volume.

After 10 minutes, everything returned to normal.

Qian stared at the ceiling emotionlessly. Youqing got him a tub of warm water, and placed it down in front of him, "Uncle Qian, please wash your face."

Qian Xiong glanced at Youqing and nodded slightly.

**Day 1412**

Mrs. Du asked Youqing to take care of Lan Yin. No one could expect that Lan Yin was the ultimate challenge at the time.

**Day 1413**

Grandpa Feng has gone out to bask in the sun.

It took Youqing 14 days to get an old man with his burial clothes ready to come out and sit in the sun.

Youqing dressed Grandpa Feng carefully and put him in a wheelchair. Everyone was shocked when they saw them in the yard. People praised them and sent their greetings to Grandpa Feng. Surprisingly, Lao Geng grinned and gave Youqing a thumbs-up, and blood returned to his face.

Dean Li wanted to reward Youqing, who said he wanted to invite the elderly and caregivers to drink something.

"What drink?" Dean Li asked.

"Whatever they want!"

"Alright."

That spring, the elderly enjoyed the warm sunshine and the beverage of their choices in the yard. And it was Mr. Li's treat.

Grandpa Feng sat in a wheelchair and took a sip of his favorite yogurt, enjoying the coolness of the sour liquid running through his throat, and the warmth of the sun shining on his face.

The caregivers and I were drinking soda on the side, letting the sunshine fall on our shoulders. At that moment we felt like gods, as if we were taking care of our children. We were the masters of all things.

I turned my head and glanced at Youqing.

The sun shone directly on Youqing's back, as he lifted a pile of sheets above his head and unfolded them out on a drying line. He smiled mysteriously while looking at everyone enjoying what he had earned for them.

Chef Zhao handed him a bottle of soda, "This one is colder, Youqing."

"I'm good, thanks. Cold drinks make me fart." Youqing said with a smile.

Chef Zhao came back over to us and gave me a quick glance.

You might think that Youqing did this to please the elderly, or to make some friends within the care workers, but I believe that he did it just to bring a little happiness to everyone... even if it was just a little.

At this moment, I received a text message on my phone. I looked at it and put down the soda in my hand.

Youqing's mom: "Mr. Ye, I can't agree to the path that Youqing has chosen. Do you really think he is strong now?"

That was the second time Youqing's mom rejected his choice, and I decided to defend for Youqing.

Mr. Ye: "When he was in school, he couldn't do without his auntie.

Later on, he couldn't do without me.

Now, Youqing can work independently, and Grandpa Feng couldn't do without him. Do you think he's strong or not?

I don't think he's stronger than before. Rather, I think this is what strong looks like. He's strong since he is irreplaceable. For Grandpa Zhu, You-qing is all that he has.

He stood out from thousands of his peers and became an irreplaceable member of the society. He pulled Feng back from the line of death, who couldn't do without him now. Even if only one person in this world who cannot do without you, you are the only one for that person.

And that's what we strive for, to be the one, nothing else.

Why would anyone think that this is not considered strong?

Because they want to look decent and have a face. What they say and what they think, are all manipulated by the thought of what others think about you, instead of what Youqing really wants.

And once you're on that path, an unrealistic path, every step that you take would be a failure.

Some might ask, 'What's real to you?'

What's real to me is what Youqing really wants. Which is the fact that he wants to take care of the elderly."

Youqing's mom: "I had a nightmare last night and my mind was not clear enough to follow your thoughts, Mr. Ye."

Mr. Ye: "We have been on our own path, an independent path, with you, Youqing's dad, Youqing, me, and a few other lonely souls on this path. But what we need to repeatedly test is whether the direction of this path is right or not. If it is right, we'll succeed in the end no matter how difficult it is. But what's the standard for testing?

Is it a divine power? Is it fate, or a dream?

None of the above. Nearly four years of hard practice proved it. Only dialectical materialism has achieved success: starting from reality, seeking truth from facts, and resolving major contradictions.

If we don't believe this one, we will fall into the quagmire of prophecy, illusion, and emotion. We would be weak, powerless, and struggling in the chaos of our thoughts.

The path that Youqing has taken is a true path of individuality. It might look tough because he is in the early stage. What's keeping him going is his love in heart.

Don't just stand across from him. Stand by his side!"

Youqing's father replied, "I support him to keep going! What awaits him in the future might just be music and doing good deeds."

––––––––––

Mr. Jia: "Youqing's figure has a kind of beauty!"

Mr. Ye: "Indeed, nothing is more beautiful than someone who is dedicated to bettering oneself. This is the first principle of aesthetics."

People grow up three times.

The third time is when you realize that even if you are shattered, there is still one thing you have to do.

In the evening, Mrs. Du gathered everyone outside the VIP room for an emergency meeting, and she signaled everyone to slow down.

Inside the room, Youqing was guiding the tyrannical Qian Xiong to change his own diaper.

Qian Xiong obediently followed the instructions and put on a clean diaper, preparing for bedtime. Seeing this scene, everyone admired Youqing even more.

I asked Youqing why he let Qian do it on his own.

"Uncle Qian is not an elder." Youqing replied with a smile.

## Day 1414

Youqing felt that his skills had passed the test and insisted on going back to the nursing home that had persuaded him to leave to prove himself. Mrs. Li was very reluctant to let her friend Qing go for revenge. Before leaving she gave Youqing a slip that read:

*Dear leaders,*

*Our intern is heading to your company for work. He has been working as an intern at my retirement home for a month. During the internship he takes the work seriously, and he has developed the skills for such a position. He is trustworthy and able to follow the various rules and procedures of the retirement home well and carry out orderly work.*

*He is strongly principle-based, with a normal level of adaptability. In daily work, he is not afraid of hardship, fatigue, or dirt. His sincere care for the elderly is especially a role model for everyone to learn from.*

*He has a certain academic atmosphere, treats every elderly per-
son politely, is diligent and enterprising in their job, and is able
to constantly adjust and adapt to new job positions in the new
environment. What's hard to come by is that he can keep his
principles and dedication while adapting to the new environment. He kept our image positive, while being an idol for me as
well as the rest of the workers here.*

*The members of our retirement home are reluctant to let him
leave, and I hope he can keep working with us for a long time.
However, he has his own will, and he is eager to show the improvements of his abilities in a short period of time. Therefore,
we hope that your company can give him a chance to prove
himself. We all believe that he can do it.*

*Sincerely, and thank you in advance.*

## Day 1419

Youqing was leaving, and the two of us went to say goodbye to Grandpa
Feng.

Feng remained silent for a long time. I asked him what he wanted to say,
and Grandpa Feng said:

"A drop of yearning tear fell down my cheek."

## Day 1420

It was May the Fourth, the Youth Day. After getting up, Youqing, the
nice youth of socialism, headed straight to the nursing home.

Outside of the nursing home, I asked Youqing:

"Have you tried working here before?"

"Yes."

"And you were fired?"

"Yes."

"Why?"

"I turned off the TV and pulled the curtains for the elderly without permission."

"The families of the elderly for whom you turned off the TV and pulled the curtains are all preparing to teach you a lesson in the nursing home. Do you still want to go in and look for a job?"

"Yes."

"Alright, let's go."

Five minutes later, Youqing learned another lesson:

Sometimes in life, there's only one opportunity.

After he was rejected, he calmly made the decision to go back to Mr. Li.

### Day 1421

Youqing's been back. Mr. and Mrs. Li welcomed him with open arms. I proposed that they should sign a labor contract, including the social insurance and housing fund. Mr. Li said that he worried that Youqing's condition would not be stable enough, suggesting that he try for one week.

Youqing went home and packed two pieces of clothes. Suddenly, he said to his mother on his way out: mom, I'll wait on you next time when I come back!"

Youqing's mother held onto the door frame, suppressing tears.

At night, the elders had already fallen asleep, and the surroundings were pitch black. As agreed with Dean Li, I left the retirement home, and Youqing took out a book for logic training at the small table in the dormitory.

The moon was bright, and there were only a few stars in the sky. I looked back as I walked out of the gate, seeing a lamp so dim and looked like a bean.

Time flew by, and I haven't heard from Youqing.

Seven days later, I went back to the retirement home. I was so careful like a little girl opening a box of candy.

I came straight to Grandpa Feng.

"How has Youqing been doing these days?"

"He is very down-to-earth in his work."

I was very happy to hear it from Feng, but I turned around and saw Mrs. Du's disappointed face. It seemed that the accident still happened: Youqing let Lan Yin fall twice while moving her in the wheelchair.

Mr. Li said: "I'm the head of the retirement home, and I have my principles. I must ensure the safety of the elderly. Therefore, I'd like to ask you to leave for a while, Mr. Ye, as we need to observe for a period of time." Some people say that bad things in life will eventually pass, but if not, it means they haven't reached the end yet.

**Day 1452**

Mrs. Li revealed to me the truth about Lan Yin's fall.

It turned out that Lan was causing trouble for Youqing. When he was holding her in a wheelchair, she intentionally fell and sat on the ground. Youqing thought it was his fault, so he apologized. Without knowing the truth, Mrs. Du made Youqing repeatedly practice the decomposition action and tried to analyze the cause of the accident.

When the accident happened again, Youqing lost all the trust he had gained from Mrs. Du and Mr. Li also put the printed contract back in the drawer.

Youqing was transferred from his job position and underwent a written self-criticism at the meeting. He lost the qualification to interact with the elderly and could only do some auxiliary work such as sweeping the floor and taking out garbage in the yard.

Two weeks later, due to his good attitude and engagement in the work, as well as his constantly making commitments to Mr. Li, Youqing earned a second chance to take care of the elderly.

There is an old Chinese saying: justice is at the mercy of the heart.

When Lan Yin did the same for the third time, Grandma Li in the bed next to her couldn't bear looking down and angrily said:

"The kid wakes up early and goes to sleep late for us every day. Are you just treating him like this? It's outrageous of you!"

Mrs. Du and Mrs. Li rushed over at the sound. The old lady trembled as she told them everything she had seen.

Mrs. Du criticized Lan Yin for her actions.

After learning about the incident later, I had a conversation with Mrs. Du.

Mr. Ye: "Lan Yin may just be expressing opposition in her own way."

Mrs. Du: "Against what exactly?"

Mr. Ye: "Have you told her about Youqing's taking care of her?'

Mrs. Du: "If she had any ideas, why not speak up directly?"

Mr. Ye: "Well, maybe the answer lies in her experience."

Lan Yin's home was in the mountains. She was born disabled and was abandoned by his parents on a mountain road.

An old lady passed by and took her home. The old lady's children opposed to it and said: "If you keep her, we'll stop taking care of you." The old lady made a tent with plastic sheets halfway up the mountain and raised Lan Yin to the age of three before passing away.

Lan Yin was taken away by a man who happened to pass by and raised her to the age of 16. She was forced to give birth to a girl with this man and the baby died soon after. Lan Yin also suffered from serious gynecological diseases. Years later, the man sold her to a neighboring county. A middle-aged man from the neighboring county, whose wife did not have children, bought Lan Yin and raised her for two years. After he found that Lan Yin had lost her ability to have children, he abandoned her on the side of the road.

A kind-hearted Buddhist friend pointed out the maze and told Lan Yin to crawl towards the temple. The abbot of the temple contacted the Buddhist Association, which was preparing to send her to a public nursing home. Then they realized that although Lan Yin was over 30 years old, she did not have her own name, let alone the ID card and household registration.

The president of the Buddhist Association named her Lan Yin, hoping that she would understand the world, forget her past troubles, and find true happiness. The local government reissued ID for her and sent her to the nursing home. Later, the nursing home disbanded, and she was transferred to this retirement home.

We are all prisoners of our past. Perhaps silent struggle might be the only way when facing the imposed fates and unexpected misfortune. Isn't it a reflection of how humans fight against nature, society, fate, and themselves?"

Mrs. Du was greatly surprised upon hearing this.

---

Mr. Jia: "How do you even know all of that?"

Mr. Ye: "Because I care. These pieces of information are easily obtainable from Mrs. Li, as long as you ask."

Mr. Jia: "Did Youqing feel very aggrieved?"

Mr. Ye: "Who hasn't experienced being misunderstood? Mrs. Li said she felt so bad at the wronged Youqing at that time, but Youqing didn't take it seriously. His chest was pounding with a heart of service, determined to devote himself to meeting everyone's needs."

**Day 1461**

Mr. Li and Youqing signed a formal labor contract.

That day, someone who grew up in contempt and ridicule gained meaning in the world.

In the evening, everyone gathered at a restaurant to celebrate.

The sword is our last resort when fighting for our freedom. It is also the first thing we shall put down once we achieve the freedom we are fighting for.

During the feast, I announced that from that moment on, the principle of education would be changed: in the future, if Youqing does not think he is wrong, he will not change.

Youqing suddenly raised his glass:

"Uncle Ye, the next step is to get me a girlfriend, right?"

Everyone present was stunned. I stood up, and toasted to the person who never gave up and always looked forward to the future:

"Come, Youqing. Let's wash away the arrogant memories with this fine wine!"

**Day 1465**

This day was my 36th birthday, and Auntie Liu, who has always been concerned about me, wrote a letter saying:

"You need to take care of yourself."

**Day 1472**

I fell ill, and the doctor couldn't find the cause.

Based on the average workload in the education industry, at the age of 36, I probably had worked for almost 60 years of work.

Whatever happened, I needed to keep working.

I reported to Youqing's parents lying in bed for the first time.

**Day 1478**

Auntie Liu wrote:

"Keep up the good work! You will succeed! Keep on working. It is not easy to be a decent human, a real human. I wish you the best once again and success will be yours!"

**Day 1480**

My illness worsened.

A Letter from Youqing's mom:

In the hearts of Youqing's dad and mine, Mr. Ye is family member to us.

**Day 1492**

Youqing got his first month's salary.

I wrote to Mr. Li:

The first salary in Youqing's life was given by Mr. Li.

Mr. Li wrote back:

He earned it through hard work, while hard work earns something un-forgettable. This is inseparable from your education and cultivation.

Youqing spent half a month's salary buying two of the most expensive thermos cups for his parents in the mall, and specially bought a red rose for his mother.

Youqing's parents deserved this gift because they taught Youqing what love was.

Besides showing filial piety to parents, Youqing only knew one way to utilize the money—to deposit it into a bank account.

Youqing's mother held the rose in her hand, and took many photos with her son in her arms, and said:

> Youqing sent me roses, which made me particularly happy. It seemed that it was not a problem for Youqing to win over women's hearts. I was too excited to sleep! Congratulations to Youqing for starting a new chapter in your life. My son, the good qualities, such as romance, nobility, kindness and perse-verance, are all going to show themselves as you grow older. I am pleased that fate has given you all these. I hope they nourish your life, and you could dedicate yourself to the great love you wished for.

Only a little bit of sweetness is needed to please a woman with a lot of bitterness in her heart.

Grandpa Zhou wrote:

> Youqing, I had some of the candy that you bought me with

*your salary. They melted in my mouth, and it was sweet in my heart. I knew how hard it was for you. You worked so hard and studied so seriously when you were with me. Grandma Han and I praised you for countless times behind your back, but I never praised you in front of you, because we didn't want you to turn arrogant. I'm pleased to know that you're great at your job.*

*Youqing, you are a kind child, with a grateful heart. I hope you will be even more filial to your parents, as they are not easy to be with you.*

*Welcome to come to Shenyang again whenever you have time. We will stay a few days together.*

*And thank you for the candy, as well as the good news you brought me.*

It was late at night, and I arrived at Youqing's dormitory. He was sound asleep in a room at 37°C with 79% humidity.

Once a person figures out what he lives for, he is capable of tolerating any kind of life.

People are jealous of such life. They want to destroy it, but at the same time they want to have it.

They understand the value of love in Youqing's heart. They don't want Youqing to become them. Instead, they want to become him. His free-will is the most beautiful and indescribable power in the universe.

To be his mentor, had made my life so much more meaningful.

At night, I dreamed that I had gone to heaven (obviously it was a fairy tale) and found that the gods were reading with great concentration. I walked up to them and saw the book was titled The Victory of Man.

—————————

Mr. Jia: "Why haven't others created miracles like yours?"

Mr. Ye: "They probably don't have such things that we have right here."

### Letter of Authorization

*Mr. Ye Zhigang has created educational miracles one after another with his innovation, persistence as well as dedication to his career. We believe that he is a teacher who directly reaches the spiritual world of the educated, a spiritual mentor who reshapes life, a hope for contemporary education that has gone astray, a blessing for every family that intersects with him, and a true mentor for students.*

*My wife and I, as guardians, authorize Mr. Ye to cultivate and educate our son Youqing in all aspects. We authorize Mr. Ye to educate Youqing at any time and place, and in any way necessary. During this period, all consequences will be borne jointly by me and my wife. When Youqing reaches adulthood, he will bear the consequences himself. If Youqing is unable to bear it, it will still be borne jointly by me and my wife.*

*For the sake of the ones who are struggling in pain just like we did, we agree that Mr. Ye Zhigang will write and publish a book based on the experience of mentoring Youqing.*

*We cherish the peaceful life now. Therefore, the three of us jointly entrust Mr. Ye with full authority on contacting and communicating with the media and the public. We fully trust and obey Mr. Ye Zhigang's judgment and decisions, and we are willing to bear all consequences.*

*The above authorization represents the wills of the three princi-
pals, and it shall remain true, valid, and irrevocable.*

Mr. Jia: "Such a great trust that they had in you!"

Mr. Ye: "My principle is to trust and entrust unconditionally. Because
there is always a gap between idea and reality. There is no other way to
cross this gap, except by taking a leap.

When I was young, I grew up next to my father's workstation. He was
the first enlightenment teacher that I've ever had in my life. He showed
me what kind of life a man can create through his own hands and honest
work.

My father used to say to me that not all ego leads to backwardness.
Among all the beneficial arrogance, the most admirable one is the ego
generated from being trustworthy."

Youqing had gained the trust of the entire retirement home. Time flew
from summer to autumn. It was time for him to take on the journey to
find love.

This is the trust my father has gained, and the certificate is kept at the
Kaizong Museum.

### 12. There are four words in the world that can withstand all hardships and misfortunes.

Day 1572

In the morning, Mr. Li called Youqing to his office and said to him with
sadness:

"Youqing, ever since you came here, both the elders and I think highly of your work. You work solidly, work hard, are polite to the elderly, and care about them meticulously. You are not afraid of dirt or fatigue. This summer, it is so hot, but you are not afraid. As a leader, I feel very proud to have employees like you.

However, Youqing, you are young, and I should consider your future. You cannot take care of the elders here for a lifetime. Follow Mr. Ye and go seeking the love that's meant for you!"

Dean Li gritted his teeth and said, "Don't come back until you get married."

Youqing ran to the VIP room to bid farewell to Grandpa Feng.

But he saw a lawyer standing in front of Feng's bed, with a tense atmosphere.

Originally, Feng had two children, but neither of them wanted to pay for Feng's alimony. The lawyer drafted a lawsuit, handed over ink, and asked Grandpa Feng to press his fingerprints to sue his children in court on behalf of Grandpa Feng.

Grandpa Feng clenched his thumb tightly and sighed in tears:

"They are all my children."

Later, according to Mrs. Li, Grandpa Feng passed away shortly after Youqing left the retirement home.

### Day 1574

Suddenly, I got a letter from home. My mom fell down by accident, suffered a bone fracture in her waist, and was bedridden. Upon receiving the news, Youqing immediately rushed to my mother's bedside, and took care of her for four months until she recovered.

**Day 1618** Panjin, at my parents'

"Mr. Ye, are you watching the news?" Youqing's mom called.
On the TV screen, a rocket sprayed flames straight into the sky.

"What is this, Youqing's mom?"

"It is the launch of the Beidou Navigation Satellite," continued You-qing's mom. "Mr. Ye, there is your contribution on this satellite."

"Wait, could it be?"

"Yes, Youqing had been with me. From childhood to adulthood, I was always concerned about him and didn't have the energy to work until I met you. I felt relieved. Over the past four years, I have devoted all my energy to scientific research. With my products on this satellite, you have put in your hard work."

**Day 1696**

On the Eve of the Chinese New Year.

My mother: "Youqing, the Spring Festival Gala is on, go and watch it."
Youqing: "No, grandma, I'll prepare a foot bath for you first and then watch it. I know that who is kind toward me, and I need to be grateful."

You can't tell someone's true character in a short amount of time.

———————

Mr. Ye: "Even though his life was turned all the way around, people still believe that someone like him can only find a disabled person to start a family in the future."

Mr. Jia: "What do you think of it?"

Mr. Ye: "People always calculate too much and think too little.
What is love?

Love is a violent chemical reaction, a desire to become better, willingness to die for the person you love.

When the sun of love rises, the rational moon is at its end.

What they are talking about is not love, but a deal. For such deals, You-qing and I can't care less."

Mr. Jia: "What kind of partner did you think that Youqing could find at that moment?"

Mr. Ye: "Someone who truly appreciates Youqing, a woman whose heart beats faster when she sees Youqing, a woman who is willing to have children for Youqing."

Mr. Jia: "How are you so certain that Youqing can get happiness?"

Mr. Ye: "I'm not certain that Youqing will always be happy. But a girl who is with Youqing will be happy."

Mr. Jia: "How come?"

Mr. Ye: "The prerequisite for a woman's happiness is that a real man is standing by her side.

There are two criteria for judgment:

He needs to have a sound life instinct, and a spiritual pursuit of self-transcendence.

Both are Youqing's celebrations."

Mr. Jia: "Youqing is indeed a person with emotions and righteousness. Did you have a certain confidence in Youqing's ability to find a girlfriend at that time?"

Mr. Ye: "I was somewhat certain about it, because as long as the male desire was strong enough and the timing was accurate, success would be achieved. It was not a problem for Youqing to have a strong desire, but the timing was a little tricky."

Mr. Jia: "You couldn't time it for him?"

Mr. Ye: "I wasn't the best candidate."

Mr. Jia: "What should we do then?'

Mr. Ye: "Find this person."

A person's personality is his/her destiny.

Miss Liu has been quiet ever since she was a child and enjoyed listening to others talk, observing their expressions. She was four years old at that time.

She loved to watch the "Traffic Lights" program on Beijing TV the most because it showed the streets and traffic flow of the big city she longed for, when she was 14 years old.

She is empathetic, but not good at expressing her emotions. She is a sentimental soul, but she looks cold and distant. She loves the person she likes in a silent and delicate way, but it is an imperceptible love.

She experienced the dark side of love—betrayal, and she never felt complete again.

Before parting, her ex-boyfriend promised, "We can be together once again in the future if we don't find anyone else better."

What she didn't know at that time was that the true meaning of "future" in the mouths of primates was "never".

Her heart turned into stone, and those three years had almost emptied her entire life. She was no longer the person she used to be, afraid of deep emotions and a big dream. She was 21 years old that year.

The one person has always lived deep in her heart, and it would hurt her every time she thought of him, but she kept that feeling there. Because she knew that she might fall in love with someone else in the future, but she wouldn't be as childish, reckless, and have the courage not to turn back without hitting the wall.

She felt that she had suffered losses in the first twenty years of her life by being too sensible, which was the biggest mistake. She would always sacrifice her own interests for others, and in the end, it was the thoughtfulness that had ruined her.

She walked towards the opposite side.

She fell in love with loving, but no longer loved any individual. She enjoyed a lot of fun but did not achieve any substantial results.

The dark night struck, and she felt like it was all a tragedy. The only problem was that she was the protagonist of this tragedy. She was 23 years old that year.

She felt that her heart was sick, and she didn't know that mental illness was indeed a disease.

She fell into the endless void, as if floating on the ocean, heading toward the deep, dark and green depths. There was nothing above her head, nothing below her feet, she was exhausted and didn't have enough energy to wake up. And with it came an unpleasant smell, the smell of sadness, feeling that she had died.

But she had not said goodbye to her mother, and she still looked beautiful in the minor. Her past life was shattered into pieces, and she has completely sunk.

Diagnosis from Peking University Sixth Hospital: **Severe depression**.

### Day 1723

A person claiming to be a "Young Talent" saw a photo of hers. "Young Talent" only glanced at her photo and determined:

This woman in the picture has experienced the joys and sorrows of life with all her passion. She has outstanding strengths and weaknesses, which are all exposed in front of people. She has her opinions on things, is resilient to temptation, and knows what suits her. She has a unique view on life and the world which she has gained from experiencing much unbelievable misery and loneliness. Deep within this lonely heart is the strongest love known to a man.

### Day 1726

She had the gift of expressing emotions through written words, though it was full of desolation throughout the lines.

He had the same gift as well and touched her heart with 1100 lines of unheard legends and stories.

"Young Talent" told her that she should start over and respect herself. She said she wanted to see photos of his, and to listen to his voice, but he refused. He said that the best part of him was already seen by her, which was his heart.

## Day 1731

"Young Talent" showed up in front of her.

She had never been clear about her criteria for choosing a spouse until she saw this "Young Talent" with her own eyes and realized that other guys couldn't be taken.

Someone asked whether it is that the more mature a person is, the harder it is to fall in love with him?

The more mature you are, the harder it is to fall in love with someone.

The more mature you get, the easier for you to tell whether it is love or not.

She fell in love with him.

"Young Talent" gave her two antidotes for depression: one is to be a mother, and the other is to help Youqing find a partner. She said she was willing to do two things at the same time.

## Day 1741

She arrived at the reed marshes on the coast of the Bohai Sea and started their journey of finding true love with Youqing.

I call this journey "The Journey of Meeting and Dating".

**Day 1749**

Nature manipulates people.

The physical examination center called and said that she was HIV positive.

How are the good days ending so soon when they barely started?

Why is my life so hard?

She felt aggrieved.

She bid farewell to her lover on the phone.

"Don't go anywhere. It's no big deal. Don't you die without AIDS? Life and death are not important, but the heart matters. If diagnosed, we will fight against AIDS together." The young talent said firmly.

Upon hearing these, she cried like a child. This was the first time in her life that she has understood the meaning of the words "what is important is the heart". At that moment, she regained her confidence in human nature.

**Day 1750**

The laboratory report from the Center for Disease Control and Prevention shows that the examination center misdiagnosed.

On the hallway of the hospital, the young talent wrote a poem:

> *Trembling hands,*
> *Tearful eyes,*
> *With a desperate soul.*

*Just yesterday,*
*Just now,*
*We came from the jaws of fate,*
*Then escaped.*
*It's not luck.*
*It's enlightenment.*
*This real spiritual experience,*
*Remind us*
*What to live for.*
*If we*
*Are not the givers of meaning,*
*The puzzle solver of fate,*
*And the savior of desperate lives,*
*How can we bear to be human beings?*

## Day 1813

She was pregnant.

Her previous pain has enabled her to have foresight, and she is adept at timing and insight into human nature. She gave her all to Youqing. She cherishes her lover even more.

## Day 1843

Diagnosis from Peking University Sixth Hospital: **No depressive state.**

---

Mr. Jia: "Why are the two antidepressants for depression that you prescribed to Mrs. Liu so effective?"

Mr. Ye: "There are four words in the world that can withstand all hardships and misfortunes. The essence of these two antidotes is precisely these four words."

Mr. Jia: "Which four?"

Mr. Ye: "Live for other people."

Mr. Jia: "How did Mrs. Liu help Youqing find a partner?"

The true help is to awaken a person's self-esteem and self-improvement.

During those days, all the miracles that happened to Youqing made him a symbol of diligence and bravery, as well as an embodiment of virtue.

But Mrs. Liu had a different perspective:

This man is a lazy person.

Why is there such a statement?

Mrs. Liu has three reasons:

Youqing is watching, but never observes.

Youqing is listening, but never hears.

Youqing is experiencing, but never thinks.

Everyone suddenly realized that she was right.

Youqing expressed his intention to change his past mistakes. But every time he brushed past Mrs. Liu, he turned back and stuck out his tongue.

Youqing didn't know that Mrs. Liu has always liked to observe people from the chrome frame, continuous reflection on the mirror surface, and even the stainless-steel spoon back.

The world is changing rapidly. On this side, it's Mrs. Liu with white teeth and red lips joking, while on the other side, it's Youqing who has been whipped by his mom and me.

What truly established Mrs. Liu's revolutionary leadership was her correctness.

Most women's love advice to men is to "offer hospitality with a heavy head" and "buy, give and be moved".

But Mrs. Liu is an outsider. She is one of the very few women who know how to flirt with girls.

She took Youqing to the mall to choose clothes, transforming his image from a gloomy young man to a sunny big boy. The artistic photos she personally took for Youqing captivated everyone and received over 9000

likes from girls online.

She took him to the dating spots for a close inspection and to experience the sweetness of love.

The birds can tell the directions because they can see the magnetic field lines of the Earth. On the first day of a formal meeting, Mrs. Liu called Youqing to her side:

"The elderly often say that foxes are valuable for their skin, cows are valuable for their meat, and people are valuable for their bones.

People who blindly cater to girls lack dignity because they lack principles. Therefore, before you start dating, you need to know what type of girls you wouldn't date."

Youqing concluded: those with an eccentric personality, a love for showing off wealth, Internet celebrities, those with extensive tattoos, those who self-harm and those who like to borrow money.

Mrs. Liu taught Youqing to navigate a dating app. Youqing was full of confidence, but he didn't know how fragile his principles were without any real experience, like falling flowers, and willows and cotton, rootless and inexplicable.

If you are tempted, you will be worried about gains and losses.

Youqing is worried that the girls he likes don't like him back.

Mrs. Liu told him: "Don't worry and keep your principles. She will come to you if you have what she wants on you. Don't be afraid of missing it. If you miss it, it means she doesn't like you enough. It's not a big deal."

Youqing was trying too hard to understand a girl in a short amount of time.

Mrs. Liu told him: "Look at her best friend who she hangs out with in the photos. Birds of a feather flock together."

Youqing met a "slow hot girl" who was slow to warm up to him.

Mrs. Liu told him: "Both 'slow hot personality' and 'cold and thin nature' are excuses.

The ones who like you can take a four-hour high-speed train to see you, while the ones who don't can't make an appointment next door. She's busy not because she's physically busy, but because you are not attractive enough for her to take time."

Youqing tried to buy them gifts.

Mrs. Liu told him: "The ones who like you wouldn't stop liking you for not giving them gifts. And the ones who don't like you, it's useless for you to keep your head down and give gifts. You can buy your way in."

Youqing bragged.

Mrs. Liu told him: "Honesty is the best strategy. Don't show off qualities you do not possess."

A girl said that she had many suitors, which made Youqing anxious.

Mrs. Liu told him: "Don't believe the ones who say they have no suitors, and don't worry about the ones who say they have too many. Just assume that those competitors don't exist. Rest assured that she's not interested in any of them, or she wouldn't have time to talk to you."

A girl said that she has no filter when she speaks, hoping Youqing forgives her.

Mrs. Liu decided quickly: "Having no filter means she doesn't like you enough. It's not her personally. Her ego and arrogance are for someone whom she doesn't like. If she meets someone she likes, she wouldn't turn caring and polite in a blink of eye."

Youqing kept pursuing a girl relentlessly though he was rejected.

Mrs. Liu handed him a bowl of mung bean smoothie and said: "The common problem among those losers is that they cannot handle psychological denial correctly. They always think: 'I have to succeed now, and I will succeed if I give it a little more.' You need to set a deadline for yourself and stop the losses in a timely manner."

Youqing was showing off.

Mrs. Liu reminded him: "A good girl who sees you so flashy would directly rule you out."

For a while, Youqing had a peach-blossom luck. The girl who liked him kept going, and hormones provided too much oxygen. He impulsively took off and plunged into illusions, which made Youqing proud.

Mrs. Liu reminded him: "Do you still remember your principles?"

Youqing took out his phone and silently deleted most of it.

Those who are not hungry cannot eat with them. To get to know girls, Youqing took the initiative to learn and use 12306, shopping apps and taxi apps on his own, and stumbled into the Internet era.

He became a social animal. During a trip, a couple argued along the way. The boy kept reasoning, while the girl became more and more anxious and cried. She was sobbing and the guy was in despair. Youqing went to him and said: "Give her a hug, man."

One minute later, when the wind died down, the broken mirror was reunited. They made up and everything was fine.

People were amazed.

Youqing's answer was very concise: Teacher Liu was my benefactor. She helped me maintain my self-esteem in love.

There is a question in *100 Modern Literature Passage for Reading Skills Training in the High School Entrance Examination*, published by Hunan Education Press.

"In our life, there are always people who give us warmth. Please describe one of them and talk about the impact they have brought you. (4 points)"

Youqing's answer was very concise: Mrs. Liu was my benefactor. She helped me maintain my self-esteem in love.

### Day 1799

A small line of text appeared on Youqing's social networking app.

"I feel like," A girl from Heilongjiang said to Youqing, "that you're mature, emitting an indescribable aura."

Xiaoxue, a poetic and picturesque name, a beautiful and generous beautician with healthy limbs, and an unforgettable fate.

Mrs. Liu quietly told Youqing: "Women love through their ears."

### Day 1811

Chatting with Youqing can be described in my words as "wasting 10 minutes listening to your words". But after 10 days of chatting with Xiaoxue in his own way, they made an appointment to meet up in Harbin.

### Day 1812

On a summer night in Harbin, the air was slightly tipsy, and Youqing and Xiaoxue strolled on the Central Street Pedestrian Street.

This old street, built in 1898, bears witness to a hundred years of history and the love of Youqing.

## Day 1870

At the first sight of joy, they still felt the hearts pounding for a long time. Xiaoxue invited Youqing to celebrate on Qixi, the Chinese Valentine's Day.

The incredible details of "The Journey of Meeting and Dating" can be found in Appendix 10 of the Chinese version of *Salvation Lies Within* published by Tsinghua University Press: Please speak with the quality of marriage except for children.

## Day 1872

His reality is the proof of his success.

Youqing earned the complete respect from his father for the very first time in his life.

At 6:15 in the morning, before leaving, his father said to Youqing:

"Goodbye, Youqing."

He took the initiative to shake his son's hand, and the father and son bid farewell.

Youqing's mother asked Youqing's father why he took the initiative to shake his son's hand, and Youqing's father said:

"Because he can endure the hardships that others cannot, and he has a girl who likes him by his side. He has grown up now."

Indeed, Youqing is steady while others are lost. He is simple while others are complicated. He is brave while others are weak. He is detached while others are greedy. He is infatuated while others are promiscuous. He speaks with his action while others are decadent. He is slow and dull, but he plays his cards the best he could, while others are wise and discerning but waste the nice cards that they dealt with. Youqing is not good at speaking, but he has a heart, while others speak eloquently but lack hearts. So, who is real person in the end?

In the years before Youqing met me, people would see the waste of emotions, and "The Journey of Talent-Cultivating" and "The Journey of Meeting and Dating" further told us the futility of reason.

We saw a grey image in the beginning, and then we walked into the void by following Youqing's steps, mocked for the human arrogance of sensibility and rationality. Apart from the attitude of self-improvement, we have nothing.

Educating someone is the first, ultimate, and the only love that I have. My miracles start with me, and end with me. Anyone who follows my path will succeed with fruitful results, and anyone who imitates my footsteps will fall into an abyss.

The young mentors behind me, don't submit to anything that looks greater than you. Without you, they're merely magnificent ruins.

Everything relies on you and your youthful lives. Everything relies on your creativity.

# Part II
# My Education Thoughts

# Chapter 10
# My Life Journey

Before I was born, the doctor gave the following diagnosis: this child was either disabled or mentally handicapped. The reason was simple: my maternal grandfather was brother of my grandmother. In 1974, with the blessings from the entire family, my parents got married. They grew up together and their innocent love was envied by many people. But just six years later, the 1980 version of the Marriage Law explains the enormous genetic risks associated with such marriages. I was born, and the doctor's judgment bore witness to the rigor of science: my head was incredibly large. The doctor said on the spot that I was either deformed or had hydrocephalus. Such a child must have low intelligence and cannot grow tall.

In April 2012, at the age of 30, I had an IQ of 128, a height of 183 cm, and I was agile. I could drive at a speed of 180 km per hour on the track and finish a 1950 km race in one go, which was equivalent to the distance from Beijing to Guilin, Guangxi.

During my childhood, I grew up in a mining area of the Liaohe Oilfield. My father was the module technician in a foundry. I looked up to him. He was the master in his field, and he enjoyed the absolute authority in it. One day, he noticed that I asked him a sharp question, "Are you the best module technician in the world?"

"My son, I heard that the Germans do the best in this area, and their outstanding product is called Mercedes-Benz."

My mother was a beautiful and strong-minded lady. After six miscarriages, she insisted on giving birth to me. She said I was a miracle.

My great grandmother was a daughter of a noble family under the Boarded Yellow Banner of the Manchuria. She had a weird temperament. She never cared much about me. The reason was: according to her palmistry, I was destined to make a fortune through hard work, but a considerable portion of this fortune was distributed to the ones who had helped me. I felt sorry for her nonrecognition of my generosity.

At the age of seven, I was sent to the elementary school of General Machinery Factory in Liaohe Oilfield and started working towards being a good student. One teacher gave me this evaluation: "This student is good at observing. He acts on his own rules and doesn't care for the social norms. He is eager to help with the teacher's work. Keep working hard!"

At the age of thirteen, I entered junior high school. My thoughts back then were to study hard and get into a good university. However, I had the following 11 discoveries in middle school as I grew up, for which I correspondingly found explanations from John Dewey down the line:

1. The contents of the books were far away from my life, and unable to answer the questions that I had within me, and gradually I lost the motivation to study.

"Knowledge is only meaningful in the real world. The textbooks in school are disconnected from the real world, and they do not suit the interests and the needs of the students. Therefore, the student can't form any passion in study."

2. Every student is assigned the exact same curriculum, do the exact same homework, and come to the exact same conclusions. We have very lim-

ited opportunities to work with each other aside from copying homework.

"Why is reading aloud in school boring? One of the reasons is that the real motivation of using language is to communicate with others. The social spirit is not cultivated, and children lack social responsibilities."

3. Some students are trying very hard to work against their parents and society.

"Children are born with a natural desire to express themselves, do things, and serve. When the desire is not satisfied, and when some other motivations take over, an anti-social spirit arises."

4. Most students have the habit of procrastinating.

"When the motivation for work is for the future instead of the present, procrastination is developed. It should be noted that everyone is enthusiastic at the ticket booth."

5. I felt selfish sometimes.

"Selfishness is the impure motive and the self-benefiting result. When a child is unable to develop interest in school, he will automatically seek some kind of stimulation to focus on their study. At best, this stimulation is his love for teachers, the good intentions of his parents or the fear of school rules. The goal is changed from making himself more perfect to surpassing others."

6. I sometimes lack judgment on important issues.

"Judgment is the interpretation of the facts. Good judgment is one of the most important weapons for our survival, and it requires constant testing in life. Simply acquiring knowledge can never develop judgment ability.

One must have the opportunity to make choices for himself and put his choices into practice, so that he can withstand the final test, which is the test of action."

7. I felt like I was wasting my life during high school.

"On the one hand, children are completely unable to fully and freely utilize the experiences they have gained outside campus. On the other hand, they cannot apply what they have learned in school in their daily lives. The discrepancy between school and life created a huge waste of life."

8. Many students have low self-esteem.

My classmate's father got full gray hair when he was in his forties for taking self-study exams. Two years later, he framed the certificate with a red stamp and hung it in the living room, and then went back to work as a welder.

"There is one type of people who are born to study, skilled in being patient and enjoying hardships. They never ask about the purpose of studying, and they have strong memories. Their motivation for learning is to cumulate the useless knowledge as a way to improve their social status. Most people are only interested in the knowledge that they can touch or use in life. In the end, most people lose the opportunity to study. Even if they might be mixed among them, they also earned the reputation of laziness, lack of effort and poor abilities, leading to a low self-esteem for the rest of their lives."

9. I feel that sometimes I lack a sense of responsibility.

"A sense of responsibility is cultivated through exploring the meaning of things step by step, and through continuous practice in action. It can ultimately be established. Students study knowledge that they do not agree with in their hearts throughout the years, and the consequence is that they are unwilling to fully understand the meaning of something and explore the truth of something, and eventually they lose their responsibilities towards things.".

10. I felt depressed sometimes.

"Long term suppression of love and engagement in work that we do not agree with in our hearts makes us particularly indifferent to our inner voices and become negative. Such people often turn their gaze to others, seeking protection through being like others, and this type of security is rotting in our personalities, making us cater to society, being afraid of standing out. Thus, our ideals, beliefs, and values are gradually buried together with the passage of time."

11. I didn't know what I was studying for.

"When a child feels that the homework is a task, he only does it because he has to. And once the outside pressure stops, their attention that is free from constraints immediately flies towards what interests them. Children who are raised on the basis of 'effort' have amazing skills. In psychology, the word "effort" is contradictory. Its theory is to replace one interest with another. The pure interest towards knowledge is replaced by the fear of the teacher's authority, the worry for punishments, impure interest in surpassing peers or hoping to receive rewards in the future."

The above 11 discoveries have made me increasingly disdainful of school education, but upon reflection, I have also received sincere help from many teachers. The two teachers left the deepest impression on me.

I remember Mr. Zhang Riguo, who enhanced my judgment in history class with countless reasons and sincere praise. He often asked me questions, not basic historical knowledge such as how and when the Opium War broke out, and why, and he encouraged me to search for answers that were not available in books. My cogitation was improved dramatically from all the sharp questions.

One day I asked him: "If Hitler died in 1938, what would the world be like today, and how would people evaluate him?" Mr. Zhang firmly said to me, "History has no ifs, and life has no ifs. So, cherish the moment."

I also remember my literature teacher Mr. Zhang Fuguang. One day, after reading Romance of The Three Kingdoms, I felt contradicted because the book praised heroes like Guan Yu and Zhao Yun, but at the same time, it also wrote: "The white-haired fisherman and woodcutters on the riverbank with ease, accustomed to watching the autumn moon and spring breeze," and "Many things from ancient to modern times would end up being casual conversations and laughter." I asked Mr. Zhang, "Is a man supposed to be a hero or to be content with mediocrity?"

Mr. Zhang said to me earnestly, "A man, a great man, walking in this world, even if he turns into a shooting star, shattered to pieces, he will still shine and illuminate the sky!" I have always remembered what he said that day.

However, I was unable to keep going on a path that I did not approve.

In 2000, I failed the college entrance examination.

In 2001, I failed my second attempt, with one point less than the entry score of the 2000 college entrance examination, leaving a mess.

My father was somewhat disappointed at me and decided to encourage me in his way.

In university, I could barely fill my stomach with the 250 Yuan that my loving father remitted each month. Standing on the balcony of my dorm, I looked into the distance and asked myself a sacred question: how can I get enough food?

The next day, I stood up and solicited translation services in the development zone. But at that time, this industry was well saturated. After a thorough investigation, I defeated most of my competitors with the following three tactics:

1. The translated manuscript was subject to the final review by the university professors to ensure optimal quality.

2. The translated manuscript was delivered to the client's doorstep, with precise timing and no delay.

3. My entrepreneurial location was in the teacher's office, and nearly zero cost.

Then, inspired by the slogans on the wall of a tiny restaurant, I came up with a fourth move to kill the last competitor: The client decided on my payment.

I became the wealthiest student.

My stomach was finally full. I stayed in five-star hotels and started having fun in recreational areas all night.

Oscar Wilde once said: "There are two tragedies in one's life: one is not getting what one wants, and the other is getting it." Soon I ran out of imagination in spending money. I got bored by the life of extravagance. I was lost and miserable. One question that hurts me the most: what exactly do I want?

I found the answer in Dr. Abraham Maslow's book. He said that people have five needs, for the most they are materials, safety, social interaction, and respect; and for the selected few, they want the realization of self-worth. There are many ways to achieve self-worth: some climb the summits in the world, some donate money to build libraries in universities, and some donate blood to the Red Cross voluntarily. I asked myself: how do I fulfill my self-worth? And when you start living with a question, the answer would appear unexpectedly.

One day, while running in the park, I noticed that there were several new benches added, which were gifted to the park by a large company. Its name was printed on the back of the chairs: Cheng Ren Da Ji Life Insurance Co. These chairs made me remember the phrase: Cheng Ren Dai Ji, which means to realize self through benefiting others.

Ten years before writing this book, I dropped out of the university in my sophomore year, went back to my hometown and started mentoring Xiaomin. At that time, he was a beast in the eyes of adults. The university president thought that I was crazy—What does a Japanese major know about education? The middle school teacher thought that I was crazy—What does someone who failed the college entrance exam know about education? The professor at the Beijing Normal University thought that I was crazy—What does a young man in Northeast China know about education? My mother thought that I was crazy—I was still a child myself!

But my education has achieved unexpected success.

After helping Xiaomin rebuild his confidence, we traveled all over the country to learn from different industries. In the rural areas of Jiangsu Province, we saw    university graduates coming to the villages to serve as grassroots cadres to help the locals. Their down-to-earth and hardworking spirit left a deep impression on us. After returning to Liaoning, Xiaomin finally set the life goal to "enter politics through the college entrance examination and serve as a village official". Xiaomin voluntarily proposed to go to a listed key high school.

In less than 14 months, Xiaomin completed the previous seven years' courses, and his ranking advanced from 811 to 140 in the entire school.

In 2005, he was admitted to a key high school in the city with a score of 756, and in 2008, he was admitted to a key university of finance and economics. He followed his dream after graduation and became a village official. Nowadays, Xiaomin wakes up at 6:00 am every day and returns home in the dark, leading the villagers towards a better life.

My story with Xiaomin came to an end on a rainy afternoon. His father told me that one day I will achieve great success, and the most precious quality in me is dedication. John Orr Young, the genius of the American advertising industry, wrote a passage in his Advertising Fantasy, which I have made some modifications to make it more suitable here:

If you are lucky enough to find young people who can start your own business with abundant energy and courage, and use such talents to serve you, you will definitely make endless profits. Great educational miracles are created by the parents relying on excellent teachers with unparalleled ambition and energy.

I have accumulated reputation, and my legendary stories spread out in the parent groups. Clients who come to you for your reputation have the utmost trust in you. You don't have to tell them too much, and they just trust you. The essence of trust is willing to trust.

The disadvantage of word-of-mouth is that the customer base is single. Most of the friends of intellectuals are still intellectuals, and they always hope that I can find a way to help their children who can get into key universities get into prestigious universities.

I soon got bored of it because I kept getting results as I expected. The best punishment for young people is to give them the exact same life every day. I wanted to know: what other kinds of children are not easy to educate?

Quickly, my assistant transformed into a property administrator in a noble community. Two weeks later, he presented me with information about all the potential customers in this community: it seemed that the challenges were diverse.

Now it seems that it was a golden age when as long as you had the courage to smash the windshield of a parked Mercedes Benz, there would be business coming to your door. I, who was restless, focused my attention on various tricky types: silent losers, the maniacs, and even the bullies.

My career was on the rise in those years. Inspired by the students, I had my weight dropped from 110 kg to 85 kg.

In 2007, the CCTV News Investigation program reported on walking schools in Jiangsu. I was shocked by the cheap and efficient educational model and magical educational effects in the film. And by contrast, I blushed for my own initiative to inspire others.

Two months later, I learned the truth about the walking school. I took a long breath and went into action lightly, but the tremendous pressure from the media left a deep impression on me.

In November 2007, the China Petroleum Daily published a full-page interview entitled "Ye Zhigang, a Master of Training Rebellious Children", which caught the attention of a child's grandfather. This family has been extremely successful for two generations, but the third generation has put them in a difficult situation.

In 2008, his grandson stepped on the right track under my education. Immediately after that, I worked hard and successfully trained the descendants of six senior predecessors. My doorstep was bustling with traffic.

In 2008, China successfully hosted the Beijing Olympics. The slogan of "Faster, Higher, Stronger" in the Olympics inspired my imagination. I asked myself: Where is the limit of education? Is it effective for mental illnesses?

I started to challenge the limit of education in the following few years.

From 2009 to 2010, with diligence and talent, I solved a bunch of problems of many children with autism, mental retardation, and depression.

During that period, I also made a new attempt: I summarized the spiritual connotation of a family and wrote a book entitled The Origin of the Chen, referring to the history of two generations of the family. With my efforts, the family has established a groundbreaking set of rules and etiquette.

The elder said that Zhigang Education not only helped to set life goals for students and solve their growth problems, but also saved the entire family, ensuring that the efforts of the ancestors in the family were not in vain. In the future, Zhigang Education will definitely make more families prosperous and their foundations evergreen.

The elder's words explained something I was unable to answer for myself: how much value does my work have?

Through the education and cultivation of heirs, the family's foundation will remain evergreen. From then on, education is no longer a challenge to personal abilities for me. Since then, I have looked at problems from a family perspective. To benefit myself through benefiting others. I benefited the Chen family, as well as myself.

On May 19, 2012, I was invited to participate in the "Very Great" program on Jiangsu TV, guessing the truth on the show. The host asked a female contestant if my story was true, and she said no. One minute later, she missed the opportunity to travel abroad. The consultation call came from all over the country.

I was invited to towering mansions throughout the capital to meet dozens of high-ranking officials and answer their questions about cultivating family heirs.

At the Zhejiang Business Club in Houhai, I met a leader of Peking University. He was looking for innovative talents like me who kept up with the times. I entered Peking University and served as the head teacher and chief lecturer of the Youth Business Leaders Class at the School of Economics, Peking University.

By then, education for the children of the elites had developed into a social problem.

On August 27, 2013, the Beijing Evening News told my story in three full pages. The Wall Street Journal and China Daily immediately followed up and invited me to contribute, and China Daily referred to me as "Manto" in subsequent reports.

On July 1, 2014, my debut book The Godfather of Peking University was published.

On March 2015, I led the writing of The Proposal of the National People's Congress on Improving the Diagnosis, Treatment, Rehabilitation and Education System for Children with Autism in China.

From 2014 to 2019, I challenged the limits of education, discovering 427 teachers, designing 618 sets of plans, and travelling over 27000 kilometers mountains and rivers, working day and night for a full 1872 days, helping a severely autistic young man with an IQ below 46 improve his IQ to 108 and restoring his reproductive system, passing the piano Level 10 Test in four months and helping him find his life goals, abilities, confidence, a job, and love.

In 2021, my second book *Salvation Lies Within* (Chinese version) was published.

On April 15, 2023, the play based on *Salvation Lies Within* premiered at the auditorium of Tsinghua University.

My dear readers, many years later today, even I myself have been shocked by this unique process of upbringing. If my experience shocked you, I could only say that: if I followed along the ordinary path that was given, I probably would've been guarding an oil well somewhere in the fields of Bohai Bay, and my story wouldn't even fill a piece of paper. I never wanted to silent my heart just because of other people's judgment. I don't want to waste the limited time repeating the lives of others. I insist on following my own path.

It is said that there is an anonymous tombstone in the tombstone forest in the basement of Westminster Abbey. On this tombstone, there is a passage that resonates with me:

When I was young, my imagination was never limited, and I dreamed of changing this world.

When I matured, I realized that I couldn't change the world. I narrowed my gaze and decided to only change my country.

When I entered old age, I realized that I couldn't change my country. My last wish was just to change my family. However, that was also impossible.

As I lay on my deathbed, I suddenly realized that if I had only changed myself at first, and then acted as a role model, I could have changed my family. With the help and encouragement of my family, I may do something for the country.

And who knows? I may even change this world.

At the bank of Weiminghu Lake and in Tsinghuayuan Garden, I have visited famous houses to understand the history of each building on the campuses and the meanings behind every name. I ran along the May Fourth Road and arrived at the gate of the red building of Peking University. I thought of Chen Duxiu and Li Dazhao in their prime, tirelessly striving to cultivate students' independent, open and progressive thinking. I couldn't help but ask myself, "What else can I do?"

I wanted to make a TV series to show the audience the tremendous changes of the children, so that they could share the joy and hardship, thus triggering public reflection on what kind of education is truly needed in our era. I wanted to give lectures all over the world and cultivate a large number of teachers with pragmatic philosophy in their minds like me, so that they can work in the places where the values of educators can be best reflected. I wanted art forms like drama, photography, painting, music, dancing, writing, sculpting and architecture to serve education, so that we all can find a direction of life.

If you ask me what my ideal is, I will tell you that my ideal is to be a teacher for a lifetime.

In my childhood, the hero I admired was my father, and I planned to become a carpenter when I grow up. But in the end, I became a teacher. I have trained excellent successors for many families, enabling them to have successors.

Those who are blessed by nature must act on their behalf.

# Chapter 11

## How to Manage Educational Institutions

Managing educational institutions is just like managing any other innovative institutes like laboratories, publishing companies or factories. They all need excellent managers.

When I was a child, I grew up next to my father's workbench. My father managed a workshop with a total of 14 workers, and they were responsible for processing materials into parts on the drawings. They worked from day to night under my father's command.

Once in a gathering with my classmates, someone told me that according to his grandfather who was the director of the factory, my father was the best young man. I often thought that I could also apply the art of leadership skills to run my educational institution if I could figure out how my father managed the workshop well.

My father was born in 1950 and has met Chairman Mao twice in his life. He was the most loyal follower of Chairman Mao. He went to the countryside in 1968, and he did physical labor during the day while studying at night under only an oil lamp. In 1970, the entire team of over 800 people anonymously voted for him to return to the city to participate in the Drilling Production Campaign of Liaohe Oilfield.

One day in 1971, the military representative told him that the organization wanted him to have the only spot to attend university. My grandfather, who worked as the chief engineer at Anshan Iron and Steel Corporation, loved his eldest son and remembered his experience as a technical authority labeled as the Rightist during the Cultural Revolution, and told my father to keep being a technical worker. My father was very filial and returned to the oil field, where he worked hard, studied techniques for thirty years and started a family.

The process of transforming a piece of wood from a pattern on paper into a delicate spare part is a leap. The manager had to order materials, plan the processing sequence, assess the workload of workers, and inspect the final quality before the parts left the factory.

Whenever complex drawings appeared in the workshop, everyone gathered around to study, and gave out their own understandings, and my father would always speak the last. Everyone was able to tell that my father's plan was always the best.

One day, the factory leader came to the workshop with some Japanese partners, who were Japanese representatives of the joint venture and urgently needed a batch of parts. The Japanese technicians took out a blueprint and spread it out on the desktop. When they saw the blueprint, everyone was dumbfounded: the Japanese blueprint and the Chinese blueprint were completely different in projection. The Japanese saw the expressions of the masters present, looking disdainful, said something in their native tones and left. My father said nothing and returned to his workbench and dove into the blueprint. Two days later, the Japanese came back and saw the parts that they had been dreaming of. My father's superb skills stunned everyone, and the factory earned its first international order since its establishment.

Father was extremely strict with work, and his inferiors feared him with respect. Now I can understand the situation at that time. Workers in state-owned enterprises generally could not be dismissed, and a mighty leader was needed for the peak efficiency.

My father demanded that I take my job seriously and do it well. During the vacation, I went to my father's workshop to do homework. Every time I was distracted, I looked around to see if I had been noticed by his sharp eagle eyes.

The technical workers would be easily irritated under immense pressure of work, and they were often impatient and engaged in arguments. Father always reminded me to pay attention to safety in the workshop. One day, when Master Liu, who entered the industry in 1958, was working, a saw suddenly flew towards him and hit his shoulder. It came from Master Xu, who thought the song was mocking him and became furious. It was at that moment that I understood what my father meant.

My father's inferiors were weird. Mr. Sui, who started working in 1954, always had his radio on while working. Instead of regular programs, he'd always listen for the news of corruption. Once he heard about such news, he would immediately stop his work, wave his tools, and loudly criticize corruption. In the skills competition hosted by Liaohe Oilfield, Master Sui defeated all the other workers in the workshop, and was rewarded with a new radio larger than the one he had.

My father never complimented others. Whoever was lucky enough to receive compliments from him would drown in joy for days. When turning to work, he would sit on the throne symbolizing his royal status, rolling up his sleeves with a red and blue pencil in hand. The masters, old or young, showed great respect for father's outstanding skills and presented their work to him humbly, looking forward to his comments. And my father's evaluation would affect their mood for the few days thereafter.

Nowadays, I tried to give compliments objectively to my subordinates, like my father did.

Foreign magazines have changed our lives. My uncle was the workshop director of cardboard factory in Liaoyang City. They often had foreign magazines coming in containers, and the pictures in the magazines had opened eyes of our whole family. My father cut out pictures of Hitachi TV, Toshiba refrigerators, Sharpe vacuums, Panasonic video recorders and Italian furniture, while my mother cut out pictures of children's clothing and women's fashion. My favorite was Victoria's Secret. After work, my mother sewed clothes for me based on the designs in the magazine, making me look like a child star in the mirror.

In the evening, my home was always crowded with friends. My father chatted with everyone and showcased various foreign household appliances, while the carpenters that came with would measure and drew the new Italian style furniture that my father had just made.

Father had zero tolerance with someone who didn't take their job seriously. He knew that these people would bring down the morale of the professionals, and even led to disintegration. I fully agreed with him. He attached great importance to standards and norms, which was shown after his retirement. He and my mother won first place in the Northeast Three Provinces International Standard Dance Competition and became national level referees. When I was a child, I often saw my father working overtime at the workbench. Some said that he was dumb, for the work could be delayed. But he always told me to keep promise to others. Over the years, I remembered my father's guidance and kept my promise no matter how much effort or how much money I had to spend.

At the National Academic Exchange Conference on System Theory, Academician Liu Yuanzhang of the Chinese Academy of Engineering said that once a Japanese told him that the working environment of Chinese people was very dirty and good products could not be produced. I thought to myself that this Japanese must have never come to my father's workshop. My father had extremely strict requirements for the working environment. During the holiday, he took a day's drive from Liaoning to Beijing Sun Palace Vacuum Equipment Factory to learn about the structure and construction of vacuum devices, and then he led the workers and made one in only two months. In his words, it had reached the international advanced level. There were no dust, sawdust or wood chips in his workshop. Everything was gathered automatically into a huge jar, and they'd sell it at the end of the month and share the profit to everyone as a reward to keep the workshop clean. None of the workers had lung problems in the 30 years. The workshop was sectioned based on functionalities and everything was organized neatly. Workers were prohibited from smoking or spitting on the ground, and clothes were prohibited from smelling sweat, and the floor was thoroughly cleaned every day.

My father told me that the most efficient organization in the world was for everyone to have his own way, and as an individual, the most efficient action was to put things back in place.

Today, I firmly ask my employees and students to keep the environment clean, and this habit has been fused into my blood.

In that era, the average salary couldn't be lower. My father would try to make money on the side, and even started a small factory in the 1990s. My mother was diligent and thrifty, and we were able to live a prosperous life at an early age.

He never concealed his wealth from me. He would count the money he earned in front of me and put them under the rug. I would count it again like he did after he walked away.

In the early 1990s, as soon as he finished work, my father would take off his work clothes, brushed himself up and down with a small broom, then combed his hair and put on the suits and shoes that grandfather bought him from Germany. He had the style of a tycoon from Shanghai beach. After returning home, he'd put a CD in the Pioneer player and rest on the European-style couch. He would dance with my mother on the top of the scarlet carpet after dinner. On the weekends, they would put on leather jackets and pants, and take the motorcycle out for a ride. Father's way of life encouraged me to make a fortune of my own.

My father often said to me, "You will be irreplaceable if you can benefit others." This sentence is the greatest teaching of my great grandfather Ye Haiting to the family. Father always reminded workers to turn off lights, maintain equipment, improve work efficiency, and recycle scraps—he wanted the factory to maximize the profit. I appreciate my father's attitude.

Out of his characteristics, his diligence left the greatest impression on me. He always worked over 60 hours a week, and his action influenced me. Those days, I always stayed with the students whether they were taking the middle school and college entrance exams, TOEFL, IELTS or SAT. I woke up before they did, and only went to sleep after them. One of the parents wrote this in a letter to show his appreciation: "I purchased talent. You gave it as a gift for dedication. I believe that the latter will have a more profound impact on my son, and you are the godfather of his life."

I was the first child in the oilfield mining area to own LEGO toys, transformers, and ride a children's bicycle. During winter vacation, my father would personally play the spinning top with me. Late at night in the fall, he would wake up and fix the blanket for me. During the winter vacation in the third grade, he rode a bicycle for an hour every day to take me to treat myopia. Six months before the high school entrance exam, he would get up early to make fried rice for me, and he put so much carrot and meat in it. When I grew taller than him in high school, he'd pat me on the shoulder and grab my clothes just to see if I was wearing enough every time we met. In the final year of high school, he rode a motorcycle for an hour every two weeks to come to school to see me, using a thermos bucket to bring hot meals made by my mother. In kindergarten, he forced me to learn elementary school Chinese and mathematics every day. (That was in 1987.)

In elementary school, he would check my homework every night. In middle school, he supervised me with household chores every noon. In high school, he would still punish me for being naughty. All of these taught me what education was.

When I grew up, I lived a wealthy life in Liaoning Province. Until one day I saw the following passage:

The achievements of genius teachers exist with their birth and disappear with their death, benefiting only those students who have personal contact with them. In the past, the contribution of such genius teachers was limited to a few students, and the waste and losses caused by this fact were incalculable. The only way we can prevent this waste in the future is to find ways to add the work that genius teachers have intuitively done, so that we can extract something from their work that can be conveyed to others.

After reading this passage, I smacked the desk and stood up and walked towards the door, thinking to myself: John Dewey was right! The next day, I picked up my pen and started writing this book. Once a year, I gather the entire staff of the institution together and report their performance of the year. Then, I told them what kind of people I appreciate. I said:

1. I appreciate the ones who are eager to face the challenges. From my observation, this type of person is most likely to become an expert in the industry.

2. I admire the ones who make money while standing tall. A parent told me in his hummer: "The most important aspect of a man is his strength." The measure of success in a market economy is the amount of money. We are teachers, but we are also men. As men, our mission is to take good care of our families. And as far as I observe, we are engaged in this industry that can create considerable wealth while being elegant.

3. I appreciate people with charismatic personalities. Some people believe that charm lies in elegant behavior and appropriate clothing. I believe that sincerity is the foundation of charm, and human touch is the highest level of charm. I have found that teachers with human touch are very busy every day. After they do their job well, they start helping others and cultivating apprentices.

4. I appreciate people who fulfill their mission and have a good start and end. These people don't measure their efforts by time. Rather, they talk about success or failure. Helping parents achieve their wishes is our duty.

5. I appreciate smart people. People who are not smart enough cannot stay in this industry for long. Of course, intelligence must be combined with rational honesty.

6. I appreciate the ones who work with a passion, or they can leave. The luckiest man is one who can make a living by doing what he loves.

After explaining my expectations to my subordinates, I told them the standard that I hold myself to.

1. I do my best to make quick and correct decisions.

2. I will do my best to develop our career.

3. I try my best to gain the maximum trust from the parents.

4. I strive to make everyone's income higher than those in the same industry, which is an indispensable reason for making our family proud of us.

5. I will do my best to fully utilize your talents.

6. I try my best to appoint a top talent in each position, which is the root cause of making us a leader in the industry.

I have no ambition to host a large organization, and that's why we only served 49 clients in the first 10 years. Pursuing the highest quality is not as profitable as pursuing quantity, but it will provide parents with the most satisfactory service.

The education industry is originally a creative industry, but the selection of talents in this ancient industry often focuses on theoretical qualities, while practical abilities are ignored. The teachers selected on this basis naturally evaluate students according to the same standards, encouraging those who are similar in nature to develop unilateral theoretical talents, rather than value practical instincts. The students they cultivate are becoming increasingly quiet and dislike crisis and competition. The children educated by these people are like squeezed oranges, both withered and uninteresting. The little ones seem to have everything but ambition.

Many people believe that cultivating excellent successors for the family through education will also invite those who are well-dressed, graduated from prestigious universities, and speak fluently. But let me tell you that I must recruit a group of creative people who are sharp, unique, and not bound by red tape. The reason for our success is that I have tolerated the arrogant attitude of a group of outstanding teachers.

The place where teachers and students are together is the school. As a leader of an organization, my success or failure depends on whether I can discover these outstanding educational talents with extraordinary talents and passionate hearts. In terms of institutional development, I am as keen as a sonar soldier on a submarine hunting ship and look forward to the emergence of excellent partners.

As Einstein said, an atom cannot produce any effect, but two atoms colliding with each other can produce the power of 130000 tons of yellow

explosive. I am eagerly looking forward to collaborating with my partner, and I believe this is the key to whether Zhigang Education can
achieve a leap forward.

Mr. Richard Branson's words reveal the true essence of business management: the key to starting a company is to meet the right people.

# Chapter 12

# How to Establish Trust Between Educational Institutions and Parents

At the beginning, I was just a private tutor in a small town in Liaoning. Today, I have become the pioneer of this industry. I invited bankers from the Wall Street to lunch and told them about my ambition to shoot an educational reality show, to present the public the real education needed in this era through the screen.

The banker's advisor and analyst at Morgan Stanley in the United States whispered to me afterwards that they conservatively estimated that this industry would generate a miracle of annual output exceeding one billion dollars and annual growth rate exceeding 100% in the future.

Advertising tycoon David Ogilvy once said: "What really determines whether consumers buy the product or not is the content of your advertising, not its form. Your most important job is to decide how you explain your product and what benefits you'd promise."

At Zhigang Education, we use the Student Growth Survey Form for the parents to write down their expectations:

> 1. Just like sailing in the ocean without knowing when to land and suddenly seeing a beacon light. You are the beacon light that guides our children to land. I have too much guilt for my child. He is smart and handsome, but when he was young, we neglected paying attention to and care for him due to my busy

work. It was the wrong educational theories that led us to some difficult paths in his growth. Now we have to make it up for him, but do not have the ability to do so. We are anxious and worried while he's growing up day by day. We sincerely hope to receive help from Mr. Ye and so that my child can find his life goals as soon as possible.

2. Help the child go back to school, take the initiative to learn, and get rid of nicotine addiction and Internet addiction.

3. Enable children to be mature, to understand parents and teachers, to understand how to care for loved ones and consider others' feelings.

4. The child lacks goals in life and academics, with no enthusiasm. He knows that learning is important but does not take actions, only hanging out with friends all day long. Being in a relationship takes a lot of time, and he doesn't understand the problem of it, which has much impact on him. Being in a relationship is good but he is not able to fully understand it. He also lacks the correct views on life and value.

5. Build confidence, attend school and study normally, and be interested in learning.

6. Establish life goals, have a clear understanding of himself, be able to return to classroom learning, and put computer games in the right position in life.

7. Find a goal in academics and life and open up from the semi self-isolation.

8. Help him regain his will to improve, go back to the right path, go back to school and take the college entrance examina-

tion, expected to last for one year.

9. Lose weight to strengthening his will, and it is best for him to make up his mind to get into a master's program at an Ivy League School and have plans for his future, with an expectation of one year, which can be extended if needed.

10. Help the child to get back up from a breakup, pick himself up and study.

11. Do you think there still is hope for him? Can he study normally?

12. Study hard and get into a key high school, change the current situation of being cynical, complacent, and having high expectations but low abilities; become a person with a positive and healthy mindset, life goals, ambition, and the courage to face challenges without fear of difficulties.

13. Change his current situation of not loving work, having no dream and liking to play. Make him have a life goal like a normal child and work hard.

14. Study actively and be lively. (Study comes before being lively.)

15. The child is 10 years old now and is still adorable, and we have great expectations for him. Looking back on my own personality and growth experience, I am full of worries about my son. I need the most professional guidance in raising children, so that my family can have successors. Expected 10 years.

Just as the purpose of a state banquet is not to eat enough, the vast majority of parents also do not aim for their children's self-improvement.

Competition is everywhere in society, and it is the mission of all living beings to have an advantage in competition. Among the 15 expectations of parents mentioned above, the word "study" appears 13 times. Parents almost unanimously agree with Friedrich Herbart's view that education is a preparation for future life.

We also have to notice that the word "goal" appears seven times, and the proportion of parents with an "expected 10 years" in our business is increasing. More and more people stopped and thought seriously, who has the greatest impact on my happiness in the second half of my life? How can I prolong my hard work? How to keep the family's wealth? Are materials the only things to be inherited?

In the Zhou Dynasty, Tai Shi, Tai Fu, Tai Bao, Shao Shi, Shao Fu and Shao Bao, led a large team to cultivate the crown prince for the imperial family. Today, education that sets life goals and the services of outstanding educational teams have become essential for families to cultivate their successors, and they are the best investments for any family with great visions.

What parents want is for their children to learn actively, while what children want is to give full play to their individuality and freedom of action, and conflicts are inevitable. What's even more troublesome is that children are the most opportunistic group in society, and they are good at circuitous warfare.

I have always believed that only when educational institutions help students find their truly recognized life goals and make them realize that learning is a necessary path on the pilgrimage will they focus on learning. They will only take action when they believe they have the ability to cope with learning. They are only willing to continue working hard when they show signs of progress in their studies. Only when learning becomes a child's need can parents and teachers truly become the spokespersons of God and the guides of heaven, as Dewey said.

My student A Long said, "I never studied before because I didn't know what to study for. Once I made up my mind to get into politics and knew that it is the only way, Uncle Ye, do you think the college entrance examination would be a problem for me?" Nine months later, his parents' expectation, which was No. 8, was fulfilled.

In my living room, Herbart and Dewey stopped arguing.

It's not hard to imagine that it is the most difficult to earn the trust of a family for the first time, because at this time, we have no other successful cases and no reputation. At this stage, it may be helpful to conduct some preliminary research for the potential clients as a promotion. It is rare for them not to be touched when we show them the results of the research.

I was much luckier. I had no other competitions when I stepped on the stage. People shrugged their shoulders and walked away when they saw someone like Xiaomin. Despite this, I took it very seriously because education is truly my greatest passion.

In the two years I spent with Xiaomin, I worked 28 days each month, 18 hours a day, sometimes even 24 hours! I got the habit of sleeping under light from then, and I also developed the habit of sitting only against the wall and facing the door when eating in a restaurant, so that I could see the oncoming person.

The parents could feel how proud we were when interacting with us. Our students came from all kinds of experts and workshops but only became better with us. Because our students came from various renowned educational institutions and expert workshops, they have been revitalized here.

When a parent decided to invest heavily in cultivating heir for his family, he invited me and the heads of other three overseas study institutions to prepare the plans, and I was the first to talk to him. I said, "I didn't prepare for anything. On the contrary, I'd like you to tell me about your troubles. Then you can meet with the other three institutions and see what they have for you. It'd be easy for you to choose if you like any of them. If not, please hire us. We will start the investigation and study how to help the child find his life goal. In our institution, investigation always comes before plans. The biggest failure of traditional education is having a plan before even meeting the student."

He took my advice. Five days later, he came back to me with the child. This made me particularly happy back then, even floating high.

However, one strategy seemed to work for any situation, which is letting the parent talk. The more focused when you listen, the smarter they think you are. Once you gain the trust of your student's parents, you can't be careless with them. You spend someone else's money, and the fate of their family is often controlled by you.

Having the experience of dealing with parents of students trained my ability to identify outstanding individuals from the crowd. I also taught it to the children. I took them to Tiantongyuan Subway Station in Beijing at 8:30 in the morning and asked them to keep their eyes fixed on the gaze of some men in the crowd. Then I'd ask them: What is the difference between these people's eyes and your father's? Some kids would come up with the answer within 10 minutes, while others might take an hour, and there would always be a little guy who suddenly answers, "Their eyes are not as ambitious as my father's."

That's right. Ambition is the origin of success.

Next, the little one who answered correctly would be taken to the shooting range, holding various world-renowned guns that have appeared in computer games for live fire shooting. Other children would stand beside him in pain, swallowing saliva and watching as shells of various calibers fell to the ground. But anyhow, all children had deeply remembered a truth: the foundation of a man's success is ambition.

David Ogilvy once wrote, "Every few years, a new big company is born. Such a company is ambitious, hardworking, and full of vitality. It takes customers from those aging companies and works very well. Through time, the entrepreneur got wealthy but also tired. The fire of creating is extinguished, becoming a dead volcano.

"These companies will continue to thrive, and the initial momentum has not yet been exhausted. It also has a strong network of relationships. But it is already too large, and the things it creates are lackluster, planning activities in the old style of winning in the past. It has withered and declined, and its business focus has shifted to providing services based on attributes to conceal the fact that the company's creative power has declined. At this stage, it begins to lose its customers to a new company that is vibrant, hardworking, and fully invested in their creative endeavors.

Think about the inevitable rise and fall pattern that goes from being full of vitality to being exhausted, and the fading ambition of the helmsman rings the death knell for the enterprise."

One of my student's parents who was very accomplished wrote down this in his diary after graduating from university:

*7 / 17 / 1986, Thursday*

*At 1:35 in the afternoon, when I stepped on the soil of my hometown, I felt so grounded and full of confidence. Although I was a bit disappointed that no one came to pick me up, I couldn't lose my ambition. Walking onto the road, I was thinking that I have returned to my hometown after four years of separation. Will there be a successful career here in the future? Can this land, which once nurtured me, belong to me in twenty years? How should I take the most important step in my life?*

*What policies, principles, and specific methods should be ad-
opted to accept the challenge of this important turning point in
life? In short, I believe in one thing: The future belongs to me!*

A few years later, I learned the ability to find parents as potential clients
among a large group of people.

At the opening ceremony of the Beijing Olympics Games in 2008, 100
thousand people were cheering in Beijing National Stadium (the Bird's
Nest). I had a premonition that someone on the southwest stands would
eventually become my student's parent one day. That turned out to be
true. Wenxi and his father were sitting in that crowd.

180 days after I took over Wenxi's education work, his father called me
and said, "I must be honest about the tremendous changes in my child.
You have achieved amazing success." 10 months later, Wenxi was admitted by a key high school.

Some of the parents that I work with are executives from large corpo-
rations. They dedicated themselves wholeheartedly to the growth of the
company and didn't have much time to spend with their children. They
always unconsciously brought the atmosphere of corporate management
into their homes, exacerbating the already fragile parent–child relationship. They buried deep apologies for their partners and children in their
hearts, and they most agreed with what Gu Long said: "When people are
in the world, they cannot help themselves."

When it comes to educating children, one after another company managers shed tears sitting across from me. Making their children happy is
their greatest wish.

I feel that one day, Zhigang Education will be treated as the highest welfare in his business by a kind entrepreneur, in return for his subordinates
who have been following him for many years.

I spend a lot of time selecting clients. Now we reject an average of 25 parents of students who we are not very willing to accept every year. I have eight criteria for selecting clients.

1. We do not accept the employment of parents unless we are confident that we will be helpful. A mine owner asked us to help his son with drug rehabilitation, but I declined because I didn't think we could do better than a drug rehabilitation institution I knew.

2. I would reject any parents who are delusional and paranoid. Most of them are scholars who started with technical skills, sensitive and extreme, lacking trust in people, and you will never meet their requirements. Now let's listen to the unreasonable demands of their representative, the Vice President of a Fortune Global 500 company in Greater China:

> The child develops a strong sense of goals, plans and discipline—expected to be completed in one or two months.

> Thoughts and ability of analyzing, in the form of having better writing skills—expected in one semester.

> Have academic achievement in the top 10 of the class (the child was studying in a key middle school, ranking last in junior high school.)—expected in one semester.

> Build the child's confidence—expected in one semester.

> Improve the child's ability to interact and communicate with others—expected in one semester.

A newly established educational institution, no matter how eager it is to obtain students, should always be able to restrain itself and reject such parents. A renowned surgeon can withstand the blow of accidentally losing a patient on his operating table, but if a young doctor encounters such an unfortunate accident, his future may be ruined. I was always afraid of it happening to us.

3. Find out if your student's parents hope that the person who serves them can live a good life.

4. If a parent appears to be unprofitable to you, can they motivate you to make excellent educational cases? I couldn't make much money from the parents of Xiaomin or the Chens, but they all gave me valuable opportunities to showcase my exceptional creativity, so that other families don't have to worry about our credit when hiring us. There is no other way to bring a new educational institution to the forefront faster than this method. The only crisis was the obsession form in society through thousands of years. The public believes that a male teacher who specializes in education must love to delve into details, feel excited and shy about talking about money. Only a few believe that one would have a high standard in all aspects if he had a high standard in one. Thanks to Haonan's father. One day, he said to me, "I heard that Xiaomin's parents paid you 1000 yuan each month, but I don't think it can measure the value of your career, so I decided to pay you 80 times as much."

5. The relationship between the teacher and the parent is like that between a doctor and his patient. Before accepting a parent, you need to figure out whether you can really get along well with him.

When a potential client comes to me for the first time, I need to make sure what type of person he or she is. If I have any reason to believe that he is not telling the truth, I'd go to the child's homeroom teacher. This happened not long ago, and the teacher told me that what the parent needed was to find a professional psychologist, not a teacher for his child.

6. I reject any parent who view education as a marginal auxiliary factor. They have an embarrassing way of doing things: they never hesitate a bit when it comes to playing mahjong, having skincare sessions or buying

luxury cars, but they become indecisive when it comes to education. I prefer parents who view education as a necessary factor in determining the future well-being of their children. Just like a doctor performing surgery, the area where we operate on these families is the indispensable brain and heart, not just any insignificant part.

Wenxi's father made astonishing remarks on this: "Mr. Ye, the value of your education highly depends on the expectations of the parents for the happiness of the latter half of their life. It also depends on whether they want to acknowledge the continuous impact of your education on the family's descendants. Pricing priceless things is the most difficult." Upon hearing these words, I stood still, unable to say a word.

7. If you have the ambition to excel in education, do not recruit "full agents". A few years ago, I met with a parent who was in a rush to meet me. "Mr. Ye," said the man across from me, "I'm here today to entrust the child with your institute."

I didn't speak about education right away. Instead, I asked him two questions:

"Who are you to this child?" He answered: "I'm a friend of his father's."

"Where are his parents?" He answered: "They are highly positioned and are extremely busy. I was fully authorized by them to handle everything about the child's education."

"No one can replace the parents to fulfill their responsibilities. I heard that the Obamas were never late for their daughter's parent teacher meeting. Mind your steps on your way out." I left right after.

Almost all the fully authorized agents have a pair of souls in need of rescue behind them. Dealing with them was just like kissing with face masks on. I can't get away from this type of parent faster enough.

8. I reject the parents who treat their children like masters. They have two problems: they can't make any decisions and are irrationally honest.

They all have a universal pattern. First, they tell you all their secrets, even cry bitterly in front of you, but before they pay the tuition, they can't help but ask their children: "My son, mom wants to hire a teacher for you. What do you think?" Or "Mom wants to sign you up for some classes. Do you even know how expensive it is?" As expected by everyone, the children will firmly say: "I won't go!"

Who is the head of the family? Who is leading the revolution? The root cause of their educational failure lies in their lack of dignity as parents. Children are the head of the family.

Some parents may suddenly say to their children when everything is going smoothly: "Son, you have to study hard because we have paid so much money!" Soon after, the parents would call me and say that they've worked on the children in order to provide assistance to my job, but the children didn't want to go anymore, and that we should do what the children want!

They do not understand the sacred role that parents play. Money is not given to teachers for free, nor is it spent on cultivating children's interests. It is spent on compensating for the losses caused by parents themselves. How can this kind of thing make children appreciate it? Once you're on the ship of Guangxu, it is difficult to get off.

No matter how much investigation you do on potential clients, it is almost impossible for you to figure out whether they possess the quality that you desire before you meet them face-to-face. Then you'll find yourself in a tricky situation. On the one hand, you're trying to make it work. On the other hand, you need more information to decide if it'll work. Speaking less and listening more usually benefits the most.

Some people say that enthusiasm is a common disease among young people, which can be cured by taking a small dose of regret internally and applying some experiential ointment externally. In the early days, I sometimes made the mistake of being too enthusiastic towards my clients. I did the same thing when I first met Haonan's father. The impression I left on him was that I was too young for the job, and that I needed more experience. It took me a long time to convince him that I was very experienced in education. Later in Beijing, I found out that one of the leaders was only two years older than me. When we went out for dinner, the younger fellows would call him uncle, but they would call me brother. The leader attributed his success to losing his hair at the age of 18 and speaking in an official tone with a cold expression.

It is exciting to earn the respect of parents, but it raises the workload of preparation. 80 hours of work per week was a lot already. But my young employees wanted eagerly to face new challenges. Besides, our education cycle was very short. Therefore, you'd bleed to death if you don't have new clients coming in.

Sometimes rejection is the best way in achieving success. I have rejected parents of students who did not meet our requirements five or six times, only to find that the rejection has actually sparked their desire to hire us. An entrepreneur proposed to hand over his son's education rights to us, but we declined because the actual head of their family was the child's grandfather. The elderly had a deep family connection and never felt that there was anything wrong with his grandson. It wasn't until the child stopped going to school that the elderly let go a little bit. When it came to children's education, the parents could not make the decision, and the child's grandfather never showed up. We didn't refuse them directly. Rather, we asked for double payment. And they accepted.

Many parents make plans for their children to study abroad. Actually, it is not the way if the children do not have the desire. There is not a chance for the children to meet the expectations in a relatively stress-free environment, and foreign education is not the answer to their problems. The key is the type of belief and faith that the children have in their hearts, as well as whether they have a goal in life, whether the purpose is found or given, and whether such purpose can fulfill their values. A way out is not what they seek. Rather, they want to fulfill their value in society.

These children usually lack guidance and companionship from their parents. They were sent to expensive international schools, or even abroad at a very young age. Failed family education usually makes the advantages go to waste.

A parent complained to me when we first met, "I thought my wealth could give my son a thousand paths to go, but in the end, I realized that without solving the motivation problem, there is no way to go."

If my students' parents have a way out, I always withdraw and ask them to take it. Most likely, we will meet again in a few years. Zhigang Education is a game of the brave. I like the parents who have no other way, and it is me who gives them nirvana.

# Chapter 13
# How to Deal with Students' Parents

Try to avoid dealing with the parents who speak badly of various people that they hired previously. You might think your extraordinary efforts can cure their narrow-minded problems, but soon you'll realize that they were born with their unsatisfaction.

Parents who work in production, finance, or make a fortune in sales will definitely suspect educational institutions because they are too skilled in calculation. There are some clumsy parents who are not good at calculation but cooperate with us quite well. We serve them tirelessly because they can make the people who serve them feel comfortable.

Make sure to spend the money on things that are visible to the parents, for hearing is false, and seeing is believing. If you hire security guards for your students, make sure to have them march in front of the parents at least once. One time, a parent sent her son to me in the afternoon. When she saw her son again in the evening, she was amazed by my superb educational skills. The mother insisted that after only an afternoon without seeing her child, he looked much wiser. I think the reason why he looked wiser is that I took the little guy to get an expensive haircut in the afternoon, which really made him look more refined. Anyways, education is invisible, but it should be preserved as tangible as possible, such as diaries, letters, videos, etc.

The program manager with high capabilities usually takes on two or three students at a time. They have a great idea when they should report to a parent with the information of all the students they're working with, to make the parents believe that they are capable. It might be damaging to the educational institutions, almost without exception, that the parents think that their own children were not taken seriously. At this point, if you want to soothe the imbalance in their parents' hearts, you will end up hitting a wall.

The Catholics believe that humans have seven original sins, namely arrogance, jealousy, anger, laziness, greed, gluttony, and lust. Outstanding teachers should pay extra attention to the jealousy coming from the children's mothers.

A master in the education industry whom I knew well in my early years was fired twice by the mother of one of his students. The first time was because he made the student feel like an adult and refuse to share one room with his mother. The second time was when the mother witnessed her son who found the teacher's diarrhea, rummaged through the boxes and found sugar and salt, prepared them at a 2:1 ratio, washed them away with warm water, and personally took a small sip to test the water temperature. Then, sweating profusely, he lifted the bowl of sugar and salt water over his head and asked the teacher to quickly take it down. After seeing all of this, the mother of the child had a strange smile on her face and said, "I've never seen my son treat anyone like this before." The next morning, the elegant lady went furious, and the teacher was immediately kicked out of the room.

I have an effective way to identify this type of woman: I would play song "Chess Pieces" by Faye Wong on the stereo while driving with my child's mother.

> I want to walk away from your controlled territory,
> But end up in the battle you have arranged.
> I don't have strong defenses,

*Nor do I have a way out.*

*I want to escape the trap you set,*
*But end up in in another predicament.*
*I don't have the courage to decide whether to win,*
*Nor do I have the luck to escape.*

*I'm like a chess piece,*
*My next move is up to you.*
*I'm not the only general in your eyes,*
*But an inconspicuous soldier.*

*I'm like a chess piece,*
*That comes and goes without control.*
*You never hesitate to move a piece back,*
*But I am under your control.*

When I hear this, I suddenly change the song. If the mother of the child insists on listening to this song, she is most likely this kind of woman.

Liu Xiaoqing has a famous saying: being a person is difficult, being a woman is difficult, being a famous woman is even more difficult, and being a single famous woman is extremely difficult. The word "you" in the lyrics refers to their husbands, and the word "I" refers to themselves. For some women, their relationships are difficult. A son is not only a son, but also a man who will not betray her. He is a tool for experiencing maternal love, and even their entire life. I try to avoid this type of mother.

I have a very talented colleague who was criticized by three parents throughout the year, and this experience deeply hurt him. There was also a male assistant who lived with Xiaomin for several late nights and was pranked by Xiaomin. He suddenly attacked and kissed him six times, one of which was his first kiss... He was furious and decided to quit education for good. Lol, you're not meant for this industry if you're easily provoked.

Our work projects are complex: investigation, diet, clothing, daily life, transportation, entertainment, security, parent–child relationship repair, academic planning, motivation enhancement, setting life goals, public relations, and even marriage planning. The reason why parents choose us to prepare the heir for them is that they believe we are their best choice, which is concluded after they understand what we can provide.

Before entrusting their children to you, parents are eager to find reassuring evidence from their interactions with you. They analyze your words, recall your actions, look at the stubble on your cheeks, and stare at the mole on your cheeks.

Nothing is perfect under the microscope. Whether the education succeeds or not depends on the teacher's talent of efforts, rather than whether he is a perfect person. Only truly discerning parents can we see that wild and unrestrained teachers can also cultivate knowledgeable and rational students.

Think about it! Even someone like me who is good at tidying up the mess has a record of resigning the parents. I don't allow my employees to be bullied by a tyrant, and I can't let the parents dictate to me to develop an education plan according to his will, unless I believe his opinion is basically feasible. If you tolerate it, your reputation will be damaged, and reputation is your greatest treasure.

In the first few years of my career, I made such a mistake. At that time, there was a person who approached me. He was a celebrity and people still talk about his achievements to this day. He lives according to his own understanding, insisting that I make his rebellious child fall in love with learning through playing table tennis, tutoring, and preaching. In fact, the disconnect between textbooks and real life determines that only bookworms will truly fall in love with learning. Even worse, he had set a circle for us, and for some inexplicable reason, the child was not allowed to leave the community they live in.

For several weeks in a row, I tried my best to explain to this father that only cognitive changes that arise from social practice truly make sense for people, and it was impossible for a child to fall in love with learning through tutoring and preaching. The child was not an idiot. But he refused to take a step back. The signal of a storm approaching has risen. His secretary warned me that if I didn't follow the instructions, I would lose them. And eventually I compromised. I kept telling myself that different paths lead to the same destination! Different paths lead to the same destination! No one knows a son better than his father! What if he was right!

I started living a regular life and paid the dumbest price in the history of education. I was embarrassed, and the morale of my team was as low as it could be. All those who witnessed this educational failure have come to the conclusion that I have no concept of how to educate children at all. Eight months later, we walked away from the community, with no one seeing us off. We deserved it. The misfortune had not ended there. The immense pressure defeated my immune system, and I had rashes and other skin problems all over my body, which I then spent a year recovering from. This tragedy taught me that it was not worth pleasing and yielding to parents when it came to principles. One tragedy in Munich was well enough.

I will fire the parents when I lack confidence in their children. I must be honest. Not all families will have successors, and the decline of some families is inevitable. It is extremely unethical for a teacher to encourage parents to play a must lose poker game.

Sadness is inevitable if you interact with parents who love vanity. The happiness of such parents lies not in how much they have gained, but in how much they have gained more than their neighbors and colleagues. A student who dropped out of school for many years made outstanding efforts to be admitted to a second- tier university. Just as everyone was happy for him, his mother cried out of embarrassment. She told her son:

"I am so embarrassed of you!" She was in the position to arrange his son into a top-tier university, which was what her colleagues did for their children, but her son refused her, and he just wanted to see what the result of his eight months of hard work was. What his mother said broke his heart, and all his joy disappeared. Clearly, she forgot that her wish was for her son to be strong-willed when she first came to us. However, this type of parents is easily identified, and their desire for quick success and instant benefits is written all over their faces. They focus on results, leaning forward with no tears in their eyes. They can't stop looking at you up and down. They treat education as a necklace around their necks, and both you and the child are just proof that they only win and never lose. They live in hell, for vanity is what the devils love the most.

Haonan's father once said to me, "Zhigang, to tell you the truth, all the parents of your students, including me, are wealthy idiots. When they were young, they traded happiness with the devil, thinking that one day they would have everything. But in the end, they found out that their children hated them. It was smart of them to seek for help. It is lucky for us that there are teachers like you."

Wenxi's father gave me advice on my development, so I respect him for always speaking his mind. The day when this outstanding scientist entrusted his only son to me was truly a significant day in my life.

Every parent that I worked with has told me about the development of their families. They arranged for me to work in their companies, allowing me to gain another perspective on the family businesses, which enriched my life.

Xiaomin's parents were my clients first, but later became close friends with me. We shared the details of our lives together.

Xiaohu's father was a respected entrepreneur, and his business management skills were taken as a classic case of MBA programs at world-renowned universities. One day, he saw his son doing a math problem and found that on the back of the grass paper was a good essay shared by his classmate. He immediately asked his son to change the paper. He said, "Respect others. Although this classmate's excellent essay is shared with everyone in the class and is useless after reading it, it is still the fruit of others' labor. Regardless of whether others know it or not, it should be preserved and not used as grass paper casually. This is different from using office paper on both sides." For someone like Xiaohu's father, the way he respected others and his attention to detail earned my respect.

The life experience of Haonan's father fascinates me. This handsome man started his business in the 1980s and earned three million yuan at the age of 19. Then he lost it all but got back up five years later. At the beginning of the new century, he turned to real estate, and established his own commercial empire.

He was already an outstanding entrepreneur when we met. His charisma came from his generosity. All his friends knew that they could count on him when they were in need.

I have personally received more parents than other educational institution bosses, because I am confident that I am a sociable person, and there is no better way to demonstrate to parents that this institution values their affairs. Even lawyers wouldn't spend so many nights preparing one education plan after another as I did.

It is worth putting in a lot of effort to investigate and understand children. The summary materials of the investigation information should contain all irrefutable facts.

However, there are still some parents who do not like my survey results. They only hope that my investigation results are consistent with their expectations. Haonan's father belongs to this category. He said that the biggest problem of his child was that he didn't like doing homework, but my information told me that his son was a combination of all troubled kids. I mean that any kind of evil behavior you say can be found in Haonan. A week later, in front of a large number of videos and recordings, Haonan's father furrowed his eyebrows and painfully grabbed his hair, smoking one cigarette after another. Finally, he forcefully extinguished the cigarette in his hand and threw all the materials into the paper basket. Even so, I will not compromise. My education must be established.

Even so, I will not compromise. My education must be based on facts and avoid being emotional.

Two years later, at the farewell banquet for Haonan's study abroad in the UK, Haonan's father said to me, "If time can turn back, if my son can go back to the past, I will listen to you." At that time, Haonan had already set great ambitions, and his family's billions of assets had a responsible successor.

Another parent who didn't want to be hurt by the facts said to me in the most mournful tone, "Mr. Ye, do what you think is right." Raymond Robbie once said, "The priceless ingredient of any product is the honesty and integrity of its producer."

# Chapter 14

## How to Get Better Services from Educational Institutions: Advice to Parents

1. A major shareholder of a large corporation sent his child to a well-known private high school in Switzerland. He spent large amount of money and was confident that he could provide his child with the best education in the world. Recently, he came to me and said that the child had quit school. He couldn't understand that spending 1.5 million yuan on cultivating life goals is much more profitable than spending 1.5 million yuan on studying abroad.

2. I have seen a teacher whose enthusiasm for educating a student is five times greater than educating another student.

3. I know of a female entrepreneur who signed up for all types of classes and workshops to solve her child's education problems. Finally, she let go of the burden of this life and became a Buddhist.

Sometimes the institutes were responsible for these tragedies, but in most cases, the parents were to blame. The type of parents dictates the type of education. I have trained heirs for many families and have had a rare chance to compare their attitudes and family traditions. Some parents behave really badly, making it impossible for any educational institution to educate their children well. Some perform well, and any educational institution will be helpful for their children's education.

In this chapter, I will write down 13 rules. If I were a parent of a child, I would follow these rules when dealing with educational institutions, and I believe you will receive the best service.

## Rule 1: Stability beats everything.

If I were a parent, I would try my absolute best to make the team that I hire feel secure, even if signing a long-term contract. Childbirth needs taking risks, but cultivating an heir needs stability.

The ideal relationship between parents and institutions is stability. To achieve stability, both parties must have it in mind from the beginning. They need to find ways to consciously merge it into the relationships.

Before firing the teacher that you hired, ask yourself the following questions.

1. So many families received excellent services from Zhigang Education. Why is that?

2. Can hiring a new teacher solve your problem, or is it only sweeping garbage under the bed? What is the root cause of the problem?

3. Have you ever insisted on educating the child according to the teachers' ideas, but you're blaming the teachers now?

4. Have you ever threatened the teachers and made them feel lost?

5. Do you have an advisor who is a conservative and not good at accepting new things?

6. Do you realize that changing teachers would disturb the children's emotions and the entire education plan, which would cause adverse effects to last up to 12 months or even more?

7. Are you frank enough with the teachers? He may work even harder if you explain your dissatisfaction to him, which will even provide a better service than you can from a new institution.

## Rule 2: Choose the right educational institution.

If you spend large amount of money on your children's education, and your happiness in the future depends on the effectiveness of education, then you have a responsibility to put in some effort to choose the best educational institution.

Parents who are not familiar with the industry would search for target schools online or with friends and compare tuition fees and the appearance of school buildings. The winners of such competitions usually are the schools that are extremely stingy with frontline teachers and in huge debt.

The most reasonable way to choose an educational institution is to hire an education professional who understands the current situation of education and can make judgments based on your wishes.

Then invite two teachers from the target educational institution to have a meal together. Let them talk freely to see if they can keep other families confidential, and if they have the courage to disagree with your out-of-place comments. Observe if they are loyal teammates or the ones who are playing tricks on each other, and if they are making grand promises to you. Are they lifeless or full of energy? Are they good at listening to others' opinions? Are they sincere?

The most important part is whether you like them or not. The relationship between the parents and teachers must be intimate. Otherwise, they can't work together.

Don't mistakenly believe that the smaller institutions are less reliable, for the employees in small institutions might be more capable and work harder.

**Rule 3: Provide the teacher with a comprehensive and thorough introduction to your situation.**

The more your teachers know about your family and your past, the more skillful their education will be. When Mr. Li, the head of a well-known media group in China, hired us to train his successor, he demonstrated the wisdom of Zhejiang people.

I asked him about his life story. He opened up to me completely, and I admire his courage. I spent days listening to him talking about his tumultuous growth journey, his reluctance to work outside when his child was young, his mistakes in life, and the glory of his current career.

What made him despair was that his only son hated him. I used my writing skills to write a biography of Mr. Li, and every night before going to bed, I read a short paragraph for his son to listen to. The little one realized that it was about his father right away, but he didn't say anything.

Two weeks later, the child called his father and apologized. Some parents are always overly careful like walking on eggshells. They don't truthfully tell the family situation to the teacher. In this case, we'd suggest they try their luck elsewhere. Because if parents are not frank, it'd increase our workload and lengthen the education cycle. This attitude will also discourage everyone who works for them.

**Rule 4: Don't compete with the teacher you hire in the field of education.**

Why to catch mice yourself if you had a cat already? Directing the professionals will inevitably kill creativity. If you do that, I'd only ask for god's blessing for you.

In 2003, when Xiaomin's mother entrusted her child to me, she said: "I'm going to ask you to take full responsibility for Xiaomin's education. I'm afraid that I'm not paying the highest fees, but I can assure you that I'll never interfere with your education if you accept my offer."

I accepted the work. Xiaomin's mother kept her promise and never interfered with my education plan. I would be solely responsible if I failed. But I didn't.

## Rule 5: Don't take studying abroad as the only way out.

The successful ones from the last generation are obsessed with one belief: Either staying domestically or studying abroad.

If a child has serious problems in their domestic life and study, studying abroad is not a lifesaver. The primary task of parents is to help their children find their own path of identification. My experience is that in terms of direction, it's best not to follow others. Every family is unique and should make the best choices based on their own situations. Don't send the child abroad just because your friends or co-workers did. Once the child has a worrying situation outside and is far away, you will know whether it is hot or cold.

## Rule 6: Cherish the talent.

A teacher is asked to cultivate heirs for a family with no successors, which may be the most sacred job that educators can encounter.

As I write this paragraph, I think of a family I once met, where eight family members spent over a decade taking care of this only frail and sickly child. By the time they met me, this family had reached a dead end. I didn't have much time either—they wanted me to reshape this child completely in six months. If I did well, my contribution to this family would be no less than what they could've done in over a decade.

It wasn't something for the beginners. It required the educator to fully understand the child in a short period of time, and to be well experienced to make the correct judgment based on the information obtained from surveys and research, while considering the costs. Additionally, he must be creative, and be able to design the most efficient plans. I believed that only very few people possessed these traits in the entire education field.

Lv Buwei once wrote: "To have ten decent horses, is not as good as to have one who knows the horses." The most difficult job in the world is dealing with people.

People who cultivate talents are first-class talents.

The talented ones in the education field are one out of a thousand, and we need to explore these talents as much as possible. But without any exception, they all have great personalities. You need to cherish them so that they can educate your child well.

**Rule 7: Don't let various voice around you interfere with your decisions.**

When you want to send your child to a unique educational institution, there are often more voices of opposition than agreement around you. Grandparents are thinking about the pain of separation, and various educational advisors who have to secure their positions by giving advice will tell you seriously: Take your time. Don't hurry.

They seem to have good reasons but have no idea how to solve the problem.

Our problem is to follow the mass, walk the smooth path, choose the safe option, and not willing to take the risk of exploring the truth. The cultivation of an outstanding successor is undoubtedly the result of the cooperation of a down-to-earth and distinctive educational team and a parent who cooperates with them harmoniously and patiently.

In 2003, following the rule of "decline right after flourish", I helped Xiaomin quit his Internet addiction. I accompanied him to play online games to the level of 140, which was the highest level of that game. Our reputation in the game ranked first in the three northeastern provinces at that time. At this time, various voices were coming from Xiaomin's family, and they couldn't understand my method. They believed that being with me not only did not improve his academic performance, but also led him into an even deeper addiction. I was under extreme pressure.

Xiaomin's father called and said, "Mr. Ye, please don't feel pressured. I support you!" With these words, I was willing to serve him for the rest of my life. One year later, I returned to him much beyond his imagination.

**Rule 8: Ensure that the educational institution serving you is profitable.**

Good educational institutions will not always lack customers. If they feel that creating value for you is not profitable, they will not send top-notch talents to serve you, and sooner or later they will find customers who can make them money to replace you.

Nowadays, it is becoming increasingly difficult for educational institutions to make money. If the student is transferred through referrals, the referrer will take 30% of the total price, which is a bad habit in the training industry. If it is a business training course, this proportion does not matter because there is no upper limit on the number of people, but it is a heavy blow to professional educational institutions that value educational outcomes as their lives.

In my experience, paying annually is the most effective method for parents to pay for this type of ability development education. The traditional monthly payment system, on the other hand, can cause educators to selectively overlook abilities that require long-term cultivation due to their eagerness to show parents the results.

**Rule 9: Be frank with each other.**

If you think the educational institution that you are hiring is performing poorly, or if you believe that an educational program is not being
executed well enough, don't beat around the bush and speak up about
your thoughts. If parents play a hide and seek with their teachers in daily
contact, the consequences would be catastrophic.

Parents are often very candid when teachers have not yet made progress
in education. When education begins to make progress and they increasingly rely on teachers, they tend to bottle everything up, and usually the
child would take notice first. They all have a radar in their minds, and
they can always sensitively capture the slightest crack between parents
and teachers, which would reduce the result of education.

Never let the teacher guess your meaning. Being straightforward will
make your teacher equally candid. Without frankness between both parties, no single partnership would work.

**Rule 10: Don't haggle with the educational institution you hire.**

If you let your drivers take advantage of you when filling the gas or re-
pairing the car but to haggle over payment issues with the educational
institution you hire, then you've made a mistake. For example, in the
early stages, you are stingy with the teacher's observing and interaction
with the child. The result would be that the teacher you hired had to
rush forward and act blindly, and you would still suffer the loss. On the
contrary, if you proactively bear the cost of the first meeting as well as
the investigation analysis, the institution will dispel their concerns and do
the initial work well with full enthusiasm, which will benefit you. If the
process of education is not as fast as imagined, then ask them to continue
working hard for a period of time, and the money will be paid by you.

In 2007, I was introduced to the chairman of a real estate group to train a successor for his family. The father told me firmly, "I only build the best house, and your task is to cultivate the most responsible successor for my family!" I replied, "Building the best house is difficult, and once your engineering supervisor inspects any problems, they need to rectify them. Education is equally difficult."

Twelve months later, he asked me, "Are there any education plans that haven't been implemented yet?" I said I still have two plans, which may take another six months. "Zhigang, I'll give you this card as well as six months of time." Such an open-minded parent cannot be perfunctory.

**Rule 11: Give sufficient time for observation.**

In the dictionary of education, the most important word is "observation". The key to education is not to break children's bad habits, but to constantly observe, discover their strengths, cultivate their abilities, and make them confident. The accumulation of confidence will make a person feel excellent, and they will pursue excellence. They will correct their shortcomings by themselves.

The purpose of observation is to discover interest, as John Dewey said. Interest is a signal and symbol of growing abilities.

I once spent five months observing Ah Xi and found that behind this face, which was skilled in disguise, deceitful, extremely isolated, and sometimes exceptionally manic, lay a tenacious, upright, kind, and brave heart. I have designed and implemented three events— "Face to Face Challenge" "Revenge in the Hotel", and "Dining with the Royal Family". In the last month of my agreement with Ah Xi's father, this small body made a loud noise: "Uncle Ye, I have decided that I want to fight. I hate being a lonely and cynical loser. I want to form a team like my father and have my own business empire!"

The effect was amazing.

Please give sufficient time for observation. We need to spend a lot of time observing children's facial expressions, movements, daytime activities, nighttime sleep, reactions in various environments, and evaluations of different things. God is in the details.

**Rule 12: When there is progress, maintain a positive attitude and do not rush forward.**

When the child is getting better, the parents should capture this opportunity to execute their plans hidden in their hearts for many years. They have already played out the scenario in their heads, but they were struggling because the child did not cooperate. They couldn't wait any longer since the child was better and the relationship between them was starting to get fixed.

I have taught a child who had been away from school for five years. One day, his mother suddenly saw her son flipping through a book! That evening, this elegant lady solemnly expressed to me: she thought her son had a full chance of getting into a key high school and eventually being admitted to an Ivy League university in the United States.

Thank goodness! In the end, her wishes came true, but back then, this idea almost made the child collapse.

When there is progress, you can feel the excitement but don't be tempted.

**Rule 13: Don't let your education budget run tight.**

Under standard atmospheric pressure, water only boils at 100 degrees Celsius. My experience is that five out of ten education budgets set by parents are low, and the parents always cut off when they see a little bit progress, which makes it difficult to reach the desired destination. Private custom education has become a necessity for the wealthy families, and the cultivation for the successor is the most important investment for any family with visions.

During the 14th to 15th centuries, the Medici family became the patron for Michelangelo, Leonardo da Vinci, Masaccio, Sandro Botticelli, Raphael, Tiziano Vecelli and many other Renaissance artists. They never had to worry about the amount of creation. Later generations exclaimed: There would be no Italian Renaissance without the Medici family. For there's only one reason:

> *Come on, give your soul to Gods, and I will give you ten thousand taels of gold.*
>
> —Giovanni de Medici

# Chapter 15
# How to Enter the Industry:
# Advice to Young People

Haonan's father often tells me to succeed early, and what he admires most is young heroes.

I'm very lucky. At the age of 21, I found a career to strive for throughout my life.

I have observed myself as well as the successful families around me for many years and I have summarized a set of behavior patterns that can quickly lead young people to success. Firstly, at the beginning, whether you graduate from a prestigious university or come from Lanxiang Technical School, your understanding of parents is the same. At this point, the only thing dictating the future is attitude.

From the very beginning, you should make up your mind to become the one who knows the professional work the best in the institution. If you are the organizer of a project, you need to know the family's history and the most distinctive personality factors that make their family successful. Go deep into the parents' factories, offices, and laboratories, understand their work, analyze their perspectives and ways of thinking about problems. Spend your weekend in their kitchens, by the poker table and the fireplace, and talk to their family and friends.

Action is eloquence. In no time, you'll understand them more than anyone else, and you'll have the power to take control of the situation.

Liao Yimei once said: "Everyone is lonely. In our lives, love and sex are not rare. What is rare is understanding." I always tried to extract the unique spiritual connotations of each family, establish a family tradition, and create a new family culture.

Imagine a scene. On countless nights, I tried to explain to parents the significance of deeper understanding of the family history: I will explain the success of the parents in a way that children could understand, awaken family pride and cohesion, establish parental authority, enhance intimate relationships, enable children to understand their own mission, and gain strength from the past of their elder generations, enhancing confidence in facing difficulties. Perhaps, children would open up to a charismatic teacher, but if you know nothing about the family, you wouldn't understand the weight of the burden on their shoulders and whether they have enough ability to carry it.

Upon hearing these, parents always talk about everything.

If you have time, you should read more autobiographies of successful people and study their lives. I mean those who dare to tell the truth in public. As I said before, five thousand years cannot change human nature. On the top of society, there are still the same people. The progress of technology has certainly brought about many changes in society, but the only thing that remains unchanged is human nature.

Many people in educational institutions are accustomed to living a regular life like in a retirement home. They are polite and finish work on time, unwilling to do such "in-depth understanding" work and satisfied with only a little understanding. Slowly but surely, they are abandoned by the parents.

In psychology, humans have an instinctive defense mechanism which manifests as fear. Therefore, the first consideration for a person in a difficult situation is to preserve strength, and they cannot step forward unless they absolutely have to.

In other words, not everyone is willing to achieve success through hard work. What they hope for is to achieve success while avoiding hard work.

In the eventful days, I worked 28 days a month, averaging 18 hours a day, and often unconsciously heard the crowing of roosters in the early morning. If you enjoy spending your time raising dogs, surfing the Internet, and even sharing family fun, I would certainly like you more, but you cannot complain that I don't value you enough. I appreciate people who bury themselves in hard work.

The outstanding teachers all have unique personalities, and successful cases are often the masterpieces of their hard work. These excellent individuals earn the most generous rewards. Among the three types of personnel in our organization, pioneers, relationship supervisors, and project organizers, pioneers are responsible for expanding the market, customer supervisors are responsible for maintaining the market and managing projects, and project organizers are responsible for organizing teams to provide corresponding services for specific projects. However, only the outstanding project organizers are immune to the threats of getting fired, as they directly create value.

Perhaps some young people are attracted by international travel, luxurious banquets and the fancy sports cars of the project organizers. But soon they'll realize that this position is not for the regulars. Great teachers are never born great. Instead, they become great through arduous trials and tribulations.

And it is much more difficult for the relationship supervisor to become famous than the project organizer, because the brilliant achievements of Zhigang Education come directly from the project organizer. I, therefore, hope that young people can become project organizers. You will find that competition in this field is not very fierce, and this position can give people a great sense of security both mentally and financially.

The bankers from Wall Street say that I'm a lot like them, for I always find the underestimated values—before someone else does. Success is imminent. When I first stepped on the stage, I made my mind to make every project I did a case of innovative success. Now it seems that I have basically achieved my goal. I did it my way, and cultivated a group of people like me. It is said that I created this industry.

Before the project organizers join our organization, they will be called together to watch my martial arts masterpiece Eighteen Dragon Subduing Palms.

This book tells the secrets of how to cultivate excellent children for successful families. These tips are not my personal assumptions, but the essence I summarized from practice.

Then I tell them that if they follow the principles I mentioned, it won't be long before they create successful educational cases with their own styles.

What is education? There are three different perspectives. The old heads say that education recognized by parents is great. The other school follows John Dewey's idea that education is growth without external motives. The students I educate are all growing well, but I'm in the third school. I believe that good education is education that both meets the parents' expectations and matches the children's psychological development. It should keep the children and parents on the same page. The social competition is the competition between families. With the support of families, children can gain an advantage in social competition.

Some people say that the experience is the gain when people cannot achieve their goals. And what I am going to introduce below is my secret recipe for creating educational miracles—if you want to work for me, it is also the 14 commandments you must abide by.

## 1. Only to teach students that you truly like.

The children must be the people that teachers can sincerely accept. Based on my observation, the results are usually not satisfactory if teachers and students cannot accept each other, even regular cultural tutoring. A lawyer may have to defend a murderer he knows is guilty of, and a surgeon can also perform surgery on someone he doesn't like, but professional detachment doesn't work in education industry. If a teacher's services to parents are to be effective, the children must have some attraction to the teacher himself.

In my career, I've had various mythical creatures brought to me, some of whom have behaved outrageously. Believe it or not, in my eyes, they all had one most significant advantage: kindness. Their parents and I were astonishingly consistent on this point.

This reminds me of a letter from a mother-in-law to her daughter-in-law: "Please understand, no matter how bad my son is, he is always the cute baby lying in the cradle to me and the mischievous little boy with a muddy face. But you showed up in my life as a mature and sensible girl. Therefore, I always find my son is easily forgiven."

The education industry is the most humane industry. What truly moves people is sincere care, sincere joy, selflessness, and a pinch of sweat. Educational technology only affects efficiency, and the "cool" high-tech monster standing alongside the truth of the universe is not popular here. We can only be influenced by the people we love.

Teachers are people who make themselves increasingly redundant. Others love their children for gathering, while our love for our children is for parting.

## 2. You need to forgive in these three areas.

Firstly, to obtain "revolutionary leadership".

Each of my cases started with the thrilling process of gaining revolutionary leadership. The anxious parents regard whether teachers can quickly gain "revolutionary leadership" as a magic weapon to distinguish between their abilities. They led you into the arena to watch you fight against the beast face to face. Teachers should be people standing behind students and doing noble work in a harmonious atmosphere. However, the reality is that most parents, unless absolutely necessary and when the situation gets out of control, do not feel that their children need education beyond basic cultural tutoring. I am not pessimistic about this at all, for I believe that the type of parents dictates the type of education.

As society develops, the parents that I work with are even more insightful. They grasp the essence of education and take preventive measures. Currently, 80% of our business comes from visionary families whose children do not have significant problems and only need professional advice.

In a word, the establishment of revolutionary leadership ultimately relies on your correctness.

At the beginning, you need to do two things well: first, make students like you; and second, let the student know that you are capable.

I have the ability to generate positive energy from wealth, which students all love.

Even if you have got autism, you cannot turn a blind eye to my living room. When the autistic teenager Wenxi first stepped into my house, he actually spoke: What a beautiful parlor! What a beautiful living room! Half an hour later, Wenxi's father left for Shanghai, and his only son would not be living with him for the first time in his life. He bid farewell to his son with deep affection, while Wenxi stood still, looking at the balcony, with his back to his father indifferently.

Qiming showed his attraction to me in the back seat of a Rolls Royce. Soon after the son of an oil businessman gave me the side on through the window of a Land Rover, a brand-new Porsche 911 Turbo S suddenly stopped right in front of him. When he saw the legendary "the root of evil"—Prince Haonan personally getting off the car and opening the door for me, his clothes draped over his shoulders and the corners of his mouth hang down. He swore to reform and inherit the family business like Brother Haonan.

The reasons why students like you are sometimes surprising. The first time Ah Xi met me, I scolded him loudly. 20 minutes later, Ah Xi told his parents that he felt very fond of me and wanted to stay with me. Later, when I asked him why, he said he had never seen such a domineering private Internet cafe in my house before. He wanted to stay and see how many hours he could play every day.

In addition, if you spend time with the children day and night, you will find them observing you 24 hours a day, which could be a challenge for gaining "revolutionary leadership", because you will find it difficult to gain leadership and even more difficult to maintain it.

These children often have innate talents, making it difficult for them to convince others. So, in such families, it is often the dominant mother who loses first when her child goes to elementary school, followed by the father who loses when the child goes to middle school. The child is like a tiger in the mountains and forests when at home.

Tiger, you can consider it both as the king of beasts and as an animal that made Wu Song famous. Sometimes challenges come from parents. Ah Long's father once said to me, "Because of Ah Long, I have met too many people in your field over the years. Whether you have the ability or

not depends on whether you can make my son willing to go with you!"
Six days later, Ah Long willingly got into my car wearing sandals. Nine
months later, he was admitted to a science and technology university.
When facing the flames, I often take long walks and contemplate, letting
my intuition and spiritual guidance flow, and redemption is within it.

Secondly, to identify the main contradiction through investigation.

Parents often ask me why their children ignore them all the time? That
is because the child has bigger problems waiting to be resolved, and they
don't think you know what the main contradiction is. Even if they listened to you, they can't solve their inner troubles. For example, Xiaomin's parents wanted him to stop gaming and focus on academics, but all
he thought about was the girl Xiaojing and the insults he had received
before. Haonan's father wanted him to finish his homework on time,
but Haonan's problem was that he couldn't feel the warmth of his family. Xiaowu's parents wanted him to participate in the college entrance
examination normally, but Xiaowu thought that there was no reward for
the efforts. Qiming's parents couldn't bear the insults from him, but they
would've never known that it was all due to a leaking window.

In domestic business, if the parents set the education cycle to a year, then
they'll have 365 days to explore education. To get to the point immediately, start investigating right away, to find the truth, to analyze the
reasons, and to try various methods to solve the problems. You need to
investigate ceaselessly from the first hour of meeting until the last hour
before parting.

From my experience, the children know their problems very well. It is
way more accurate than therapy, without need for sand tables or hypno-
tizing. They will tell you what their problems are once you become the
people whom they trust. The choice of weapon depends on the type of
people who use it. In order to eliminate the target, the most incompetent
person launches a nuclear bomb from thousands of miles away, while the

expert can get the job well done sitting and chatting right next to you.

In the process of investigation and understanding, patience always pays off. I once spent five months observing Ah Xi and found that behind this face, which was skilled in disguise, deceitful, extremely isolated, and sometimes exceptionally manic, lay a tenacious, upright, kind, and brave heart. I have designed and implemented three events— "Face to Face Challenge" "Revenge in the Hotel", and "Dining with the Royal Family". In the last month of my agreement with Ah Xi's father, this small body made a loud noise: "Uncle Ye, I have decided that I want to fight. I hate being a lonely and cynical loser. I want to form a team like my father and have my own business empire!" Ah Xi's family has regained vitality. Be patient! Haste is the agility of a fool.

The parents usually don't know the truth. Parents have a mixed understanding of the main causes of their children's abnormalities. Xiaomin's mother thought it was fate; Haonan's father thought it was bad habits; Qiming's family thought it was Internet addiction; Ah Xi's parents thought it was laziness; Ah Long's parents thought it was willfulness; Xiaowu's parents thought it was a dislike of learning. Only Wenxi's father guessed the right answer: it was autism. However, who would've guessed wrong? Some parents even show me the slips written by the so-called masters, saying that it's all fate. Whenever I hear that, I'd tell them loudly that in my eyes, fate is the right for wolves to eat meat and the excuse for dogs to eat shit.

Explore bravely, but do not take it lightly. People say that simplifying complex problems is a fundamental quality of a genius. After you enter our profession, you will find that fools are those who simplify complex things casually.

Thirdly, to resolve the main conflict through social activities.

The most important principle of organizing activities is to ensure the safety of students.

I remember when I was teaching Xiaomin, every weekend I had to take my bike and Xiaomin's to an old guy at the entrance of the community for maintenance and upkeep. He was called Lao Yao, who had a strange temper and never talked to people easily. He only repaired bikes and used his left hand to tell you the price after they were repaired. He would ask you to pay as much as he wanted without bargaining. Once you ever did, he immediately waved his hand and asked you to leave and never to repair your bike again.

Nearby people all knew that Lao Yao was good at fixing bikes. He was serious about it and kept a reasonable price, so his business was always booming. On a breezy evening, I went to his store to pick up my bike, Lao Yao spoke up! "I heard that you're a teacher, educating children from wealthy families. Do you know what the most important job of a teacher is?" He asked me as he worked. I thought about for a second and replied, "Educate them well, and fulfill my duty." He shook his head.

"What do you think then?" I asked curiously.

He waved to signal me to leave. The next morning, I waited early at the location of his business, and he showed up not long after I got there. When Lao Yao had arranged everything and sat down on a small stool, I respectfully lit a top-quality cigarette for him.

He looked at the cigarette in his hand, and then said to me: "I heard you educate children from wealthy families who are difficult to discipline, but I see that you are also a child, so at first, I didn't believe it. Later, your student came to pick up the bike several times and I saw the huge changes in him. I think you are a very diligent child, so I asked you a question yesterday to remind you to pay attention to."

"Uncle Yao, what do you mean?"

"Nowadays, every family has only one child, and your most important job is to ensure the safety of your child. Everything else is secondary!"

I suddenly realized!

"Uncle Yao, you're right. What measures should I take? Please teach me."

It was the most unforgettable morning of my life. A bike technician waved away all his customers and had a long conversation with a 21-year-old young man. He used a pack of cigarettes to give away his experience of working as a security guard for the high-rank officials in his youth.

The most important thing in organizing activities is to ensure the safety of the customer's family heirs. The biggest danger is not being able to see the danger. Anyone who regards accidents as the worst humiliation to personal dignity will not encounter accidents.

Although the success of an event largely depends on adequate preparation, behind any success lies luck as well. "Man proposes and god disposes." For many years, I have been constantly adjusting my plans for every event I organized, but the goals of the event must not change. Sometimes, if the changes are too sudden, the results might come out unexpectedly. At this point, inspiration is needed to seize opportunities. Inspiration is a reward obtained through tenacious labor, while opportunity is a gap that tests people's agility and resilience.

### 3. To help students establish life goals is fundamental.

I've read a remarkable book that said more than 2300 years ago, Mengzi from Zoucheng, Shandong Province, gave three criteria for judging "who is the real man". The first criterion was: neither riches nor honors can lead one astray.

I tightened my legs and quickly looked at the comment below, "Lust: Confused." Mengzi believed that having a definite life goal and not feeling lost even when wealthy was the primary characteristic of being a real man.

The essence of setting life goals is to choose which career to pursue in the future. What I want to do in the future and what profession I want to take determine what kind of person I will become. Education that helps students establish life goals is the most fundamental form of education.

The American educator John Dewey gave me tremendous theoretical support.

Interest is not something simple. It represents the fact that a process of action, a job, or a profession can completely attract a person's ability. The opposite of profession, as individuals, is the accumulation of blindness, fickleness, and lack of experience; as in society, it is baseless boasting about oneself and relying on others to live a parasitic life.

Career is the only thing that can balance an individual's exceptional talent with their social services. Finding a career suitable for an individual and obtaining opportunities to implement it is the key to happiness. The saddest thing in the world is that a person cannot discover his true career throughout his life, or when he fails to discover that he has already gone with the flow or are forced by the environment to pursue a career that does not align with his interests. The so-called appropriate profession simply means that a person's abilities tend to be appropriately utilized, and they can work with minimal friction and maximal satisfaction. For other members of society, this appropriate action certainly means that they receive the best service that this person can provide.

Occupation gives us a chance that connects a multitude of diverse details. It keeps the details of various experiences, facts, and information well-organized. Lawyers, doctors, laboratory researchers in a certain branch of chemistry, parents, and citizens who are enthusiastic about local public welfare all have a frequently effective stimulus that makes them pay attention to and connect with everything related to their careers. They start from the motivation of their profession and unconsciously need to collect all relevant information and save it. Professions absorb information like magnets and preserve it like glue.

### 4. You need to reason calmly.

You need to reason calmly, keep accounting, and explain the benefits of doing so, even if such a small effort can bring such a big return. To speak over and over again, without getting tired of it. If this doesn't make them change their mind, just wait for the tragedy to happen, because anything that goes against the rules will be punished. If you can't wait, try to think of some way to accelerate the tragedy, and they will naturally change their mind. Next time they will even come to you in advance to discuss. Remember, seeking benefits and avoiding harm is the instinct of all creatures. They did not change their mind because they felt that the loss was less than the profit. What you need to do is to show them how great the benefits are. If they are indifferent to profits, you need to repeatedly confirm the reason for it. If it was because they were not interested in it, you need to look for new directions. If this indifference is due to laziness, let him witness the unexpected losses.

Some people only cherish the warmth of their family after experiencing the cruelty of society.

### 5. If your life is not exciting enough, education will inevitably fail.

No matter what product you sell, you're selling yourself. Education is a way of life, a culture, and even a belief. The process of teachers educating students can be understood as process of the church preaching to the people. An empty church cannot save the soul.

Some people say that former US President Carter was a dull person, and if he spoke into the fire, it would soon go out. So, after Carter accompanied the leaders of Egypt and Israel to live in Camp David for a short period of time in 1978, the archenemy quickly signed the first peace agreement in history.

We cannot use Carter's experience. Be sure to make your education full of modern consciousness and keep pace with the thoughts and emotions of young people. Most of the teachers I have trained are young people, and they understand the mental activities of young people better than I do.

### 6. To trust, but to verify.

Any work requires good judgment to do well. What is judgment? Judgment is the interpretation of facts. In the dictionary of education, the most important word is "verifying". Constantly observe, investigate, verify, and check until the truth emerges.

I remember when Xiaomin and I worked day and night, we needed to hire a housekeeper to clean our rooms. We were very picky about the people around us. As a last resort, we used the "trust, but verify" method to audition all the housekeeping companies on the market. We collected 9.85 Yuan worth of coins, including nine 1-yuan, eight 1-jiao, and one 5-fen, 18 coins in total. We scattered them in corners of the rooms, making it look like they were accidentally lost there. Then, we called all the housekeeping companies and asked them to tidy up our house without supervision. They were only trustworthy if the coins were returned to us after cleaning the rooms. If less than 18 coins were returned, it indicated that they lacked attention to details. If the coins were gone, it indicated that they could not be trusted.

The results shocked us. In Xinglongtai District, Panjin City, Liaoning Province in 2003, none of a company passed the test! We ran out of coins very soon after we started the experiment. The results of this survey made Xiaomin, and I feel very insecure. One afternoon, disappointed, I found two women at the entrance of the park who were tightly covering themselves. I walked towards them, and it turned out that they came from the countryside to work in the city. I asked them to clean the rooms for me. One hour later, 18 coins were polished shiny and placed in the hands of Xiaomin. The various facilities in the room were spotless, and they stood at the door with a blush on their faces, smiling kindly. Until now, they are still serving me, but I am no longer their only customer.

Character is the attitude and habits that society needs. Once you have a verified attitude or habit, no matter what industry you enter, you are more likely to achieve success. Remember, people lie, but science doesn't.

**7. Don't engage in education that you don't want your family to know about.**

If you won't mistreat your own child, please do not mistreat my child. What you don't want someone to do something to you, do not do it to others.

If you mistreat a student, you will be discovered sooner or later, either by me or by the parents. Believe it or not, students discover it before anyone else does, for they all have radars in their heads. If I find out, you will be called to talk to me. If the parents find out, they will punish you by making you unemployed. If discovered by the students, you will lose their trust.

Teachers should set examples. As the most capable individual in a group, every second you spend with students has an impact on them. You need to become a role model, but please pay attention to what kind of role model it is.

## 8. To discover strengths and protect personality.

Is it only by surname that people are distinguished from each other? No, it's personality. The fundamental reason for the significant difference in status between dogs and wolves is the dog's tendency to eat shit. Five thousand years cannot change human nature. At the top of society, there are still the same people.

At the 6th National Conference of Chinese Psychologists, a psychologist asked me, "How did you change a child's nature?" I was startled into cold sweat. The advancement of technology has certainly brought about many changes in education, but the only thing that remains unchanged is the human heart. Xiaomin has a hot temper but is extremely hardworking; Qiming seems weak but has a tenacious personality; Ah Xi is stubborn but can tolerate humiliation. Although Ah Xi looks unrefined, he has outstanding abilities and a meticulous heart. If you understand their family history, you can easily find that every advantage of them is a gift from their ancestors, and each generation in their respective families has completed the continuation of their family through these advantages. I won't put in any effort to change Xiaomin's irritability, Qiming's seemingly softness, Ah Xi's ostensible obedience, and Ah Long's slovenliness. I just dug out their strengths and constantly amplified them, and soon they all achieved success.

In 2008, Xiaomin was sent to the hospital for bravery and righteousness. When I arrived, I heard relatives and friends who came to visit exclaim to Xiaomin's father, "This child is really your son!" Xiaomin's father was extremely proud. But I've never taught Xiaomin to act bravely in righteousness before.

John Dewey once said:

Pathological education only focuses on preventing and correcting students' past behaviors but does not know that inducing students to engage in legitimate activities can naturally suppress bad habits. If prevention and suppression are seen as more important than the positive force that induces good deeds, it is equivalent to acknowledging that death is more valuable than life, denial is more valuable than affirmation, and sacrifice is more valuable than service. This is clearly a fallacy. The so-called formality refers to the general practice of teaching kindness without substance in schools, where students are indifferent and often pretend to be kind, without any emotional or ideological impact, and are unable to establish firm moral character.

Some people say that the greatest word invented by humans is "genetics", and no matter what shortcomings you have, you can blame genetics. In my opinion, what is most worthy of praise is the unique personality that students have inherited from their ancestors, which has helped their family overcome hardships in various periods of history. In my eyes, these personalities are like huge diamonds hanging around their necks, so dazzling that it's hard not to be noticed. The cultivation of heirs is a long-term investment in the Y chromosome. In education, the most important law to remember is that the world is easy to change, but the nature is not.

## 9. Do not stop innovating.

Samuel Ullman said: Youth is not a matter of peach blossom, red lips, or soft knees, but a matter of deep will, grand imagination, and passionate emotions. And my realization: the most beautiful manifestation of youth is innovation. Especially in terms of innovative methods for entering children's minds and setting life goals, these two fields fascinate me the most. I touched Xiaomin's heart through fortune telling, helped the outstanding student to go to Yale University through comparing alumni records, touched Qiming's heart through writing poetry on the wall, set life goals for Ah Xi through dining with the royal family, won the trust of Ah Long through staying up for five days and nights, and transformed Haonan and Wenxi completely through an ordinary family life.

Innovation is also reflected in the use of people. In my early years, I challenged the limits of education and took over a child with intellectual disabilities. In order to select a tutor for him, I conducted an audition, and excellent teachers came in a continuous stream. Finally, Mrs. Wu, a teacher from Heilongjiang, spoke with a heavy accent and told me that she could teach all three subjects, including language and mathematics. However, during the trial lecture, I found that Mrs. Wu made mistakes in English pronunciation, Chinese writing, spelling, and even occasionally miscalculate elementary school application problems of mathematics!

In the end, I chose to let her serve as the tutor for this intellectually disabled student because she had a distinct advantage: particularly, extremely, and quite patient. She taught my student this way:

"Child, you left home at 6:00 o'clock in the morning and it took you 30 minutes to arrive at school. What time did you arrive at school?"

"Huh?"

"I asked you what time you arrive at school?"

"Our school requires to be there by 7:30."

"No, the teacher asked you, you left home at 6:00 o'clock in the morning and took 30 minutes to arrive at school. So, what time did you arrive at school? Then you need think this way. Draw a clock for 6:00 o'clock on paper. The hour hand moved from 0 to 6, which means it is 6:30 when you arrive at school. Do you understand?"

"I understand."

"If you leave home at 8:00 o'clock in the morning, and walk for half an hour, when will you get to school?"

"My home is far away from the school. It takes an hour to walk, and if we leave at 8:00 o'clock, we will get to school by almost 9:00 o'clock."

"No, let me tell you..."

It was the morning of the fourth day when the student learned to watch. Do you know how many times Mrs. Wu has talked about this question? 33 times. It's nothing, while the most amazing thing is that the 33rd time was as patient and friendly as the first time.

With the help of Mrs. Wu, Xiaoyu successfully passed the strict junior high school entrance examination in Beijing. I was very lucky that my first project Xiaomin was a huge success. Mr. Richard Branson's words resonated within me.

"Having success on the first case will bring you many problems. It makes you falsely believe that you have learned all the truth, but later you will realize that you were simply lucky. Nothing is that easy."

If you only have one hammer, then you have to see all the problems as nails. Don't be afraid of innovation. Use all your imagination, and education doesn't have a right answer nor a limitation. Only the shallow ones can give out answers at will. Express your passion. Any kind of personality can create glory in this great industry! Failure is certainly painful, but maintaining the status quo is even more tragic.

## 10. Be honest.

A parent once told me: Money has no personality. It looks like whoever holds it.

Education is the same. Whenever I meet a child, I can feel the personality of the teachers and parents behind him. The influence they had on the child is as pungent as the smell of urine on the trunk of a cheetah's territory.

The greatest resource for teachers is themselves, and the key to the success or failure of education lies in what kind of people the educators are. The premise of making students become themselves and the masters of their own lives is that educators first dare to seek their true selves and become the masters of their own lives. Those who become themselves do not overly focus on others' evaluations of themselves. They build a sense of value on themselves. Not easily influenced by the negative emotions of others, and not easily incited by their passion. Have one's own judgment on things and people, not follow the crowd. When given the right to choose, don't panic and know what to choose and why. Education is an art, so to be an artist, you must know who you are and truly showcase yourself. In contemporary times, what children are most vigilant about is whether the people who educate them are consistent in their appearance. Most parents and teachers who are not appreciated by their children do not meet this standard.

The sanctity of a teacher does not lie in being a perfect person. Don't hide your shortcomings. In this regard, my experience is similar to that of Miss Gabrielle Chanel: defects should not be deliberately hidden, since the more they are concealed, the more they will highlight this area.

### 11. Educating people with social reality.

How to learn to swim? Jump in the water!

Practical education philology shortens the distance between thinking and doing. The benefit of receiving education is to fit in the society better. This determines that teaching with practical education is more convincing. To judge whether an equation is modern is to see whether it can lead to a social practice effectively. Real education only has one form which is to make students realize the truth of life and love it.

## 12. Make good use of talents.

John Dewey said: Teachers, especially teachers with strong abilities, usually attract students with their strong points. They replace the attractions of the contents of actives with personal influences. They realize from their own experience that when lessons can't capture students' attention, personal attraction usually works well. In this way, he increasingly utilizes the latter, to the point that the relationship between students and teachers nearly replace the relationship between students and subjects. In this circumstance, the teacher's personal influence will make the student reliant and soft, and make students not treat the values of the subjects seriously enough.

Teachers should pay more attention to their own habits of thought and to prevent negative influences. Otherwise, it might lead to students only studying the teacher's characteristics instead of the subject. Students will cater to the expectations of the teachers passionately, instead of studying the subject. When students think about the problems, they think about whether the answer can satisfy the teacher instead of actually solving the problems. Of course, for the students to study the personal characteristics of the teacher is not valueless, but they should not have their intellectual thoughts moved by others' will.

## 13. Don't make promises about the results no matter how confident you are.

I've had an arrogant performance. After thoroughly understanding a student, I made the prediction in front of the parents: that it would not be a problem for the child to advance 200 places in the next exam!

The child studied hard for the entire month. The problems in the exam were done many times before. I was full of confidence, and the mother even bought a cake for celebration. However, after the results came out, the child only advanced one place. I felt ashamed and couldn't figure out how to solve it. Later, I went to the psychological counseling room of my child's high school and accidentally came across an attention testing software on the computer. The child went up and tested it: severe distraction.

Do not predict the future with a crystal ball, and do not play Russian roulette with parents. Education is an empirical science, but not a precise science. Success always has the element of luck no matter how confident we are. Like John Dewey said:

"We cannot predict the future, and we also cannot teach the children for the future. What we say about having the children prepare for the future, is to enable them to manage themselves, train them fully and always use their full energy." His eyes, ears and hands should be tools. His judgment has to understand when he can make use of it. His action ability has to be trained to act efficiently."

### 14. To create a hard-earned success.

A great teacher can always make the student experience hard-earned success. Friedrich Nietzsche said: What is happiness? It feels stronger and resistance is overcome.

If my apprentice became a relationship supervisor without listening to my advice, I will give him some advice like this.

1) People who can excel in this field, I believe, can excel in any industry because they possess both the meticulous observation of scientists and profound skills in interacting with people.

2) The parents who hired you will oppose you eventually. Maybe it's because they don't like you, you are too straightforward, or they blame you for others' faults. Do not be sad when this happens. Read the short poem "IF" by Joseph Rudyard Kipling. I know a great relationship su-

pervisor who didn't break down after being opposed by the parents three times within a year.

3) If you don't know how to make quality proposals to the parents, there is no way you can be a great relationship supervisor. Great relationship supervisor understands humanity. They can discover the hidden needs and satisfy the parents. Based on my years of observation, they share a common characteristic: They can always think from other people's perspective, and help parents realize that interacting with us is their best choice.

4) Do not treat the parents like enemies. This is a common mistake. Some parents might show off their wealth aggressively and speak harshly. I always see these actions as crying for help. It's like a jumping deer when running for its life. Even though it's risky, it's still willing to take the risk, for it equals telling the cheetah: "Don't you dare to kill a deer as strong as me." Parents are also trying to tell us: "Other than educating my child, you'll never be better than me."

Tell them that you are their friend, treat yourself as a member of their family, and that all people need is love. Smile at them more, dine with them more, but don't get involved in internal conflicts within their families.

Don't think the parents are irresponsible for the children. Knowing that every parent that I've met, no matter how big a failure they might look as parents, you'll know that they tried their best if you know them. We all thought that we'd have everything one day, like Raggy Dick who was a young boy from Alger's book. We did everything right in the beginning, but then…

5) When briefing with the parents, you need to get off the details for the bigger picture. Someone who can sacrifice on the small things, is hard to be ignored when speaking out on something important.

6) Do not speak about the parents in the elevator, and keep your files locked up as the family secrets are in your hands. Not keeping them safe will destroy you.

7) If you want the project organizer or the pioneer to accept an idea, speak with them softly. In my flock, tough people are not welcomed.

8) Bravely take on your mistakes in front of parents and colleagues will earn their respect. Honesty and subjectivity are what we need the most.

9) Keep a good attitude instead of rushing for success. Go slow because nothing is easy.

10) I have to admit that time kills gratitude faster than beauty. Stepping out after success is the ways of heaven.

I have a few more words for the project organizer.

Firstly, in a word, the key to receiving praise is that your requirements for the product exceed the expectations of the customer. Haonan's father wanted him to complete his homework on time, but Haonan broke free from his bad habits and returned home to inherit the family business. Wenxi's mother only wanted her child to go to school normally, but as a result, Wenxi not only had excellent character and education, but also regained his male instincts. As always, the bright future of Zhigang Education depends on all of you. I am well aware of the difficulty of exceeding parental expectations in this industry, as the standards for outstanding individuals are already high, and parental expectations are bound to skyrocket.

Secondly, some people say that the difference between good and very good lies in the details, and I think the difference lies more in what you believe can be better. In the pursuit of excellence, I have my own set: I have recorded a DVD for myself, which contains videos of various characters creating miracles, and these people seem so relaxed when creating miracles. Whenever I feel complacent, I play this DVD alone, which inspires my ambition to surpass myself.

Thirdly, find a good wife like me. Good education requires hard work, and a happy family can provide you with the best rest.

Zhigang Education is a job, a career, and even a way of life, but anyway, remember that your value is much higher than your classmates in other industries.

There is a story that says two wolves came to the grassland, and one of them was very disappointed because it couldn't see meat. The other wolf was very excited because it knew that with grass, there would be sheep. This is the difference of vision. As Gustave Moreau said, "We are all prisoners of our own experience." Expand your horizons, go out and explore art more.

Psychologists say that everyone needs a hobby. I recommend education. Turn your vision towards areas beyond the reach of others, choose a good topic, work hard to study, and become an expert in this field. Write a good article every year, send it to me, and I will give you real feedback. My email address is: tm007jmf@163.com. The areas worth exploring include new ways to enter children's hearts, how to find life goals faster, and so on.

Once you become an expert in these troublesome fields, you can rise all the way. In one word, work hard to move forward. A parent said to me: "People only judge you on your achievements regardless of how much effort you have put in."

# Chapter 16

# My Education Thought: To Help Children Find Their Life Goals

I am a frontline teacher. In the many years of challenging the limits of education, I formed a series of firm educational beliefs.

The two questions "How to educate people" and "What a human is" are closely connected, and a teacher's choice of educational methods is based on his understanding of human nature.

What is human?

To answer this question, we need to delve into "What are the most essential characteristics of human beings?" and "What are the most inner needs of human beings?"

Some people say that the most essential characteristic of human beings is the ability to use tools, but Burmese macaques often use stone tools.

Some people say that the most essential characteristic of human beings is the ability to walk upright, but Tyrannosaurus Rex once walked upright for 50 million years.

Some people say that the most essential characteristic of human beings is the ability to use language. It should be noted that not only do dwarf lemurs use language, but different groups also have their own dialects. After a male Japanese lemur moves, he will consciously learn the dialect of his new residence to avoid conflict.

In fact, the most essential characteristic of human beings is "flexibility".

It is precisely because of this that human beings have defeated other animals. Other animals are inherently fixed. They are only fixated on their own nature. People have the possibility to develop in all directions. They can change themselves, shape themselves, and create their own essence.

What is the most inner need of a person?

It is a life goal.

The secret to living is not in being alive itself, but in why one lives. When there is nothing to say about why being alive, one cannot continue to live.

A person must establish a goal for their life in order to live like a person. When his survival lacks a goal, he feels like he's just an animal.

Therefore, the most inner need of a person is their life goal. Only by finding a life goal can one truly become a person, and achieving a goal is one's achievement.

Human flexibility and the desire to reach a goal make it possible for everyone to find his own life goal, but most humans are never mature enough to find a goal.

Therefore, people need education, and the purpose of education is to help people find their life goals.

The greatness of Mr. Li Shuqing was not reflected in his teaching of the Four Books and Five Classics. He handed a book to Mao Zedong, who was then 14 years old. The first sentence at the beginning of the book was: "Alas! China is about to perish!" Mao Zedong remembered this sentence for the rest of his life.

The success of Mr. Gao Panzhi was not reflected in the open geography classes. During the era of Yan'an, a foreign journalist asked Zhou Enlai, "How did you embark on the path of revolution?" Zhou Enlai replied, "When I was young, I studied in Shenyang and received the guidance of Mr. Gao Panzhi, which laid the foundation for me to embark on the path of revolution."

The ability of Mr. Xi Pinsan is not reflected in his writing of the Eight Part Essay. He not only inspired the patriotic thoughts of his student Zhu De, but also convinced his family to send him to a new school. What's even more touching was that he raised funds for Zhu De when he was studying.

The value of these three teachers was not in giving lessons, but in helping students find their life goals.

Can all kinds of students find their own life goals?

Not really. A person who wants to find his life goal needs to have a prerequisite, which is that they must be a real person.

It's not easy to be a real person. The fashion of the times and public opinion will not only oppose you, but also assimilate you. How many people can maintain the original intention regardless of the evaluation from others?

The hypocrites are the worst threat to humanity. Because their existence comes at the cost of sacrificing both themselves and the future.

In the 24th year of the founding of the Soviet Union, teacher Anton Makarenko wrote about his discovery.

In fact, we did not educate students. Our students have discipline to abide by, but there is no discipline to struggle with. We have to wait until the students make mistakes to start educating them. We do not notice those students who have not made mistakes. They may seem normal on the surface, but we do not know or are not good at discovering what kind of people they will develop into. Our teachers did not pay attention to some of the most common personalities, such as honest people, misers, slippery people, lethargic people, careless people, courteous people, people who love to take advantage, selfish people, people who love to fantasize, and bookworms. Sometimes we can also notice their presence, but first, they don't hinder us much. Secondly, we don't know what to do with them anyway. And in fact, it is the students with these personalities who later become the black sheep, rather than those mischievous students.

52 years after Makarenko's discoveries, the Soviet Union fell apart.

In later generations, the reasons for the disintegration of the Soviet Union were attributed to institutional flaws, incorrect routes, and the influence of the West.

No, no, it's not the institution, routes, and conspiracy that led to the disintegration of the Soviet Union. It's people, honest people, misers, slippery people, lethargic people, careless people, courteous people, opportunists, selfish people, fantasists, and bookworms who buried the Soviet Union. It's their hypocritical personalities that buried the Soviet Union, and it's the teachers of these people that buried the Soviet Union.

Teachers are responsible for the fate of the country.

Perhaps as Professor Makarenko said, we did not educate our students.

We were busy with giving lessons, grading homework, writing lesson plans, and preaching, but we weren't busy helping students find their own life goals. We weren't busy helping them become real people. We weren't busy fighting against real enemies and hypocrisy in human nature.

Take a look around us, those children who go to school every day, how many of them know why they need to study? How many of those few children who know why they study give it their all?

The person walking on their chosen path must strive forward. On the contrary, procrastination indicates inner unwillingness. Isn't it a sign of a lack of life goals?

Year after year, misunderstandings of educational goals, neglect of life goals, and indulgence in hypocritical personalities have led generations of teenagers to walk by us, becoming citizens and parents. This kind of loss—the loss of humans, is immeasurable.

Three days before his death, Makarenko said to his comrades on stage, "In the past five years, they have sent me some students who are stubborn troublemakers. Their fathers have cars, medals, phonographs, and money. Please try to educate such children, for it was way more difficult."

This is why those large families chose me to cultivate their successors.

Because it was way more difficult.

Later I paused this service.

Because it wasn't difficult enough.

Education issues, like technological bottlenecks such as engines and chips, are essentially design capability issues.

To enhance this ability, one needs to be extreme.
People deepen their understanding of things in extreme environments,

and the depth of their understanding is directly proportional to the degree of extremism.

One day, one of the main characters in this book, Youqing came to me, and I realized that he was extreme, truly extreme.

I couldn't stop thinking, "Does he have will?" "What is human?" "What is the most essential characteristic of human beings?" "What are human beings seeking?" "What is the purpose of education?" "Do life goals also work to him?" "Can anyone find life goals?" "What is the essence of love?" "Will anyone fall in love with him?"

I stepped into loneliness with doubts and creativity.

Yes, he is the summit of the Himalayas, the ultimate test for a master. If you take a glance at the summit, turn around and leave, you can't help but think: does the truth at the foot of the mountain still work on the summit?

Yes, he is at the core of the earth, where everything will be re-evaluated.

The end of humans is the beginning of education.

In 1872 days, 427 teachers, 618 sets of plans, over 27000 km of traveling.

Youqing found his goals, abilities, confidence, a career, love… maybe they are just one thing—himself.

My students have always been an indescribable existence. They were seen as outliers. Sigmund Freud walked over, lit a cigar, and said they had various illnesses.

I don't see it that way.

# CHAPTER 16

Above the horizon, one thing stands in front of everyone, and it is called normal.

Most people submit to it. But he questioned it and stopped.

He is so different, but being different is a mistake. He is too incomprehensible, but that is absurd.

Compared with his peers, he risked more and rebelled more. He challenged normality. He had experienced the most hardships in life and suffered the most humiliation.

I don't want to argue for him, but he would rather die than do something he doesn't recognize. This is truthfulness, this is bravery, and this is owning the future.

I knew that he only needed a goal, a decent goal.

Those who fail to find their life goals throughout their lives either pursue careers that do not align with their interests or flaunt themselves in vain while relying on others for a parasitic life. This is a tragedy of being human.

They are unable to know, believe, and love themselves throughout their lives, and their hearts are filled with resentment. Even if they do good deeds, their resentment will manifest in every good deed, for only the self-loved ones can love, and only the wealthy can give.

A parent said to me when we first met, "I thought my wealth could give my son a thousand paths to walk on, but in the end, I realized that he has nowhere to go if he can't find a life goal."

I like parents who have nowhere to go. I'll let them survive in dire straits.

Looking around the world, one could see the revolution in education has begun.

The task of a teacher is no longer just to impart knowledge, but to help students find their own life goals.

A teacher's job is not only in the classroom anymore. More and more teachers joined the unknown on the path of exploration.

The standard for a good teacher is no longer a professional title or certificate. Rather it is a simple "Loved by students and supported by parents".

Educational books do not give answers. Instead, they record the honesty and bravery of the those who explore life and reflect the path of exploration.

The incredible educational miracles were created by the ambitions and energy of the young teachers.

Therefore, take actions, young people. Be loyal to yourself. In the post-industrial era where it is filled with "modernization", consuming becomes a symbol, algorithm controls our minds, and commercials create illusions. This world doesn't need one more educational institution, no more ordinary vain people. It needs one more teacher who can help children find their life goals, and another citizen who can push society forward. And your happiness is not elsewhere. It is in your hometown. Go help your fellow villagers around you, and help their children become themselves.

Take actions, young people. Believe in yourselves. Don't try to prove to others that you are doing a legitimate job, and don't push your head in the textbooks anymore. In the education industry, what can be quantified and replicated is just fleeting shadows and clouds. Lead children who cannot be educated by others to exceed the expectations of their parents, enhance your ability to design in education, and let everything revolve around your blueprint. It is your creativity that determines your value.

Take actions, young people. Return to the foundation of education and become teachers who can help children find their life goals. Innovating in "how to enter a child's heart" and "how to help him find his life goals", what you need is forgiveness, instead of permission. Your creative hard work dictates the number of owners in this world, and it dictates the future of humanity.

Take actions, parents. Don't get lost in the name and scale of educational institutions anymore. The true motive of any educational institutions is the passion and skills of their frontline teachers.

Take actions, parents, to find that young man. At this moment, what you are holding in your hand is not a book, but a horn. Pass it to the one next to you and tell them loudly that you want the young man in this book to be the teacher for your child, and that you need the young man in the book to help your child find his life goal.